ALSO BY STEPHANIE AND WILLIAM LASKA

The DIRTY, LAZY, KETO® Cookbook:
Bend the Rules to Lose the Weight!
by Stephanie Laska, MEd, and William Laska (Simon & Schuster, 2020)

The DIRTY, LAZY, KETO® Dirt Cheap Cookbook:
100 Easy Recipes to Save Money & Time!
by Stephanie Laska, MEd, and William Laska (Simon & Schuster, 2020)

DIRTY, LAZY, KETO®: Get Started Losing Weight While Breaking the Rules
by Stephanie Laska (St. Martin's Essentials, 2020)

DIRTY, LAZY, KETO® Fast Food Guide: 10 Carbs or Less
by William Laska and Stephanie Laska (2018)

THE DIRTY, LAZY, KETO®

NO TIME TO COOK COOKBOOK

100 Easy Recipes Ready in under 30 Minutes

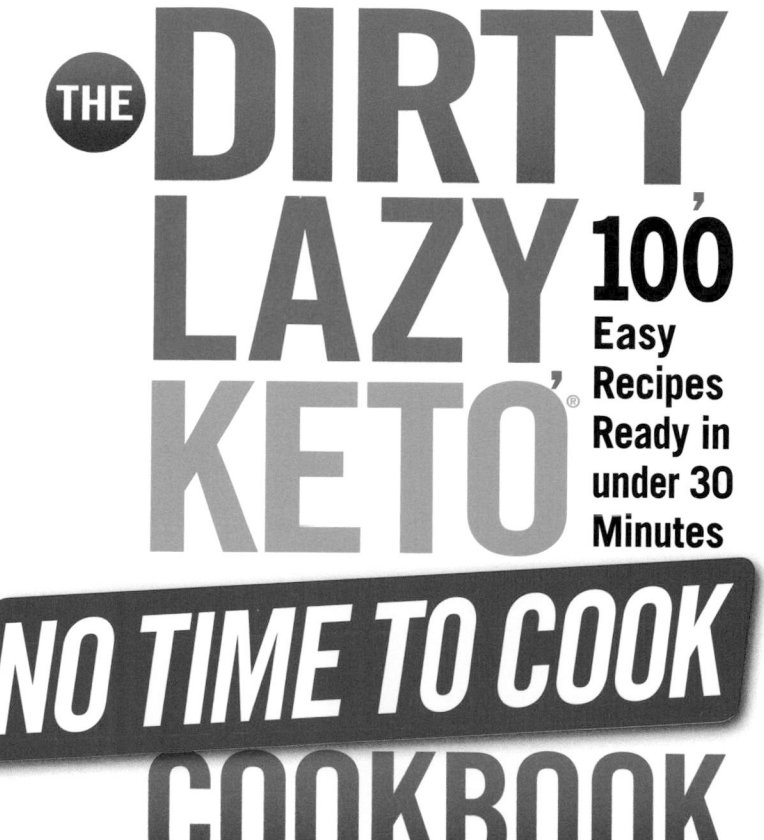

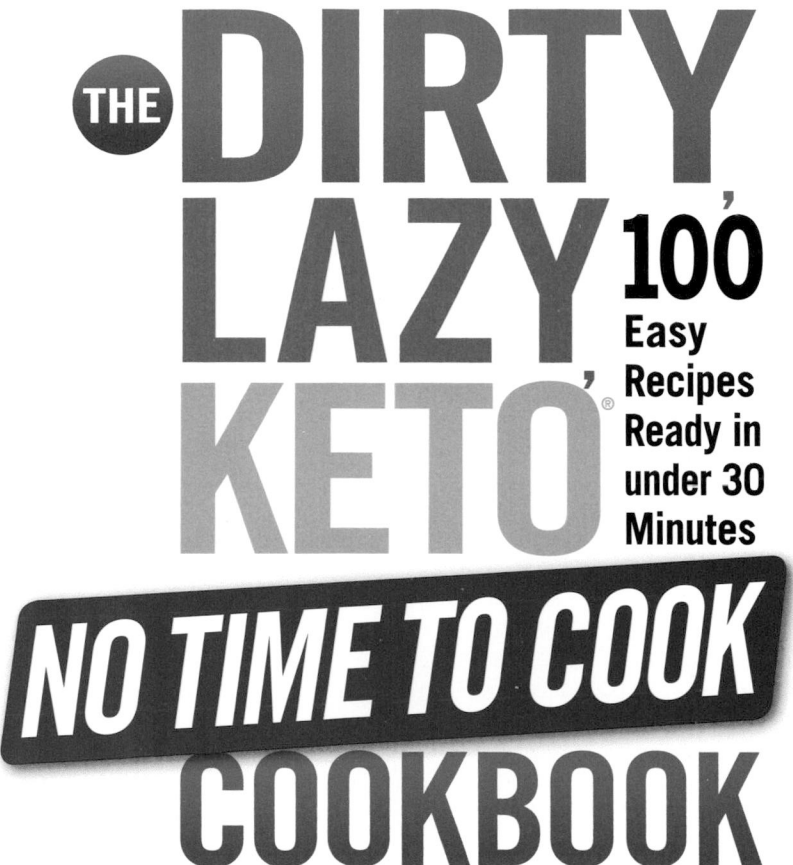

THE •DIRTY, LAZY, KETO®

100 Easy Recipes Ready in under 30 Minutes

NO TIME TO COOK

COOKBOOK

Stephanie Laska, MEd, and **William Laska**

ADAMS MEDIA

New York London Toronto Sydney New Delhi

Adams Media
An Imprint of Simon & Schuster, Inc.
100 Technology Center Drive
Stoughton, MA 02072

Copyright © 2021 by Stephanie Laska and William Laska.

All rights reserved, including the right to reproduce this book or portions thereof in any form whatsoever. For information address Adams Media Subsidiary Rights Department, 1230 Avenue of the Americas, New York, NY 10020.

First Adams Media trade paperback edition January 2021

ADAMS MEDIA and colophon are trademarks of Simon & Schuster.

For information about special discounts for bulk purchases, please contact Simon & Schuster Special Sales at 1-866-506-1949 or business@simonandschuster.com.

The Simon & Schuster Speakers Bureau can bring authors to your live event. For more information or to book an event contact the Simon & Schuster Speakers Bureau at 1-866-248-3049 or visit our website at www.simonspeakers.com.

Interior design by Colleen Cunningham
Interior photographs by James Stefiuk
Interior images © Getty Images/maglyvi, nadyaillyustrator, Serhii Sereda, Nadzeya_Dzivakova, petite_lili, LanaMay; 123RF/sudowoodo, macrovector, Aksana Chubis, Mikalai Manyshau
Author photos by Stephanie Laska

Manufactured in the United States of America

4 2022

Library of Congress Cataloging-in-Publication Data
Names: Laska, Stephanie, author. | Laska, William, author.
Title: The DIRTY, LAZY, KETO® no time to cook cookbook / Stephanie Laska, MEd, William Laska.
Description: Avon, Massachusetts: Adams Media, 2021. | Series: DIRTY, LAZY, KETO® | Includes bibliographical references and index.
Identifiers: LCCN 2020034709 | ISBN 9781507214275 (pb) | ISBN 9781507214282 (ebook)
Subjects: LCSH: Reducing diets. | Ketogenic diet. | Quick and easy cooking. | LCGFT: Cookbooks.
Classification: LCC RM237.73 .L374 2021 | DDC 641.5/12--dc23
LC record available at https://lccn.loc.gov/2020034709

ISBN 978-1-5072-1427-5
ISBN 978-1-5072-1428-2 (ebook)

Many of the designations used by manufacturers and sellers to distinguish their products are claimed as trademarks. Where those designations appear in this book and Simon & Schuster, Inc., was aware of a trademark claim, the designations have been printed with initial capital letters.

DIRTY, LAZY, KETO® is a registered trademark of Stephanie Laska and William Laska.

Always follow safety and commonsense cooking protocols while using kitchen utensils, operating ovens and stoves, and handling uncooked food. If children are assisting in the preparation of any recipe, they should always be supervised by an adult.

The information in this book should not be used for diagnosing or treating any health problem. Not all diet and exercise plans suit everyone. You should always consult a trained medical professional before starting a diet, taking any form of medication, or embarking on any fitness or weight training program. The author and publisher disclaim any liability arising directly or indirectly from the use of this book.

DEDICATION

I keep a box under my desk filled with letters from readers. I look at them again and again (especially in the wee hours when I'm writing). I feel comforted knowing that I'm not alone in struggling with my weight. For many of us, fighting obesity has been the biggest challenge of our lives.

The letters (okay, emails) come from all over the world, but they share the same themes—Hope. Relief. Inspiration!

> The success stories are far and wide. Readers are losing weight and reversing chronic health conditions with DIRTY, LAZY, KETO. *This is exciting.* We're onto something here, folks. Something big.

The secret is out and it's working. You can have your sugar-free cake and eat it too! It turns out *you don't have to be perfect to be successful.*

To all the weight loss rebels out there, this book is for you.

—Stephanie (*140 pounds, 8 years and counting!*)

In this book you'll find DIRTY, LAZY, KETO easy and economical recipes that still taste AMAZING. Join my family in the DLK kitchen, and let's do this together!

Special thanks to my social media advisors and liveliest recipe testers, Charlotte and Alex. Thank you for your patience and understanding while Mom and Dad embark on this keto journey to spread the word of this unbelievable way of eating that has such profound potential to change and save lives.

—#KetoOn! Bill

CONTENTS

10. MAIN DISHES 149

11. DRINKS AND DESSERTS 185

PREFACE

A decade ago, if you would've told me I'd be publishing a *third* cookbook (about weight loss, nonetheless!), I would've thrown my head back and roared with laughter.

"Preposterous!" I would've yelled, shaking one fist in the air (while the other hand clutched a cold can of full-sugar Mountain Dew). That would've been the most outrageous prediction—*on so Many Levels*.

You see, I've always struggled with my weight.

> From second grade to my second marriage, I tended to weigh more than anyone else in the room.

I never had the time (or so I believed) to address the problem. After all, I was a busy mom of two—and working full-time. My schedule didn't have room for spending all day in the kitchen cooking fancy meals. I was more like a drive-thru or microwave type of girl, if we're being completely honest!

It's not like I could blame my weight on having kids. I gained more weight *after*, not during, my two pregnancies. It wasn't that I *wanted* to be morbidly obese. I just didn't know what to do about it. I weighed close to 300 pounds and felt stuck.

I stumbled into this way of eating, quite literally. I had just finished drinking a beer (or maybe two) at a friend's barbecue when I ran smack into her husband. I barely recognized him; he had lost so much weight! I was honestly surprised. You can guess what happened next. I quickly pulled him aside and whispered.

"*HOW* did you do it?"

His response was short and sweet. The secret to his losing forty pounds was eating only grilled chicken (while still drinking beer). Hmmm… *That's not at all what I expected.*

His menu recommendation didn't solve my weight problem (that's for sure). But ironically, I did walk away from that conversation feeling just a teensy, tiny bit inspired (and maybe a little buzzed). He made it sound so easy. Perhaps I too could take another crack at this whole dieting business. Maybe…*just maybe*…I would try to lose weight *one more time.*

That chance conversation, my friends, was the spark of inspiration that led me to create DIRTY, LAZY, KETO. With a lot of experimentation, I figured out that a matrix of higher-fat, moderate-protein, and lower-carb foods would help me to lose roughly ten pounds a month for a year and a half straight. Now don't get mad when I tell you this, but it wasn't that hard. I wasn't slaving over a hot stove all day. I didn't meander around a farmers' market smelling and squeezing produce (that's just weird). Rather, I learned to quickly shop for ingredients at "normal people" stores *and make healthy meals fast*!

> Here's the clincher though, folks: To achieve weight loss success, I finally realized I couldn't follow anyone else's rules about dieting. I had to do it in my own way.

I ended up losing 140 pounds total, or about half of my entire body weight. I've kept that amount of weight off for eight years now. *Eight!* (That's the equivalent of, like, 800 in dieting years.) With this kind of track record, it seems I've conquered the impossible. Ironically, I've managed to do this without changing the amount of time I spend in the kitchen. I'm still a busy working mom. That part didn't change!

I don't plan on keeping my methods a secret. I feel passionately that I'm onto something really big here. My mission is to fight obesity, not just at my house, but at your house too. I won't shut up about DIRTY, LAZY, KETO. In fact, it's pretty much all I talk about!

Folks new to DIRTY, LAZY, KETO usually start off by asking me one question:

"What do you eat?"

The conversation quickly morphs, however, into a deep discussion about much more than food. Losing weight isn't an exact science. You can't just eliminate carbs, "say no to bread," and become skinny overnight. It doesn't happen that way (unfortunately!). Making meaningful changes is a much more complicated process.

> DIRTY, LAZY, KETO isn't a temporary quick fix; it's a lifestyle.

My books and support groups have helped literally hundreds of thousands of people to lose weight *just like I did*. **My method works!**

To get started on your weight loss journey, you'll need an experienced guide. There's no time to waste. I'm going to be that person for you. Trust me to help you, and I'll show you the way.

We will do this together, my friend. Let's fight one carb at a time and make meals in 30 minutes or less. You CAN do this.

#KetoOn!

Stephanie

INTRODUCTION

No time to cook? *No problem!* Put down the takeout menus—I'm here to help.

I lost 140 pounds and have kept the weight off for eight years by taking shortcuts in the kitchen. I live by the mantra "You don't have to be perfect to be successful." I may not be a professionally trained chef, but I sure am an experienced eater!

I created DIRTY, LAZY, KETO when I was working full-time while managing a hectic household. At the end of a busy day, I had to get dinner on the table—*fast!* There was no time to waste preparing unnecessary ingredients, or worse, making a meal my family wouldn't like. Instead, I got to work creating quick-fix DIRTY, LAZY, KETO meals that would help me to lose weight while being delicious enough for my whole family to enjoy (even my picky eaters!).

With lots of humor and practical tips, I'm here to share my fast and favorite family recipes. Inside *The DIRTY, LAZY, KETO® No Time to Cook Cookbook,* you'll find 100 great-tasting recipes—all 10 grams net carbs or less—that you can make in 30 minutes or less. *That's including prep time, people!* As always, the ingredients can even be found at discount grocery stores—nothing fancy required. That's just not how I roll. With simple, stress-free instructions, you'll have dinner ready and on the table before a delivery guy could possibly arrive at your doorstep.

Each dish is created from the DIRTY, LAZY, KETO basics: healthy fats, lean protein, and slow-burning carbs. You'll find:

- Recipes that can be prepared in under 30 minutes, including prep time!
- Helpful shortcuts for food prep and execution
- Suggestions to add variety or adjust the recipe to your tastes
- Macronutrients in line with DIRTY, LAZY, KETO principles
- Recipes that are no more than 10 grams net carbs per serving
- Tasty, time-saving "remixes" that transform yesterday's leftovers into an entirely new meal or snack to enjoy today
- One pot/one bowl recipes that save you tons of cleanup time

The DIRTY, LAZY, KETO® No Time to Cook Cookbook has everyone covered—from meals for picky eaters or big eaters, to fancier meals for guests and vegetarian-"ish" options (that don't contain meat, but may contain dairy or eggs). I designate how recipes meet a variety of needs by assigning these handy-dandy icons throughout the cookbook:

 REBOOT: It's a *"twofer"*! Make extra and use part for another meal.

 LESS MESS: One pot—one bowl? *Minimal* dish-washing.

 I'M HANGRY! Big-eater meals to *fill you up*!

 PICKY EATERS? *He likes it! She likes it!* Crowd-pleasing favorites.

 FANCY ENOUGH FOR GUESTS: *Ooh la la…* Looks impressive and tastes great!

 VEGETARIAN-"ISH": *"Kinda"* meatless, but may still call for dairy and/or eggs.

DIRTY, LAZY, KETO is a flexible, honest, real-world approach to losing weight while still living a normal life.

You'll find shortcuts throughout this cookbook to save you time and help you get food on the table in 30 minutes or less. Losing weight doesn't have to be complicated or time-consuming!

The DIRTY, LAZY, KETO® No Time to Cook Cookbook empowers you to keto your own way—in a style and on a schedule that works for *you*. Recipes in this judgment-free cookbook support your unique path to sustainable weight loss, *not perfection*.

Let's get started!

DIRTY, LAZY, KETO
SHORTCUTS

No Time? No Problem!

CHAPTER 1

DIRTY, LAZY, KETO CHECK-IN

KEEP IT REAL—START WHERE YOU'RE AT

Growing up, my husband and I both ate the same rotation of meals for dinner. Even though we lived a world apart, our families were equally *uncreative* in the kitchen (sorry, Mom!). We ate a similar conga line of basic American meals: spaghetti, hamburgers, tacos, lasagna, meat and potatoes, and, let's not forget, *leftovers*. Neither of us were exposed to any kind of fancy cooking; if we were experts at anything, it was *eating*.

Even without formal training, everyone knows what good food tastes like. That is all that matters when you're learning how to cook. Why spend time making food if you don't like the end result? The meal has to be worth your while. At the same time, most people don't want to spend an arm and a leg on ingredients or be chained to a stove all day long. There has to be a balance.

> DIRTY, LAZY, KETO recipes aren't complicated, time-consuming, or expensive.

You don't need to take out a second mortgage to buy ingredients or take the afternoon off work to figure out what to do. The stress of cooking healthier shouldn't cause you to bow out and sign up for a meal delivery service. You can do this on your own! No matter what your comfort level is in the kitchen, I'm going to help you get in and out of the kitchen fast—*one DIRTY, LAZY, KETO meal at a time*.

I lost 140 pounds and have maintained my weight loss for eight years by making recipes like these. The meals, snacks, and desserts are easy to make, and just as important, taste fantastic.

> I'm not missing out on "old favorites" because I am still enjoying them—I can make a modified low-carb version of just about anything!

Unlike other strict diets, DIRTY, LAZY, KETO is a complete lifestyle that you can follow forever. It's flexible, practical, and sustainable for the long haul. I'm living proof!

WHAT IS DIRTY, LAZY, KETO?

In my world, Dirty Keto means anything goes. No foods are "off the table" as long as you stay within your daily target amount of net carbs. If you want to eat a hot dog for lunch or drink a Diet Coke with dinner, then I say *do it*. Who am I to judge? Personally, I enjoyed many of these *so-called* "taboo" foods and I still lost weight. It's your choice whether or not to eat "Dirty Keto" foods like low-carb tortillas, shredded cheese, lunch meat, alcohol, sugar-free candy, low-carb ice cream, or zero-carb energy drinks. Only you can make that call. I won't judge your lifestyle for even a second.

Only you get to decide what to eat. Go ahead and show the keto police the door. Their criticism is not welcome here. *Buh-bye!*

To lose weight with DIRTY, LAZY, KETO, you don't have to follow rigid macronutrient guidelines. Lazy Keto is just as effective as the Strict Keto diet. Maybe even more so! You don't have to count calories, fat grams, amounts of protein, *and* net carbs to be successful with weight loss. **Lazy Keto means only tracking net carbs.** That was my strategy, and I found it extremely effective; I've helped thousands of others to do the same.

If my way sounds too loosey-goosey to be effective with your personality type, that's okay too. Some people find that strict counting of macronutrients helps them be more accountable. It's important that you follow your instincts. You can be strict with counting and "dirty" with ingredient choices if that tickles your fancy. DIRTY, LAZY, KETO supports you either way. In fact, here in this cookbook, I provide expanded nutrition information for every recipe. You will find accurate net carb counts per serving as well as the number of calories, and grams of fat, protein, sodium, fiber, carbohydrates, and sugar.

All methods are welcome here. Have a seat and get comfortable.

If the mere mention of doing complicated math causes your blood pressure to skyrocket, however, let me provide you with some reassurance. *You are not alone!* I can't handle advanced math problems either. I lost my weight without ever counting a single calorie, protein gram, or fat gram. I didn't use an app, nor did I make graphs or charts; I only kept track of net carbs. I ate 20–50 grams of net carbs per day. That's it! *I consistently lost weight.* That's Lazy Keto in a nutshell, folks.* I could talk about this all day long—no other topic gets me this excited!

DIRTY, LAZY, KETO is so simple, yet it works.

Before we start cooking, let's review a couple of basics, including how to calculate net carbs, the DLK food pyramid, foods to avoid, and approved drinks. We need to level-set our knowledge so everyone is on the same page.

First, you'll need to identify the key markers of a nutrition label with DIRTY, LAZY, KETO. Let's get started.

1 Notice the serving size.
2 Find the Total Carbohydrate number.
3 Subtract the amount of Dietary Fiber.
4 Subtract the amount of Sugar Alcohols (if applicable).
5 The result is the NET CARBS per serving.

Here's an example:

Nutrition Facts

Serving Size 1/2 Cup (64g)
Servings Per Container 4

Amount Per Serving

Calories 80	Calories from Fat 25
	% Daily Value*
Total Fat 2.5g	**4%**
Saturated Fat 1.5g	**8%**
Trans Fat 0g	
Cholesterol 45mg	**15%**
Sodium 110mg	**5%**
Total Carbohydrate 13g	**4%**
Dietary Fiber 2g	**8%**
Sugars 6g	
Sugar Alcohol 5g	
Protein 5g	**10%**
Vitamin A 2%	Vitamin C 0%
Calcium 10%	Iron 2%

*Percent Daily Values are based on a 2,000 calorie diet.

13
−2
−5
6

I wish I could tell you the magic number of net carbs you'll need to eat to ensure weight loss, but I believe that number is different for everyone. Age, activity level, hormones, and gender affect our metabolism.

TIER 1   **FRUITS, NUTS, AND SEEDS**   EAT JUST A HANDFUL

TIER 2   **FULL-FAT DAIRY**   LIMIT—USE COMMON SENSE

TIER 3   **NIGHTSHADE VEGETABLES**   EAT WITH CAUTION

  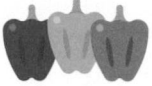

TIER 4   **NONSTARCHY VEGETABLES, HEALTHY FATS, LEAN PROTEINS**   WILL HELP KEEP YOU FULL

TIPS

Eat lots of nonstarchy vegetables!

Eat fats with your vegetables to make them more enjoyable.

Use fat only for satiety and satisfaction, not as a goal or as a food group.

AVOID

Bread   Pasta   Sugar   Milk   Corn   Beans   Rice

Water   Diet Soda   Tea   Coffee   Dry Wine   Spirits

To help explain why DIRTY, LAZY, KETO is so effective, I wrote a full support guide, *DIRTY, LAZY, KETO®: Get Started Losing Weight While Breaking the Rules* (St. Martin's Essentials, 2020). In this DLK handbook, I go into detail about how to start and make recommendations for what to eat. I give you the framework for success, but with helpful girlfriend advice to consider when things get rough. After all, we know food is just one part of the weight loss riddle!

WHAT'S REALLY STOPPING YOU?

Who's ready to start cooking? Are you PUMPED UP? Wait a minute… Why isn't anyone raising their hand?

You have a cookbook in front of you, but I notice you haven't started cooking yet. What are you waiting for?! Okay, *okay*…instead of harassing you, let me try a more empathetic approach. I might be able to guess why you're procrastinating. If you haven't cooked in a while (or ever!), you may be feeling a bit lost or intimidated. Those are valid feelings. It can be scary to try new things. Is that all, though?

> Sometimes we tell ourselves little fibs to stall for time. If that describes your situation, let me help pull the wool away from your eyes. Let's evaluate and debunk common myths about cooking that may be blocking your culinary progress.

I'm Not a Good Cook

To get you over the hump, let's redefine *cooking* to mean "fixing." Good cooks don't have to be gourmets; they just have to follow directions. I make DIRTY, LAZY, KETO recipes doable for everyone. Using easy-to-follow terms, I'll walk you through the exact steps needed to make one hundred scrumptious recipes. I promise to "keep it real" at all times. Strategies I use in *The DIRTY, LAZY, KETO® No Time to Cook Cookbook* are:

- Keep directions simple (not elaborate)
- Assemble already prepared ingredients (as opposed to making them from scratch)
- Take shortcuts (no wasting time)
- Simple execution (avoid unnecessary steps)

I'm Too Tired to Cook

It can be challenging to lose weight if you are constantly eating restaurant food. Portion control, limited menu choices, questionable ingredients, and social pressure all contribute to weight loss mayhem. *That's just not going to work!*

Additionally, many people mistake ordering takeout or eating meals at restaurants for bona fide "rewards" when they feel tired.

"I've worked a long day; I deserve to go out to eat."

Does that sound familiar?

> Food is not a treat (unless you are a dog). Instead, substitute healthier ways to reward yourself by *making more time for you.*

I Don't Know How to Cook

Start where you're at. No one is judging you! Set small, realistic goals. In fact, I recommend you aim *as low as possible* (don't laugh!). I use this technique often when trying to build up my confidence. By setting the bar low, I find it easier to become an overachiever. For instance, you could set a goal to make one meal per week from the cookbook. That sounds easy enough, right?

By expecting progress (not perfection) from yourself, you are much more likely to succeed. Interestingly, the pride and confidence that grow from learning a new skill (like cooking) will spill into other areas of your weight loss journey. Today, you conquer roasting a chicken, but tomorrow, *the world!*

Cooking Is Expensive

DIRTY, LAZY, KETO recipes are more affordable than going out to eat (for any ultra-cheapskates out there, you'll have fun poking around our last book, *The DIRTY, LAZY, KETO® Dirt Cheap Cookbook*). Every ingredient called for here is most likely something you're already familiar with. You probably have it in your kitchen right now! *Nothing fancy or expensive is required here.* Ingredients are available at your local grocery store.

Aside from your grocery bill, think about the money you'll save in the long run by losing weight. Healthier people don't get sick as often. Your overall quality of life will improve. *How much is that worth to you?*

I'll Have to Make Separate Meals

Everyone in your family can enjoy the same meal. DIRTY, LAZY, KETO recipes taste so decadent and delicious that folks will likely become suspicious about how these will help you lose weight! To help meet the needs of varying tastes, though, I provide suggested tips and tricks throughout the cookbook for you to make desired modifications. Recipes are designated with convenient "callouts" for specific audiences too. At the top of each recipe, symbols are used to inform you when a dish is perfect for picky eaters, guests coming over for dinner, those feeling extra hungry, and even those wanting something vegetarian-"ish" (no meat but may contain dairy/eggs).

I Have No Time

We all lead busy lives. At first glance, your packed schedule might seem too full for home cooking. I understand. But what happens when you take a closer look? Sometimes freeing up a window of time to cook is as simple as moving routines around or delegating tasks to others.

If that's not the case, though, and you're still pushing back about not having any free time, I suggest you have a more honest conversation with yourself. Is it possible your day is overscheduled on purpose? As a form of procrastination, many of us put personal needs last on the list. This is a sneaky way to avoid taking action.

Prioritizing your health is a decision that only you can make.

Once you commit, however, I'll be there to help you the rest of the way. (I promise it won't take all day either.) *The DIRTY, LAZY, KETO® No Time to Cook Cookbook* gives you all the immediate tools necessary to make healthy meals—and *fast*! I'll help you deliver results in 30 minutes or less.

DLK PEP TALK

I'm sensing you're finally ready to get started. This is going to be quite the adventure. Roll up your sleeves, my friend, because it's time to get down and dirty in the kitchen! (Don't worry, I'll give you tips for cleanup too.) With *The DIRTY, LAZY, KETO® No Time to Cook Cookbook* in hand, you'll learn how to prep your kitchen for maximum efficiency and execute meals at lightning speed. I'll be coaching you with specifics from the sidelines. As an added bonus, I promise to tell entertaining and encouraging stories every step of the way.

CHAPTER 2

GET READY FOR ACTION!

SET THE STAGE FOR SPEED

Organization is the name of the game for fast cooking. You need the right tools, sure, but more important, you need them at your fingertips. The 30-minute clock is ticking and we can't waste time looking for something.

Before you even think of preheating the oven, it's time to tidy up. You're going to need space to work, after all. I don't know about you, but my kitchen island is like a magnet for everything *unrelated* to cooking. Mail, homework, art projects, and dog leashes keep showing up, *no matter how many times I put them away*. It's maddening! In order to have a functioning kitchen, though, you have to stake your claim on the kitchen real estate and keep out trespassers.

> Removing unnecessary clutter from countertops
> is imperative for speedy cooking.

Now that you have cleared a space to work, you're going to cover the counters with all of your kitchen gadgets, cookware, and packaged food from your pantry. Yes, get *everything* out! Crawl under cabinets, empty the drawers, and unpack every shelf. Keep going! Don't stop until the cupboards are bare. Yes, we're getting all Marie Kondo in your kitchen, but we'll be doing it *DIRTY, LAZY, KETO style*.

A surprising reward for completing this activity is the likelihood of finding hidden treasures. Like the missing sock vortex in the laundry room, every kitchen has a black hole of forgotten items. Who knows what you might find? When cleaning out my own cabinets, I found a partially wrapped air fryer from last Christmas. *Score!* You might discover items you assumed were lost, or even better, stumble upon sentimental heirlooms. I know you'll find at least one surprise. *Press on.*

DO THE THREE-STEP SHUFFLE

Once you see everything you own, it's time to **analyze, evaluate, and organize**. Start by grouping similar items together—appliances in one spot, canned goods in another, for example. Did you discover anything obvious to get rid of? Getting rid of damaged equipment, duplicate items, or expired food is an easy place to start. Determining what *else* to get rid of, though? Well, that can be tricky.

As you evaluate what's spread out on the countertops, think about the current needs of your household. Ask yourself guiding questions to help you decide what stays and what goes: *How often is this used? Do I throw big parties? How many people do I serve at once? Does this have important sentimental value?*

Step 1. Let It Go!

Once you make a decision to get rid of something, remove it immediately. Load donations right away into the trunk of your car and fill the trash can with the rest.

- To charity—donate duplicate kitchen tools, junk food, items you don't use or no longer need.
- To the trash—send expired food, and broken or damaged equipment.

Step 2. Make It "Purty"

Clean the bare shelves and cabinets. How often are they empty like this, after all? Cleaning the space can be as simple or as elaborate as you'd like. At the very least, use the extension arm on your vacuum to suck out floating dust bunnies and spills from spices. If you have more energy, consider lining the shelves. Take note of anything that needs repairing, like broken hinges or knobs. The goal here is to maximize your available space; make sure every bit of storage space can be utilized.

Step 3. Create Workstations

Before you start shoving items back into your (now clean!) cabinets, I'm going to challenge you to have an open mind and consider a new organizational system. Instead of putting things back in the same place they've always been, let's do something different.

> Organize tools by their intended purpose and in a cabinet/drawer closest to where they will be used.

This strategy eliminates time searching for what you need. You'll have what you need and where you'll need it from the get-go. This method saves oodles of time!

Don't worry, I'll provide suggestions for how to organize your space. Not all of my ideas will apply (or appeal to your household). *That's okay!* Not everyone drinks coffee or has an outdoor grill; my suggestions aren't mandatory. I encourage you to create workstations based on your unique family needs. Be creative!

Before we begin, let me share a few caveats. Don't stress if you don't have the items I describe. They aren't necessarily required. I'm only trying to help you organize what you may have on hand. Later, I will provide a list of "must-have" items. *Stay tuned!* Second, don't be surprised that items often overlap. Expect intentional duplicates (when appropriate) in your workstations. I keep packages of sugar-free sweetener in two stations—my coffee area and my baking station. I store aluminum foil in *both* my grilling section *and* food packing drawer. The convenience of having the exact item where it's needed is worth the expense and trouble of stocking the same item in two places.

With efficiency in mind, carefully select the most appropriate spot for each station. You know your kitchen better than anyone else. How can you best use your space?

VEGETABLE PREP AREA
Choose a location nearest the sink to house cutting boards, colanders, and related kitchen tools (sharp knives, peeler, and so on). If

you don't have a kitchen drawer or cupboard for utensils next to your sink, think outside the box—place the items in a decorative cup instead (be careful with knives—safety first!).

BAKING SECTION

Gather all currently owned baking ingredients and cookware to store in one spot. Unless you bake often, the baking section could be off the beaten path in your kitchen. Baking hardware found in this section might be a mixer, mixing bowl, muffin tin, whisk, spring pan, nonstick baking sheet, Pyrex baking dish, measuring cups, measuring spoons, and so on. Common baking ingredients also stored here include coconut flour, almond flour, baking soda, baking powder, artificial sweetener, unsweetened coconut, 100% cocoa powder, and nonstick cooking spray.

MAIN MEAL STATION

Stow essential dinner-making tools next to the cooking area (stovetop, oven, and microwave). Examples include pots, pans, skillets, and specialty cooking trays (like a pizza pan). Helpful gadgets to stash in this section include a can opener, spatula, tongs, measuring cups, measuring spoons, pizza cutter, rubber spatula, oven mitts, and meat thermometer. Include food items here too, like cooking oils and spices.

FOOD PACKING

Organize available food storage containers (but only with matching lids!) to improve efficiency. In the same spot, keep a supply of disposables (aluminum foil, parchment paper, Ziploc bags, plastic wrap, and so on). Twist ties, lunch sacks, and permanent markers are helpful too.

KITCHEN APPLIANCE STORAGE

Shelve practical appliances you love (and know how to use!) alongside their ancillary parts in one centralized location (waffle maker, pressure cooker, slow cooker, blender, mixer, food processor, electric wok, and air fryer).

Instead of crawling on my hands and knees on the floor of the kitchen trying to find a particular kitchen appliance (and its accessories!), I finally had the bright idea to move them all to one spot, *out in the open*. I have my kitchen appliances lined up on a stainless steel rack next to my kitchen table. Yes, this shelf is a bit of an eyesore, I'll admit. But the time I've saved by being able to grab what I need? *It's so worth it.*

COFFEE AND TEA CART
Store coffee- and tea-related items adjacent to your coffee maker or teapot (mugs, ground coffee, immersion blender, filters, stir sticks, artificial sweetener packets, flavored sugar-free syrups, tea bags, and so on).

OUTDOOR GRILLING
Secure outdoor cooking–related items in one location. These include barbecue tools, an apron, long matches, outdoor foil, oven mitts, and so on.

PARTY SUPPLIES
Pack rarely used items (disposable party napkins, themed paper plates, birthday candles, holiday platters, tablecloths, travel potluck containers, etc.) out of the way, *relocated out of the kitchen altogether* if you have the space. I keep party decorations in my hall closet, and party platters and travel food containers are in my garage.

EATING STATION
In the space closest to the dishwasher (and the area where you eat meals), stack serving plates, silverware, and glasses, in addition to disposable plates, napkins, and cups.

CLEANUP SUPPLIES
Keep cleaning products (trash bags, antibacterial soap, dish soap, dishwasher soap, pot scrubber, antibacterial wipes, bleach spray, paper towels, and so on) stocked and accessible to help maintain a healthy and clean cooking environment.

FILL IN THE GAPS

Now that you have a better understanding of what's available in your kitchen, you can get to work filling in any gaps. Remove any potential barriers in your path to fast cooking. If you need a pressure cooker to make cooking easier, then so be it!

> Having a fully functioning kitchen is an investment
> in your health.

Go ahead and make a list of the outstanding tools you need. Replacing broken, outdated, or missing kitchen items doesn't have to break the bank. You won't need to max out your credit card. Before heading to the mall, try stopping by a thrift store first. You might be surprised at the selection of donated kitchen tools and quality bakeware. You never know what treasure you'll find! Shopping at discount (or dollar) stores is another viable option, especially for smaller, inexpensive items. Lastly, don't be afraid to ask for help. Send an email to friends and family with your wish list or offer to do a trade.

> Upgrade your kitchen supplies over time; for now,
> just start with acquiring the basics.

STEPHANIE'S FAST COOKING ESSENTIALS

- **Tools and Gadgets:** colander, sharp knives, pizza cutter, julienne vegetable peeler, silicone spatula, kitchen shears, meat thermometer, immersion blender, whisk
- **Cookware:** nonstick baking sheet, skillet, pots/pans, glass Pyrex dishes, muffin tin, pizza pan
- **Appliances:** pressure cooker with accessories (steamer basket, muffin tin), slow cooker, blender, mixer, waffle maker, microwave, air fryer, food processor
- **Duplicates:** mixing bowls, measuring cups, measuring spoons, food storage containers, small dishwasher-safe cutting boards
- **Disposables:** Ziploc bags in all sizes, parchment paper, extra-large heavy-duty aluminum foil, aluminum foil sheets, heavy-duty plastic wrap

Now that your kitchen is efficiently prepared and organized to support speedy cooking, you're ready to tackle the next step: food!

CHAPTER 3

CLOCK'S TICKIN'—30 MINUTES OR LESS

SECRET SAUCE FOR FAST COOKING?

Finally! We're ready to talk about my favorite part—*food*! You'll quickly discover how important it is to buy the *right ingredients* at the store. By *right*, I mean "correctly packaged." Cauliflower is sold a dozen ways, for example, and the subtle nuances between each choice affect how much time is required for prepping and cooking (and net carb count too!). To help you avoid any potential pitfalls, I'll share my DIRTY, LAZY, KETO shopping hacks for selecting the perfect time-saving ingredients.

To start, you'll need to arm yourself with a strategic shopping list. You don't want to waste your precious time aimlessly meandering down every aisle looking for something that "looks good." An itemized list isn't the only thing you'll need. You must also bring a sharp and critical mind. Judiciously choose what ingredients to buy. Challenge every purchase decision.

"Will *this* help me cook fast?"

If the answer is no, *put that sucker back.*

Too often, we get caught up in the shopping experience. We become distracted by discounts or begin romanticizing what we're willing or capable of doing in the kitchen. In the produce aisle, a

BOGO cauliflower promotion tempts you to fill up your cart with a dozen heads. *It's on sale, right?* You might become delusional, thinking of spending the afternoon making organic riced cauliflower with a Cuisinart food processor (and you don't own one!). Slap both cheeks and wake up from that fantasy! I don't want you feeling bad when those dreams turn into a nightmare of moldy cauliflower.

You don't have to make ingredients from scratch to lose weight.

> Unlike other strict diets, DIRTY, LAZY, KETO empowers you to cheat with artificial ingredients and time-saving tricks in the kitchen.

Food doesn't have to be locally sourced, organic, or 100 percent homemade for you to lose weight. Let me assure you that it's okay to cut corners! I lost 140 pounds by using tricks like these on a regular basis. Stop trying to be Martha Stewart already and *just be you*. Embrace these dirty or lazy tips and free yourself from judgment.

TAKE INGREDIENT SHORTCUTS

At the store, I shop for ingredients that help make cooking fast. *Do they cost more?* Sometimes, yes, but not always. There are plenty of ways to buy shortcut ingredients at discounted prices. When I stumble upon a good sale, I take advantage and buy extra. My pantry and freezer are chock-full. I'm also flexible with meal planning. I've been known to spontaneously change my dinner plans after discovering a tempting sale. Occasionally, when it's important to me, I choose to spend more money when I know it will save me time later. Ingredient shortcuts to consider:

- **Precooked Meats.** Rotisserie chicken, cooked shrimp, and precooked sausage make meal assembly a snap. Check the inventory of your grocery store deli and you might discover a wide variety of precooked meats at competitive prices.
- **Prewashed, Precut Veggies**. Speed up meal prep by taking produce shortcuts. Buy shredded coleslaw, bags of prewashed spinach, or freshly cleaned and sliced mushrooms and bypass meal prep. I even buy jars of preminced garlic to skip a step while cooking.

- **Frozen Foods.** Fresh is not always the best choice when it comes to speedy cooking. Vegetables like riced cauliflower, zoodles, or fajita mix can transform a meal in seconds—*straight from the freezer!* May I remind you that frozen berries don't need washing? Flash-frozen (individually portioned) meats also save time without ever sacrificing flavor.
- **Premade Sauces.** Stock your pantry or fridge with assorted sauce starters: Alfredo sauce, no-sugar-added marinara sauce, or Indian simmer sauces.
- **Jarred or Canned Items.** With virtually no prep time needed, canned foods reduce cook time. I sometimes prefer the flavor of canned versus fresh. Examples of my favorites include canned green beans, artichoke hearts, and coconut milk.
- **Direct-to-Microwave Vegetables.** More and more vegetables are being sold in microwave-ready packages. You don't even have to stab the package with a fork to vent the bag before heating! (Can you get lazier than that?) So far, I've discovered Brussels sprouts, green beans, riced cauliflower, and broccoli florets sold in these miraculous, time-saving pouches.

MENTALLY PREPARING

Having the right ingredients on hand is only half the battle when it comes to speed cooking. What you do with them next is equally important. To make recipes in 30 minutes or less, you'll need to apply time-saving strategies in the kitchen *at every step*. For me, this starts with meal planning.

Hunt and Gather

Before I go to bed at night, I think about what I'll eat the next day (don't judge). I spend a few minutes in the kitchen looking for needed ingredients, making notes of any missing items on a shopping list. I pull required items from the pantry and glance at the spice rack to make sure I have everything I need. In one messy pile, I dump the ingredients onto the kitchen counter. Depending on what I'm making, I'll drag out necessary cooking gadgets (like a slow cooker) and add it to the heap. Lastly, before I head to bed, I transfer frozen meat to the fridge to safely thaw.

When I wake up the next day, I have a smile on my face. I'm prepped for success! I've removed any anxiety or guesswork about what to eat for dinner. Sure, I might have to stop by the store for any missing ingredients (let's be realistic, this happens), but aside from any hiccups, I'm ready for action.

Before You Start

Cooking a meal goes much more smoothly when everything is ready from the get-go. Assemble all necessary ingredients in one spot before you start. Prep ingredients ahead of time with speed in mind.

- Start with thawed meat.
- Buy smaller cuts of meat to begin with (smaller pieces cook faster).
- Transform larger cuts of meat into smaller sizes (pound into thin slices, cut into smaller pieces or strips).
- Prep vegetables (wash, clean, cut) ahead of time.
- Chop food into smaller, evenly sized pieces (for even cooking time).
- Open every package at once.

FLASH COOKING METHODS

When it's time to actually cook the food, choose methods that speed up the process. You don't have to sacrifice flavor during this step. Think about ways you can bring the heat to get the job done in the most efficient way possible.

- **Be "Spacy."** Spread out food so it cooks efficiently and evenly, both horizontally and vertically. Strive for thin layers of food; thicker cuts require additional cook time.
- **Fat Is Your Friend.** Don't be afraid to use fats like oil when cooking. Remember, DIRTY, LAZY, KETO recommends using fat to make healthy food taste better! In addition to helping with satiety, fat helps food to cook faster.
- **Execute.** Turn up the heat! Use hot methods of cooking to get the job done quicker. While it might seem obvious, some methods of cooking are faster than others, including:
  - Outdoor grilling
  - Baking in the oven at higher temperatures

- Broiling food on high
- Stovetop cooking on medium to high heat
- **Go, Go, Gadget!** Don't be afraid to use plug-in gadgets to help you cook faster. Some might surprise you (like an air fryer)! Overall, gadgets speed up cooking by helping you to multitask. They also free up valuable stovetop space. Here are some that I find very helpful.
  - Pressure cooker
  - Air fryer
  - Electric wok
  - Waffle maker
- **Multitask.** Get more done (in less time) by doing several jobs at once. This doesn't have to be stressful. Multitasking can be as simple as precooking vegetables in the microwave while stir-frying meat on the stovetop. Don't be afraid to use unconventional cooking methods. Get creative and #breaktherules. For example:
  - Instead of cooking bacon in a frying pan, bake it in the oven.
  - Use a pressure cooker to make hard-boiled eggs.
  - Microwave scrambled eggs.
  - Use a waffle maker to grill sausage.

DOUBLE OR NOTHING

Think several steps ahead when prepping for a meal. If you're cleaning one stalk of celery, why not clean two? Better yet, prep all the vegetables for the week at once. As long as you're planning on using the food in the immediate future, doubling up on a job now saves time later. Additionally, I recommend you reboot entire portions of your meal from one day to the next. Call it leftovers or creative meal planning, but taking practical shortcuts like these saves valuable time.

- Make double portions of a meal and freeze the second one for later.
- Cook or chop double the amount of an ingredient to use again later in the week.
- Recycle leftovers from today's meal. Enjoy again tomorrow.

BE A TECHNO

Use hands-free available technology to help problem solve in the kitchen. You won't have to stop what you're doing to look something up.

"Alexa, how many tablespoons are in a cup?"

"Alexa, how do you make pesto?"

Pair cooking with music or listening to a podcast to make it more enjoyable.

"Alexa, play Italian cooking music on Spotify."

Set cooking timers and reminders with Siri and Alexa to keep yourself on schedule.

"Alexa, remind me to defrost steaks for dinner at six a.m. tomorrow."

"Siri, set a 10-minute bacon timer."

When you're not in the kitchen, plan ahead for what to make. Use your iPad or other digital device to search and store recipes. This is much faster than flipping through cookbooks (this cookbook excluded, of course!).

TIME TO EAT? BUT I'M NOT HUNGRY.

Stop making meals just because you feel like *you are supposed to*. If your family is too busy (or not interested) in eating a big dinner, then don't make one! Or maybe your family would prefer to sit down for lunch instead? Society's norms may not apply to you—*and that's just fine*. Not a morning eater? Skip breakfast, I say! By empowering yourself to follow your own rhythm, you'll eat DIRTY, LAZY, KETO foods when you actually feel hungry, not because it's "time." This strategy will save you crazy amounts of time (and frustration) in the kitchen.

Stop making meals no one wants to eat; #BreaktheRules! Eat breakfast for dinner, leftover dinner for lunch, or lunch foods for breakfast.

Do what works for you and your body, and do it on your own schedule.

CHAPTER 4

NO MESS COOKIN'

BE FAST, EFFICIENT, EFFECTIVE...AND FABULOUS

In my kitchen, we maintain order (and sanity!) by operating under one guiding principle: "Start clean, end clean." Yes, there might be some swear words yelled when the bacon burns—*language doesn't count*—but with everything else, we try our best to keep the kitchen tidy.

How does that work on a day-to-day basis? At my house, I expect the kitchen to look tidy *before* I even start cooking. Clean dishes from the dishwasher are put away, the sink is empty, and counters are cleared of distractions and interferences *before* I start making a meal. It's like a painter sitting down to create a masterpiece. He wants to start with fresh brushes and a blank canvas, right? If you're going to create a work of art in the kitchen, you too need a clean slate.

From a practical standpoint, I've had to break the "start clean, end clean" message down to specifics to avoid any confusion about what I'm asking for. Don't laugh, but sometimes folks need clear directions.

- You ate it? *You clean it up.* Walk your dishes back to the sink.
- Rinse your plate/cup/silverware after use and load directly into the dishwasher.
- Push food scraps down the disposal with running water until it magically disappears.

- Instead of complaining that the trash smells, take the bag out to the curb!
- When the milk carton is empty (or anything else in the fridge, for that matter), throw it away but add that item to the grocery list.

Your house rules may be different from mine. Everyone has different hot buttons. One of mine, for example, is the necessity to cover the food inside the microwave. It only takes a second for a nuclear-style explosion to occur. Using an inexpensive food cover or removable tray in the microwave is an insurance policy for easy cleanup, but it's only effective when people actually use it. Otherwise, mayhem occurs. No one ever admits to causing a marinara sauce detonation!

Maintaining order like this requires teamwork. Rather than leaving standards up to interpretation, I recommend being direct and blunt with your expectations (and maybe even LOUD!).

"Do you want dinner or *NOT*, people?"

You're not asking for much here, so stop feeling guilty. No one is doing *you* a favor by cleaning up after *themselves*. **Keeping the kitchen clean is about common decency and courteousness.** These are life skills needed for adulthood. Your family should be thanking you!

MINIMIZE MESS

Do yourself a favor. Do more with less *from the get-go*.

Intentionally streamlining your cooking methods will help you get in and out of the kitchen fast. I'll teach you how to make DIRTY, LAZY, KETO meals in 30 minutes or less, and in a way that reduces any unnecessary cleanup afterward.

My favorite "clean" cooking methods require a limited number of pots or pans. When you're finished cooking, there shouldn't be a pile of dirty pots and pans left behind in the sink.

ONE-STOP SHOP

- **Sheet Pan.** Line a 12" × 18" (or equivalent) baking sheet pan with extra-large aluminum foil or parchment paper and bake all of the ingredients you need at the same time. Clean up *in seconds* by simply throwing away the lining. *Hello!*
- **Disposables.** Use disposable aluminum trays for cooking or leave them behind at a potluck or barbecue for your host to reuse.

PIONEER MODE

- **Grill.** After you're finished cooking on the barbecue, crank up the heat *caveman-style* and burn off any remaining food that was stuck to the grill. Done.
- **Cast Iron Skillet.** Remove food scraps using a spatula. Next, reheat the cast iron skillet and scrub the surface with coarse salt and oil. That's it!

ONE AND DONE

- **Plug and Play.** Cook the entire meal, snack, or dessert all at once inside a single device like a pressure cooker, air fryer, or slow cooker, leaving only one item to be cleaned afterward.
- **First Apartment Style.** I moved into my first place without much cookware. As a result, I had to get creative when fixing something to eat. My breakfast might be cooked and served in the same cup I used earlier to drink my morning coffee. This unique method is perfect for making personalized portions like a mug cake dessert!

CLEAN AS YOU GO

My family is always being pulled many different directions. As soon as dinner is over, the whole family (including the dog) walks our son to swim practice. There isn't a lot of extra time to waste on cleanup—I'm sure you can relate. Your time is valuable.

Instead of waiting until the meal is finished to determine who will do the dishes, let me suggest an alternative. Tidy up as you go! This isn't as hard (or painful) as you might think. Follow these easy suggestions and stop arguing over whose turn it is. The kitchen will be clean in seconds flat.

- **Wet and Wild.** Keep dirty dishes wet. A little soap and water added NOW prevent the dreaded crustiness from occurring LATER!
- **Multitask.** In between cooking steps, make productive use of your time. Rinse/dry/put away dishes that were only lightly used (like a measuring cup used to measure dry ingredients or a cutting board used briefly to chop vegetables). Not every dish needs to be run through the dishwasher. Sometimes, a quick rinse and dry is all it needs. If an item requires a deeper clean, like after touching raw meat, quickly give it a rinse and immediately load it into the dishwasher.
- **Family Rule.** As a household, agree that eating a meal doesn't begin until an agreed-upon standard has been met. For example, "No one eats dinner until all pots and pans that were used are washed and dried" or "All dishes (currently in the sink) must be loaded into the dishwasher before anyone sits down at the table." It's amazing how motivated and helpful your family can become when they are hungry!

ASK FOR HELP...(OR NOT)?

My kitchen is tiny. Since there isn't a lot of room, I tend to ferociously protect my space. Inviting others into my domain under the guise of "helping" would backfire and ultimately slow me down. With such limited real estate, there is literally no room available for an extra pair of hands. A crowded kitchen might cause an accident (or a fight, let's be honest). Besides, I've already got the dog underfoot as my dance partner. Even though she sometimes causes me to trip, her 100 percent success rate of cleaning up spills and dropped food makes the interference tolerable.

It's not that I don't want assistance; I really do. But I've discovered more effective ways to get the help I need for cleaning up the kitchen:

- **"I Called It!"** Household members can elect to manage certain cleanup responsibilities permanently. I have found that there are jobs that some people just *like*, and I recommend you capitalize on enthusiasm. As many of you know from reading *The DIRTY, LAZY, KETO® Dirt Cheap Cookbook*, my husband (God bless him!) is the thriftiest person I know. He promptly removes and sorts disposed kitchen packaging, turning so-called "trash" *into cold hard cash*. His commitment to recycling is not only helpful; it's downright AMAZING!

- **Alternate.** Assign specific days to family members for tasks to get done. For example, on odd dates, males are in charge of cleanup, while on even dates, females take over. Be creative to meet your family's needs and lifestyle. A division of labor doesn't have to be fifty-fifty for this strategy to work. You may only cook on weekends, and your partner weekdays, or vice versa. In some relationships, one person cooks, but the other shops and cleans. Do what works for your schedule and individual family dynamic. There is no right or wrong way to divide up kitchen duties as long as everyone is left feeling happy.

- **Routines.** In my experience, tasks that occur at the same time every day are more likely to be completed. Taking out the trash every night after dinner, even if it's not really needed, helps keep up the routine long term. Don't believe me? Try asking a teenager to take out the trash "when it's needed," and you'll watch him transform into a human trash compactor to avoid doing the job. *As needed* often gets lost in translation. In fact, my son believes that phrase means, "I'll take out the trash when Mom threatens to take away my Xbox." To avoid frustration, rely on consistent routines instead. Examples of effective routines include: Never go to sleep with dishes still in the sink, wipe table and counters after every dinner, and so on.

- **Throw It Away.** I realize this last suggestion is extremely controversial. Using disposable paper and cooking products is definitely NOT good for the environment. *You're right about that!* My family diligently recycles everything (as mentioned previously), so in my household, at least, we try to balance using disposable products with painstaking, thorough sorting and recycling of what's in our trash. I don't think trying to be perfect should stop you from taking shortcuts to start cooking. If your decision to eat healthier depends on using paper plates and napkins, then I say, *do it.*

STEPHANIE'S TOP TEN HACKS

Cleanup doesn't have to be a drag. With a little teamwork and planning, you can become more efficient and *even speedy* during kitchen cleanup. My goal is to help you cook healthy meals, true, but I also want to help you simplify mealtime (while having fun). This strategy ensures you'll be likely to repeat the process *all over again*! Feel free to borrow one of my top ten workflow hacks to help keep things speeding along. Share your tips with me too! Post on social media using: @dirtylazyketo #dlkcookbook

1 **Trash Bowl.** Instead of making what seems like hundreds of trips to the kitchen trash can during meal prep, toss dribs and drabs as they arise into a designated trash bowl placed on the countertop (the trash bowl is just a pot or bowl you already dirtied while cooking). Empty the contents of your trash bowl to the main kitchen trash only once, at the very end of cooking your meal.

2 **Extra Trash Bags.** Instead of searching for replacement trash bags, keep extra bags at the bottom of the can. Additionally, toss a few fresh-smelling dryer sheets at the bottom of the trash can to combat foul odors.

3 **Mini Trash Trips.** Where I live, disposable plastic grocery bags from the grocery store are a thing of the past. I covet these disposable bags and store them under my kitchen sink stuffed inside an empty plastic milk jug. These mini grocery bags are perfect for trash that can't wait—that stinky or leaky trash that needs to go to the outside garbage receptacle pronto.

4 **Play Music.** Cleaning is much more fun while your favorite songs are playing!

5 **Silverware Mash-Up.** Instead of manually sorting clean silverware into categories (knife, spoon, fork), store mixed utensils together in a giant heap. *Who really cares?*

6 **Foil.** I buy three sizes of aluminum foil: a standard-sized roll for everyday use regular-sized precut sheets to line small trays, and a heavy-duty, extra-large-sized foil roll for lining baking sheets or (sometimes) the grill. Mama loves a quick, disposable cleanup!

7 **Wipes.** In addition to buying spray disinfectant cleaner and paper towels, I keep dispensers of premoistened disinfectant wipes on hand. I find they are easier (and safer) for my kids to use when wiping down counters or mopping up spills. (In case you're wondering why I buy the more expensive premoistened wipes, I've learned the hard way that little boys and spray bottles don't go together!)

8 **Silicone Bakeware.** Upgrade your Teflon cupcake tins (and other baking dishes) to modern silicone bakeware. Say goodbye to paper cupcake liners; your muffins will pop out fast and easy with a flexible twist of the pan, just like when emptying an ice cube tray.

9 **White Towels.** I replaced my mismatched decorative kitchen towels with more practical white flour-sack towels. They are super absorbent, inexpensive to buy in bulk, and easy to bleach clean in the laundry.

10 **Reusable Cups and Straws.** I thank my teenage daughter for introducing me to washable reusable straws and insulated thermal cups. Rather than pull out a fresh glass each time they want to pour a drink (leaving behind a sink full of barely used cups), my children each have their own Hydro Flask for refilling. They each take great pride in caring for their custom bottle, even going so far as to decorate it with stickers. Reusable cups are great for cleanup, and helpful to the environment.

THE DIRTY, LAZY, KETO RECIPES

Short on Time, Long on Flavor

CHAPTER 5

BREAKFAST

In the morning, I do a lot of *skedaddling*. I'm constantly rushing from one end of the house to the other. The clock is ticking and I'm desperately trying to maximize every second. Did the dog go out yet? *Yes.* Is my lunch packed? *Check.* Is there anything left in the kids' backpacks I need to look at? *Ooops!* I'll have to text the kids—they just left for school. Okay, what about dinner? I glance up at the clock…*I should've left by now!*

If your mornings are as stressful as mine, I'm sure you could benefit from some uberfast tips on how to make a DIRTY, LAZY, KETO breakfast quickly and get out the door fast. **A healthy meal doesn't have to be complicated.** Sometimes food can be made the night before—a quick reheat in the microwave and you're ready to go! Other times, pulling out something from the freezer works just as well. I make yummy treats like chaffles on the weekend (when I have more time) and freeze the extra portions. I can quickly reheat a fabulous breakfast as I'm about to walk out the door.

Redefining what breakfast looks like or how it's made is equally helpful when you're pressed for time. My husband (and coauthor) introduced me to the concept of microwaving scrambled eggs when we first got married. At first I was offended by his bachelor ways! Who scrambles an egg in the microwave? *That's ridiculous.* Two kids and a career later, though? I've embraced the technique. **Speed is sometimes more important than perfection.**

During a recent *DIRTY, LAZY, Girl* podcast recording, my cohost, Dr. Tamara Sniezek, blew my mind when talking about eating a salad for breakfast. A *salad*. Really! Once I stopped laughing, I realized maybe she was onto something here. Who says we have to eat cereal, oatmeal, or toast for breakfast? That advice didn't work out well for me! I've decided to be more open-minded about what I eat in the morning.

When I'm pinched for time, or eating breakfast on the go, eating healthy food is all that matters.

HOT-FOOTED HOMESTYLE "POTATOES"

Sometimes you may feel like your family isn't being supportive. Changing the habits of other people can be an uphill battle. It's possible, however, that your family isn't trying to be malicious—they just may not understand what DIRTY, LAZY, KETO is all about. For example, my in-laws regularly make homestyle potatoes for breakfast when we come to visit. Potatoes are a vegetable, right? Not so fast! They were curious to try this lower-carb alternative using the potato's distant low-carb cousin—*the radish!*

¼ cup unsalted butter

2 cups chopped (¼"–½" chunks) radishes

½ cup chopped green onions

½ cup thinly sliced green bell pepper

2 tablespoons water

1 teaspoon Creole seasoning

1 In a medium skillet over medium heat, melt butter.

2 Stir in all remaining ingredients and cook 20 minutes covered, stirring regularly until radishes are starting to brown and all liquid has been absorbed.

3 Serve warm on a plate.

NET CARBS

2G

SERVES 4

PER SERVING:

CALORIES	117
FAT	11G
PROTEIN	1G
SODIUM	376MG
FIBER	1G
CARBOHYDRATES	3G
NET CARBS	2G
SUGAR	2G

TIME

PREP TIME:	10 MINUTES
COOK TIME:	20 MINUTES
TOTAL TIME:	30 MINUTES

TIPS & OPTIONS

Radishes are what I call one of the Seven Wonders of DIRTY, LAZY, KETO. Darn if they don't taste just like fried potatoes.

For added fiber and fullness, keep the skin on these gems during preparation.

Reboot Hot-Footed Homestyle "Potatoes" in No-Bake "Potato" Soup (see Chapter 6).

NET CARBS

2G

SERVES 4

PER SERVING:

CALORIES	457
FAT	40G
PROTEIN	17G
SODIUM	638MG
FIBER	1G
CARBOHYDRATES	3G
NET CARBS	2G
SUGAR	1G

TIME

PREP TIME:	10 MINUTES
COOK TIME:	15 MINUTES
TOTAL TIME:	25 MINUTES

TIPS & OPTIONS »

If a perfectly shaped poached egg is NOT important to you, take a shortcut and poach multiple eggs simultaneously. Cut away and dispose of any egg white strands coming off the poached eggs.

Reboot leftover Hollandaise Sauce by enjoying ASAP Asparagus with "Holiday" Sauce (see Chapter 9).

You have my permission to skip going to the gym today. All that whisking counts as a workout.

When poaching eggs, fresh are best. Make friends with neighbors that have chickens. *That's what I did!*

Enjoying a rich sauce like Hollandaise on my Early Eggs with Benefits feels so rich and decadent! Contrary to what many of us were taught, eating fat will help, not hurt, your weight loss efforts.

Poached Eggs

1 tablespoon white vinegar

4 large eggs

Hollandaise Sauce

2 large egg yolks

½ cup unsalted butter, melted

1 tablespoon 100% lemon juice

¼ teaspoon salt

⅛ teaspoon ground black pepper

Toppings

4 slices Canadian bacon

4 slices Boogie Bread (see recipe in this chapter)

1 teaspoon chopped fresh parsley

1 Make the Poached Eggs: In a large saucepan over medium heat, bring 3"–4" of water to a boil. Stir in vinegar.

2 Over a small bowl, carefully crack 1 egg into a small strainer, draining and discarding any loose egg white. Transfer intact egg yolk with membrane from strainer to a small bowl. Repeat process, creating four small bowls of strained eggs.

3 Using a slotted spoon, gently create a slow swirling vortex in the boiling water in the saucepan. Gently pour 1 egg at a time into the center of the vortex and allow swirling water to cook egg 3½ minutes. Remove poached egg using slotted spoon and set aside. Repeat for remaining eggs.

4 Make the Hollandaise: In the bottom of a double boiler over medium-high heat, add 1" water. Heat until water begins to boil.

5 In the top pan of the double boiler, whisk together egg yolks.

6 Slowly, pour melted butter into sauce, whisking rapidly until desired thickness is achieved. Add lemon juice, salt, and pepper and stir.

7 Remove from heat and set aside.

8 On a large microwave-safe plate, spread out Canadian bacon and microwave on high 1 minute. Place 1 slice bacon on top of 1 slice Boogie Bread. Top bacon slice with 1 poached egg. Repeat with remaining bacon, eggs, and bread.

9 Dollop generous portions of Hollandaise Sauce onto each stack. Sprinkle with parsley. Serve immediately.

ALARM CLOCK CEREAL

NET CARBS

2G

SERVES 1

PER SERVING:
CALORIES	140
FAT	11G
PROTEIN	3G
SODIUM	1MG
FIBER	6G
CARBOHYDRATES	8G
NET CARBS	2G
SUGAR	1G

TIME

PREP TIME:	6 MINUTES
COOK TIME:	2 MINUTES
TOTAL TIME:	8 MINUTES

TIPS & OPTIONS

Take Alarm Clock Cereal on the road to enjoy while traveling. Simply prep the dry ingredients at home, pouring a single serving inside a snack-sized Ziploc bag. Use the in-room coffee maker to heat up the needed water. Clever, right?

Reboot unused portions of Alarm Clock Cereal as Accelerated Acai Bowl toppings (see recipe in this chapter).

Feeling fancy? Top your cereal with sugar-free chocolate chips. Lily's, ChocZero, and Hershey's all make varieties of sugar-free chocolate chips you can try.

Even on the weekends, I'm an early riser. I'm excited to jump out of bed and *start the day*. My family, on the other hand, doesn't always share my enthusiasm. They would prefer I don't bang pots and pans to make breakfast while they are still sleeping. Slackers! When I'm trying to be considerate, my go-to "quiet" meals are either a cup of yogurt (in the summer) or a warm bowl of Alarm Clock Cereal (in the winter). *Shhhh!*

½ cup water

1 tablespoon chia seeds

1 tablespoon unsweetened shredded coconut

1 tablespoon crushed pecans

3 (1-gram) packets 0g net carbs sweetener

⅛ teaspoon ground cinnamon

1 In a microwave-safe cup, add water and microwave on high 2 minutes until boiling.

2 Combine all dry ingredients in a large coffee cup.

3 Carefully add boiling water to cereal mixture and stir. Let cool 4–5 minutes, stirring occasionally until cool enough to eat. Enjoy!

PROMPT PROTEIN PANCAKES

The number of available protein powders on the market is startling. At the grocery store, I've been known to stand in a complete stupor trying to figure out which is which. What a time waster! It's become so ridiculous that I now force myself to only order protein powder online (where I can quickly zero in on the product I want). Don't get me wrong; protein powder is worth the added effort and expense. I find the ingredient invaluable for making morning smoothies and recipes like my favorite Prompt Protein Pancakes. These pancakes give me more energy than Pop-Tarts ever did!

- 4 large eggs, beaten
- ¼ cup full-fat cream cheese, softened
- 1 teaspoon baking powder
- 3 (19-gram) scoops low-carb vanilla protein powder
- ¾ cup unsweetened almond milk
- ⅛ teaspoon salt

1. In a food processor, pulse all ingredients 30–60 seconds until completely blended.

2. Heat a large nonstick skillet over medium heat.

3. Pour pancakes of desired size in skillet, using half the batter, and flip after 3–5 minutes, when bubbles are showing.

4. Remove after 2–3 minutes when starting to brown. Repeat with remaining batter.

5. Serve warm.

NET CARBS

1G

SERVES 4

PER SERVING:

CALORIES	172
FAT	10G
PROTEIN	16G
SODIUM	403MG
FIBER	1G
CARBOHYDRATES	2G
NET CARBS	1G
SUGAR	1G

TIME

PREP TIME:	10 MINUTES
COOK TIME:	16 MINUTES
TOTAL TIME:	26 MINUTES

TIPS & OPTIONS

I recommend topping with butter while still warm.

Feeling frisky? A dollop of rebooted Swoop Cream (see Chapter 11) and a few strawberries will start the day just right! Other creative toppings include sugar-free chocolate chips, blueberries, or (*gasp!*) sugar-free chocolate syrup.

Have you found a sugar-free pancake syrup yet? My all-time favorite is Mrs. Butterworth's. I find it to be the thickest of the available low-carb options on the market.

DELIVERY DONUTS

When I was a kid, my sibling and I clamored to be first to open the door when Gram came to visit. Like any good grandparent, she brought more than just hugs and kisses. Perhaps most important (sorry, Gram!), she held a large container full of homemade red velvet donuts. Everyone tried to steal those Delivery Donuts! My keto-friendly donut recipe has just as much pizazz, but without so many carbs.

½ cup 0g net carbs sweetener

½ cup superfine blanched almond flour

¼ cup coconut flour

2 tablespoons unsweetened 100% cocoa powder

1 teaspoon baking powder

1 teaspoon xanthan gum

⅛ teaspoon ground cayenne pepper

⅛ teaspoon salt

½ cup heavy whipping cream

1 tablespoon full-fat sour cream

1 teaspoon pure vanilla extract

1 large egg, beaten

3 tablespoons coconut oil, melted

2 tablespoons sugar-free chocolate chips

⅓ cup Frantic Vanilla Frosting (see Chapter 11)

2–4 drops red food coloring

1. Preheat oven to 350°F. Grease six donut molds thoroughly with nonstick cooking spray.

2. In a large bowl, combine sweetener, almond flour, coconut flour, cocoa powder, baking powder, xanthan gum, cayenne, and salt and mix well.

3. In a medium bowl, whisk together all remaining ingredients except chocolate chips, frosting, and food coloring.

4. Whisk wet ingredients into dry ingredients. Fold in chocolate chips until thoroughly blended.

5. Transfer batter to a large Ziploc bag and snip 1" from corner.

6. Evenly pipe mixture into prepared donut molds, making six donuts. Bake 23–24 minutes until cooked throughout and starting to brown.

7. In a small bowl, combine frosting and food coloring until well blended and desired color is achieved.

8. While donuts are still warm, spread each with equal amounts of frosting. Frosting will melt like a glaze as donuts cool.

NET CARBS

5G

SERVES 6

PER SERVING:	
CALORIES	272
FAT	24G
PROTEIN	6G
SODIUM	177MG
FIBER	5G
CARBOHYDRATES	13G
NET CARBS	5G
SUGAR	2G
SUGAR ALCOHOL	3G

TIME

PREP TIME:	6 MINUTES
COOK TIME:	24 MINUTES
TOTAL TIME:	30 MINUTES

TIPS & OPTIONS

Top with chopped nuts, shredded unsweetened coconut, or sugar-free chocolate chips before frosting dries to "lock 'em in good."

Gallon-sized or freezer-grade Ziploc bags work best for makeshift pastry bags. Anything smaller is likely to split at the seams when pressure is used to squeeze out the batter.

BOOGIE BREAD

NET CARBS

1G

SERVES 2

PER SERVING:
CALORIES	150
FAT	14G
PROTEIN	5G
SODIUM	131MG
FIBER	1G
CARBOHYDRATES	2G
NET CARBS	1G
SUGAR	0G

TIME

PREP TIME:	5 MINUTES
COOK TIME:	10 MINUTES
TOTAL TIME:	15 MINUTES

Intermittent fasting (also referred to as I.F.) is all the rage these days. It can be interpreted different ways, but in my mind, I.F. is a fancy way of saying, "No eating after dinner, Stephanie." Call it whatever you want, but this strategy is effective. No good decisions about food are made late at night—*at least in my kitchen*! Plus, as an added benefit, I wake up the next morning motivated (and hungry!) to make a quick, healthy breakfast like Boogie Bread.

1 large egg, beaten

1 tablespoon water

2 tablespoons superfine blanched almond flour

1½ tablespoons full-fat mayonnaise

⅛ teaspoon baking powder

1 Lightly grease a waffle maker with nonstick cooking spray and preheat.

2 In a medium bowl, whisk all ingredients together.

3 Pour half the batter in center of waffle maker and close. Cook 3–5 minutes until solid and browning. Remove and repeat for second Boogie Bread.

4 Serve warm.

TIPS & OPTIONS

Since Boogie Bread is savory, not sweet, use as "toast" to accompany your morning eggs.

Top Boogie Bread with butter, peanut butter, or sugar-free jam. One of my favorites is Smucker's Sugar Free Seedless Blackberry Jam, which has 3 grams net carbs per 1-tablespoon serving.

Prefer a breakfast sandwich to go? Use Boogie Bread as the "bread" with eggs, sausage, and cheese stuffed inside.

Reboot Boogie Bread in Rush In Reuben (see Chapter 10) or Early Eggs with Benefits (see recipe in this chapter).

DOUBLE-QUICK DOUBLE-CHOCOLATE CHAFFLES

As a kid, I remember thinking frozen waffles were such a waste of time. All I really wanted was the syrup! I can't imagine going back to those kinds of habits. A plate full of carbs, carbs, and topped with more carbs? No thanks. I want to be awake in an hour, not feeling my blood sugar go haywire. This adult version of DIRTY, LAZY, KETO waffles, Double-Quick Double-Chocolate Chaffles, fulfills my desire for morning sweets but without leaving me in a blood-sugar crash.

- 2 tablespoons superfine blanched almond flour
- 2 tablespoons full-fat cream cheese, softened
- 1 tablespoon unsweetened 100% cocoa powder
- 1 tablespoon sugar-free chocolate chips
- 1 large egg, beaten
- 2 (1-gram) packets 0g net carbs sweetener
- 1 teaspoon pure vanilla extract

1   Lightly grease a waffle maker with nonstick cooking spray and preheat.

2   In a medium bowl, whisk all ingredients together.

3   Pour half of batter in center of waffle maker and close. Cook 3–5 minutes until solid and browning. Remove and repeat for second chaffle.

4   Serve warm.

NET CARBS

2G

SERVES 2

PER SERVING:	
CALORIES	167
FAT	13G
PROTEIN	7G
SODIUM	88MG
FIBER	4G
CARBOHYDRATES	8G
NET CARBS	2G
SUGAR	1G
SUGAR ALCOHOL	2G

TIME

PREP TIME:	10 MINUTES
COOK TIME:	10 MINUTES
TOTAL TIME:	20 MINUTES

TIPS & OPTIONS

In case the Double-Quick Double-Chocolate Chaffles don't have enough chocolate for ya (*is there ever such a thing as too much chocolate?*), try topping with a dollop of Swoop Cream (see Chapter 11) and Hershey's Sugar-Free Syrup (1 gram net carbs per 1-tablespoon serving).

SWIFT CINNAMON ROLLS

NET CARBS

2G

SERVES 6

PER SERVING:

CALORIES	248
FAT	20G
PROTEIN	8G
SODIUM	326MG
FIBER	2G
CARBOHYDRATES	9G
NET CARBS	2G
SUGAR	1G
SUGAR ALCOHOL	5G

TIME

PREP TIME:	10 MINUTES
COOK TIME:	20 MINUTES
TOTAL TIME:	30 MINUTES

TIPS & OPTIONS »

If you've ever been to a Cinnabon Bakery, you'll know the employees ask if you want frosting on top of your roll. *Who in their right mind says no?* I won't be able to sleep tonight unless I share how to make Frantic Vanilla Frosting (see Chapter 11) for this recipe.

If your rolls don't cooperate during cutting, try freezing the dough for a few minutes to firm up.

Research from a perfume company proved what I already knew to be true: The scents of vanilla and cinnamon are preferred over all other scents. My personal market research was unofficially conducted at the mall the other day when I found myself blindly drawn to the wafting smells from the Cinnabon walk-up. I'm like a moth to a flame when it comes to *deliciousness* of this caliber. Fix up a batch of Swift Cinnamon Rolls and watch your family swarm around.

Dough

3 tablespoons full-fat cream cheese

1 cup shredded whole milk mozzarella cheese

⅔ cup superfine blanched almond flour

3 tablespoons 0g net carbs sweetener

1 large egg, beaten

1 teaspoon pure vanilla extract

½ tablespoon baking powder

⅛ teaspoon salt

Buttery Sweetener

¼ cup unsalted butter, melted

2 tablespoons 0g net carbs sweetener

1 teaspoon ground cinnamon

1 Preheat oven to 375°F. Grease a baking sheet.

2 In a medium microwave-safe bowl, add cream cheese and mozzarella and microwave on high 30 seconds. Stir until blended.

3 Add remaining Dough ingredients and stir to combine until a dough forms. Roll the dough flat on a large piece of plastic wrap. Form a rectangle approximately 10" × 6" and no more than ¼" thick. Dough will be sticky.

4 In a small bowl, combine Buttery Sweetener ingredients. Whisk to mix thoroughly.

5 Brush half the Buttery Sweetener on Dough and roll tightly starting at one of the short sides, creating a loaf 6" long.

6 Using a serrated knife or thin string (like dental floss), cut loaf into six rolls, 1" wide. Carefully transfer rolls to baking sheet and top with remaining Buttery Sweetener.

7 Bake 15–18 minutes until golden.

8 Let cool slightly and serve warm.

MINUTE MUG OMELET

Mornings can be stressful. Trying to get everyone ready and out the door on time can lead to hasty decision-making when it comes to healthy eating (making that break room pastry look ever so tempting!). You won't go down that path, though, if you embrace a few shortcuts in the morning. Put your hair in a ponytail *or man-bun* and start crackin' some shells. Cooked in the microwave, this Minute Mug Omelet will be ready in no time.

2 large eggs

2 tablespoons unsweetened almond milk

2 tablespoons shredded Cheddar cheese

2 tablespoons diced green bell pepper

1 tablespoon chopped ham

⅛ teaspoon salt

⅛ teaspoon ground black pepper

1 Grease a large microwave-safe coffee mug.

2 Add eggs to prepared mug and beat, using a fork.

3 Beat in remaining ingredients until completely mixed.

4 Cover and microwave omelet on high 45 seconds.

5 Stir, cover, and microwave again 30 seconds.

6 Enjoy warm right out of the mug.

NET CARBS

1G

SERVES 1

PER SERVING:

CALORIES	148
FAT	10G
PROTEIN	12G
SODIUM	594MG
FIBER	1G
CARBOHYDRATES	2G
NET CARBS	1G
SUGAR	1G

TIME

PREP TIME:	5 MINUTES
COOK TIME:	1 MINUTE, 15 SECONDS
TOTAL TIME:	6 MINUTES, 15 SECONDS

TIPS & OPTIONS ≫

Additional ingredients to consider are crumbled bacon, ground sausage, chopped spinach, sliced mushrooms, sliced jalapeños, or olives.

It's fun to play around with flavors in a Minute Mug Omelet. Broccoli and cheese? Spinach and feta? Think of what type of omelet you like to order in restaurants for inspiration.

FLEETING FRENCH TOAST

Hands down, French toast brings back the best memories from childhood. Whenever it was my turn to choose what we were having for dinner (which was pretty rare!), I chose French toast. Topped with a snowy drift of confectioners' sugar, it was pastry in disguise. One of the best parts of DIRTY, LAZY, KETO is that I don't have to give up any of these indulgences. The only difference is that I've learned how to remake my breakfast favorites in a healthier way.

Bread

1½ tablespoons unsalted butter, melted

2 tablespoons coconut flour

1 tablespoon full-fat cream cheese, softened

1 large egg, beaten

½ teaspoon baking powder

French Toast Coating

1 large egg, beaten

2 tablespoons heavy whipping cream

¼ teaspoon ground cinnamon

1 teaspoon 0g net carbs sweetener

¼ teaspoon pure vanilla extract

1 In a medium microwave-safe dish, add all Bread ingredients and stir to combine.

2 Microwave on high 1½ minutes, then remove from microwave and allow to cool. Cut in half.

3 In a separate medium bowl, whisk together all French Toast Coating ingredients until sweetener is dissolved. Pour mixture onto a plate.

4 Place both pieces of bread on the plate to soak. Flip after 30 seconds to soak other side.

5 Heat a medium nonstick skillet over medium heat. Add both pieces of bread and fry 2–3 minutes on each side until brown and crispy.

6 Serve warm.

NET CARBS

3G

SERVES 2

PER SERVING:

CALORIES	256
FAT	21G
PROTEIN	9G
SODIUM	230MG
FIBER	3G
CARBOHYDRATES	7G
NET CARBS	3G
SUGAR	2G
SUGAR ALCOHOL	1G

TIME

PREP TIME:	10 MINUTES
COOK TIME:	7 MINUTES, 30 SECONDS
TOTAL TIME:	17 MINUTES, 30 SECONDS

TIPS & OPTIONS

Some great suggestions for toppings are pecans, sliced strawberries, or sugar-free pancake syrup.

When you fool the eye, you fool the palate. Sprinkle confectioners'-style 0g net carbs sweetener on top of your serving of Fleeting French Toast for the most dramatic and authentic presentation.

ACCELERATED ACAI BOWL

On family vacations, we often stop at a food court for lunch. Everyone can get what they want, right? One meal in particular was a showstopper. My daughter waited in the longest line (with all the cool kids) and brought back a lunch that looked more like a dessert than a meal. The color scheme alone was impressive! I spent the rest of our trip trying to pronounce acai (ah-sah-EE) and scheming how to make a low-carb version back at home.

1½ cups plain full-fat Greek yogurt

½ teaspoon acai powder

2 teaspoons 0g net carbs sweetener

1 tablespoon chia seeds

¼ cup sliced strawberries

¼ cup raspberries

2 tablespoons crushed pecans

1 tablespoon unsweetened shredded coconut, toasted

½ tablespoon finely chopped dark chocolate, 92% cacao

1 In a small bowl, whisk together yogurt, acai powder, sweetener, and chia seeds.

2 Divide mixture evenly between two medium bowls.

3 Top bowls with remaining ingredients in an artful manner.

4 Cover and let chill in the refrigerator at least 20 minutes to allow chia seeds to soften.

5 Serve chilled.

NET CARBS
9G

SERVES 2	
PER SERVING:	
CALORIES	268
FAT	18G
PROTEIN	17G
SODIUM	60MG
FIBER	3G
CARBOHYDRATES	12G
NET CARBS	9G
SUGAR	8G

TIME	
PREP TIME:	30 MINUTES
COOK TIME:	0 MINUTES
TOTAL TIME:	30 MINUTES

TIPS & OPTIONS

Acai berries are mainstream, baby! Forget the health food store; find this superfood at supermarkets everywhere.

Carefully design your Accelerated Acai Bowl with the goal of posting a picture of it on social media (you're one of the cool kids now).

In case you're curious, the potent acai berries come from the acai palm, which thrives in the Amazon River delta. Not only does the tree provide berries rich in antioxidants, but the core of the palm is harvested for heart of palm, a delicious (though arguably pricey) noodle alternative.

SHORTCUT CINNAMON TOAST STICKS

NET CARBS

1G

SERVES 3

PER SERVING:
CALORIES	162
FAT	11G
PROTEIN	13G
SODIUM	281MG
FIBER	1G
CARBOHYDRATES	2G
NET CARBS	1G
SUGAR	1G

TIME

PREP TIME:	10 MINUTES
COOK TIME:	9 MINUTES
TOTAL TIME:	19 MINUTES

TIPS & OPTIONS

When coating the strips with the cinnamon mixture, spoon mixture on top as you turn the strips to get sweetener inside the square "waffle" holes. *Every bite matters!*

Instead of syrup, spread a portion of rebooted Frantic Vanilla Frosting (see Chapter 11) onto these sticks. Good call, right? I know how to do breakfast, people.

A surefire way to get my kids up and moving before school is to make Shortcut Cinnamon Toast Sticks. There is something about the blended aromas of vanilla and cinnamon in the air—the smell is so tantalizing it can wake up the dead (or very tired teenagers… *so*, basically the same thing). Serve these warm with sugar-free pancake syrup as a dip.

> 2 large eggs, beaten
> 1 cup shredded whole milk mozzarella cheese
> 2 tablespoons 0g net carbs sweetener
> 1½ teaspoons ground cinnamon

1. Grease a waffle maker with nonstick cooking spray and preheat.

2. In a medium mixing bowl, whisk eggs and mozzarella.

3. If using a single waffle maker, pour one-third of egg mixture into waffle maker and cook 3 minutes until browned and solid throughout. Transfer to a plate and slice into even strips no more than ¾" wide. Repeat with remaining batter.

4. While first piece of toast is cooking, combine sweetener and cinnamon on a shallow plate.

5. Roll still-warm toast strips in cinnamon mixture. Coat both sides and shake off any excess.

6. Serve immediately.

CHAPTER 6

SOUPS AND SALADS

It may be due to my middle-aged hormone problems—I'm not sure—but the temperature outside often dictates the method I prefer to cook with. When I'm freezing, I crave warm soups, stews, and chilis; slow cookers and stockpots become my best friends. On the other hand, hot weather makes me run from the kitchen. I refuse to even turn on my oven during the summer months! Because of my erratic inner thermostat, I often waver between making DIRTY, LAZY, KETO soups or salads for dinner.

You can revise any of your family's favorite soup recipes to become DIRTY, LAZY, KETO by following a few simple steps. Substitute offending high-starch ingredients like rice, potatoes, or beans with a low-carb alternative. Riced cauliflower (added at the last minute) fools the mouth and brain into thinking that you are eating rice. Boiled radishes or softened cauliflower florets resemble potato chunks when floating in sauce. Lastly, instead of making soup with high-carb black beans, try low-carb black soybeans instead. *Be creative!* Next, to increase the amount of fats in your soup, add intense flavor by stirring in additional cream cheese, olive oil, or cream to the soup stock. *That's it!* Simple and fast.

Quickly assembling a DIRTY, LAZY, KETO salad is all about having the right ingredients on hand. Once you stock these items in your fridge, it takes only a few minutes to toss desired flavors together and artfully present them on a plate. Salad ingredients I keep on hand include prewashed bagged salad greens, assorted cheeses, and leftover protein (hard-boiled eggs, grilled chicken, turkey lunch meat, etc.). Berries, nuts, and various chopped veggies make tasty additions to an otherwise "blah" salad. Don't be afraid to cut corners by using store-bought salad dressings either. When I'm pressed for time, I gladly pour purchased low-carb salad dressings (like ranch or blue cheese) over my salad and get started with the fun part—*eating*!

GASSED-UP CHILI

"This tastes like nothing," my son said to me when describing cauliflower. And you know what? He is right. Cauliflower magically takes on the flavors of whatever foods surround it, making it the most versatile vegetable in the DIRTY, LAZY, KETO universe. When added to this Gassed-Up Chili dish, the florets provide the perfect amount of bulk and texture without sacrificing taste.

1 medium head cauliflower, cut into bite-sized florets

2 tablespoons unsalted butter

1 medium yellow onion, peeled and chopped

1 large green bell pepper, seeded and chopped

1 recipe Ready, Set, Go Ground Beef (see Chapter 10)

2 (8-ounce) cans no-sugar-added tomato sauce

½ tablespoon minced garlic

2 teaspoons chili powder

1½ teaspoons ground cumin

¼ teaspoon paprika

¼ teaspoon salt

¼ teaspoon ground black pepper

1 In a medium microwave-safe bowl, add cauliflower and microwave on high 4–5 minutes until tender.

2 In a large soup pot over medium heat, melt butter. Stir in onion and bell pepper and cook 5 minutes until softened.

3 Stir in cauliflower and remaining ingredients and bring to a boil. Reduce heat to low and simmer covered 10 minutes.

4 Remove from heat and let cool uncovered. Serve warm.

NET CARBS

8G

SERVES 6

PER SERVING:

CALORIES	211
FAT	9G
PROTEIN	20G
SODIUM	664MG
FIBER	6G
CARBOHYDRATES	14G
NET CARBS	8G
SUGAR	6G

TIME

PREP TIME:	10 MINUTES
COOK TIME:	20 MINUTES
TOTAL TIME:	30 MINUTES

TIPS & OPTIONS

Make a chili dog! Reboot Gassed-Up Chili over hot dogs from the grill to make Convenient Chili-Cheese Dogs from Chapter 7.

Serve chili in a bag? Yes, you can! Crush a bag of Quest Nacho Cheese Tortilla Style Protein Chips. Carefully cut open the bag with scissors along the top. Pour chili inside the bag and serve.

NO FUSS PHO

You may wonder why I include so many Asian dishes in the DIRTY, LAZY, KETO cookbooks. On the whole, I find Eastern cuisine embraces vegetables much more than the Western diet, where French fries are practically their own food group. Since I believe that vegetables are the magic elixir needed for weight loss, I look for as many ways as possible to incorporate low-carb veggies into my meals. Dishes like No Fuss Pho are a quick and obvious vehicle to make this possible.

½ cup chopped green onions, divided

1 tablespoon minced fresh ginger

6 cups beef broth

½ tablespoon minced garlic

1 tablespoon soy sauce

2 (8-ounce) packages shirataki noodles

1 pound flank steak, thinly sliced

¼ cup bean sprouts

1 medium jalapeño pepper, seeded, deveined, and sliced in rings

½ tablespoon chopped fresh cilantro

½ tablespoon chopped fresh basil

1 In a medium nonstick skillet over medium heat, add ¼ cup onion and ginger. Cook 5 minutes while stirring until brown. Transfer to a large soup pot.

2 Place soup pot over medium heat. Add broth, garlic, and soy sauce. Bring to a boil, then reduce heat to low and simmer 10 minutes.

3 Divide remaining ingredients evenly among four bowls.

4 Carefully ladle broth mixture into bowls. The near-boiling broth will cook meat as well as other vegetables.

5 Enjoy when cool enough to taste.

NET CARBS

1G

SERVES 4

PER SERVING:

CALORIES	221
FAT	8G
PROTEIN	29G
SODIUM	1,632MG
FIBER	4G
CARBOHYDRATES	5G
NET CARBS	1G
SUGAR	1G

TIME

PREP TIME:	15 MINUTES
COOK TIME:	15 MINUTES
TOTAL TIME:	30 MINUTES

TIPS & OPTIONS

Pho isn't just fun to eat; it's an interesting word to say. *Pho* is pronounced *fuh*.

I don't usually eat shirataki noodles, but for this pho dish, I make an exception. Fans of these fishy noodles asked me to create a pho recipe, and I aim to please. If you're like me and the scent of these throw you for a loop, try substituting zucchini noodles (zoodles) instead.

Pick up your bowl and slurp away—totally acceptable in Vietnamese culture.

NET CARBS
6G

SERVES 6

PER SERVING:

CALORIES	285
FAT	20G
PROTEIN	15G
SODIUM	685MG
FIBER	1G
CARBOHYDRATES	7G
NET CARBS	6G
SUGAR	3G

TIME

PREP TIME:	10 MINUTES
COOK TIME:	20 MINUTES
TOTAL TIME:	30 MINUTES

TIPS & OPTIONS »

Once a week at the grocery store, I buy a rotisserie chicken. Having the precooked protein on hand makes cooking dinner a snap! In my community, Costco sells cooked "astronaut chickens" for less than five bucks a bird.

YOU SNOOZE, YOU LOSE ALFREDO SOUP

Eating healthy doesn't have to take up a lot of time. Once you have the right ingredients on hand, putting them together becomes easier. Aside from fresh vegetables, there's a handful of ingredients I'm never without: butter, cream cheese, eggs, Parmesan cheese, and heavy whipping cream. I don't eat these in excess, mind you, but I find that most recipes call for one or another of these from this list. As demonstrated by this You Snooze, You Lose Alfredo Soup, cooking with full-fat ingredients creates a rich and satisfying taste. I feel fuller faster and end up eating less food overall as a result.

2 tablespoons unsalted butter

1 medium yellow onion, peeled and chopped

2 teaspoons minced garlic

6 tablespoons full-fat cream cheese

⅔ cup heavy whipping cream

½ cup grated Parmesan cheese

2 cups chopped Grab and Go Chicken Breasts (see Chapter 10)

2½ cups chopped broccoli florets

2 cups chicken broth

2 teaspoons Italian seasoning

¼ teaspoon salt

⅛ teaspoon ground black pepper

1 In a large soup pot over medium heat, melt butter.

2 Stir in onion and garlic and cook 5 minutes until soft.

3 Stir in remaining ingredients and bring to a boil while stirring. Reduce heat and simmer covered 15 minutes, stirring regularly.

4 Serve warm.

MINESTRONE ZIPPY ZOODLE SOUP

Zoodles fascinate me. How can a zucchini become a noodle? It's amazing! The best part is how quickly you can make a zoodle. (Don't get swept up in the hype about commercial zoodle makers, now!). A simple julienne peeler is all you need to create spiralized noodles in under a minute. They will cook in a flash and take your Minestrone Zippy Zoodle Soup to the next level.

1 tablespoon olive oil

1½ cups chopped celery

2 tablespoons chopped green onion

½ tablespoon minced garlic

4 cups chicken broth

2 tablespoons white vinegar

¼ teaspoon salt

⅛ teaspoon ground black pepper

1 pound boneless, skinless chicken breasts

1½ cups spiralized zucchini

1 Add oil to Instant Pot® and heat using Sauté function at Less setting. Stir in celery, green onions, and garlic and cook 5 minutes while stirring.

2 Stir in broth, vinegar, salt, and pepper until combined. Arrange chicken breasts evenly over mixture.

3 Put on lid and close pressure release. Cook on High Pressure 10 minutes.

4 Carefully quick-release pressure and remove lid to cool.

5 Using two forks, shred cooked chicken in Instant Pot®.

6 Add zucchini and stir to combine. Using Sauté function at Normal setting, cook 5 minutes while stirring.

7 Turn off heat and let cool with lid off. Serve warm.

NET CARBS

2G

SERVES 6

PER SERVING:

CALORIES	132
FAT	4G
PROTEIN	19G
SODIUM	769MG
FIBER	1G
CARBOHYDRATES	3G
NET CARBS	2G
SUGAR	2G

TIME

PREP TIME:	10 MINUTES
COOK TIME:	20 MINUTES
TOTAL TIME:	30 MINUTES

TIPS & OPTIONS

If you can swing it, add fresh herbs like minced fresh parsley, rosemary, and thyme to the broth. It will smell *ahhhhhhmaaaazzzinnnng*!

My family loves when I make a theme-night dinner like Unlimited Soup and Salad. It sounds special and we all fill up on healthy food.

Reboot leftover zoodles to make the EZ Zoodle Noodle "Spaghetti" recipe in Chapter 10.

FAST-TRACK FRENCH ONION SOUP

NET CARBS

5G

SERVES 4

PER SERVING:

CALORIES	238
FAT	16G
PROTEIN	14G
SODIUM	1,286MG
FIBER	1G
CARBOHYDRATES	6G
NET CARBS	5G
SUGAR	2G

TIME

PREP TIME:	8 MINUTES
COOK TIME:	22 MINUTES
TOTAL TIME:	30 MINUTES

TIPS & OPTIONS »

Instead of white wine, substitute a splash of brandy in your broth à la Julia Child style.

Make the soup vegetarian-"ish" by using vegetable broth instead of beef.

If you don't want to buy a whole package of Gruyère cheese, try buying just the right amount at the fresh deli counter inside your supermarket.

Gruyère is a bit of a "grown-up" cheese (and subsequently can be pricey or hard to find). Feel free to substitute sliced Swiss cheese.

There are a few topics that really get the keto police riled up. Diet soda, carrots, and onions rank right up there. (*Sad but true! Get a life, people.*) The food police love to share unsolicited nutrition advice like, "Onions are NOT keto!" I'm going to fight back here with my Fast-Track French Onion Soup. If enjoyed in moderation, onions add flavor and fun to my cooking. This recipe is my way of saying, "Nanny nanny boo boo" to all the negative ninnies who criticize my beloved onion.

2 tablespoons unsalted butter

1 medium white onion, peeled and thinly sliced

1 bunch green onions (approximately 6), trimmed and chopped

1 tablespoon minced garlic

⅛ teaspoon salt

4 cups beef broth

¼ cup white wine

¼ teaspoon ground thyme

2 bay leaves

½ teaspoon ground black pepper

4 (1-ounce) slices Gruyère cheese

¼ cup grated Parmesan cheese

1 In a medium skillet over medium-low heat, melt butter.

2 Add onions, garlic, and salt. Cook until caramelized, about 10 minutes.

3 While onion mixture is cooking, in a microwave-safe bowl, add broth. Microwave on high 2–3 minutes until boiling.

4 Add broth to skillet, then add all remaining ingredients except cheeses. Reduce heat to low and simmer an additional 10 minutes.

5 Preheat broiler to high.

6 Place four small oven-safe bowls inside a large baking dish (for transporting to broiler).

7 Evenly distribute soup among four bowls. Remove bay leaves. Top each bowl with 1 slice Gruyère, draping over edges of bowl. Top with equal amounts Parmesan.

8 Place tray of soups under broiler 1–2 minutes until cheese browns. Serve warm.

NO PATIENCE POLLO SOUP

NET CARBS

5G

SERVES 4

PER SERVING:

CALORIES	317
FAT	18G
PROTEIN	25G
SODIUM	1,060MG
FIBER	4G
CARBOHYDRATES	9G
NET CARBS	5G
SUGAR	3G

TIME

PREP TIME:	10 MINUTES
COOK TIME:	20 MINUTES
TOTAL TIME:	30 MINUTES

TIPS & OPTIONS

To make the soup heartier, add riced cauliflower.

Sour cream, shredded Cheddar cheese, and olives are suggested low-carb soup toppings.

If you don't have a pressure cooker, make No Patience Pollo Soup on your stovetop using a large covered stockpot. Boil until chicken is thoroughly cooked, about 30 minutes for boneless thighs and 45 minutes for bone-in thighs.

Cooking with a pressure cooker is life-changing. It's removed all of my excuses for not having enough time to make dinner! I mean, really. The fact that you can cook a frozen piece of meat in just minutes is shocking. Who figured this out? *Someone hungry, that's who!* I don't want to spend all day in the kitchen making dinner. I want to throw a handful of ingredients into a pot without much fuss. No Patience Pollo Soup looks fancy and tastes yummy, but most important, it cooks quickly while I check *Facebook*.

1 pound boneless, skinless chicken thighs, sliced

1 (10-ounce) can no-sugar-added diced tomatoes and green chiles

2 cups chicken broth

2 tablespoons unsalted butter

¼ cup chopped green onion

2 teaspoons minced garlic

½ tablespoon onion powder

1 teaspoon chili powder

½ teaspoon ground cumin

½ tablespoon paprika

½ medium jalapeño pepper, seeded, deveined, and diced

½ teaspoon salt

1 medium avocado, peeled, pitted, and sliced

1 tablespoon chopped fresh cilantro

1 In Instant Pot®, combine all ingredients except avocado and cilantro. Stir to mix.

2 Put on lid and close pressure release. Cook on High Pressure 20 minutes. Carefully quick-release pressure and remove lid. Stir to mix well.

3 Serve warm topped with avocado slices and sprinkle of cilantro.

LIGHTNING-SPEED SLAW

I get SUPER excited at social events when my DIRTY, LAZY, KETO dishes rub shoulders with high-carb counterparts on the buffet line. I can almost feel the scrutiny and suspicion from critical family members and friends deciding how to fill their plate (trying to avoid suspicious "diet food"). I see this as a challenge to prove them wrong. Lightning-Speed Slaw is so rich and satisfying, even Grandma will think it's *the real thing*.

1 (16-ounce) bag coleslaw mix

⅓ cup full-fat mayonnaise

1 tablespoon apple cider vinegar

1 teaspoon 100% lemon juice

1 tablespoon 0g net carbs sweetener

¼ teaspoon salt

⅛ teaspoon ground black pepper

1 In a large bowl, add coleslaw mix.

2 In a medium bowl, combine all remaining ingredients. Stir to thoroughly mix.

3 Using a spatula, add dressing to coleslaw mix. Stir to combine.

4 Cover and put in refrigerator until ready to serve. Serve chilled.

NET CARBS	
4G	

SERVES 5	
PER SERVING:	
CALORIES	124
FAT	11G
PROTEIN	1G
SODIUM	225MG
FIBER	2G
CARBOHYDRATES	7G
NET CARBS	4G
SUGAR	3G
SUGAR ALCOHOL	1G

TIME	
PREP TIME:	10 MINUTES
COOK TIME:	0 MINUTES
TOTAL TIME:	10 MINUTES

TIPS & OPTIONS

Adjust the sweetener to your taste.

Adjust the vegetables and spices as you wish. Green onion, red onion, and parsley are all great choices.

Sometimes I top my coleslaw with a tablespoon of sunflower seeds. They add just the right amount of crunch with a punch of salt to the sweet dressing.

NO-BAKE "POTATO" SOUP

DLK is full of surprises. For example, there's no potato in this soup, but the cauliflower florets and vibrant radish skins will fool you into thinking that there is. Radishes are the ideal potato substitute. I'm certain they will become a keto staple in your household too. I use radishes so often in recipes that now I keep extra servings of this prepped veggie on hand for moments like this. (See the Hot-Footed Homestyle "Potatoes" recipe in Chapter 5.) Radishes are truly the secret ingredient of No-Bake "Potato" Soup!

1 (12-ounce) bag frozen cauliflower pieces, broken into bite-sized florets

2 tablespoons unsalted butter

1 cup finely chopped radishes

1 cup sliced zucchini

½ cup chopped green onions, divided

1 tablespoon minced garlic

4 cups chicken broth

½ cup full-fat cream cheese

2 (3.7-gram) chicken-flavored bouillon cubes

⅛ teaspoon ground black pepper

2 cups shredded Cheddar cheese

¼ cup cooked bacon bits

1 In a large microwave-safe dish, add cauliflower. Cover and microwave on high 4–5 minutes until tender.

2 While cauliflower cooks, in a large soup pot over medium heat, melt butter. Add radishes, zucchini, ¼ cup onion, and garlic. Sauté 3–4 minutes until softened.

3 Add cauliflower, broth, cream cheese, bouillon, and pepper to soup pot. Bring covered pot to a boil, then reduce heat to low and simmer 20 minutes while stirring.

4 Using an immersion blender, pulse soup ingredients 1–2 minutes to desired consistency.

5 Add Cheddar to soup and fold in.

6 Pour into six small bowls and top with equal amounts bacon bits and remaining green onion. Serve immediately.

NET CARBS	
5G	
SERVES 6	
PER SERVING:	
CALORIES	310
FAT	22G
PROTEIN	15G
SODIUM	1,354MG
FIBER	2G
CARBOHYDRATES	7G
NET CARBS	5G
SUGAR	4G

TIME	
PREP TIME:	5 MINUTES
COOK TIME:	25 MINUTES
TOTAL TIME:	30 MINUTES

TIPS & OPTIONS

For a heartier soup, top with your choice of protein. I like to add leftover taco meat, shredded chicken, or basically any leftovers from last night's meal.

Don't have an immersion blender? Though messy (and hot!), here is a work-around. Transfer soup to a standing blender in small batches and pulse until desired consistency is achieved.

Be careful not to over-blend your soup. Bites of cauliflower and radish will fool your brain into thinking you're eating baby red potatoes.

HURRY UP HOUSE SALAD WITH RANCH

NET CARBS

4G

SERVES 8

PER SERVING:
CALORIES	92
FAT	8G
PROTEIN	1G
SODIUM	83MG
FIBER	1G
CARBOHYDRATES	5G
NET CARBS	4G
SUGAR	3G

TIME

PREP TIME:	15 MINUTES
COOK TIME:	0 MINUTES
TOTAL TIME:	15 MINUTES

TIPS & OPTIONS »

Substitute your favorite low-carb salad vegetables and toppings. Go heavy on what's in season and available in your fridge.

Set some dressing aside for later in the week to use as a dip when it's time for pizza! Or chicken! Or…just about anything!

Ranch is like a food group when you come from the Midwest. Don't judge, but we like ranch on just about everything, from pizza to wings to veggies. As such, I take my ranch dressing seriously. There was a time in my life when on my way home from work, I would drive out of the way just to get to the best pizza parlor, simply because it had the most spectacular ranch dressing. I've had to endure hundreds of taste tests (such a rough job) to get this one right.

DLK House Salad

1 (24-ounce) bag salad mix

1 medium red onion, peeled and chopped

1 cup grape tomatoes, halved

DLK House Ranch Dressing Mix

¼ cup dried parsley flakes

2 tablespoons 0g net carbs sweetener

3½ tablespoons dried garlic flakes

1½ tablespoons onion powder

1½ tablespoons lemon pepper

1 tablespoon dried dill

1 teaspoon salt

DLK House Ranch Dressing

¼ cup full-fat mayonnaise

¼ cup full-fat sour cream

1 tablespoon 100% lemon juice

1 tablespoon DLK House Ranch Dressing Mix

2 tablespoons water

2 tablespoons heavy whipping cream

⅛ teaspoon ground black pepper

1 In a large salad bowl, add all DLK House Salad ingredients.

2 In a medium bowl, add all DLK House Ranch Dressing Mix ingredients and stir until mixed. For storage, put in an airtight container (preferably a transparent one, so mix can be seen). Store in the spice rack with the rest of your spices.

3 In a medium bowl, whisk all DLK House Ranch Dressing ingredients together.

4 Using a rubber spatula, pour the DLK House Ranch Dressing on top of the DLK House Salad and toss well to coat. Cover and put in refrigerator until ready to serve.

5 Serve chilled in fancy salad bowls.

INSTAMATIC CUCUMBER SALAD

One of my favorite mantras with DIRTY, LAZY, KETO is to "use fat to make healthy food taste better." Let's face it. Most of us don't wake up in the morning craving a cucumber. *Let's be real!* But when it's chopped up into Instamatic Cucumber Salad with full-fat mayonnaise and sour cream? Now that's a whole different story. Fat makes everything taste better. Use that to your advantage! Pair fats with low-carb veggies and watch your waistline shrink.

2 medium cucumbers, skin on and sliced

½ medium red onion, peeled and chopped

2 tablespoons full-fat sour cream

2 tablespoons full-fat mayonnaise

2 teaspoons 100% lemon juice

1 medium clove garlic, peeled and minced

¼ teaspoon salt

⅛ teaspoon ground black pepper

2 teaspoons finely chopped fresh cilantro

1 In a medium bowl, add cucumbers and onion.

2 In a small bowl, whisk to combine remaining ingredients.

3 Pour dressing on top of vegetables and stir to coat.

4 Cover with wrap and put in refrigerator. Give final stir prior to serving chilled.

NET CARBS

6G

SERVES 4

PER SERVING:

CALORIES	87
FAT	6G
PROTEIN	1G
SODIUM	195MG
FIBER	1G
CARBOHYDRATES	7G
NET CARBS	6G
SUGAR	3G

TIME

PREP TIME:	10 MINUTES
COOK TIME:	0 MINUTES
TOTAL TIME:	10 MINUTES

TIPS & OPTIONS

I like to keep the skin on my cucumbers for added fiber.

Instamatic Cucumber Salad is the perfect summer barbecue side dish. Pair with any meat from the grill.

Instead of cilantro, try using fresh dill. It makes for a snappy, refreshing alternative.

COUNTDOWN CURRY CHICKEN SALAD

NET CARBS

6G

SERVES 4

PER SERVING:

CALORIES	648
FAT	59G
PROTEIN	17G
SODIUM	554MG
FIBER	5G
CARBOHYDRATES	11G
NET CARBS	6G
SUGAR	4G

TIME

PREP TIME:	10 MINUTES
COOK TIME:	0 MINUTES
TOTAL TIME:	10 MINUTES

TIPS & OPTIONS

Interesting fact: The original Waldorf Salad was created in 1893 by Oscar Tschirky, the maître d'hôtel of the Waldorf Astoria in New York City.

Enjoy Countdown Curry Chicken Salad while watching one of my favorite movies filmed at the Waldorf Astoria: *Catch Me If You Can*, *Serendipity*, or *Scent of a Woman*.

Any apple variety will do. Feel free to peel the apple if you prefer.

My twist on the traditional Waldorf salad leaves raisins behind and introduces bright yellow curry to the mix. This combination offers a hint of savory flavor to an already sweet dish, but perhaps more important, it just looks *perty*! Impress your guests by whipping up stunning Countdown Curry Chicken Salad in just 10 minutes flat.

> 2 Grab and Go Chicken Breasts, cubed (see Chapter 10)
>
> 1 cup full-fat mayonnaise
>
> 1 cup chopped celery
>
> ½ medium Granny Smith apple, cored and chopped
>
> 4 ounces chopped walnuts
>
> 4 (1-gram) packets 0g net carbs sweetener
>
> 1 tablespoon curry powder
>
> 1 tablespoon white vinegar
>
> ⅛ teaspoon salt
>
> 1 (10-ounce) bag prewashed spinach

1 In a medium bowl, combine all ingredients except spinach.

2 Stir to combine and completely coat chicken.

3 Evenly divide spinach among four salad bowls.

4 Top each bowl with one-fourth of chicken curry mix. Cover with wrap and put in refrigerator.

5 Serve chilled.

THAI TIME CRUNCH SALAD

In my "previous life" (when I weighed close to 300 pounds), I frequented Panera Bread for lunch. I ordered the Spicy Thai Salad with Chicken (thinking I was being healthy), a giant Candy Cookie (knowing I wasn't), and washed both down with a Diet Coke (which made up for indiscretions). Little did I know that my meal contained about 100 grams of carbs! That's not even counting the dozen bagels I bought on my way out the door. These days, when I want a fast and casual lunch, I make this Thai Time Crunch Salad.

Dressing

1 tablespoon no-sugar-added peanut butter

1 tablespoon soy sauce

1 tablespoon water

5 (1-gram) packets 0g net carbs sweetener

2 teaspoons apple cider vinegar

⅓ cup sesame oil

⅛ teaspoon ground ginger

½ teaspoon sesame seeds

¼ teaspoon red pepper flakes

¼ cup salted peanuts, crushed

Salad

6 cups shredded cabbage mix (**green cabbage, red cabbage, carrot blend**)

¼ cup chopped green onion

¼ cup chopped fresh cilantro

1½ cups shredded Grab and Go Chicken Breasts, cold (**see Chapter 10**)

1. In a medium bowl, whisk together all Dressing ingredients except crushed peanuts. Cover and set aside.

2. In a large mixing bowl, combine cabbage mix, green onion, and cilantro and stir. Add chicken and mix again.

3. Add Dressing to Salad. Toss to fully coat.

4. Divide equally among four bowls. Top with equal amounts of crushed peanuts.

5. Serve chilled.

SERVES 4	
PER SERVING:	
CALORIES	323
FAT	24G
PROTEIN	16G
SODIUM	308MG
FIBER	4G
CARBOHYDRATES	9G
NET CARBS	5G
SUGAR	4G

TIME	
PREP TIME:	10 MINUTES
COOK TIME:	0 MINUTES
TOTAL TIME:	10 MINUTES

TIPS & OPTIONS

Lettuce can be substituted for the cabbage. A 12-ounce bag (four servings) of pre-washed salad mix will make the job even easier. But don't forget the cilantro! That herb really seals the deal.

For a slightly different twist (not to mention time-saver), reboot leftover Peanut Sauce from the Vietnamese Spring Rolls to Go recipe in Chapter 7, or vice versa, you could reboot the Dressing recipe here to accompany your Vietnamese Spring Rolls to go.

JUST PRESS START "POTATO" SALAD

NET CARBS

3G

SERVES 6

PER SERVING:

CALORIES	141
FAT	11G
PROTEIN	5G
SODIUM	340MG
FIBER	2G
CARBOHYDRATES	5G
NET CARBS	3G
SUGAR	2G

TIME

PREP TIME:	10 MINUTES
COOK TIME:	4 MINUTES
TOTAL TIME:	14 MINUTES

TIPS & OPTIONS 〉〉

Hard-boil your eggs in the Instant Pot® and they will easily peel "like buttah."

Sprinkle fresh dill on top of your Just Press Start "Potato" Salad to add some excitement to your plate.

Potatoes are a food of the past with DIRTY, LAZY, KETO. Even sweet potatoes are crossed off my list! They are both just too starchy for my liking, with 26 and 23 grams of carbs, respectively. Just Press Start "Potato" Salad keeps all the taste of a traditional potato salad, but without unnecessary carbs. That's a win-win in my book!

1 (12-ounce) bag cauliflower florets

3 large eggs, hard-boiled, peeled, and chopped

½ cup chopped celery

½ cup finely chopped red onion

¼ cup full-fat mayonnaise

¼ cup full-fat sour cream

1 tablespoon yellow mustard

½ teaspoon salt

¼ teaspoon ground black pepper

1 In a medium microwave-safe bowl, add cauliflower. Microwave on high 4 minutes. Let cool.

2 Add cauliflower to a large bowl and stir in the remaining ingredients; mix well.

3 Cover and let cool in refrigerator. Serve chilled.

CHAPTER 7

SNACKS

It's almost embarrassing how often I talk about food. When thinking about fast snack ideas to share with you, my mind was flooded with hundreds of helpful tips. Seriously, I had to rein in my excitement! Having DIRTY, LAZY, KETO snacks on hand has been crucial to maintaining my 140-pound weight loss.

> Nibbling on healthy food helps keep the edge off.
> I make better decisions (about everything, really) when
> I'm not feeling so *hangry*.

What makes the perfect DIRTY, LAZY, KETO snack, you ask? I believe snacks should be simple yet filling. That's the whole point, right? Snacks, by design, should get you through the empty transition period in between meals.

If you're like me, when you're hungry, you want something fast. I want a snack to curb a hunger craving without having to do a lot of work. In the past, that meant I reached for mostly unhealthy convenience food like chips or crackers. Unfortunately, those high-carb foods never hit the spot. Since starch, just like sugar, is quickly metabolized by the body, foods like chips and crackers sent my blood sugar levels spiraling out of control. I would end up eating more, not less, making the whole snack experience pointless.

Now my snack options consist of foods with higher amounts of fat, moderate levels of protein, and low carbohydrate numbers. I find DIRTY, LAZY, KETO snacks stop the hunger beast in its tracks. I am able to eat a healthy snack and then move on with my day. You'll notice many of my snack recipes contain vegetables too. The high amount of fiber in slow-burning carbs keeps my metabolism on point. They fill me up and keep me from overeating (which has always been my challenge).

I also drink a lot of water with my snacks. That wouldn't make for a very exciting recipe, but it's worthy of mentioning here! In between meals, I aim to consume as much water as possible. It helps with digestion, keeps me full, and prevents dehydration symptoms (more commonly referred to as the "keto flu").

TURKEY TORRENT MEATBALLS

There is nothing more disappointing than making meatballs that fall apart during cooking. You do so much work to mix and shape the ingredients, only to have a giant crumbly mess in the pan—*frustrating*. Without using bread crumbs as a binder, what's a girl to do? There are plenty of effective DLK options to try. Parmesan cheese, crushed pork rinds, and mozzarella cheese work wonders to maintain the meatball shape. And, as seen in these Turkey Torrent Meatballs, egg and oil also do the trick.

1 pound 85% lean ground turkey

½ (10-ounce) bag frozen riced cauliflower

1 large egg, beaten

1 medium clove garlic, peeled and minced

½ teaspoon ground ginger

¼ teaspoon salt

⅛ teaspoon ground black pepper

1 teaspoon sesame oil

2 tablespoons water

1 In a large bowl, using your hands, combine all ingredients except oil and water. Form fifteen to twenty uniform balls approximately 1" across.

2 In a medium skillet over medium heat, heat oil. Add meatballs and fry 10 minutes, turning regularly, until browned on all sides. Drain any fat from skillet.

3 Add water to skillet and bring to a boil. Reduce heat to low, cover, and simmer 10 minutes.

4 Serve warm.

NET CARBS
1G

SERVES 4	
PER SERVING:	
CALORIES	286
FAT	17G
PROTEIN	27G
SODIUM	253MG
FIBER	1G
CARBOHYDRATES	2G
NET CARBS	1G
SUGAR	1G

TIME	
PREP TIME:	10 MINUTES
COOK TIME:	20 MINUTES
TOTAL TIME:	30 MINUTES

TIPS & OPTIONS

When it comes to flavor, fat matters. Choose 85% lean ground turkey for a much better taste than the rubbery, low-fat variety.

Serve with Asian stir-fry veggies like bok choy, bean sprouts, mushrooms, and bamboo shoots.

Chopsticks make a meal special. Even the most un-coordinated family members can stab a meatball with their sticks!

AGILE "APPLE" CRISP

NET CARBS	
8G	

SERVES 4

PER SERVING:

CALORIES	405
FAT	33G
PROTEIN	7G
SODIUM	82MG
FIBER	8G
CARBOHYDRATES	24G
NET CARBS	8G
SUGAR	5G
SUGAR ALCOHOL	8G

TIME

PREP TIME:	7 MINUTES
COOK TIME:	23 MINUTES
TOTAL TIME:	30 MINUTES

TIPS & OPTIONS

Chayotes come in two forms: prickly and smooth.

If you want a stronger apple taste, add 2 teaspoons apple extract or mix in a peeled, cored, and diced medium Granny Smith apple with the chayote (for an increase of 4–5 net carbs per serving).

It's not just the fruit of the chayote plant that's edible. You can eat the tendrils and flowers from the vine too!

Years ago, we moved into a house with a suspicious vine overtaking the front yard. I woke up every morning to find the spiky vine had grown at least another foot, like I was in some kind of twisted "Jack and the Beanstalk" story. Little did I know this was a producing chayote plant. With a bushel of this low-carb fruit at my disposal (4g net carbs per cup), I started getting creative in the kitchen. We ate a lot of chayote that year! Agile "Apple" Crisp was the champion recipe of the season.

Almond Crumble

¾ cup superfine blanched almond flour

5 tablespoons 0g net carbs sweetener

2 tablespoons coconut flour

½ teaspoon ground cinnamon

⅛ teaspoon salt

¼ cup cold unsalted butter, cubed

Chayote Filling

4 large chayotes, peeled, cored, and diced

¼ cup unsalted butter, melted

3 tablespoons 0g net carbs sweetener

3 tablespoons 100% lemon juice

1 teaspoon ground cinnamon

½ teaspoon ground nutmeg

¼ teaspoon ground allspice

1 Preheat oven to 375°F. Grease a 9" × 7" baking dish.

2 In a medium nonstick skillet over medium heat, add almond flour. Toast almond flour 3 minutes while stirring.

3 In a medium bowl, combine toasted almond flour, sweetener, coconut flour, cinnamon, and salt. Stir to combine well.

4 Using two knives or a pastry blender, cut in butter until the mixture resembles coarse crumbs and butter is fully incorporated.

5 Add all Chayote Filling ingredients to prepared baking dish. Stir to combine and coat completely.

6 Top with even layer of Almond Crumble and bake 15–20 minutes covered until cooked throughout. Serve warm.

FLY OFF THE PLATE ROOSTER WINGS

Wings are the perfect pizza alternative at my house. Every Friday night, my kids insist on eating Little Caesars pizza. If I want a night off from the kitchen, I'll tack on a request for wings to their order. It's not hard to make my own, though. Ironically, it's faster too! My plate of Fly Off the Plate Rooster Wings is ready in less time than it takes to jet across town and back with takeout.

> 6 ounces (approximately 4–6) chicken wing sections, drumette or "flat"
>
> 2 tablespoons olive oil, divided
>
> 1 tablespoon baking powder
>
> 1 teaspoon ground fresh chili paste
>
> ¼ teaspoon salt
>
> 1 medium clove garlic, peeled and minced
>
> 2 tablespoons rebooted DLK House Ranch Dressing (see Hurry Up House Salad with Ranch in Chapter 6)

1 Preheat air fryer to 400°F.

2 On a medium plate, brush chicken wings with 1 tablespoon oil. Generously sprinkle both sides of wings with baking powder.

3 Spread out wings on crisper tray. Cook in air fryer 15–20 minutes, tossing once halfway through until dry and golden.

4 In a medium bowl, whisk to combine remaining 1 tablespoon oil, chili paste, salt, and garlic.

5 Add cooked wings to sauce mixture and toss until completely coated.

6 Serve warm with DLK House Ranch Dressing in a dipping bowl on the side.

NET CARBS
6G

SERVES 1

PER SERVING:

CALORIES	663
FAT	57G
PROTEIN	30G
SODIUM	2,373MG
FIBER	0G
CARBOHYDRATES	6G
NET CARBS	6G
SUGAR	1G

TIME

PREP TIME:	5 MINUTES
COOK TIME:	20 MINUTES
TOTAL TIME:	25 MINUTES

TIPS & OPTIONS

Anyone who has perusedthe DIRTY, LAZY, KETO cookbooks knows about my husband's love affair with the "rooster" chili paste called Sambal Oelek, made by Huy Fong Foods. (It has the famous fowl as its logo.) He puts it on almost everything he eats, including wings.

The wings should only be lightly coated in sauce, just enough to give them flavor.

Serve wings with celery stalks, ranch dressing, and lots of napkins!

VIETNAMESE SPRING ROLLS TO GO

NET CARBS

6G

SERVES 4

PER SERVING:

CALORIES	171
FAT	13G
PROTEIN	7G
SODIUM	266MG
FIBER	5G
CARBOHYDRATES	11G
NET CARBS	6G
SUGAR	3G

TIME

PREP TIME:	15 MINUTES
COOK TIME:	2 MINUTES
TOTAL TIME:	17 MINUTES

TIPS & OPTIONS

Give the sauce some kick by adding sriracha sauce and red pepper flakes.

Add 1 teaspoon crushed peanuts to the sauce for more texture.

To save on carb count, try using powdered peanut butter (3g net carbs per 2-tablespoon serving). I've been experimenting with great success using Simply Nature Organic Peanut Butter Powder.

In truth, spring rolls are just a vehicle for me to eat more peanut sauce. I could probably eat this peanut sauce every day—no exaggeration—because I love it so much. It deserves a DIRTY, LAZY, KETO gold star! For me, it's like the ranch dressing of Vietnamese food. Use fat to make healthy food taste better, right?

4 cups water

4 outer leaves from medium head green cabbage, trimmed

4 (1-gram) packets 0g net carbs sweetener

½ teaspoon sesame seeds

Peanut Sauce

⅓ cup no-sugar-added creamy peanut butter, softened

1½ tablespoons water

1 tablespoon soy sauce

½ tablespoon 100% lime juice

1 teaspoon white vinegar

1 teaspoon ground ginger

1 medium clove garlic, peeled and minced

Filling

½ cup mung bean sprouts

½ cup shredded cabbage

½ cup shredded cucumber

½ medium avocado, peeled, pitted, and thinly sliced

¼ cup finely chopped green onion

1 tablespoon chopped fresh cilantro

1 Boil water in a large saucepan. Carefully add cabbage leaves to boiling water. Boil cabbage 2 minutes, stirring and rearranging leaves using metal tongs to cook evenly.

2 Drain cabbage and cool leaves by running cold tap water into saucepan.

3 In a small microwave-safe bowl, whisk all Peanut Sauce ingredients until mixed and sweetener is dissolved. If peanut butter is stiff, microwave covered sauce 10–20 seconds until softened and whisk again. Evenly divide sauce among four small serving bowls.

4 Put 1 cabbage leaf on each of four dinner plates.

5 On one half near the center, top each leaf evenly with one-fourth of each of the Filling ingredients.

6 Roll up each cabbage leaf like a burrito into a spring roll.

7 Serve immediately with Peanut Sauce.

SUPERSONIC SUSHI-STYLE ROLLS

Japanese restaurants can be intimidating when you're eating low carb. Every dish seems to come with rice! Look closer at the menu, however, and you'll notice there are many more options beyond the traditional sushi roll. Edamame, sashimi, and ahi salad are part of my standing order, but you may also consider yakiniku (boneless short rib), yakitori (skewered chicken), wakame sarada (seaweed salad), or miso soup. If I'm really craving a true sushi roll, I make my own using thinly sliced cucumber or seaweed as a wrap.

1 (10-ounce) bag frozen riced cauliflower

2 tablespoons full-fat cream cheese, softened

2 teaspoons sesame oil

¼ teaspoon salt

2 sheets sushi nori seaweed, 7½" × 8½" each

¼ pound raw salmon steak (no skin), thinly sliced

½ cup matchstick-sliced cucumber

½ cup matchstick-sliced red bell pepper

½ medium avocado, peeled, pitted, and thinly sliced

1 tablespoon toasted sesame seeds

1   In a medium microwave-safe bowl, add cauliflower and microwave on high 4–5 minutes until tender. Let cool and place on clean kitchen towel. Wrap up cauliflower and squeeze out any excess water.

2   Return to bowl and mix in cream cheese, sesame oil, and salt.

3   Lay out a large piece of plastic wrap on counter. Place two pieces mostly square seaweed on plastic wrap, side by side, and moisten with water.

4   Evenly spread a thin layer (about ¼") cauliflower mixture on both sheets of seaweed.

5   Next, evenly spread salmon, cucumber, bell pepper, avocado, and sesame seeds on cauliflower mixture.

6   Starting at the side closest to you, slowly roll each seaweed sheet. If parts of seaweed are dry and brittle, brush with water. Cut each roll in half and refrigerate covered.

7   Place one 4" roll on each of four plates. Serve.

NET CARBS

4G

SERVES 4

PER SERVING:

CALORIES	180
FAT	12G
PROTEIN	9G
SODIUM	204MG
FIBER	4G
CARBOHYDRATES	8G
NET CARBS	4G
SUGAR	3G

TIME

PREP TIME:	15 MINUTES
COOK TIME:	5 MINUTES
TOTAL TIME:	20 MINUTES

TIPS & OPTIONS

For best results, start the rolling process at the edge closest to you (lift the edge of the plastic wrap to get it started).

Your roll should only overlap the opposite side by ¼"–½" (which helps seal the roll closed).

Serve with soy sauce and wasabi.

Roasted seaweed snacks have become all the rage with millennials. Instead of salty chips, be one of the cool kids and munch on a snack pack of nori seaweed chips.

NIMBLE "NACHOS"

Eating nachos and losing weight? I'm determined to revise and revive old favorites in a new, healthier way. Nachos are just one example.

SERVES 8

PER SERVING:

CALORIES	170
FAT	11G
PROTEIN	10G
SODIUM	593MG
FIBER	1G
CARBOHYDRATES	4G
NET CARBS	3G
SUGAR	1G

TIME

PREP TIME:	9 MINUTES
COOK TIME:	21 MINUTES
TOTAL TIME:	30 MINUTES

"Tortilla" Chips

2 cups riced cauliflower

1 cup grated Parmesan cheese

1 teaspoon DLK House Ranch Dressing Mix (see Hurry Up House Salad with Ranch in Chapter 6)

⅛ teaspoon salt

⅛ teaspoon ground black pepper

Cheese Sauce

1½ cups shredded Cheddar cheese

¼ cup full-fat cream cheese, softened

¼ cup unsweetened almond milk

½ teaspoon ground cumin

½ teaspoon salt

½ teaspoon chili powder

Toppings

1 small jalapeño pepper, steamed, seeded, deveined, and thinly sliced into rings

½ tablespoon chopped fresh cilantro

TIPS & OPTIONS

Optional toppings are diced tomato, sour cream, sliced olives, and chunks of avocado.

Nachos are best enjoyed while sipping a low-carb beer. Some of my favorites are Corona Premier, Michelob Ultra, or Miller Lite (all have 3 grams net carbs per 12-ounce serving).

In a hurry? Make "chips" in the air fryer. Brush low-carb tortillas with oil and salt, cut into triangles, and bake 4–6 minutes at 400°F until crispy, stopping every couple of minutes to shake the basket.

1 Preheat oven to 375°F.

2 In a medium microwave-safe bowl, add cauliflower and microwave on high 4–5 minutes until tender. Let cool and place on a clean kitchen towel. Wrap up cauliflower and squeeze out any excess water.

3 Return to bowl and add Parmesan, DLK House Ranch Dressing Mix, salt, and pepper. Mix until a moist dough is formed.

4 Place dough on a large piece of parchment paper and place a second piece of paper on top of dough. Use a rolling pin to flatten dough to the thickness of a Dorito.

5 Remove top piece of paper. Use a pizza cutter to cut dough into triangles, roughly the size of Doritos.

6 Transfer parchment paper with chips on it to a large baking sheet.

7 Bake 15 minutes until golden brown.

8 In a medium microwave-safe bowl, combine all Cheese Sauce ingredients. Microwave on high 30 seconds. Stir and microwave another 30 seconds until smooth.

9 Put all chips in a medium decorative bowl and top with Cheese Sauce. Garnish with jalapeño slices and cilantro.

CLIP CHIPS AND SALSA

NET CARBS

10G

SERVES 4

PER SERVING:
CALORIES	182
FAT	12G
PROTEIN	6G
SODIUM	727MG
FIBER	14G
CARBOHYDRATES	24G
NET CARBS	10G
SUGAR	5G

TIME

PREP TIME:	10 MINUTES
COOK TIME:	15 MINUTES
TOTAL TIME:	25 MINUTES

TIPS & OPTIONS

No time to make your own salsa? Take a shortcut today and buy a jar of La Victoria Thick 'n Chunky Salsa Verde Medium (6 grams net carbs per ¾-cup serving). I won't tell anyone your salsa is not homemade.

In general, green salsa (verde) is lower in net carbs compared to red salsa.

Resist the temptation to blend the Salsa Verde too long, creating a lifeless soup. A little texture/lumpiness gives it character.

Are you an experienced diner? (Don't laugh, but I once heard that question posed during a hotel room TV infomercial in Las Vegas.) Seriously, though, my advanced palate should be awarded a Michelin star for its ability to discern among junk food flavors. Diet Pepsi versus Diet Coke? That's too easy. McDonald's fries versus Burger King fries? Amateur hour. Give me a real challenge. Let's talk about chips! I can discern the subtle nuances among tortilla chips served at every chain restaurant, with Clip Chips and Salsa being my favorite (and from my own kitchen!).

Chips

3 tablespoons olive oil

1 tablespoon 100% lime juice

½ teaspoon chili powder

½ teaspoon ground cumin

⅛ teaspoon garlic powder

¼ teaspoon paprika

½ teaspoon salt

4 low-carb flour tortillas or reboot Tempo Tortillas (see Chapter 8)

Salsa Verde

1 pound medium tomatillos, peeled, stemmed, and quartered

2 medium jalapeño peppers, seeded, deveined, and minced

¼ medium yellow onion, peeled and minced

2 teaspoons minced garlic

1 tablespoon 100% lime juice

¼ cup chopped fresh cilantro

¼ teaspoon salt

⅛ teaspoon ground black pepper

⅛ teaspoon ground cumin

1. Preheat oven to 425°F. Line a baking sheet with parchment paper.

2. In a small bowl, whisk to combine oil and lime juice.

3. In a separate small bowl, whisk to combine remaining Chips ingredients except tortillas.

4. Using a basting brush, coat both sides of four tortillas with oil mixture.

5. Evenly dust both sides of moistened tortillas with chili powder mixture.

6. Using a pizza cutter, slice tortillas into eight triangles.

7   Evenly distribute tortilla slices on prepared baking sheet without touching. Bake until crunchy, 8–10 minutes, flipping chips over halfway through.

8   Preheat broiler to high. Cover a baking sheet with greased foil.

9   Place tomatillos, jalapeños, onion, and garlic on prepared baking sheet and broil on high 4–5 minutes, stirring every minute until starting to char.

10 In a food processor, add roasted vegetables and remaining Salsa Verde ingredients. Pulse 30–60 seconds until desired consistency is achieved.

11 Pour Salsa Verde into a small decorative dipping bowl.

12 Transfer chips to a large decorative platter and serve with bowl of Salsa Verde in the center.

CLOSE THE KITCHEN EARLY QUESADILLAS

A rotisserie chicken is a weekly staple on my shopping list. Every grocery store in my community sells these precooked beauties, all at a similar, reasonable price point. I want to remove any potential excuses that might pop up about cooking dinner. Rotisserie chickens are such a time-saver! Having precooked chicken at my fingertips makes it easy to whip up meals like Close the Kitchen Early Quesadillas.

Barbecue Sauce

⅔ cup no-sugar-added ketchup

1 tablespoon olive oil

1 tablespoon white vinegar

1 tablespoon 100% lemon juice

½ teaspoon minced garlic

1 teaspoon paprika

½ teaspoon ground chili powder

¼ teaspoon salt

2 (1-gram) packets 0g net carbs sweetener

⅛ teaspoon xanthan gum

Chicken Quesadillas

2 cups cooked and shredded chicken (from rotisserie)

1 cup shredded Cheddar cheese

¼ cup chopped green onion

4 (8") low-carb flour tortillas

2 tablespoons unsalted butter

½ cup full-fat sour cream

2 tablespoons chopped fresh cilantro

1. In a large skillet over medium heat, heat all Barbecue Sauce ingredients 10 minutes, stirring regularly to thicken. Sprinkle in xanthan gum slowly to prevent clumping.

2. Fold in chicken, Cheddar, and onion until combined.

3. Divide mixture evenly among four tortillas on four dinner plates. Place mixture evenly on one half of each tortilla and fold in half.

4. In a large skillet over medium heat, melt butter. Add two quesadillas to the skillet and fry 2 minutes until golden. Flip and cook another 2 minutes. Repeat for second batch and transfer to dinner plates.

5. Top each quesadilla evenly with a dollop of sour cream and chopped cilantro. Serve warm.

NET CARBS

8G

SERVES 4

PER SERVING:

CALORIES	435
FAT	26G
PROTEIN	34G
SODIUM	1,190MG
FIBER	12G
CARBOHYDRATES	20G
NET CARBS	8G
SUGAR	4G

TIME

PREP TIME:	10 MINUTES
COOK TIME:	18 MINUTES
TOTAL TIME:	28 MINUTES

TIPS & OPTIONS

Try using the brand Olé Mexican Foods Xtreme Wellness! Tortilla Wraps, which have 5 grams net carbs per tortilla.

In a hurry? Skip a step by using store-bought G Hughes Sugar Free BBQ Sauce (available in Honey, Hickory, Sweet & Spicy, Mesquite, Maple Brown, Carolina Style Sweet Heat, or Original flavors).

As a side dish, heat up a can of low-carb Eden Organic Black Soy Beans (available online) at 1 gram net carbs per ½-cup serving.

Instead of buying a rotisserie chicken, reboot Grab and Go Chicken Breasts (see Chapter 10) here.

HIGH-SPEED SAUSAGE BITES

NET CARBS
3G

SERVES 4

PER SERVING:

CALORIES	211
FAT	17G
PROTEIN	12G
SODIUM	830MG
FIBER	0G
CARBOHYDRATES	3G
NET CARBS	3G
SUGAR	0G

TIME	
PREP TIME:	3 MINUTES
COOK TIME:	6 MINUTES
TOTAL TIME:	9 MINUTES

TIPS & OPTIONS »

Bring a platter of High-Speed Sausage Bites to your next get-together. Serve with decorative toothpicks in lieu of silverware.

Don't have a waffle maker? Heat sausage bites on an outdoor grill or in a skillet (filled with a small amount of water) on the stovetop.

I prefer Aidells brand of smoked sausages. Some of my favorite smoked chicken flavors include Chicken & Apple and Artichoke & Garlic. For smoked pork sausage, I recommend the Aidells Cajun Style Andouille.

I'm always on the lookout for creative ways to maximize the efficiency of my counter space. Kitchen appliances, in particular, are one of my sore spots. They take up too much room! In order to claim a permanent spot on my limited real estate, a gadget must multitask. I was about to relocate my waffle maker to a "weekend only" cabinet when it hit me: I could use this gadget to heat up sausages for tonight's dinner, George Foreman–style! High-Speed Sausage Bites (with minimal prep and execution) are ready in seconds flat.

> 2 tablespoons full-fat mayonnaise
>
> ½ tablespoon yellow mustard
>
> 1 teaspoon sriracha
>
> 1 teaspoon minced garlic
>
> ⅛ teaspoon ground paprika
>
> ⅛ teaspoon salt
>
> ⅛ teaspoon ground black pepper
>
> 1 (12-ounce) package low-carb precooked chicken sausage links, sliced lengthwise in half and then into ½"–¾" pieces

1 Grease a waffle maker with nonstick cooking spray and preheat.

2 In a medium bowl, whisk together all ingredients except sausage bites until well blended.

3 Working in batches, distribute sausage bites on waffle maker and close. Cook 3 minutes. Repeat process until all sausages are cooked.

4 Add hot sausage bites to bowl with sauce and toss to coat.

5 Serve warm in four medium fancy bowls.

CONVENIENT CHILI-CHEESE DOGS

Dirty Keto catches a lot of heat in the media. Critics think we're just eating bunless, triple-bacon burgers from the drive-thru on our way to shop for skinny pants. This couldn't be further from the truth (well, maybe keep the skinny pants part). In reality, the "dirty" part of DIRTY, LAZY, KETO means we are open-minded with ingredient choices. Don't confuse that with eating low-quality foods 24/7! Instead, it's about flexible options. I can have a Convenient Chili-Cheese Dog with a side of organic vegetables if I want to—*nothing is off limits.*

Chili

1 pound 90% lean ground beef

½ cup diced yellow onion

1 teaspoon minced garlic

1 (1.25-ounce) packet chili seasoning mix

1 (14.5-ounce) can no-sugar-added diced tomatoes, undrained

1 (15-ounce) can no-salt-added black soybeans, undrained

¼ teaspoon salt

Cheese Dogs

4 beef hot dogs

4 (19-gram) slices Cheddar cheese

1. In a medium nonstick skillet over medium heat, add beef, onion, and garlic. Cook 10–15 minutes while stirring until beef is no longer pink. Drain fat.

2. Add remaining Chili Ingredients to skillet and cook 5 more minutes while stirring.

3. On a medium microwave-safe plate, place all 4 hot dogs and microwave on high 1½ minutes.

4. Using tongs, place each hot dog on a separate plate and top each with 1 slice Cheddar.

5. Top each cheese-covered dog with ¼ cup hot Chili.

6. Serve warm.

NET CARBS
10G

SERVES 4

PER SERVING:

CALORIES	578
FAT	31G
PROTEIN	44G
SODIUM	1,294MG
FIBER	10G
CARBOHYDRATES	20G
NET CARBS	10G
SUGAR	5G

TIME

PREP TIME:	5 MINUTES
COOK TIME:	22 MINUTES
TOTAL TIME:	27 MINUTES

TIPS & OPTIONS

Don't worry about over-microwaving the hot dogs and having them split. No one will notice! The cheese and chili will hide any accidents.

In a hurry? Use chili from a can! A popular low-carb brand is Skyline Original Chili with 2 grams net carbs per cup.

Reboot extra servings of Gassed-Up Chili (see Chapter 6) in this recipe.

Black soybeans are a relatively new phenomenon. I buy Eden Organic Black Soy Beans with no salt added in 15-ounce can online. Miraculously, they have only 1 gram net carbs per ½-cup serving and 3.5 grams net carbs per 15-ounce can.

DEADLINE DEVILED AVOCADOS

NET CARBS

2G

SERVES 4

PER SERVING:

CALORIES	140
FAT	12G
PROTEIN	1G
SODIUM	224MG
FIBER	5G
CARBOHYDRATES	7G
NET CARBS	2G
SUGAR	1G

TIME

PREP TIME:	10 MINUTES
COOK TIME:	0 MINUTES
TOTAL TIME:	10 MINUTES

TIPS & OPTIONS 〉〉

Catch a sale on a bag of mini avocados? Make a whole platter of Deadline Deviled Avocados for an appetizer.

For variety, add cold baby shrimp as a topper.

Presentation is everything, right? These Deadline Deviled Avocados are so darn cute. I love food served in surprising ways! Bring a platter of these to your next party or serve for a ladies' luncheon and you'll be certain to get a boatload of compliments. Eating healthy doesn't have to be boring. Dress up your plate, even if it's just to impress yourself. You're worth the effort!

2 large avocados, halved and pitted (leave the skin on)

1 tablespoon full-fat mayonnaise

½ tablespoon 100% lemon juice

1 tablespoon sriracha sauce

¼ teaspoon garlic salt

⅛ teaspoon ground black pepper

⅛ teaspoon ground paprika

1 For each avocado half, carefully scrape out about half of the avocado flesh from the center, leaving a thick border all the way around the shell. Transfer scooped-out avocado flesh to a medium bowl.

2 Thoroughly mash avocado and mix in remaining ingredients, except paprika, until combined.

3 Divide mixture evenly among avocado halves and top with sprinkle of paprika.

4 Cover and put in refrigerator. Serve chilled.

STEP ON IT PICKLE STACKERS

Commercial cheese-and-egg wraps are all the rage these days. These quick substitutions for sandwich making are tempting for newbies who are still in mourning over cutting bread from their diet. Personally, I find these substitutions hard to find and often expensive. Wrapping my "sandwich" in lettuce leaves, sliced deli meat, or even pickles as shown here, is just as effective (and novel). And it saves me a trip to the store.

1 pound deli-sliced turkey breast

¼ cup full-fat mayonnaise

2 teaspoons yellow mustard

2 strips no-sugar-added bacon, cooked and crumbled

2 cups shredded iceberg lettuce

½ cup chopped tomato

¼ cup finely sliced red onion

½ cup shredded Cheddar cheese

2 large whole dill pickles

1 Divide turkey evenly into four portions and arrange on plates. If multiple slices are on a plate, organize so they form a circle no more than 4"–5" across and are an even thickness as much as possible.

2 In a small bowl, combine mayonnaise and mustard. Spread evenly on turkey wrappers.

3 Evenly layer all remaining ingredients, except pickles, on turkey slices.

4 Roll each turkey deli wrap.

5 Slice each pickle lengthwise into four long, flat slices each (eight slices total). These will serve as the "buns."

6 Insert each turkey deli wrap inside a pair of pickle slices. Secure with toothpick. Cover and put in refrigerator.

7 Serve chilled.

NET CARBS	
7G	
SERVES 4	
PER SERVING:	
CALORIES	312
FAT	18G
PROTEIN	26G
SODIUM	1,948MG
FIBER	2G
CARBOHYDRATES	9G
NET CARBS	7G
SUGAR	4G

TIME	
PREP TIME:	10 MINUTES
COOK TIME:	0 MINUTES
TOTAL TIME:	10 MINUTES

TIPS & OPTIONS

Adjust mayonnaise and mustard amounts to your particular tastes.

Instead of mustard, substitute a spoonful of pesto. When mixed with the mayonnaise, this creates a delightful zing! I buy a jar of fresh pesto every time I visit Costco—the competitive price on this pesto beats buying the required ingredients to make fresh pesto at home.

SPEEDY SEVEN-LAYER DIP

NET CARBS

4G

SERVES 6

PER SERVING:
CALORIES	219
FAT	12G
PROTEIN	19G
SODIUM	224MG
FIBER	0G
CARBOHYDRATES	4G
NET CARBS	4G
SUGAR	2G

TIME

PREP TIME:	10 MINUTES
COOK TIME:	15 MINUTES
TOTAL TIME:	25 MINUTES

TIPS & OPTIONS

Suggested toppings are cilantro, avocado, and jalapeño rings.

Scoop this dip with my very own Clip Chips and Salsa recipe in this chapter.

Serve with a platter of hearty fresh veggies for dipping, like cauliflower florets or bell pepper slices. Better yet? Bring a plastic spoon. No one likes double-dippers!

I always bring a dish to parties, even when I'm not asked. First of all, I think bringing a gift is a nice thing to do, but more important, I want to make sure I have something low-carb to eat. Sure, what I bring depends on the type of get-together, but I find a casual dish like Speedy Seven-Layer Dip goes well with whatever the person is planning.

1 pound 93% lean ground beef

1 tablespoon taco seasoning

¾ cup full-fat sour cream

½ cup shredded iceberg lettuce

½ cup shredded Mexican-style cheese blend

½ cup diced tomato

2 tablespoons chopped green onion

2 tablespoons diced black olives

½ cup no-sugar-added salsa

1 Grease a 9" × 9" × 2" baking dish and set aside.

2 In a medium skillet over medium heat, cook beef 10 minutes while stirring.

3 Stir in taco seasoning and cook 5 more minutes.

4 Evenly spread meat in prepared baking dish.

5 Next, in this order, layer sour cream, lettuce, cheese, tomato, onion, olives, and salsa.

6 Cover and put in refrigerator until ready to serve. Serve chilled.

CHAPTER 8

BREADS AND PIZZA

Raise your hand if you have a bread-making machine somewhere in the bowels of your kitchen. Anyone, *anyone?* You're not alone. I too was brought up with the false belief that if I ate bread that was homemade—or even better, made with whole wheat—I was on my way to picture-perfect health. Boy, was I wrong! ...*on all counts.*

As it turns out, for many of us, bread of any kind causes more harm to our health than good. (At least that's been my experience.) Interestingly, despite knowing how many carbs are in each serving of bread, many people struggle finding a satisfactory alternative. They become stuck before even starting DIRTY, LAZY, KETO.

"How do you make a sandwich?" they ponder.

"What about pizza?" they question.

"How do you hold a hot dog?" and so on, and so forth.

I empathize. Cutting out long-standing traditions like morning toast or a PB&J sandwich seems downright *un-American*. I agree! But what if there is another way? One of the reasons I've been so successful in maintaining my 140-pound weight loss *for eight years* is that I've fully embraced cheap, easy, and tasty bread-swap options.

Instead of buying overpriced loaves of "cardboard" from the Internet, I make my own tasty rolls, crackers, and breads. I don't buy expensive "keto" pizza crusts; I create a low-carb version at home. I don't feel deprived, because I'm not missing out! I continue to cook and eat "normal foods" just like everybody else.

I will admit, however, that my bread habits have evolved over time. I've learned to swap out some breads altogether for my *new* favorites. For lunch, I enjoy an *unwich* wrapped in lettuce. My favorite pizza crust is now made from chicken! These substitutes taste delicious. In fact, I love these breadless versions even more than their original. By becoming open-minded and taking risks to try familiar favorites in a new way, I've created my own *new normal* with DIRTY, LAZY, KETO. Be brave and come join me!

PROCRASTINATOR PIZZA CASSEROLE

You can tell a lot about a person by peeking into their freezer. Mine is overstocked (some might say "crammed") with the most unusual items. Call me overprepared, but if a pizza hankering comes on, I won't be calling for delivery.

NET CARBS

5G

SERVES 6

PER SERVING:
CALORIES	229
FAT	14G
PROTEIN	16G
SODIUM	799MG
FIBER	3G
CARBOHYDRATES	8G
NET CARBS	5G
SUGAR	4G

TIME

PREP TIME:	10 MINUTES
COOK TIME:	20 MINUTES
TOTAL TIME:	30 MINUTES

Crust

2 (10-ounce) bags frozen riced cauliflower

1 large egg, beaten

¾ cup shredded Cheddar cheese, softened

1 medium clove garlic, peeled and minced

1½ teaspoons Italian seasoning

¼ teaspoon salt

⅛ teaspoon ground black pepper

Toppings

1 cup no-sugar-added pasta sauce

1 teaspoon Italian seasoning

1 medium clove garlic, peeled and minced

¼ teaspoon salt

2 cups shredded whole milk mozzarella cheese

8 slices pepperoni

1 teaspoon dried parsley

1 Preheat oven to 420°F. Grease a 9" × 9" baking dish.

2 In a medium microwave-safe bowl, add cauliflower and microwave on high 4–5 minutes until tender. Let cool and place on a clean kitchen towel. Wrap up cauliflower and squeeze out any excess water.

3 In a large bowl, combine cauliflower with remaining Crust ingredients. Stir until dough forms.

4 Place dough ball in prepared baking dish. Using your hands, spread the dough evenly, pushing firmly into place (dough will be somewhat loose).

5 Bake 8–10 minutes until crust is golden and crispy. If crust overbrowns too early, cover with foil and return to oven.

6 In a medium bowl, whisk together pasta sauce, Italian seasoning, garlic, and salt until well blended.

7 Remove crust from oven and evenly spread sauce mixture on top. Next, evenly top with mozzarella. Finally, top evenly with pepperoni slices.

8 Return to oven 3–5 minutes to melt cheese.

9 Cut into six slices, sprinkle evenly with parsley, and serve.

TIPS & OPTIONS

Quickly drain cauliflower mixture by "smooshing" (that's a technical kitchen word, by the way) it in a fine-mesh strainer using a spatula, repeatedly pressing down to eliminate remaining moisture.

I like to sneak vegetable toppings onto my pizza. Whether I want them there or not isn't the issue—the added fiber and overall "healthiness" helps prevent me from overeating too many slices.

Some of my favorite low-carb pizza toppings include sliced mushrooms, broccoli, black olives, green bell pepper, zucchini, and spinach.

NET CARBS

5G

SERVES 6

PER SERVING:

CALORIES	452
FAT	27G
PROTEIN	39G
SODIUM	797MG
FIBER	1G
CARBOHYDRATES	6G
NET CARBS	5G
SUGAR	2G

TIME

PREP TIME:	10 MINUTES
COOK TIME:	20 MINUTES
TOTAL TIME:	30 MINUTES

TIPS & OPTIONS

If you're using jalapeños from a can or jar then there is no need to remove the seeds. The pickling process removes some of the heat.

After the final baking step (and pizza has cooled down enough to eat), you can top your slice with fresh lettuce, tomatoes, and onions. *Build it like its namesake, the taco!*

Don't be shy. Enjoy salsa, sour cream, or sliced avocado with your meal.

TICK TACO PIZZA

The two dinners my family can agree on are pizza and tacos. One day I figured, why not have them both at the same time? This fun twist on traditional favorites is executed quickly and sure to please even the pickiest of eaters at your dinner table.

Crust

5 large eggs, beaten

2 cups shredded whole milk mozzarella cheese

Toppings

3 tablespoons no-sugar-added tomato paste

1 tablespoon taco seasoning

2 cups shredded Cheddar cheese

1 recipe Ready, Set, Go Ground Beef (see Chapter 10)

½ cup diced red onion

¼ cup thinly sliced jalapeño peppers

1 Preheat oven to 400°F. Line a round 16" pizza pan with parchment paper.

2 In a medium bowl, add eggs and mozzarella. Stir to combine thoroughly.

3 Spread batter on pizza pan in the shape of a circle approximately ¼" thick.

4 Bake 15 minutes until crust is golden and firm. Let cool.

5 Raise oven temperature to 450°F.

6 In a small bowl, combine tomato paste and taco seasoning. Spread mixture evenly on crust.

7 Evenly spread Cheddar; Ready, Set, Go Ground Beef; onion; and jalapeños (in that order) on crust.

8 Bake 5 minutes until cheese is melted and vegetables are soft.

9 Cut into six pieces and serve warm.

MARGHERITA PRONTO PIZZA

When I was younger, I thought there was something wrong with Margherita-style pizza. "What's the deal with the giant white globs of cheese?" I wondered, thinking someone had made a mistake. It wasn't until adulthood that I began to appreciate the subtle nuances of different pizza styles. Made in a new lower-carb fashion, Margherita Pronto Pizza continues to be one of my favorites.

Crust

1 cup superfine blanched almond flour

2 cups shredded whole milk mozzarella cheese

2 tablespoons full-fat cream cheese

1 large egg, beaten

¼ teaspoon salt

Toppings

⅓ cup no-sugar-added tomato sauce

2 teaspoons Italian seasoning

3 (21-gram) slices whole milk mozzarella cheese, broken into 1"–2" circular pieces

1 tablespoon chopped fresh basil

1. Preheat oven to 425°F. Line an ungreased 16" round pizza pan with parchment paper.

2. In a large microwave-safe bowl, combine almond flour, mozzarella, and cream cheese. Microwave on high 1 minute. Stir and microwave another 30 seconds.

3. Fold in egg and salt until dough forms.

4. Put dough on pizza pan and flatten in a circular shape to no more than ¼" thickness.

5. Bake 7–10 minutes until top begins to brown. Remove from oven.

6. In a small bowl, combine tomato sauce and Italian seasoning. Mix well. Evenly spread sauce on crust. Evenly distribute mozzarella pieces over top.

7. Return to oven and bake 5 minutes to melt cheese.

8. Top with fresh basil. Using a pizza cutter, cut into six even slices. Serve warm.

NET CARBS

4G

SERVES 6

PER SERVING:

CALORIES	294
FAT	22G
PROTEIN	16G
SODIUM	505MG
FIBER	2G
CARBOHYDRATES	6G
NET CARBS	4G
SUGAR	2G

TIME

PREP TIME:	10 MINUTES
COOK TIME:	16 MINUTES, 30 SECONDS
TOTAL TIME:	26 MINUTES, 30 SECONDS

TIPS & OPTIONS

Serve with grated Parmesan, garlic, or red pepper flakes.

Instead of chopping the fresh basil, cut the leaves into ribbons. Tightly roll a handful of fresh basil leaves (into a shape like a pencil) and slice every $\frac{1}{8}$" or so. The leaves unroll into elegant ribbons for you to top the pizza with. *Fancy, right?*

PORTOBELLO PACED PIZZA

NET CARBS

5G

SERVES 4

PER SERVING:
CALORIES	207
FAT	15G
PROTEIN	9G
SODIUM	738MG
FIBER	3G
CARBOHYDRATES	8G
NET CARBS	5G
SUGAR	5G

TIME

PREP TIME:	10 MINUTES
COOK TIME:	20 MINUTES
TOTAL TIME:	30 MINUTES

TIPS & OPTIONS »

If you partially cover the vegetables with a little cheese prior to baking, they cook faster.

Sprinkle red pepper flakes, if desired, on top prior to serving.

Mushrooms contain a lot of water. By slightly elevating them on a baking rack (also called a roasting rack) during the cooking process, you avoid the dreaded soggy-bottom pizza crust.

Ladies and gentlemen, we have to broaden what we think of as pizza if this is going to work. En Vogue reminds me, "Free your mind and the rest will follow" (from one of my favorite 1992 songs, "Free Your Mind"). If that helps, sing along. Let the creativity flow when it comes to pizza. No, that's not a slice of deep-dish pizza on your plate; it's a Portobello Paced Pizza created from a giant mushroom cap. *No joke.*

1 cup no-sugar-added pasta sauce

1 tablespoon Italian seasoning

1 medium clove garlic, peeled and minced

¼ teaspoon salt, divided

4 large portobello mushroom caps

2 tablespoons olive oil

1 cup shredded whole milk mozzarella cheese

¼ cup sliced black olives

¼ cup sliced red bell pepper

2 tablespoons grated Parmesan cheese

1 Preheat oven to 425°F. Grease a 9" × 12" × 2" baking dish. Place a baking rack inside.

2 In a medium bowl, whisk together pasta sauce, Italian seasoning, garlic, and ⅛ teaspoon salt.

3 Scrape black gills out of each mushroom cap and rinse. Pat dry and brush top (round part) of each cap with a heavy coating of oil. Sprinkle oil-coated cap (round side) with remaining salt.

4 Place caps on baking rack in baking dish, gill side up, and evenly fill each with one-fourth of sauce mixture.

5 Divide mozzarella evenly among four caps and top with olives and bell peppers. Dust with Parmesan.

6 Bake 15–20 minutes until caps are softened throughout and cheese is melted. Cover with foil halfway through when browning starts.

7 Serve warm.

GO GO GRILLED CHEESE

There are a handful of meals that people commonly mourn when starting DIRTY, LAZY, KETO. For some reason, grilled cheese is one of them. I'm not sure if it's due to nostalgia or taste, but people love this sandwich! For all those guys and gals, this one's for you.

> 2 large eggs, beaten
>
> ¼ cup full-fat mayonnaise
>
> 1 cup crushed pork rinds
>
> 1 cup shredded whole milk mozzarella cheese
>
> ½ cup shredded Cheddar cheese, divided

1. In a medium bowl, whisk to combine eggs and mayonnaise. Fold in pork rinds and mozzarella to form dough.

2. Divide dough into four even balls. Form each dough ball into a flat patty ¼"–½" thick.

3. Heat a large nonstick skillet over medium heat.

4. Cook two patties at a time in the skillet 3–5 minutes until bottom is golden. Flip both and top one with ¼ cup Cheddar. Cook 3–5 minutes until firm and bottoms are golden.

5. Remove to a plate and top cheese-covered bun with bun top (hot side down to continue melting cheese).

6. Repeat for second Go Go Grilled Cheese. Serve warm.

NET CARBS
2G

SERVES 2

PER SERVING:

CALORIES	783
FAT	59G
PROTEIN	50G
SODIUM	1,476MG
FIBER	0G
CARBOHYDRATES	2G
NET CARBS	2G
SUGAR	1G

TIME	
PREP TIME:	5 MINUTES
COOK TIME:	20 MINUTES
TOTAL TIME:	25 MINUTES

TIPS & OPTIONS

Pair Go Go Grilled Cheese with a warm bowl of Minestrone Zippy Zoodle Soup (see Chapter 6) for the ultimate comfort food experience.

Bread substitute recipes can be calorie-dense. Be sure to add lots of vegetables to your meal to keep a healthy balance.

Want to take the ultimate shortcut? Reboot Boogie Bread (see Chapter 5) and slap on a slice of cheese. *Done.*

NET CARBS

4G

BARBECUE CHICKEN FLYING FLATBREAD

SERVES 6

PER SERVING:

CALORIES	326
FAT	22G
PROTEIN	22G
SODIUM	502MG
FIBER	2G
CARBOHYDRATES	6G
NET CARBS	4G
SUGAR	1G

TIME

PREP TIME:	10 MINUTES
COOK TIME:	16 MINUTES, 30 SECONDS
TOTAL TIME:	26 MINUTES, 30 SECONDS

TIPS & OPTIONS »

Need more zip? Add sautéed onions and bell peppers to the sauce.

Serve with a mini cup of homemade DLK House Ranch Dressing (see recipe for Hurry Up House Salad with Ranch in Chapter 6).

Instead of buying barbecue sauce for this dish, reboot the homemade Barbecue Sauce from Close the Kitchen Early Quesadillas (see Chapter 7).

For variety, prior to baking, sprinkle bacon bits or red onion on top of your pizza.

Enjoying homemade pizza on a regular basis has helped me to stay on track with DIRTY, LAZY, KETO. I don't feel resentful about missing out on favorite foods. In fact, I get fired up when challenged to create a low-carb alternative. My Barbecue Chicken Flying Flatbread recipe tastes just as good as what you'd experience at any restaurant— maybe even better, now that I think of it, as you can enjoy it at home in your slippers, *guilt-free*. You can't put a price on that!

Crust

1 cup superfine blanched almond flour

2 cups shredded whole milk mozzarella cheese

2 tablespoons full-fat cream cheese

1 large egg, beaten

¼ teaspoon salt

½ teaspoon baking powder

Toppings

¼ cup sugar-free barbecue sauce

2 Grab and Go Chicken Breasts, shredded (see Chapter 10)

½ cup shredded whole milk mozzarella cheese

1 medium clove garlic, peeled and minced

1 Preheat oven to 425°F. Line a baking sheet with parchment paper.

2 In a large microwave-safe bowl, combine almond flour, mozzarella, and cream cheese and microwave on high 1 minute. Stir and microwave another 30 seconds.

3 Mix in egg, salt, and baking powder until a dough forms.

4 Put dough on prepared baking sheet and flatten to no more than ¼" thickness in an oblong shape.

5 Bake 8–10 minutes until top begins to brown.

6 In a medium bowl, combine barbecue sauce and chicken. Mix well to coat.

7 Evenly spread barbecue chicken on crust. Top with mozzarella and garlic. Bake 5 minutes to melt cheese.

8 Cut into six even slices using a pizza cutter and serve warm.

NAAN NOW

Indian food and DLK are a match made in heaven. Many of the sauces (like my favorite Butter Chicken) are rich with healthy fat and protein (but low in carbohydrates). The conundrum about Indian food lies in the starchy side dishes—Indian buffets offer rice or naan bread with every meal. I sidestep these sides altogether and instead choose shredded lettuce or my homemade Naan Now bread. *Namaste.*

1½ tablespoons plain full-fat Greek yogurt

2½ cups shredded whole milk mozzarella cheese

2 medium eggs, beaten

2 teaspoons baking powder

1¼ cups superfine blanched almond flour

2 tablespoons unsalted butter, melted

1 medium clove garlic, peeled and minced

1 tablespoon finely chopped fresh cilantro

1 Preheat oven to 400°F. Line a baking sheet with parchment paper.

2 In a medium microwave-safe bowl, add yogurt and mozzarella and microwave on high 1 minute. Stir and microwave again 1 minute.

3 In a separate medium bowl, whisk eggs, baking powder, and almond flour together.

4 Stir egg mixture into cheese mixture until dough forms.

5 Cut dough into four equal pieces and form each into a ball. Press dough onto prepared baking sheet until they are in typical naan oval shape and ¼"–½" thick.

6 Bake 7–10 minutes until golden and firm.

7 In a small bowl, whisk butter, garlic, and cilantro until combined.

8 Remove naan from oven. Brush tops with garlic butter and bake again 12 minutes until starting to brown.

9 Serve warm.

NET CARBS

5G

SERVES 4

PER SERVING:

CALORIES	528
FAT	41G
PROTEIN	27G
SODIUM	720MG
FIBER	4G
CARBOHYDRATES	9G
NET CARBS	5G
SUGAR	2G

TIME

PREP TIME:	6 MINUTES
COOK TIME:	24 MINUTES
TOTAL TIME:	30 MINUTES

TIPS & OPTIONS

If the dough is too dry, stir in a teaspoon of water until it's workable (but not sticky). Chill in fridge if needed to firm up and remove stickiness.

Get inspired by the variety of naan served in restaurants. Garlic, onion, and cilantro are popular styles of naan.

Tandoori breads like this are traditionally cooked on the walls of high-temperature clay ovens. The final appearance looks scarred, bubbled, and often charred, making it one of the most forgiving dishes to make!

TEMPO TORTILLAS

Walking away from tortillas can be excruciating for some. When a food like naan, rice, or tortillas is ingrained into your culture, removing it from the diet can seem sacrilegious. If a food represents more to you than just flavor, I recommend finding a new, healthier way to make the dish. You don't want a single food to cause any resentment, right? Tempo Tortillas quickly cut the carbs while maintaining the form and function of a tortilla.

- **4 large egg whites**
- **1 tablespoon olive oil**
- **3 tablespoons coconut flour**
- **¼ teaspoon baking powder**
- **⅛ teaspoon salt**
- **⅛ teaspoon ground black pepper**

1 In a medium mixing bowl, combine all ingredients and whisk to fully blend.

2 In a small nonstick skillet over medium heat, add half of the batter. Using a silicone spatula, carefully spread dough to edges of pan, creating a circular shape approximately 6" in diameter. Cook 3–4 minutes until tortilla bottom begins to brown. Use spatula to pry up edge and flip over, cooking 3–4 minutes more on opposite side. Remove.

3 Repeat to create second tortilla. Serve warm.

NET CARBS

3G

SERVES 2

PER SERVING:

CALORIES	138
FAT	8G
PROTEIN	9G
SODIUM	322MG
FIBER	4G
CARBOHYDRATES	7G
NET CARBS	3G
SUGAR	3G

TIME

PREP TIME:	4 MINUTES
COOK TIME:	16 MINUTES
TOTAL TIME:	20 MINUTES

TIPS & OPTIONS

You also have the option of making larger tortillas (like for making a burrito). Use a bigger skillet and double or quadruple the recipe to make the desired shape.

Serve warm as a side dish or use as a soft taco and insert your favorite toppings.

These days, there are many low-carb tortilla options available at the grocery store (some tasting better than others!). La Tortilla Factory brand has never let me down.

READY OR NOT CORN BREAD

I've had an ongoing battle about corn with one of my family members. He happens to be from Nebraska, where corn is an economically important crop. Just because corn is a vegetable doesn't mean it's healthy (at least for me, anyway!). Corn is too starchy and high in carbs for my liking. I can survive without it. (Though I'm still a little sad about popcorn, I'll admit.) I made Ready or Not Corn Bread to prove my point.

- 1 cup superfine blanched almond flour
- 2 tablespoons coconut flour
- ½ tablespoon baking powder
- ½ teaspoon salt
- 2 tablespoons full-fat sour cream
- ¼ cup unsalted butter, melted
- 2 medium eggs, beaten
- 12 drops liquid 0g net carbs sweetener
- ½ cup shredded Cheddar cheese
- 3 tablespoons unsalted butter
- ¼ cup sugar-free pancake syrup

1. Preheat oven to 375°F. Grease a 9" × 7" baking dish.

2. In a medium mixing bowl, whisk together flours, baking powder, and salt.

3. In a separate medium mixing bowl, stir to combine sour cream, melted butter, eggs, and sweetener.

4. Stir dry mixture into wet mixture until thoroughly combined.

5. Fold in Cheddar until thoroughly mixed and then spread evenly in prepared baking dish.

6. Bake 25 minutes until firm and golden.

7. Slice and serve warm with remaining butter and sugar-free pancake syrup drizzled on top of each serving.

NET CARBS	
2G	

SERVES 9	
PER SERVING:	
CALORIES	214
FAT	18G
PROTEIN	6G
SODIUM	287MG
FIBER	2G
CARBOHYDRATES	5G
NET CARBS	2G
SUGAR	1G
SUGAR ALCOHOL	1G

TIME	
PREP TIME:	5 MINUTES
COOK TIME:	25 MINUTES
TOTAL TIME:	30 MINUTES

TIPS & OPTIONS

Serve with barbecued chicken and grilled veggies for an A+ summertime experience.

Butter and syrup make everything taste better. No one will notice the lack of corn with a little bit of *deliciousness* on top!

ZUCCHINI ZOOM ZOOM BREAD

NET CARBS

1G

SERVES 12

PER SERVING:

CALORIES	123
FAT	10G
PROTEIN	4G
SODIUM	141MG
FIBER	2G
CARBOHYDRATES	3G
NET CARBS	1G
SUGAR	1G

TIME

PREP TIME:	5 MINUTES
COOK TIME:	25 MINUTES
TOTAL TIME:	30 MINUTES

TIPS & OPTIONS

I love a little butter and jam on my zucchini bread. *Don't knock it till you try it!* I keep a bottle of Smucker's Sugar Free Strawberry Preserves in my refrigerator for moments like this. It has 2 grams net carbs per tablespoon. Other Smucker's sugar-free preserve flavors you might enjoy include red raspberry, blueberry, orange marmalade, and apricot.

One Christmas a couple of decades ago (am I THAT old?), I received a fancy-pants bread maker for my "big gift." Boy, did I put that gift to use! My kitchen smelled like a bakery for months. I had fallen victim to the marketing ploy that food from scratch was somehow "healthier." I even convinced myself that homemade *whole-wheat* bread would help me lose weight. Boy, was I wrong on both counts. Since DLK, I have had to become more open-minded about what constitutes bread in order to cut the carbs—lettuce leaves, low-carb tortillas, and Zucchini Zoom Zoom Bread are now among my favorites.

1½ cups shredded zucchini

3 large eggs

¼ cup unsalted butter, softened

½ teaspoon pure vanilla extract

¼ cup 0g net carbs sweetener

¾ cup superfine blanched almond flour

3 tablespoons coconut flour

½ teaspoon baking soda

½ teaspoon baking powder

¼ teaspoon salt

¼ teaspoon ground cinnamon

⅛ teaspoon ground nutmeg

¼ cup chopped walnuts

1 Preheat oven to 350°F. Grease a twelve-cup muffin tin.

2 Using a cheesecloth, squeeze excess moisture from zucchini.

3 In a medium mixing bowl, whisk together eggs, butter, vanilla, and sweetener.

4 In a separate medium bowl, combine all dry ingredients except nuts. Combine wet and dry ingredients in one bowl and mix well. Lastly, fold in zucchini and nuts.

5 Scoop equal amounts of batter into prepared muffin cups. Bake 23–25 minutes until firm and a toothpick comes out dry when poked into the middle of one.

6 Serve warm.

CHAPTER 9

SIDES

Side dishes are important accessories to the main event. They're like a terrific pair of earrings, a necklace, or a matching bracelet that accentuates your ensemble. Sides can complement (or ruin!) the whole look of what you're pulling together. With a little planning, I'll help you design the perfect DIRTY, LAZY, KETO outfit.

High-carb sides dishes (like rolls, chips, or toast) are easy to dismiss. You can tell the waiter, "No rice or tortillas, please" and be done worrying about carbs, right? *Not so fast.* Sometimes your meal is much more complicated to plan. Higher-carb side dishes can be difficult to identify. They look seemingly "healthy" but are actually quite high in carbs. Take vegetables, for example. Often some of the most offensive side dishes contain higher-carb vegetables such as corn on the cob, peas, or sweet potatoes. Since these are touted as "good for you," they might slip under your DIRTY, LAZY, KETO radar. *You've been warned!*

But more often than not, higher-carb side dishes are easy to spot. In my previous "heavier life," every entrée was served with a heavy starch as its side dish. Rice, potatoes, pasta, or bread hogged at least half of my dinner plate! If the starch wasn't on the side, it was hiding underneath, like a plate of noodles under spaghetti sauce or a bed of rice with curry sauce poured on top. Most entrées, it seemed, were pre-programmed to have a starchy best friend. The two seemed inseparable. It was illogical to NOT eat these foods together!

Learning to redefine side dishes took time. At first, I wouldn't let go. I searched high and low for a lower-starch version of the same item. These exist but are usually hard to find in stores (and quite expensive). Like you, I tried the "fake" *fishy* noodles and low-carb *cardboard* bread. *So disappointing!* Eventually, I gave up looking for a miracle product. I learned to create my own DIRTY, LAZY, KETO low-carb version of side dishes or pair an old favorite with a new food altogether. This shift in mindset has increased my overall happiness level (and ability to "stick with it") a hundred times over. I encourage you to do the same.

GOBBLE GOBBLE GREEN BEAN CASSEROLE

Holidays don't have to be boring just because you're committed to DIRTY, LAZY, KETO. In fact, you can still enjoy many traditional favorites, like Gobble Gobble Green Bean Casserole! All it takes is a little creativity when it comes to the ingredients. Instead of the *carb-loaded* fried onion topping many of us grew up with, try sprinkling a tablespoon of crumbled bacon or crushed pork rinds on top after the bake. This dish is sure to replace Grandma's version without any complaints.

- 1 teaspoon olive oil
- 1 cup thinly sliced mushrooms
- ¼ cup chopped green onion
- 1 teaspoon minced garlic
- 1 pound fresh green beans, steamed, trimmed, and cut into 1" sections
- ½ tablespoon Italian seasoning
- 2 strips no-sugar-added bacon, cooked and crumbled
- ½ cup heavy whipping cream
- ½ tablespoon soy sauce
- ¼ cup shredded whole milk mozzarella cheese
- ⅛ teaspoon ground black pepper
- 1 teaspoon grated Parmesan cheese

1 Preheat oven to 375°F. Grease a 9" × 9" baking dish.

2 In a large skillet over medium heat, heat oil. Stir in mushrooms, onion, and garlic. Cook 4–5 minutes, stirring occasionally, until mixture starts to brown.

3 Add green beans and remaining ingredients, except Parmesan, and stir to combine.

4 Pour into prepared baking dish, cover with aluminum foil, and bake 10 minutes. Remove foil and return to oven to bake 5 minutes more to brown top.

5 Let cool slightly. Stir and serve warm with sprinkle of Parmesan on top.

NET CARBS

3G

SERVES 6

PER SERVING:

CALORIES	139
FAT	10G
PROTEIN	5G
SODIUM	183MG
FIBER	3G
CARBOHYDRATES	6G
NET CARBS	3G
SUGAR	3G

TIME

PREP TIME:	10 MINUTES
COOK TIME:	20 MINUTES
TOTAL TIME:	30 MINUTES

TIPS & OPTIONS

Use canned mushrooms or canned green beans instead. Even frozen green beans can be substituted for fresh in this recipe, as long as they are cooked and ready to go!

This is a great dish for sneaking in vegetables. They kind of disappear in the thick and creamy sauce—all that people will see are the green beans. Broccoli, cauliflower, bell peppers, and even eggplant can be buried in this dish. Of course, if relatives are expecting the *traditional* green bean casserole, this strategy might cause an uproar.

ASAP ASPARAGUS WITH "HOLIDAY" SAUCE

Asparagus spears are the French fries of DIRTY, LAZY, KETO. *Seriously!* When cooked right, they can be just as crispy and delicious as fries from Micky D's. (Come on, folks, work with me a little.) Want to make asparagus irresistible? Add hollandaise sauce to the equation. Holla!

Asparagus

1½ pounds large asparagus spears, trimmed

¼ teaspoon salt

⅛ teaspoon ground black pepper

"Holiday" Sauce

2 large egg yolks

½ cup unsalted butter, melted

1 tablespoon 100% lemon juice

¼ teaspoon salt

⅛ teaspoon ground black pepper

1   Preheat oven to 400°F. Line a baking sheet with parchment paper.

2   In a large microwave-safe bowl, add asparagus and microwave on high 3–4 minutes until tender. Toss with salt and pepper and let cool.

3   In the bottom of a double boiler over medium-high heat, add 1" water. Heat until water begins to boil. Reduce heat to low.

4   In the top pan of the double boiler, whisk together egg yolks.

5   Very (very!) slowly, pour melted butter into sauce, continuing to whisk at a rapid pace until desired thickness is achieved. Add lemon juice, salt, and pepper and stir.

6   Remove from heat and set aside.

7   Spread out asparagus on prepared baking sheet and bake 10–12 minutes until starting to get crispy, turning halfway through.

8   Place asparagus on a serving platter and top with "Holiday" Sauce. Serve warm.

NET CARBS

3G

SERVES 6

PER SERVING:

CALORIES	176
FAT	16G
PROTEIN	4G
SODIUM	200MG
FIBER	2G
CARBOHYDRATES	5G
NET CARBS	3G
SUGAR	2G

TIME

PREP TIME:	10 MINUTES
COOK TIME:	16 MINUTES
TOTAL TIME:	26 MINUTES

TIPS & OPTIONS

For a crispier asparagus, lightly coat each spear with cooking oil.

If you are a master of the broiler feature in your oven, try cooking the asparagus on high 5–6 minutes per side. You have to really babysit it, though! At least at my house, the broiler has a tendency to burn my food if I look away even for a second.

Save time and reboot Hollandaise Sauce from Early Eggs with Benefits (see Chapter 5).

GALLOPING GRITS

NET CARBS

3G

SERVES 4

PER SERVING:
CALORIES	148
FAT	6G
PROTEIN	17G
SODIUM	839MG
FIBER	2G
CARBOHYDRATES	5G
NET CARBS	3G
SUGAR	2G

TIME

PREP TIME:	5 MINUTES
COOK TIME:	25 MINUTES
TOTAL TIME:	30 MINUTES

TIPS & OPTIONS

Don't have any shrimp on hand? Don't trip! Substitute a different protein of your choice.

I recommend that you keep multiple bags of riced cauliflower in your freezer. They don't take up much room and are perfect for a multitude of recipes. To save time, I try to only buy the brands that can be micro-waved directly in the bag.

When I'm out traveling, I make it a habit to stop by local grocery stores to pick up regional spices. They're inexpensive and easy to pack in my suitcase! On a recent trip to New Orleans, I bought a jar of "Slap Ya Mama" Cajun Seasoning. Call me sentimental, but sprinkling this spice on my Galloping Grits recipe makes the whole dish sing like a Dixieland band. Plus, when I run out of the souvenir spice, I have an excuse to go back.

- 1 (10-ounce) bag frozen riced cauliflower
- 2 tablespoons unsalted butter
- 1 pound medium (41–60 per pound) shrimp, peeled and deveined
- 1 tablespoon Cajun seasoning
- 1 teaspoon minced garlic

1. In a medium microwave-safe bowl, add riced cauliflower and microwave on high 4–5 minutes until tender.
2. In a large skillet over medium heat, melt butter. Stir in shrimp and seasoning and cook 10 minutes covered while stirring.
3. Add riced cauliflower and garlic. Stir to combine.
4. Cook covered 10 minutes, stirring regularly.
5. Serve warm.

HELP ME OUT HUSH PUPPIES

Don't get your knickers in a knot. You can still enjoy southern-style food and lose weight! Set up the table on the porch because I'm *a-fixin'* "K.F.C." Keto Fried Chicken (from *The DIRTY, LAZY, KETO® Cookbook*), Help Me Out Hush Puppies, and a pitcher of Snappy and Sweet Iced Tea (see Chapter 11) for supper tonight.

3 tablespoons full-fat cream cheese, softened

2 tablespoons unsalted butter, melted

2 large eggs, beaten

2½ tablespoons coconut flour

2 tablespoons grated yellow onion

½ teaspoon baking powder

½ teaspoon Creole seasoning

½ teaspoon minced garlic

1 Preheat oven to 375°F. Line a baking sheet with parchment paper.

2 In a large bowl, whisk together cream cheese, butter, and eggs.

3 Stir in remaining ingredients until completely mixed.

4 Form six even patties of dough no more than ½" thick. Carefully place on baking sheet ½" apart. Bake 20–25 minutes until golden and firm. Flip halfway through.

5 Serve warm.

NET CARBS	
2G	
SERVES 6	
PER SERVING:	
CALORIES	96
FAT	7G
PROTEIN	3G
SODIUM	209MG
FIBER	1G
CARBOHYDRATES	3G
NET CARBS	2G
SUGAR	1G

TIME	
PREP TIME:	5 MINUTES
COOK TIME:	25 MINUTES
TOTAL TIME:	30 MINUTES

TIPS & OPTIONS

I use a cheese grater to grate small amounts of vegetables like the onion in this recipe (which saves so much time compared to hauling out my Cuisinart food processor and cleaning it afterward).

Prefer a firmer shape? Bake hush puppies inside well-greased cupcake tins.

Alternatively, you can fry your Help Me Out Hush Puppies. Any high-temperature oil will do: avocado, canola, corn, grape-seed, peanut, sunflower, and so on.

FASTEN YOUR SEATBELTS FONDUE

NET CARBS
3G

SERVES 8

PER SERVING:

CALORIES	159
FAT	10G
PROTEIN	8G
SODIUM	446MG
FIBER	1G
CARBOHYDRATES	4G
NET CARBS	3G
SUGAR	2G

TIME

PREP TIME:	10 MINUTES
COOK TIME:	20 MINUTES
TOTAL TIME:	30 MINUTES

TIPS & OPTIONS

The spinach and artichoke hearts added to the cheese mixture can be fresh, frozen, or canned. They will meld with the cheeses so no one will be able to tell the difference.

Instead of a traditional fondue pot (what, you don't have one of these?), serve cheese dip in a mini Crock-Pot (with temperature on low).

Pre-make the fondue and bring to your next party! Serve with skewers of veggies and maybe even fresh bread for non-DLK folks.

To my family's horror, I once dragged them to a fondue-style restaurant. Everything protein on the menu came to the table raw with pots of boiling oil and long skewers used to cook it yourself. "It will be fun!" I insisted. My husband disagreed. "Why would anyone want to prepare their own food at a restaurant?" He may have been right. Touching raw chicken and steak while eating out? Kind of gross, actually. Today's Fasten Your Seatbelts Fondue recipe removes all the ick but keeps the novelty. Only veggies and cheese today, friends!

> 2 teaspoons minced garlic
> 1 cup dry sauvignon blanc wine
> 1 cup finely chopped spinach
> ¾ cup chopped artichoke hearts
> 1 cup shredded Cheddar cheese
> 1 cup shredded whole milk mozzarella cheese
> 6 tablespoons full-fat cream cheese, softened
> 1 teaspoon 100% lemon juice
> ¼ teaspoon salt
> ⅛ teaspoon ground black pepper
> 1 cup sliced zucchini rounds
> 1 cup bite-sized celery pieces
> 1 cup bite-sized broccoli florets

1. In a large nonstick skillet over medium heat, add garlic. Cook 2–3 minutes while stirring until soft.

2. Stir in wine, spinach, and artichokes and bring to boil. Reduce heat to low and simmer 5 minutes.

3. Slowly stir in cheeses, cream cheese, lemon juice, salt, and pepper. Keep stirring over low heat 12 minutes until smooth.

4. Put zucchini, celery, and broccoli in three separate small bowls.

5. Transfer cheese mixture to a fondue pot and serve while still smooth and warm with bowls of vegetables. Each person gets a skewer to use for dipping the vegetables.

BROCCOLI-BOOSTED CHEESE FRITTERS

NET CARBS

1G

SERVES 6

PER SERVING:
CALORIES	92
FAT	2G
PROTEIN	6G
SODIUM	303MG
FIBER	1G
CARBOHYDRATES	2G
NET CARBS	1G
SUGAR	1G

TIME

PREP TIME:	5 MINUTES
COOK TIME:	24 MINUTES
TOTAL TIME:	29 MINUTES

TIPS & OPTIONS

Stick a toothpick in each of these and serve to guests with assorted sauces on the side. Recommendations include DLK House Ranch Dressing (see recipe for Hurry Up House Salad with Ranch in Chapter 6), ground fresh chili paste (spicy), sugar-free barbecue sauce, or no-sugar-added ketchup.

My son helps me a lot in the kitchen. He hopes to open his own restaurant someday, and therefore, I hope to eat there for free (perks of knowing the boss). Despite his career aspirations, I consider my littlest Laska a picky eater. Sometimes it's a struggle to get him to eat heathy vegetables. Does that sound familiar? If so, I've got a solution: Broccoli-Boosted Cheese Fritters. They're like bite-sized healthy nuggets of *deliciousness*. As my teenager said (while popping the whole batch in his mouth before I could even eat one), "I could totally eat ALL of these!"

1 cup frozen riced broccoli

½ cup shredded whole milk mozzarella cheese

¼ cup superfine blanched almond flour

1 large egg, beaten

2 tablespoons finely chopped green onion

2 strips no-sugar-added bacon, cooked and finely crumbled

1 teaspoon minced garlic

½ teaspoon Creole seasoning

⅛ teaspoon salt

1. Preheat oven to 400°F. Line a baking sheet with parchment paper.

2. In a medium microwave-safe bowl, add broccoli and microwave on high 3–4 minutes until tender. Let cool and put in a colander to drain.

3. In a large bowl, add all ingredients and stir to combine.

4. Make 1" balls using a tablespoon and spread them out no less than 1" apart on prepared baking sheet.

5. Bake 20 minutes. Serve warm.

SHORT ORDER SRIRACHA BRUSSELS SPROUTS

I first fell in love with roasted Brussels sprouts when I ordered them from the BJ's Brewhouse appetizer menu. How did they get them so charred and delicious, yet so creamy? Up until then, I had only enjoyed them steamed (which is really boring in comparison). This five-gold-star recipe (awarded by myself, *to myself*) took several attempts on my part. I had to master the charring abilities of my broiler. I guarantee Short Order Sriracha Brussels Sprouts will become one of your all-time favorites too!

Brussels Sprouts

1 (12-ounce) bag Brussels sprouts

1 cup water

¼ cup olive oil

½ teaspoon salt

Sweet Sriracha Sauce

½ cup full-fat mayonnaise

1 teaspoon sriracha sauce

4 (1-gram) packets 0g net carbs sweetener

1 Preheat broiler to high. Line a baking sheet with foil. Grease foil with nonstick cooking spray.

2 Fit the metal trivet into an Instant Pot®. Add Brussels sprouts to steamer basket and place on trivet. Add water, put on lid, and close pressure release. Cook on High Pressure 5 minutes.

3 Carefully quick-release pressure and remove lid. Drain sprouts in a colander until cool enough to handle. Transfer sprouts to a medium bowl.

4 Add oil and salt. Toss to coat.

5 Spread sprouts out on prepared baking sheet. Broil 1–2 minutes until turning crispy. Turn and broil another 1–2 minutes until crispy on the other side.

6 In a small bowl, whisk all Sweet Sriracha Sauce ingredients until combined and sweetener is dissolved. Transfer to a small dipping bowl.

7 Serve warm Brussels sprouts on a large plate with bowl of Sweet Sriracha Sauce.

NET CARBS

5G

SERVES 4

PER SERVING:

CALORIES	344
FAT	33G
PROTEIN	3G
SODIUM	511MG
FIBER	3G
CARBOHYDRATES	8G
NET CARBS	5G
SUGAR	2G

TIME

PREP TIME:	5 MINUTES
COOK TIME:	9 MINUTES
TOTAL TIME:	14 MINUTES

TIPS & OPTIONS

If your sprouts come in microwave-safe packaging, then skip the Instant Pot® cooking steps and follow the cooking instructions on the bag.

Of course, the seasonings can be adjusted to your family's personal tastes (especially the amount of sriracha added for heat).

Smaller-sized Brussels sprouts (when halved) may not need to be "precooked" in the Instant Pot® as they will cook quickly and completely under the broiler.

Have an air fryer? Cook and crisp 15 minutes at 380°F.

ONION RUN RINGS

Comfort food cravings don't go away just because your eating habits become healthier. After all, we eat for reasons beyond hunger, right? I've had great success in my own weight loss journey by leaning in to these cravings as opposed to fighting them. By re-creating comfort food classics like onion rings with lower-carb ingredients, I'm able to stay on track with weight loss and maintenance without skipping a beat.

2 large yellow onions, peeled and sliced into ½" rings

1¼ cups superfine blanched almond flour

½ tablespoon baking powder

½ tablespoon Creole seasoning

½ cup half and half

½ cup water

1 large egg, beaten

1½ cups finely crushed pork rinds

2 cups vegetable oil

1   Separate all onion slices into rings and save acceptable rings of at least 1" diameter.

2   In a medium mixing bowl, combine almond flour, baking powder, and seasoning.

3   In a large Ziploc bag, add onion rings and 1½ tablespoons dry mixture. Seal and shake bag until all rings are coated.

4   Add half and half, water, and egg to remaining dry mixture and whisk until mixed thoroughly. Spread pork rinds on a large dinner plate.

5   In a medium skillet over medium heat, preheat oil to 375°F. Line a large plate with paper towels.

6   Dip each onion ring completely in batter and shake off excess. Transfer to plate with pork rinds and coat completely.

7   Gently drop coated rings in hot oil and deep-fry 2 minutes each until golden. Deep-fry 4–6 at time, approximately 20 minutes total. Transfer to lined plate to drain and cool.

8   Serve warm.

NET CARBS	
4G	

SERVES 8	
PER SERVING:	
CALORIES	256
FAT	20G
PROTEIN	10G
SODIUM	363MG
FIBER	2G
CARBOHYDRATES	6G
NET CARBS	4G
SUGAR	3G

TIME	
PREP TIME:	10 MINUTES
COOK TIME:	20 MINUTES
TOTAL TIME:	30 MINUTES

TIPS & OPTIONS

Don't skip the Ziploc bag step for coating the onion rings. It's necessary to remove moisture from the exposed surfaces of the onion and will help the batter to stick.

Use tongs to dip rings in batter. Set down coated rings on the plate of crushed pork rinds, then spoon rinds over the top to fully coat. Shake off loose rinds that aren't attached.

Dip your cooked rings in rebooted homemade DLK House Ranch Dressing (see recipe for Hurry Up House Salad with Ranch in Chapter 6) or rebooted Wasabi Ranch Dip (see recipe for Drive-Thru Nuggets with Wasabi Ranch Dip in Chapter 10).

BRISK BROCCOLI ALFREDO

NET CARBS

9G

SERVES 4

PER SERVING:
CALORIES	323
FAT	28G
PROTEIN	6G
SODIUM	310MG
FIBER	2G
CARBOHYDRATES	11G
NET CARBS	9G
SUGAR	3G

TIME

PREP TIME:	10 MINUTES
COOK TIME:	14 MINUTES
TOTAL TIME:	24 MINUTES

TIPS & OPTIONS

For a more robust meal, top with your favorite protein (grilled shrimp, chicken, and so on).

Just like at Olive Garden, everything tastes better with grated Parmesan cheese sprinkled on top. Go for it!

Freeze leftover portions of your homemade Alfredo sauce to enjoy another time. If properly sealed, it will last weeks in the freezer.

I learned about the Brisk Broccoli Alfredo combination on a recent trip to Olive Garden. My family was digging into plates of all-you-can-eat pasta while I sat disappointed with my unlimited bowl of salad (definitely not the same thing). Then it hit me… Alfredo sauce! Adding Alfredo sauce to, well, anything really tastes like heaven. It's impossible to feel deprived when enjoying Alfredo sauce on broccoli, salmon, *or even your spoon.*

> 1 (12-ounce) bag broccoli florets
> 2 tablespoons unsalted butter
> 1 cup heavy whipping cream
> ¼ cup grated Parmesan cheese
> ¼ teaspoon minced garlic
> ¼ teaspoon salt
> ⅛ teaspoon ground black pepper

1 In a medium microwave-safe bowl, add broccoli and microwave on high 3–4 minutes until softened but not mushy.

2 In a large skillet over medium heat, melt butter. Add broccoli and cook 5 minutes while stirring to lightly brown.

3 Stir in remaining ingredients and cook an additional 5 minutes.

4 Serve warm on four plates.

STRAIGHTAWAY SHEET PAN VEGETABLE MEDLEY

If you find yourself saying "I hate vegetables," this might be the recipe for you to try first. Even the pickiest eaters cave after tasting *roasted* vegetables. There is something magical about cooking them at high temperatures. Many vegetable flavors become sweeter (surprising, right?). Now that I've piqued your curiosity, let's get cookin' with Straightaway Sheet Pan Vegetable Medley.

¼ cup sesame oil

2 tablespoons balsamic vinegar

1 tablespoon chopped fresh basil

1 medium clove garlic, peeled and minced

½ teaspoon ground ginger

¼ teaspoon salt

¼ teaspoon ground black pepper

2½ cups bite-sized broccoli florets

1½ cups bite-sized cauliflower florets

1 medium green bell pepper, seeded and chopped

½ large red onion, peeled and sliced in rings

1 cup chopped zucchini

1. Preheat oven to 400°F. Line a baking sheet with parchment paper.

2. In a large bowl, whisk together oil, vinegar, basil, garlic, ginger, salt, and black pepper. Add all vegetables to bowl and stir until completely coated.

3. Transfer vegetables to baking sheet. Space them out so vegetables can cook on all sides.

4. Bake 15–20 minutes, turning regularly, until vegetables start to brown. Cover with foil if they start to brown before they are tender.

5. Serve warm.

NET CARBS

6G

SERVES 6

PER SERVING:

CALORIES	118
FAT	9G
PROTEIN	2G
SODIUM	121MG
FIBER	2G
CARBOHYDRATES	8G
NET CARBS	6G
SUGAR	3G

TIME

PREP TIME:	10 MINUTES
COOK TIME:	20 MINUTES
TOTAL TIME:	30 MINUTES

TIPS & OPTIONS

Use whatever vegetables you have on hand. Be creative! The sheet pan strategy is perfect for using up assorted leftover fresh veggies.

Try different spices or dipping sauces to make eating vegetables more fun (or tolerable, depending on your perspective).

Cut the vegetables into small bite-sized pieces (or smaller) to ensure that they cook completely.

STOPWATCH SPANISH "RICE"

NET CARBS

4G

SERVES 4

PER SERVING:

CALORIES	85
FAT	5G
PROTEIN	2G
SODIUM	267MG
FIBER	3G
CARBOHYDRATES	7G
NET CARBS	4G
SUGAR	3G

TIME

PREP TIME:	10 MINUTES
COOK TIME:	20 MINUTES
TOTAL TIME:	30 MINUTES

Cauliflower is the most miraculous of all DIRTY, LAZY, KETO ingredients. It takes on the flavor of whatever surrounds it, and it can be cooked in at least a dozen ways. It's affordable and available year-round, too, which removes all excuses. Even so, I find myself stocking up on frozen riced cauliflower whenever I catch a good sale. Having the right ingredients on hand makes it that much easier to cook a quick dish like Stopwatch Spanish "Rice."

2 tablespoons unsalted butter

1 (10-ounce) bag frozen riced cauliflower

½ medium green bell pepper, seeded and finely chopped

¼ cup chopped green onion

½ cup no-sugar-added diced tomatoes with green chiles, drained

1 tablespoon taco seasoning

1   In a large skillet over medium heat, melt butter. Stir in cauliflower and cook 10 minutes while stirring.

2   Stir in remaining ingredients and cook an additional 10 minutes while stirring to remove excess moisture.

3   Serve warm.

TIPS & OPTIONS ≫

Cook a little longer uncovered to boil off the liquid if the dish is still too "soupy." The finished product should be crumbly and resemble a dry rice dish.

Buy small portions of frozen riced cauliflower in "direct to microwave" packaging to save time.

Frozen riced cauliflower (purchased in bulk bags) can be poured directly into a frying pan. (There is no need to defrost ahead of time.)

Prefer fresh? Make your own riced cauliflower by running heads of cauliflower through your food processor. Scrape with a rubber spatula often, and gently pulse machine for best results.

CHAPTER 10

MAIN DISHES

I have a confession to make. Last year at Thanksgiving, I didn't *aaaaaactually* make the turkey! (Sorry, Mom.) This might not be a big deal for most folks, but *helllloooo!* I'm a cookbook writer! *That's really embarrassing.* It's not that I didn't know how to bake the bird; I just chose not to. At the time, I felt overwhelmed with work. I was up against a deadline and running out of time. I needed to cut a few corners with meal planning to keep afloat. I made my favorite side dishes, but the main event? I called an outsider for help. *Gobble, gobble!*

In today's world, where all of us are pressed for time, we need to embrace more shortcuts in the kitchen to stay sane. Whether or not you own up to these tricks *in front of guests* is entirely up to you! (Maybe your mother-in-law doesn't need to know ALL of your secrets.) Either way, let's cut a few corners and stop wasting our valuable time. *Wash and chop romaine?* Buy a bag of prewashed lettuce instead. *Forget to thaw meat for dinner?* Toss the meat, solid as a rock, into the pressure cooker.

> You don't have to be perfect in the kitchen to be successful at weight loss.

Part of the reason I've been able to maintain my 140-pound weight loss for eight years is that I focus on the big picture: *eating healthy.* The details behind how this is executed are up for discussion. I don't stress over buying 100 percent fresh or only organic ingredients. The fish I grill probably isn't line-caught (unless reeling it from the bottom of my freezer counts?). Not every part of my meal is homemade either. No, this pesto isn't from scratch—*it's from Costco!* I don't rice my own cauliflower; no, ma'am. It's cheaper *and* faster to buy it frozen. I buy what's on sale. I cook with fresh, frozen, *and* canned ingredients. I am open-minded and realistic about taking cooking shortcuts.

There is no judgment with DIRTY, LAZY, KETO. Getting dinner ready is important, yes, but you've got to do it on your own terms.

READY, SET, GO GROUND BEEF

When I first met my husband, his fridge was full of jumbo cottage cheese containers. I was like, "What's with this guy? Nobody likes cottage cheese this much!" To my surprise, these containers were full of ingredients like cooked ground beef he was planning to use in his recipes. We were a match made in heaven. He taught me how to cook ahead (and be more budget-minded), and in exchange, I upgraded his bachelor ways to a more sophisticated food storage system—clear containers, to start with. It's much easier to utilize leftovers when you can actually see what's inside.

1 pound 93% lean ground beef

⅛ teaspoon salt

⅛ teaspoon ground black pepper

1 In a medium nonstick skillet over medium heat, cook beef 10 minutes while stirring.

2 Stir in salt and pepper and continue to cook 5 more minutes.

3 Let cool and refrigerate in an airtight container up to 4 days until ready to add to a meal.

NET CARBS

0G

SERVES 4

PER SERVING:

CALORIES	166
FAT	7G
PROTEIN	24G
SODIUM	143MG
FIBER	0G
CARBOHYDRATES	0G
NET CARBS	0G
SUGAR	0G

TIME

PREP TIME:	5 MINUTES
COOK TIME:	15 MINUTES
TOTAL TIME:	20 MINUTES

TIPS & OPTIONS

Freeze unused portions to reboot for later meals. Use leftovers safely by thawing frozen meat (for reuse) in the refrigerator. When it's time for reheating, be sure the internal temperature reaches a minimum of 165°F or higher.

When storing leftovers safely in the refrigerator, airtight storage is key. Sealed Ziploc bags, secure plastic wrap, or plastic containers with properly fitting lids prevent bacteria from growing and keep your food safe.

This recipe (and storage tips) applies to all types of ground meat: turkey, chicken, pork, and so on.

GRAB AND GO CHICKEN BREASTS

NET CARBS

0G

SERVES 4

PER SERVING:
CALORIES	102
FAT	1G
PROTEIN	19G
SODIUM	111MG
FIBER	0G
CARBOHYDRATES	0G
NET CARBS	0G
SUGAR	0G

TIME

PREP TIME:	5 MINUTES
COOK TIME:	25 MINUTES
TOTAL TIME:	30 MINUTES

TIPS & OPTIONS »

Prefer the pressure cooker method? For the laziest chefs (like me!), cook boneless chicken breasts in an Instant Pot® on high pressure 8 minutes per pound.

Freeze unused portions to reboot for later meals. Use leftovers safely by thawing frozen meat (for reuse) in the refrigerator. When it's time for reheating, be sure the internal temperature reaches a minimum of 165°F or higher.

Ultra-lazy cooks can skip this recipe altogether and buy a precooked rotisserie chicken from the grocery store. Some stores even sell the meat already pulled from the bone in tidy packages. Now THAT'S convenient!

Cooking chicken ahead of time is just common sense. I use this ingredient in so many recipes, I'd be a fool to cook it over and over again throughout the week. *That's just too many dishes, people.* My time is valuable. If I can knock out a task in one sitting, sign me up! Plus, I find it convenient and cost-effective to cook chicken in bulk when I catch a good sale. The cooked leftovers are also easy to freeze for future meals.

4 (4.2-ounce) boneless, skinless chicken breasts
⅛ teaspoon salt
⅛ teaspoon ground black pepper

1 Preheat oven to 375°F. Grease a 9" × 12" × 2" baking dish.

2 Season breasts with salt and pepper and cook covered 25 minutes, flipping halfway through.

3 Let cool and refrigerate up to 4 days in an airtight container until ready to add to a meal.

BAM! BACON BURGERS

Is there any dish more American than a cheeseburger? I didn't think so! BAM! Bacon Burgers will be a hit with everyone in your household. If your family has been hesitant to support your new lifestyle change, make them this dish. After just one bite, you'll recruit a full team of volunteers to help "test" your recipes. Be sure to reboot leftover Onion Run Rings (see Chapter 9) and homemade DLK House Ranch Dressing here (see recipe for Hurry Up House Salad with Ranch in Chapter 6) for a complete DLK dining experience.

1 pound 93% lean ground beef

¼ cup grated yellow onion

2 tablespoons half and half

1 large egg, beaten

1 medium clove garlic, peeled and minced

½ teaspoon salt

¼ teaspoon ground black pepper

4 ounces sharp Cheddar cheese, cut into ¼"–½" cubes

½ pound thin-sliced no-sugar-added bacon, cut in half to make 3"–4" sections

1 Preheat oven to 400°F. Line a baking sheet with parchment paper.

2 In a medium bowl, thoroughly combine beef, onion, half and half, egg, garlic, salt, and pepper.

3 Use a scoop to form 1" balls. Push your index finger into the center of each ball and hide cube of cheese there. Pinch sides of hole you created to close and form back into ball with cheese cube sealed inside.

4 Wrap each ball in two half strips of bacon. Alternate directions, one right to left and second up and down, to ensure full coverage around ball.

5 Place on prepared baking sheet spaced at least ½" apart and bake 25 minutes, turning and draining fat regularly until meat is cooked throughout and bacon is crispy.

6 Serve warm.

NET CARBS	
2G	
SERVES 6	
PER SERVING:	
CALORIES	278
FAT	16G
PROTEIN	27G
SODIUM	630MG
FIBER	0G
CARBOHYDRATES	2G
NET CARBS	2G
SUGAR	1G

TIME	
PREP TIME:	5 MINUTES
COOK TIME:	25 MINUTES
TOTAL TIME:	30 MINUTES

TIPS & OPTIONS

I prefer the thin-sliced bacon as it forms better around the balls and also will be easier to bite through.

Use a simple box grater to shred the onion. Don't create a ton more work for yourself by dragging out your humongous food processor from storage and turning your house upside down searching for the right shredder attachment.

RUSH IN REUBEN

After finishing the New York City Marathon, I craved three things: a shower, an ice-cold Diet Coke, and a hot Reuben sandwich. I'd had 26.2 miles to think about what I wanted; nothing was going to get in my way (well, except the 52,812 other runners). I may not be in New York City anymore, but my Rush In Reuben recipe takes me back to the glory I felt after finishing the race. Rush In Reuben is the sandwich of champions.

Chaffle Buns

¼ cup superfine blanched almond flour

¼ cup full-fat cream cheese, softened

½ teaspoon baking powder

½ teaspoon garlic salt

2 large eggs, beaten

1 tablespoon unsalted butter, melted

Sandwich Toppings

½ pound sliced corned beef

½ pound sauerkraut, drained

2 (1-ounce) slices Swiss cheese

1 tablespoon Thousand Island dressing

2 tablespoons full-fat mayonnaise

1 Grease a mini waffle maker with nonstick spray and preheat.

2 In a medium bowl, whisk together Chaffle Buns ingredients and pour one-fourth of batter in center of hot waffle maker and close. Cook 3 minutes and remove bun to plate. Repeat for three more buns.

3 In a medium microwave-safe bowl, add corned beef and microwave on high 1½ minutes.

4 In a separate medium microwave-safe bowl, add sauerkraut and microwave on high 1½ minutes.

5 Place 1 bun on each of two plates. Top each with half of meat first, then half of sauerkraut, and finally, a slice of Swiss.

6 In a small bowl, stir to combine dressing and mayonnaise.

7 Spread each of remaining buns with half of dressing mixture. Place each bun, dressing side down, on each sandwich. Serve warm.

NET CARBS

7G

SERVES 2

PER SERVING:

CALORIES	848
FAT	65G
PROTEIN	40G
SODIUM	2,815MG
FIBER	5G
CARBOHYDRATES	12G
NET CARBS	7G
SUGAR	5G

TIME

PREP TIME:	10 MINUTES
COOK TIME:	15 MINUTES
TOTAL TIME:	25 MINUTES

TIPS & OPTIONS

Skip making the Chaffle Bun steps by rebooting Boogie Bread (see Chapter 5).

Be sure to purchase fresh sauerkraut (sold in the deli section of your grocery store) to enjoy the natural probiotic benefits from fermentation. Probiotics help maintain strong intestinal health. Emerging research suggests that balanced bacteria in the gut reduces overall inflammation and can prevent or treat a variety of illnesses. *Huh!*

Thousand Island dressing is higher in carbs compared to my usual DLK favorites (ranch or blue cheese dressing). This is why I "water it down" with mayonnaise.

NET CARBS

5G

SERVES 4

PER SERVING:

CALORIES	50
FAT	1G
PROTEIN	3G
SODIUM	203MG
FIBER	3G
CARBOHYDRATES	8G
NET CARBS	5G
SUGAR	5G

TIME

PREP TIME:	10 MINUTES
COOK TIME:	2 MINUTES
TOTAL TIME:	12 MINUTES

TIPS & OPTIONS

I've never had any luck with commercial spiralizers. If you like them, great. Otherwise, stick with a julienne peeler like me. This inexpensive handheld tool is much cheaper and doesn't take up any counter space.

Reboot leftover zoodles with the Minestrone Zippy Zoodle Soup recipe (see Chapter 6).

Instead of boiling your zoodles for 1 minute, try the stir-fry method instead. Heat a tablespoon of oil in a skillet over medium heat and gently toss zoodles until they reach desired softness.

EZ ZOODLE NOODLE "SPAGHETTI"

I've tried many brands of shirataki noodles with little success. No matter how much rinsing I do, a fishy smell persists. This works well in seafood or broth recipes like pho, but definitely not with Italian-style spaghetti! Instead, I prefer making noodles from zucchini. This bland vegetable doesn't compete with flavors from added sauces. As an added bonus, zucchini is inexpensive, readily available, and quick to manipulate. For a recipe like EZ Zoodle Noodle "Spaghetti," zucchini is the best overall choice.

3 cups water

4 medium zucchini, ends trimmed

½ cup pesto

½ cup no-sugar-added pasta sauce

4 teaspoons grated Parmesan cheese

1   In a medium saucepan over medium heat, boil water.

2   To make zoodles by hand, use a julienne vegetable peeler and apply light pressure lengthwise down the entire (unpeeled) zucchini. Continue making long, thin strips until you work your way through the entire vegetable. Carefully add to boiling water for *1 minute only* to prevent them from getting too soft. Drain and divide evenly among four plates.

3   In a medium microwave-safe bowl, whisk pesto and pasta sauce together. Microwave on high 30 seconds. Stir and microwave again 30 seconds.

4   Top each mound of zoodles evenly with sauce. Sprinkle Parmesan on top.

5   Serve warm.

QUICK COVER UP COTTAGE PIE

A cottage pie is usually made with beef, while a shepherd's pie contains lamb. Either way, you're covering up a meat pie, people. What makes the DLK version special is how I change up the mashed potato "frosting." Mashed cauliflower, combined with rich cream and cheese, is a superior substitute, making this classic dish a homespun home run. As an added bonus, the "frosting" covers up the mystery meat, allowing you to sneak in leftovers from last night's dinner.

1½ (12-ounce) bags cauliflower florets, thawed

½ pound lean ground turkey

½ cup diced tomatoes

¼ cup chopped celery

⅓ cup chopped green onions

1 teaspoon minced garlic

½ cup heavy whipping cream

¼ cup shredded whole milk mozzarella cheese, softened

1 teaspoon Italian seasoning

¼ teaspoon salt

⅛ teaspoon ground black pepper

1 Preheat oven to 400°F. Grease a 9" × 7" × 2" baking dish.

2 In a large microwave-safe bowl, add cauliflower and microwave on high 5 minutes. Let cool.

3 While cauliflower is microwaving, in a medium nonstick skillet over medium heat, add turkey, tomatoes, celery, green onions, and garlic. Cook 10 minutes while stirring until soft and browning.

4 In a food processor, add cauliflower, cream, mozzarella, Italian seasoning, salt, and pepper. Pulse two to four times until desired "mashed potato" consistency is reached.

5 Spread even layer of meat mixture in baking dish. Top with even layer of cauliflower mixture.

6 Bake 10 minutes. Serve warm.

NET CARBS

5G

SERVES 4

PER SERVING:

CALORIES	255
FAT	17G
PROTEIN	17G
SODIUM	277MG
FIBER	4G
CARBOHYDRATES	9G
NET CARBS	5G
SUGAR	5G

TIME

PREP TIME:	10 MINUTES
COOK TIME:	20 MINUTES
TOTAL TIME:	30 MINUTES

TIPS & OPTIONS

Any ground protein, even tofu, can be substituted or even added to this dish. Also, get creative with the vegetables used. No one is going to say, "You can't do that!"

Baby eggplant, chayote, or jicama? These are all unusual vegetables that are right at home in a baked dish like this.

Quick Cover Up Cottage Pie may look shallow in a 9" × 7" baking dish, but using this size allows the dish to cook faster.

PRESTO CHICKEN PARMESAN

NET CARBS

4G

SERVES 4

PER SERVING:

CALORIES	471
FAT	31G
PROTEIN	38G
SODIUM	969MG
FIBER	2G
CARBOHYDRATES	6G
NET CARBS	4G
SUGAR	2G

TIME

PREP TIME:	9 MINUTES
COOK TIME:	21 MINUTES
TOTAL TIME:	30 MINUTES

TIPS & OPTIONS »

The breasts are pounded to ensure that there are no thick pieces that won't have enough time to cook.

Keep it simple and please everyone at the table tonight. Serve Presto Chicken Parmesan with a Hurry Up House Salad with Ranch (see Chapter 6), and there will be no complaints (or leftovers, sorry!).

I avoided eating Italian food for the longest time. I was under the mistaken belief that plates of pasta had to accompany every meal—*or else*! I had to get over myself. The Italians have so much more to offer. I've learned to try the new Italian flavors of capers, anchovies, fresh herbs, and olives. Nevertheless, sometimes I crave a traditional favorite like Presto Chicken Parmesan.

¾ cup full-fat mayonnaise

¾ cup grated Parmesan cheese

1 medium clove garlic, peeled and minced

½ teaspoon salt

¼ teaspoon ground black pepper

4 (4.2-ounce) boneless, skinless chicken breasts

2 tablespoons unsalted butter

1 cup no-sugar-added pasta sauce

1 cup shredded whole milk mozzarella cheese

1 In a medium bowl, combine mayonnaise, Parmesan, garlic, salt, and pepper. Whisk until blended.

2 Place a large piece of parchment paper on your counter. Place chicken breasts on top and pound chicken to no thicker than ¾".

3 Pat dry and dredge breasts in mayonnaise mixture, being sure to coat both sides. Shake off extra.

4 In a large skillet over medium heat, melt butter. Fry all four breasts together for 10 minutes until golden. Flip and fry another 10 minutes.

5 In a medium microwave-safe bowl, add pasta sauce and microwave on high covered 30 seconds. Stir and microwave again for 30 seconds.

6 Remove each breast to a dinner plate. Spoon pasta sauce over chicken and top with equal amounts of mozzarella. Serve warm.

TIME PRESSURE COOKER BEEF STEW

NET CARBS

2G

SERVES 6

PER SERVING:

CALORIES	196
FAT	6G
PROTEIN	27G
SODIUM	628MG
FIBER	2G
CARBOHYDRATES	4G
NET CARBS	2G
SUGAR	2G

TIME

PREP TIME:	10 MINUTES
COOK TIME:	20 MINUTES
TOTAL TIME:	30 MINUTES

TIPS & OPTIONS

Time Pressure Cooker Beef Stew often tastes better the next day after all of the flavors bloom and the stew thickens.

Enjoy your stew with a side of Ready or Not Corn Bread (see Chapter 8) and Hurry Up House Salad with Ranch (see Chapter 6).

There is nothing inherently wrong with comfort food. I bristle when experts suggest otherwise. Having emotional connections to food is normal! A delicious smell alone can take me back to childhood or remind me of a happy place in time. As long as I'm not baking cookies for comfort, I don't see anything wrong with nostalgia. Time Pressure Cooker Beef Stew is one of those recipes that warms the heart and fills your kitchen with memories.

- 1½ pounds rump roast, trimmed of fat and cubed into ¾" pieces
- ½ cup chopped celery
- 1 small carrot, peeled and thinly sliced
- ½ large yellow onion, peeled and chopped
- 2 tablespoons no-sugar-added tomato paste
- 1 cup beef broth
- 1 teaspoon salt
- ½ teaspoon ground black pepper
- 1 teaspoon xanthan gum

1. In a large bowl, add all ingredients except xanthan gum. Stir to combine and coat meat.

2. Put mixture in the Instant Pot®.

3. Put on lid and close pressure release. Cook on High Pressure 20 minutes. Carefully quick-release pressure and remove lid.

4. Sprinkle xanthan gum slowly into mixture while stirring to combine. Serve warm in soup bowls.

CHOP SUEY EXPRESS

"Get off the couch and see the world!" is one of my *Stephanie-isms*, or guiding life principles. I have so much energy after losing 140 pounds that on weekends, instead of watching TV, I drag my family on adventurous day trips. San Francisco's Chinatown tops the list as a family favorite. Walking up and down the hills gives us a good workout while we visit local shops, enjoy cultural parades, and of course, sit down to lunch. The menu is printed in Chinese, but I can still find my favorite Chop Suey (which, surprisingly, means "leftovers"!).

- ½ cup water
- 2 tablespoons unsalted butter, melted
- ½ cup chopped green bell pepper
- ½ cup sliced mushrooms
- ¼ cup chopped green onion
- ¼ cup chopped celery
- ½ cup snow peas, trimmed and cut in 1" sections
- 2 teaspoons minced garlic
- ¼ teaspoon ground black pepper
- ¾ cup soy sauce
- ½ tablespoon grated fresh ginger
- ¼ teaspoon ground cinnamon
- 2 pounds chuck roast beef, trimmed and diced into cubes no larger than ¾"

1. In a large bowl, add all ingredients. Stir to mix and coat meat.
2. Put mixture in the Instant Pot®.
3. Put on lid and close pressure release. Cook on High Pressure 20 minutes. Carefully quick-release pressure and remove lid.
4. Remove the trivet and give the pot a final stir. Serve warm.

NET CARBS
4G

SERVES 6

PER SERVING:

CALORIES	274
FAT	10G
PROTEIN	37G
SODIUM	1,841MG
FIBER	1G
CARBOHYDRATES	5G
NET CARBS	4G
SUGAR	1G

TIME

PREP TIME:	10 MINUTES
COOK TIME:	20 MINUTES
TOTAL TIME:	30 MINUTES

TIPS & OPTIONS

This is best served on a bed of cooked riced cauliflower.

Make sure that you serve with the very tasty gravy that is in the bottom of the pot. Slowly stir in ¼ teaspoon xanthan gum at a time to thicken if desired.

TURKEY TROT DRUMSTICKS

Though admittedly morbid, I find myself thoroughly entertained by stories of Thanksgiving turkeys gone wrong. Still-frozen turkeys, non-injury deep-fryer explosions, or dropped birds? I just can't help myself; I have to know more! Hearing horror stories like these immediately makes me feel like I'm doing a good job preparing the big meal. It can be stressful, right? Sometimes a laugh is just what we need to put it all in perspective. My Turkey Trot Drumsticks recipe will have your holiday meal on the table safe, sound, and stress-free.

6 cups peanut oil

1 tablespoon Creole seasoning

2 medium turkey legs (drumsticks)

2 ounces injectable Creole butter marinade

1 In a large soup pot over medium heat, preheat oil to 375°F. Line a plate with paper towels.

2 Rub Creole seasoning all over turkey legs.

3 Inject 1 ounce butter marinade into each leg (using included syringe) in several places under skin.

4 Carefully lower both legs into oil and deep-fry 15–20 minutes until internal temperature of the turkey legs reaches at least 165°F.

5 Remove legs from oil and place onto lined plate to drain and cool.

6 Serve warm.

NET CARBS

0G

SERVES 2

PER SERVING:

CALORIES	682
FAT	46G
PROTEIN	55G
SODIUM	2,914MG
FIBER	0G
CARBOHYDRATES	0G
NET CARBS	0G
SUGAR	0G

TIME

PREP TIME:	5 MINUTES
COOK TIME:	20 MINUTES
TOTAL TIME:	25 MINUTES

TIPS & OPTIONS

Double or triple this recipe to make good use of the prepared frying oil.

Don't worry if you don't have a plastic syringe to inject the butter marinade. Do your best to push the hard butter under the skin. Stand the leg on a plate with the fat end up. Pull the skin as loose as you can and push the butter down. Some will drain out when you lay the leg back down, so add sparingly. If you can, seal the butter marinade inside with toothpicks or food-grade string, and then *play on, playah!*

SNAPPY STUFFED SALMON

The first time I had this dish, I was dining at the top of the Space Needle in Seattle. I'm slightly afraid of heights, but I forgot all about my fears when a gorgeous plate of spinach-stuffed salmon arrived at the table. *Hello, beautiful!* I spent the rest of the evening trying to figure out how I could make it myself when I got home from my trip without spending all day in the kitchen. When choosing your fillets for this dish, make sure they are thick enough to slice horizontally and allow for stuffing.

NET CARBS

2G

SERVES 4

PER SERVING:

CALORIES	442
FAT	27G
PROTEIN	40G
SODIUM	506MG
FIBER	0G
CARBOHYDRATES	2G
NET CARBS	2G
SUGAR	1G

TIME

PREP TIME:	15 MINUTES
COOK TIME:	12 MINUTES
TOTAL TIME:	27 MINUTES

TIPS & OPTIONS ≫

No air fryer? No problem. Place salmon in a well-greased baking dish, cover with aluminum foil, and bake at 350°F about 30 minutes until fillets are flaky throughout.

Be sure to take out the trash tonight. No one wants to wake up to fish smell the next day.

Want another trick to save prep time in the kitchen? Instead of making the Salmon Stuffing from scratch, substitute fresh spinach-artichoke dip purchased from the deli. *Shhh!*

Salmon Stuffing

½ cup chopped spinach

6 tablespoons full-fat cream cheese, softened

¾ cup shredded whole milk mozzarella cheese

2 teaspoons minced garlic

¼ teaspoon salt

⅛ teaspoon ground black pepper

Salmon Glaze

2 tablespoons olive oil

1½ tablespoons 100% lemon juice

⅛ teaspoon salt

⅛ teaspoon ground black pepper

Salmon Fillets

4 (6-ounce) salmon fillets

1   Grease bottom rack of air fryer drawer, then preheat air fryer to 400°F.

2   In a medium bowl, combine all Salmon Stuffing ingredients. Stir until well mixed.

3   In a small bowl, whisk to combine all Salmon Glaze ingredients.

4   Brush both sides of all 4 salmon fillets with Salmon Glaze.

5   Using a sharp knife, carefully slice each salmon fillet horizontally to create a deep pocket for stuffing.

6   Using a silicone spatula, slide equal amounts of Salmon Stuffing into each fillet.

7   Place fish on greased bottom rack in air fryer basket with plenty of space around each fillet.

8   Cook 10–12 minutes until fillets are flaky throughout. Serve warm.

HURRIED JALAPEÑO HOLLA CASSEROLE

NET CARBS

5G

SERVES 6

PER SERVING:
CALORIES	467
FAT	28G
PROTEIN	40G
SODIUM	590MG
FIBER	0G
CARBOHYDRATES	5G
NET CARBS	5G
SUGAR	4G

TIME

PREP TIME:	10 MINUTES
COOK TIME:	20 MINUTES
TOTAL TIME:	30 MINUTES

TIPS & OPTIONS

Serve squares of Hurried Jalapeño Holla Casserole on plates of shredded lettuce. I buy bags of prewashed, pre-shredded lettuce for occasions just like this. Not only does it help with the "presentation" of dinner, but having the lettuce underneath encourages me to eat more vegetables.

Holla that a jalapeño casserole is on the table and prepare for a stampede at your house. My husband gets so excited about spicy food, he even loves jalapeño jelly. (Spicy jam? That's just wrong, people!) I, on the other hand, learned to love exotic food later in life. Once the burn of excessive Jolly Rancher eating wore off, my new and improved low-carb tongue was ready to take on new flavors. Unbeknownst to me, dishes like Hurried Jalapeño Holla Casserole would become my new normal. It's fast and easy to make, which makes me want to *holla* for more!

1 large cooked rotisserie chicken

¾ cup full-fat cream cheese, softened

1 cup half and half

3 tablespoons chicken broth

1 medium clove garlic, peeled and minced

¼ teaspoon salt

⅛ teaspoon ground black pepper

1 cup shredded Mexican-style cheese blend

1 cup sliced (in rings) jalapeño peppers

6 slices no-sugar-added bacon, cooked and crumbled

1   Preheat oven to 400°F. Grease a 9" × 9" baking dish.

2   Remove all meat from chicken and shred. Be sure not to include any skin or bones.

3   In a medium bowl, whisk cream cheese, half and half, broth, garlic, salt, and pepper.

4   Spread shredded chicken evenly in baking dish. Spread cream cheese mixture evenly over chicken.

5   Sprinkle cheese on top followed by jalapeños and bacon.

6   Bake 15–20 minutes until browning on top.

7   Serve warm.

DRIVE-THRU NUGGETS WITH WASABI RANCH DIP

When I find something delicious that works for me (easy to make, affordable, and within my net carb count), I tend to put that meal on repeat. Will Drive-Thru Nuggets with Wasabi Ranch Dip become your repeat offender?

NET CARBS

6G

SERVES 4	
PER SERVING:	
CALORIES	610
FAT	47G
PROTEIN	30G
SODIUM	604MG
FIBER	2G
CARBOHYDRATES	8G
NET CARBS	6G
SUGAR	2G

TIME	
PREP TIME:	10 MINUTES
COOK TIME:	12 MINUTES
TOTAL TIME:	22 MINUTES

Chicken Nuggets

1 cup vegetable oil

¾ cup full-fat mayonnaise

3 teaspoons apple cider vinegar

1¼ cups superfine blanched almond flour

½ teaspoon salt

¼ teaspoon ground black pepper

1½ pounds boneless, skinless chicken breasts, cut into 2" strips no thicker than ½" (about 24 pieces)

Wasabi Ranch Dip

⅓ cup full-fat sour cream

2 tablespoons heavy whipping cream

½ tablespoon wasabi paste

½ tablespoon 100% lemon juice

½ tablespoon DLK House Ranch Dressing Mix (see recipe for Hurry Up House Salad with Ranch in Chapter 6)

¼ teaspoon ground black pepper

1 Line a large plate with paper towels.

2 In a large skillet over medium heat, heat oil until temperature reaches 350°F–375°F.

3 In a medium shallow bowl, combine mayonnaise and vinegar.

4 In a separate medium shallow bowl, combine almond flour, salt, and pepper.

5 Dredge chicken chunks first through the mayonnaise batter, coating all sides. Shake off any excess.

6 Next, rub all sides of chicken in almond flour mixture.

7 Add half of breaded chicken nuggets to hot oil and fry 2–3 minutes on each side until golden and cooked throughout. Repeat process for remaining nuggets. Place on lined plate to drain.

8 In a medium mixing bowl, whisk all Wasabi Ranch Dip ingredients together. Divide evenly among four dipping bowls.

9 Evenly distribute the nuggets onto four plates and serve each plate with bowl of dip. Serve warm.

TIPS & OPTIONS

Less adventurous palates might prefer homemade DLK House Ranch Dressing for dipping their chicken nuggets (see recipe for Hurry Up House Salad with Ranch in Chapter 6).

Random fact: Chicken nuggets are perfect for learning how to use chopsticks!

If you're looking for a sweeter dip, try rebooting leftover Barbecue Sauce from Close the Kitchen Early Quesadillas (see Chapter 7).

Prefer less mess? Preheat air fryer to 400°F and air-fry breaded chicken nuggets six at a time 10–12 minutes until fully cooked and golden, turning over halfway through.

LATE TO DINNER LASAGNA

I've learned to appreciate the merits of cabbage while on trips to Hawaii. It's readily used in place of lettuce because of cost and its ability to stay fresh for longer periods of time. In my community, a head of cabbage costs around a buck. *What a steal!* It's so versatile too. In this Late to Dinner Lasagna recipe, cabbage leaves replace noodles as a hearty, stable alternative.

1½ pounds Ready, Set, Go Ground Beef (see recipe in this chapter)

1 teaspoon minced garlic

2 cups no-sugar-added pasta sauce, divided

¼ teaspoon salt

⅛ teaspoon ground black pepper

2½ cups shredded whole milk mozzarella cheese, divided

1½ cups ricotta cheese

¼ cup grated Parmesan cheese

2 large eggs, beaten

2 teaspoons Italian seasoning

1 large head green cabbage, cored, leaves separated and steamed

1 Preheat oven to 375°F. Grease a 9" × 12" × 2" baking dish.

2 In a large skillet over medium heat, combine meat, garlic, 1½ cups pasta sauce, salt, and pepper and cook 5 minutes while stirring.

3 In a medium bowl, stir to combine 2 cups mozzarella, ricotta, Parmesan, eggs, and Italian seasoning until blended.

4 Evenly spread remaining ½ cup pasta sauce in prepared baking dish.

5 Layer half cabbage leaves next, no more than two leaves thick.

6 Evenly spread half of cheese mixture, followed by half of meat sauce.

7 Next, top with final cabbage layer, no more than two leaves thick. Follow with layer of remaining cheese mixture and remaining meat sauce.

8 Top with remaining ½ cup mozzarella.

9 Bake 15 minutes until cheese is starting to brown on top. Slice into ten servings and serve warm.

NET CARBS

8G

SERVES 10

PER SERVING:

CALORIES	356
FAT	18G
PROTEIN	34G
SODIUM	705MG
FIBER	4G
CARBOHYDRATES	12G
NET CARBS	8G
SUGAR	6G

TIME

PREP TIME:	10 MINUTES
COOK TIME:	20 MINUTES
TOTAL TIME:	30 MINUTES

TIPS & OPTIONS

Leaves can be steamed or boiled. To boil, bring 4 cups water to a rolling boil in a large soup pot. Using metal tongs, dip cabbage leaves in boiling water a few at a time until they soften, 2–3 minutes.

Shop for marinara sauce wisely. Many brands contain added sugar! I prefer Hunt's Pasta Sauce No Added Sugar (from the dollar store!) or Rao's Homemade Marinara Sauce (found at local supermarkets, warehouse stores, and superstores).

HOT 'N' READY TINFOIL DINNER

NET CARBS

3G

SERVES 4

PER SERVING:

CALORIES	400
FAT	27G
PROTEIN	27G
SODIUM	527MG
FIBER	2G
CARBOHYDRATES	5G
NET CARBS	3G
SUGAR	2G

TIME

PREP TIME:	5 MINUTES
COOK TIME:	25 MINUTES
TOTAL TIME:	30 MINUTES

TIPS & OPTIONS

Suggested toppings are sour cream and bacon bits.

You could also substitute steak instead of chicken.

Kids love making Hot 'n' Ready Tinfoil Dinner. Encourage them to participate in making their individually wrapped dinner packets.

During winter, my children and I have cooked Hot 'n' Ready Tinfoil Dinner in our living room fireplace on the coals (Parental Supervision Required).

I spent countless summers of my youth around a campfire, both as a camper and later as a camp counselor. Not surprisingly, my favorite part of summer camp was the outdoor cooking. Planning the meals took a ton of work, especially for the little ones, and I had to find recipes that were simple to prepare and cook. Hot 'n' Ready Tinfoil Dinner fit the bill! You don't have to be camping or have a campfire to enjoy this meal. It's quick and easy to prepare on an outdoor grill.

- 5 tablespoons unsalted butter, melted
- 1½ tablespoons DLK House Ranch Dressing Mix (see recipe for Hurry Up House Salad with Ranch in Chapter 6)
- ¼ teaspoon salt
- ⅛ teaspoon ground black pepper
- 2 (8-ounce) bags radishes, trimmed and halved
- 1 pound boneless, skinless chicken thighs, diced into 1" chunks
- 1 cup shredded Cheddar cheese
- 1 tablespoon chopped fresh cilantro

1. Preheat an outdoor grill over medium heat. Grease four large pieces of foil with nonstick cooking spray.

2. In a small bowl, whisk together butter, DLK House Ranch Dressing Mix, salt, and pepper.

3. In a medium bowl, add radishes and top with half of butter mixture. Toss to coat.

4. Divide chicken and radish pieces evenly among the four pieces of foil. Top with remaining butter mixture.

5. Fold each piece of foil around chicken and radishes. Make sure it's sealed (double wrap if necessary) and cook on closed grill (or over campfire coals) 25 minutes until internal temperature is 170°F. Check regularly and stir to mix. Reduce heat if needed.

6. Transfer to four plates. Open packets, sprinkle with Cheddar and cilantro, and serve warm.

QUICKIE WEDDING CHICKEN

My friend Lori and I are ladies who lunch. Once a month, we venture out to gossip and eat delicious food together. We always claim to want to try new restaurants, but we end up going to the same place every time. Don't laugh, but we order the exact same dish too—Wedding Chicken! I think we would even lick the bowl if no one was looking. It's that good! Now you too can experience this dish. No reservations required, and ready in 30 minutes!

- 1 cup water, divided
- ½ cup full-fat cream cheese, softened
- 1 Grab and Go Chicken Breast, shredded (see recipe in this chapter)
- 1 (7-ounce) can chipotle peppers in adobo sauce, drained and finely chopped
- 2 (3.7-gram) chicken bouillon cubes
- ½ tablespoon xanthan gum

1. In a medium saucepan over medium heat, combine ¾ cup water and all remaining ingredients except xanthan gum.

2. Cook 15 minutes, stirring regularly until well combined.

3. In a medium bowl, whisk to combine remaining ¼ cup water and xanthan gum until thoroughly blended. Sprinkle xanthan gum mixture into saucepan slowly to prevent clumping.

4. Stir to thicken the Quickie Wedding Chicken for an additional 5 minutes.

5. Serve warm.

NET CARBS	
5G	
SERVES 4	
PER SERVING:	
CALORIES	171
FAT	9G
PROTEIN	7G
SODIUM	1,247MG
FIBER	7G
CARBOHYDRATES	12G
NET CARBS	5G
SUGAR	5G

TIME	
PREP TIME:	10 MINUTES
COOK TIME:	20 MINUTES
TOTAL TIME:	30 MINUTES

TIPS & OPTIONS

I recommend serving Quickie Wedding Chicken with a hearty green salad. The rich sauce demands something lighter as a side dish, and chopped greens seems to pair perfectly.

If you have more time on your hands, you can also make this dish in a slow cooker. You don't need to chop the chipotle peppers using this method, because after a couple of hours cooking on low heat, the peppers all but disappear on their own into the Quickie Wedding Chicken sauce.

PER SERVING:

CALORIES	238
FAT	15G
PROTEIN	21G
SODIUM	405MG
FIBER	2G
CARBOHYDRATES	6G
NET CARBS	4G
SUGAR	1G

TIME

PREP TIME:	10 MINUTES
COOK TIME:	15 MINUTES
TOTAL TIME:	25 MINUTES

TIPS & OPTIONS »

If using wooden skewers, soak them in water just prior to use to prevent skewers from burning on the grill.

To reduce carb count, substitute powdered peanut butter for regular no-sugar-added peanut butter. PBfit Peanut Butter Powder has 2 grams net carbs per 2-tablespoon serving compared to 6 grams net carbs per 2-tablespoon serving of Jif Creamy Peanut Butter. *Simply add water (and/or oil) and stir!*

TWO-STEP SATAY WITH PEANUT SAUCE

My kids will eat just about anything when it's served in an unusual way, like how I prepare Two-Step Satay with Peanut Sauce. I like to mix it up, and skewers are an easy way to go. This tip might seem trivial, but I've found that variety (or lack thereof) affects my motivation to cook.

Two-Step Satay

2 (4.8-ounce) chicken breasts, cut in strips no thicker than ½" (make strips as uniform as possible)

6 ounces unsweetened canned full-fat coconut milk

1 tablespoon soy sauce

1 teaspoon minced garlic

½ teaspoon ground cumin

½ teaspoon ground ginger

½ teaspoon sesame seeds

Peanut Sauce

⅓ cup no-sugar-added creamy peanut butter

1½ tablespoons water

1 tablespoon soy sauce

½ tablespoon 100% lime juice

1 teaspoon white vinegar

1 teaspoon ground ginger

1 medium clove garlic, peeled and minced

4 (1-gram) packets 0g net carbs sweetener

1 Preheat outdoor grill over medium heat.

2 In a large Ziploc bag, place chicken and remaining Two-Step Satay ingredients except for sesame seeds. Squeeze out any air and seal the bag.

3 Knead bag to fully coat every chicken strip with seasonings. Put in the refrigerator to marinate while making Peanut Sauce.

4 In a medium bowl, whisk together all Peanut Sauce ingredients until mixed and sweetener is dissolved. If peanut butter is stiff, microwave covered sauce 10–20 seconds until softened and whisk again. Evenly divide sauce among four small bowls.

5 Divide chicken evenly into eight portions. Thread chicken pieces onto eight skewers.

6 Cook all skewers on the grill simultaneously 13–15 minutes, turning occasionally until golden.

7 Serve two skewers per plate. Sprinkle with sesame seeds and include a bowl of Peanut Sauce for dipping.

WIKIWIKI MAHI-MAHI

1G

SERVES 4

PER SERVING:

CALORIES	340
FAT	27G
PROTEIN	22G
SODIUM	500MG
FIBER	0G
CARBOHYDRATES	1G
NET CARBS	1G
SUGAR	0G

TIME

PREP TIME:	10 MINUTES
COOK TIME:	12 MINUTES
TOTAL TIME:	22 MINUTES

TIPS & OPTIONS ≫

If mahi-mahi fillets are not available in your community, substitute your favorite mild, firm fish. Suggestions include halibut, tuna, shark, or swordfish.

Save time and buy flash-frozen bags of individually portioned fish to keep on hand for dinners like Wikiwiki Mahi-Mahi. You can defrost only what you need and will always have the right ingredients on deck.

If you listen to my *DIRTY, LAZY, Girl* podcast, you'll remember that my New Year's resolution was to cook fresh fish once a week for dinner. My goal, however, might have been too aggressive. I don't always have time (or money!) to buy fresh fish fillets. Instead, I've modified my goal to include frozen fish. What really matters most to me is that I'm regularly eating delicious dinners like Wikiwiki Mahi-Mahi.

Fire Aioli

½ cup full-fat mayonnaise

2 teaspoons 100% lemon juice

½ teaspoon yellow mustard

1½ teaspoons minced garlic

¼ teaspoon salt

¼ teaspoon ground cayenne pepper

¼ teaspoon red pepper flakes

Mahi-Mahi Fillets

1 pound mahi-mahi fillets

⅛ teaspoon salt

⅛ teaspoon ground black pepper

2 tablespoons unsalted butter

1 In a medium bowl, whisk together all Fire Aioli ingredients until well blended. Cover and refrigerate until needed.

2 Lay fish fillets on a large plate and sprinkle both sides with salt and pepper.

3 In a large skillet over medium heat, melt butter. Add fillets so there is no overlapping and cook 4–6 minutes on each side until cooked throughout.

4 Divide fillets evenly among four dinner plates and top each with 2 tablespoons Fire Aioli. Serve.

ASIAN-INSPIRED TAKE-OUT TACOS

My days of ordering Chinese take-out are behind me. My standing order of sweet and sour chicken, cream cheese rangoons, and fried rice translates to carbs, carbs, *and oh, another side of carbs*. No more! I'm much happier (and thinner) eating an order of homemade Asian-Inspired Take-Out Tacos instead. I don't spend all day in the kitchen making this either. Time is on my side—I can knock out this meal in 30 minutes.

- 1 tablespoon unsalted butter
- 4 (4.2-ounce) boneless, skinless chicken breasts, cut in ¼" strips
- 1 teaspoon minced garlic
- 1½ teaspoons grated fresh ginger
- 1 tablespoon chopped green onion
- 2 tablespoons soy sauce
- ½ tablespoon rice vinegar
- 1 tablespoon peanut oil
- ¼ teaspoon red pepper flakes
- 10 drops liquid 0g net carbs sweetener
- 6 low-carb flour tortillas or reboot Tempo Tortillas (see Chapter 8)

1 In a large skillet over medium heat, melt butter. Add chicken, garlic, and ginger to skillet and cook 5–7 minutes, stirring until browned. Reduce heat to low.

2 Stir in remaining ingredients except tortillas. Cover and cook 15 minutes, stirring regularly.

3 Place 1 tortilla on each of six plates. Top each with one-sixth of meat mixture from the skillet. Serve warm.

NET CARBS
5G

SERVES 6	
PER SERVING:	
CALORIES	176
FAT	7G
PROTEIN	23G
SODIUM	602MG
FIBER	11G
CARBOHYDRATES	16G
NET CARBS	5G
SUGAR	0G

TIME	
PREP TIME:	8 MINUTES
COOK TIME:	22 MINUTES
TOTAL TIME:	30 MINUTES

TIPS & OPTIONS

Make it a Pan-Asian theme night. Start today's meal with Thai Time Crunch Salad (see Chapter 6).

Serve a steaming side dish of low-carb Asian vegetables. Bok choy, mustard greens, or daikon come to mind.

RAPID-FIRE CHILI RELLENOS

Peppers scare my children. They have spent a lifetime watching their dad eat dangerously; he orders the spiciest food on any menu. *The hotter, the better!* No wonder my kids act suspicious when I start cooking poblano peppers to make Rapid-Fire Chili Rellenos. There is no convincing the little Laskas that dinner tonight is in fact quite mild and kid-friendly.

6 large whole poblano peppers

4 large eggs, beaten

⅔ cup green enchilada sauce

½ teaspoon salt

¼ teaspoon ground black pepper

1 pound Ready, Set, Go Ground Beef (see recipe in this chapter)

2 teaspoons taco seasoning mix

1 cup shredded Cheddar cheese

1 cup shredded Monterey jack cheese

¼ cup sliced black olives

1 Preheat oven to 425°F. Grease a 9" × 12" baking dish.

2 Turn all gas stovetop burners to medium-high heat.

3 Lay all peppers directly on flames (no pan). Cook peppers 1–2 minutes to completely char on all sides, using tongs to turn as needed.

4 Transfer hot charred peppers to a large Ziploc bag and seal 1 minute to steam and loosen charred skin.

5 In a medium bowl, whisk eggs, enchilada sauce, salt, and black pepper together.

6 Under cold water, remove charred skin from peppers and slice lengthwise. Remove stem, core, and seeds. Splay to create a single bottom layer in prepared baking dish.

7 In a medium skillet over medium heat, combine beef with seasoning mix. Stir 3–4 minutes until warm.

8 Top peppers with even layers of remaining ingredients: first Cheddar, then meat, egg mixture, Monterey jack, and finally olives.

9 Bake uncovered 16 minutes. Cover when browned to your satisfaction. Serve warm.

NET CARBS	
5G	
SERVES 9	
PER SERVING:	
CALORIES	279
FAT	15G
PROTEIN	25G
SODIUM	566MG
FIBER	3G
CARBOHYDRATES	8G
NET CARBS	5G
SUGAR	1G

TIME	
PREP TIME:	5 MINUTES
COOK TIME:	25 MINUTES
TOTAL TIME:	30 MINUTES

TIPS & OPTIONS

Consider serving with Stopwatch Spanish "Rice" (see Chapter 9) as a side dish. *The more vegetables, the better, I say!*

Need a low-carb starter? Go for a theme night with Clip Chips and Salsa (see Chapter 7).

Don't have a gas stovetop? Char chiles under the broiler on high or outside on a barbecue. Even easier, you may substitute a can of drained diced green chile peppers for the bottom layer.

Chef's choice! Use red or green enchilada sauce, both 4 grams net carbs per ¼-cup serving.

CLOCK'S TICKIN' VODKA CHICKEN

NET CARBS

5G

SERVES 4

PER SERVING:
CALORIES	339
FAT	17G
PROTEIN	32G
SODIUM	264MG
FIBER	1G
CARBOHYDRATES	6G
NET CARBS	5G
SUGAR	4G

TIME

PREP TIME:	6 MINUTES
COOK TIME:	24 MINUTES
TOTAL TIME:	30 MINUTES

TIPS & OPTIONS

Riced cauliflower will pair perfectly with this dish, giving you all the more tools to sop up the sauce.

Serve with Hurry Up House Salad with Ranch (see Chapter 6).

Mashed faux potatoes (made with cauliflower, cream, and salt) would also make a lovely side dish to accompany this.

The first time I made Clock's Tickin' Vodka Chicken I think I drank as much alcohol as was required for the recipe. I figured it would get me in the right mood for cooking. Not surprisingly, *it worked*! You don't have to have cocktails to enjoy this dish, however. Any added alcohol to the recipe is burned off during the cooking process. It's ready in under 30 minutes, looks pretty enough for company, and doesn't require much prep work. That's a triple win in my book!

1 tablespoon unsalted butter

1 tablespoon minced garlic

4 (4.2-ounce) boneless, skinless chicken breasts

¼ teaspoon salt

⅛ teaspoon ground black pepper

1 tablespoon finely chopped green onion

2 large eggs, beaten

1½ cups half and half

¼ cup 100% lemon juice

½ cup unflavored vodka

½ teaspoon Italian seasoning

½ teaspoon xanthan gum

1 tablespoon chopped fresh basil

1 In a large skillet over medium heat, melt butter. Add garlic, chicken, salt, and pepper and cook chicken 5–7 minutes on each side until browned.

2 Add remaining ingredients except xanthan gum and basil and stir until combined. Sprinkle in the xanthan gum slowly to prevent clumping and stir. Cover and cook 10 minutes, stirring regularly.

3 Serve warm on four dinner plates and top with fresh basil.

WARP-SPEED SAUSAGE AND SAUERKRAUT

Oktoberfest happens year-round at my house. I've never met a beer-drinking holiday that I didn't like! There are plenty of low-carb beers to choose from. Corona Premier, Michelob Ultra, and Miller Lite are a few of my favorites since they have only 3 grams net carbs per 12-ounce serving. I've learned to keep a cold brew in my hand while barbecuing German sausages. If the grill starts to flame up, a quick pour of beer extinguishes the fire with a side benefit of flavoring the meat. *Noch ein Bier, bitte!* (Another beer, please!)

4 uncooked German sausages (14 ounces total)

1 (12-ounce) bottle low-carb beer

1 tablespoon unsalted butter

½ cup sliced yellow onion

1 teaspoon minced garlic

16 ounces sauerkraut

1½ cups apple cider vinegar

1½ tablespoons 0g net carbs brown sugar substitute

1 Preheat outdoor grill to medium heat.

2 Grill sausages 15 minutes while turning until cooked. Don't forget to have your beer ready for flare-ups! Divide evenly among four plates.

3 In a large skillet over medium heat, melt butter. Add onion and garlic and brown 2 minutes while stirring.

4 Stir remaining ingredients into skillet and cook 8 minutes, stirring regularly.

5 Top sausages with sauerkraut mixture and serve warm.

NET CARBS	
4G	
SERVES 4	
PER SERVING:	
CALORIES	366
FAT	18G
PROTEIN	13G
SODIUM	1,595MG
FIBER	4G
CARBOHYDRATES	14G
NET CARBS	4G
SUGAR	3G
SUGAR ALCOHOL	6G

TIME	
PREP TIME:	5 MINUTES
COOK TIME:	25 MINUTES
TOTAL TIME:	30 MINUTES

TIPS & OPTIONS

If outdoor grilling isn't an option, toss all of the ingredients into a slow cooker and walk away. Add washed and trimmed radishes to the pot while you're at it. With just 2 grams net carbs per 1-cup serving, radishes make a terrific baby potato substitute when "cooked to death" like inside a slow cooker. They pair perfectly with sausage and sauerkraut too!

GENERAL TSO'S SHORTCUT CHICKEN

NET CARBS

2G

SERVES 6

PER SERVING:

CALORIES	223
FAT	13G
PROTEIN	22G
SODIUM	763MG
FIBER	1G
CARBOHYDRATES	3G
NET CARBS	2G
SUGAR	0G

TIME

PREP TIME:	10 MINUTES
COOK TIME:	20 MINUTES
TOTAL TIME:	30 MINUTES

TIPS & OPTIONS

General Tso's Shortcut Chicken can be served on a bed of riced cauliflower or salad greens.

Live a little. Serve with chopsticks!

Try sprinkling toasted sesame seeds on top just prior to serving for added flavor.

It's doubtful the *original* General Tso's Chicken was created in China (I'm guessing more like Panda Express!). I've cut the carbs from this popular takeout classic by using low-carb alternatives like almond flour for breading and sugar substitute to sweeten the sauce. These tricks are not an ancient Chinese secret. You too can learn to re-create old favorites.

Chicken

1½ pounds boneless, skinless chicken thighs, cubed

½ cup superfine blanched almond flour

2 large eggs, beaten

1 teaspoon minced garlic

¼ teaspoon salt

⅛ teaspoon ground black pepper

½ teaspoon xanthan gum

2 cups vegetable oil

Sauce

¼ cup soy sauce

¼ cup chicken broth

2 tablespoons 0g net carbs sweetener

1 tablespoon minced garlic

½ teaspoon red pepper flakes

¼ teaspoon ground ginger

2 teaspoons sesame seeds

1 In a large resealable bag, add all Chicken ingredients except xanthan gum and oil. Seal and shake until all chicken is coated with seasoning. Sprinkle xanthan gum in slowly to prevent clumping and shake the sealed bag again to thoroughly coat.

2 Line a large plate with paper towels.

3 In a large skillet over medium heat, heat oil. Carefully add chicken and fry 7–10 minutes, turning until golden.

4 Remove chicken to lined plate.

5 In a large bowl, whisk all Sauce ingredients together.

6 In a clean large skillet over medium heat, add Chicken and Sauce and cook 10 minutes, stirring regularly.

7 Evenly serve warm on six dinner plates.

BARELY ANY WORK BEEF AND BROCCOLI BOWL

Sometimes I overthink dinner. I stand in front of the fridge with both doors wide open in a complete daze. It's like I'm hoping the food will shout out a dinner idea to me. This has yet to happen, but I keep trying the technique. *Am I alone?* If you too find yourself in a refrigerator stupor, remember these two words: *Beef* and *Broccoli*. These bowls are simple, easy to make, and will please everyone in your family.

1 tablespoon olive oil

1 pound skirt steak, thinly sliced

¼ cup soy sauce

1 teaspoon 100% lime juice

2 tablespoons 0g net carbs brown sugar substitute

2 teaspoons minced garlic

1 teaspoon ground ginger

¼ teaspoon ground black pepper

3 cups bite-sized broccoli florets

¼ cup chopped green onion

1 teaspoon sesame seeds

1   In a medium skillet over medium heat, heat oil.

2   Add steak and cook 10 minutes, stirring regularly.

3   In a medium bowl, whisk together soy sauce, lime juice, brown sugar substitute, garlic, ginger, and pepper. Add broccoli and toss to coat completely. Stir this mixture into skillet. Cook an additional 10 minutes while stirring.

4   Serve warm topped with a sprinkle of green onion and sesame seeds.

NET CARBS

4G

SERVES 4

PER SERVING:

CALORIES	245
FAT	13G
PROTEIN	24G
SODIUM	85MG
FIBER	2G
CARBOHYDRATES	12G
NET CARBS	4G
SUGAR	2G
SUGAR ALCOHOL	6G

TIME

PREP TIME:	10 MINUTES
COOK TIME:	20 MINUTES
TOTAL TIME:	30 MINUTES

TIPS & OPTIONS

Other than skirt, my recommended cuts of steak to use here are hanger or flank steak.

Are you trying to cut back on eating red meat? Chicken, pork, or even shrimp would make a nice substitute here.

CHAPTER 11

DRINKS AND DESSERTS

Can a drink or dessert ever be too sweet? My answer, sadly, is *no*. Food can never be sweet enough. I don't think I've ever spit out a sip of sweet tea for having too much sugar or turned away a piece of strawberry pie for having too much glaze. Who does that? Not me! I was always the one adding "just a little more sugar" to get the sweetness level up to the big leagues…*to cavity level*!

No wonder my taste buds are so warped! Surely I wasn't born this way. When I look back at pictures from my childhood, though, I start to learn clues that might explain my lifetime addiction to sweets. As a toddler, my bottles were filled with bright-red "bug juice." I could barely walk or talk, but I recognized the dancing pitcher of punch on television busting through a wall. That was my hero, the Kool-Aid Man.

It seems I was doomed from the start. To complicate things further, when I craved sweets, I became impatient. I would reach for the first sugary option within reach.

My addiction to sugar went on for decades. From chocolate milk in the hot lunch line to chasing the ice cream truck down the block after school let out, I couldn't get enough. Mentally, I knew sugary drinks and desserts contributed to my weight problem, but still, I couldn't stop consuming them. Go cold turkey? No way. For me, that's never been a realistic option. I suspect you, too, might relate.

DIRTY, LAZY, KETO has been a godsend. I finally figured out a way I could make my sugar-free cake *and eat it too*! And the best part? I learned how to make substitute treats FAST. I'm able to enjoy modified desserts or drinks with flavors I'm used to without a lot of fuss in the kitchen. I don't feel deprived or resentful for having to give up my favorite foods. Instead, I quickly whip up a DLK version to enjoy in minutes flat.

When you know better, you do better. It may have taken me a really long time, but I've finally arrived.

SWOOP CREAM

It's almost comical how excited people get when they find out that whipped cream is DLK-approved. They become giddy with excitement. It doesn't matter how old you are; everyone loves to stand in front of the refrigerator and squirt whipped cream into their mouth, straight from the can. I don't know if it's due to the can or the taste, but even dogs are getting in on the game (*I'll have a Puppuccino, please!*). It's time to class up our act, people. Let's stop eating from the can and make a proper dish of Swoop Cream.

1 cup heavy whipping cream

¼ teaspoon 0g net carbs liquid sweetener

½ teaspoon pure vanilla extract

1   In a medium bowl of an electric mixer, whip all ingredients on high speed 1–2 minutes until soft peaks form.

2   Serve cool.

NET CARBS

1G

SERVES 8

PER SERVING:

CALORIES	103
FAT	10G
PROTEIN	1G
SODIUM	11MG
FIBER	0G
CARBOHYDRATES	1G
NET CARBS	1G
SUGAR	1G

TIME

PREP TIME:	10 MINUTES
COOK TIME:	0 MINUTES
TOTAL TIME:	10 MINUTES

TIPS & OPTIONS

Chill the electric beater attachment and mixing bowl first (at least 30 minutes in the refrigerator or 10 minutes in the freezer) to create a longer-lasting Swoop Cream.

Swoop Cream doesn't have to go solo. Use your imagination here… Just like they do at a coffee shop, sprinkle a dusting of cocoa powder, cinnamon, or even crushed (sugar-free) candy on top for added flair.

Reboot leftover Swoop Cream to top fresh berries, hot cocoa, or even a smoothie.

NET CARBS

6G

SERVES 2

PER SERVING:

CALORIES	231
FAT	16G
PROTEIN	14G
SODIUM	287MG
FIBER	2G
CARBOHYDRATES	8G
NET CARBS	6G
SUGAR	4G

TIME

PREP TIME:	2 MINUTES
COOK TIME:	0 MINUTES
TOTAL TIME:	2 MINUTES

TIPS & OPTIONS »

Unless I catch an amazing sale, I tend to stick with Premier Protein or Quest brand low-carb protein powders. They both come in a variety of flavors, but I find the vanilla and chocolate flavors to be the easiest to work with.

Want to substitute frozen strawberries for fresh? *You got it.* Reduce the amount of ice—and maybe add more liquid to compensate (or risk burning out your blender's motor).

As always, every drink looks and tastes better when presented with a dollop of homemade Swoop Cream on top (see recipe in this chapter).

STAMPEDE STRAWBERRY MILKSHAKE

I could easily eat a pound of strawberries in one sitting. After all, they're a "low sugar" fruit, right? *Yes and no.* A serving of strawberries has 8 grams net carbs, but that's just for 1 cup. The plastic clamshells that many of us buy at the supermarket hold a pound of strawberries—that translates to 2¾ cups, or 22 grams net carbs. Bottom line? The net carbs add up fast. Instead of eating a bowl of berries by themselves, I use them as a topping (or an ingredient that I can measure), as in Stampede Strawberry Milkshake.

1 cup crushed ice cubes

½ cup sliced strawberries, divided

¼ cup heavy whipping cream

1 tablespoon full-fat cream cheese, softened

2 cups unsweetened vanilla almond milk

1 scoop low-carb vanilla protein powder

1 teaspoon pure vanilla extract

4 (1-gram) packets 0g net carbs sweetener

1 In a blender, add ice, then remaining ingredients, holding back 2 strawberry slices, and blend 1–2 minutes until creamy.

2 Divide evenly between two tall glasses. Garnish each glass with 1 strawberry slice. Serve immediately.

BUSY BEE BLUEBERRY SMOOTHIE

NET CARBS

9G

SERVES 1

PER SERVING:
CALORIES	328
FAT	19G
PROTEIN	27G
SODIUM	360MG
FIBER	3G
CARBOHYDRATES	12G
NET CARBS	9G
SUGAR	7G

TIME

PREP TIME:	3 MINUTES
COOK TIME:	0 MINUTES
TOTAL TIME:	3 MINUTES

TIPS & OPTIONS »

Instead of heavy whipping cream, try an avocado.

Frozen or fresh blueberries? Either will do.

When using protein powder, I recommend Quest or Premier Protein brands. Quest comes in a variety of flavors, but Premier Protein offers both liquid (ready to drink) and powder formulations.

I like sneaking spinach into my smoothies. I forget it's even there! But if the vegetable flavor bothers you (or gets caught up in your reusable straw), feel free to omit this ingredient.

Busy morning tomorrow? No excuses! Assemble the Busy Bee Blueberry Smoothie ingredients right now while you still have the motivation (which we all know can be fleeting at the crack of dawn!). Add the dry ingredients to your blender and refrigerate the whole kit and caboodle until tomorrow. When you wake up, add the ice and liquids and blend. Your homemade Busy Bee Blueberry Smoothie will be tastier, quicker, and certainly healthier than any trip to a drive-thru.

> 1 cup ice cubes
> ¼ cup blueberries
> 1 cup spinach
> 1 cup unsweetened vanilla almond milk
> 1 scoop berry-flavored low-carb protein powder
> 3 tablespoons heavy whipping cream
> ½ teaspoon pure vanilla extract
> 4 (1-gram) packets 0g net carbs sweetener

1 In a blender, add ice, then remaining ingredients.

2 Pulse 1–2 minutes until desired consistency is reached.

3 Serve immediately.

COMMUTER CARAMEL MACCHIATO

I have a very good friend who visits Starbucks every day (well, twice a day if we're being 100 percent honest!). That kind of regime takes commitment, not to mention a lot of time in your car. Myself? I'd rather brew up a quick Commuter Caramel Macchiato at home. It's affordable, faster, and there's never a line. I have all the tools I need to be an expert barista. Just like Starbucks, I keep a clear set of salt and pepper shakers next to my coffee pot, one full of cinnamon, the other, powdered cocoa. Dress up your coffee, but do it on the cheap.

14 ounces brewed macchiato, hot and unsweetened

¼ cup heavy whipping cream

½ teaspoon pure vanilla extract

1 (1-gram) packet 0g net carbs sweetener

2 tablespoons sugar-free caramel syrup

1 Add all ingredients to a blender and pulse 15–30 seconds to blend.

2 Serve immediately in two coffee mugs while still hot.

NET CARBS

5G

SERVES 2

PER SERVING:

CALORIES	125
FAT	11G
PROTEIN	1G
SODIUM	41MG
FIBER	0G
CARBOHYDRATES	5G
NET CARBS	5G
SUGAR	1G

TIME

PREP TIME:	3 MINUTES
COOK TIME:	0 MINUTES
TOTAL TIME:	3 MINUTES

TIPS & OPTIONS

Serve over ice for a refreshing summer treat.

Torani makes all sorts of fun sugar-free flavored syrups.

Heavy whipping cream is a common culprit behind a weight loss stall. If you find that the needle on the scale stops moving, take a close look at how much cream you're actually consuming.

Instead of getting your blender dirty, invest in an inexpensive handheld immersion blender. It's a much faster cleanup (just rinse and dry), but mostly, *it's fun to froth*!

PACE YOURSELF PIÑA COLADA

I'm a multitasker with busy fingers. In fact, it's impossible for me to just sit and do nothing at all. I need something for my idle hands to do or else I start reaching for food (and I'm not even hungry!). Much to my family's chagrin, I decided to pick up the ukulele. Strumming this simple instrument keeps me out of the popcorn bowl and calms me down more than any snack ever could. I'm immediately transported to happy memories from past vacations. One of the first songs I learned to play is, you guessed it, "Escape (The Piña Colada Song)"!

- **1½ cups ice**
- **½ teaspoon Sugar-Free Pineapple Drink Enhancer**
- **1 cup unsweetened canned coconut milk (12–14% coconut fat)**
- **1 (1½-ounce) shot unflavored white rum**
- **1 teaspoon 100% lemon juice**
- **4 whole raspberries**
- **2 green leaves from a pineapple crown**

1. In a blender, add ice, then remaining ingredients except raspberries and pineapple leaves.

2. Pulse 1–2 minutes until desired consistency is reached, adding water if needed. Divide evenly between two tall glasses.

3. Using a toothpick, pierce two raspberries and one pineapple leaf. Balance garnish on lip of glass. Repeat for second glass. Serve immediately.

NET CARBS

2G

SERVES 2

PER SERVING:
CALORIES	199
FAT	15G
PROTEIN	2G
SODIUM	60MG
FIBER	0G
CARBOHYDRATES	2G
NET CARBS	2G
SUGAR	0G

TIME

PREP TIME:	3 MINUTES
COOK TIME:	0 MINUTES
TOTAL TIME:	3 MINUTES

TIPS & OPTIONS

For a Virgin Pace Yourself Piña Colada, omit the rum.

There is no need to buy an actual pineapple for this recipe. Simply pluck two leaves off of one of the fruits in the store and call it a day.

If you don't have canned coconut milk on hand, substitute 2 tablespoons Swoop Cream (see recipe in this chapter) and 1 cup unsweetened, unflavored coconut milk from a carton.

An alternate source of pineapple flavoring is Jordan's Skinny Syrups Pineapple or Torani Sugar Free Pineapple Syrup.

SNAPPY AND SWEET ICED TEA

NET CARBS

2G

SERVES 4

PER SERVING:

CALORIES	6
FAT	0G
PROTEIN	0G
SODIUM	34MG
FIBER	0G
CARBOHYDRATES	2G
NET CARBS	2G
SUGAR	0G

TIME

PREP TIME:	5 MINUTES
COOK TIME:	0 MINUTES
TOTAL TIME:	5 MINUTES

I used to drink Diet Coke at every meal—*even breakfast!* Nowadays, I keep a twelve-pack in the garage (which lasts for a month). I tell myself I can "still have it," of course, but having to walk *alllllllllll the way to the garage* (followed by a trip to the fridge for a cup of ice) is often too much of a hassle. I did this on purpose, you see. Making diet soda inconvenient pushes me to drink caffeine-free beverages like a glass of Snappy and Sweet Iced Tea. I keep a pitcher cold inside the fridge.

> 4 cups unsweetened brewed herbal tea, chilled
>
> 4 cups sugar-free lemonade, chilled
>
> 3 (1-gram) packets 0g net carbs sweetener
>
> 8 thin slices lemon

1. In a pitcher, add all ingredients and stir to combine until sweetener is dissolved.

2. Divide evenly among four tall glasses and serve immediately while still chilled.

TIPS & OPTIONS ≫

Adjust the tea, lemonade, and sweetener levels to suit your tastes.

Get crazy and use lime slices in addition to (or in place of) the lemon slices. The vitamin C will do you good.

Don't forget to wash the lemon or lime before you slice it. The outer peel will be in your beverage, after all.

MAMA'S MOVIN' FAST FUDGE

I spent the summers of my youth visiting Mackinac Island, Michigan, the fudge capital of the United States, so I consider myself to be a trained expert. (There was a lot of fudge eating on those vacations, you see!) Mama's Movin' Fast Fudge recipe ranks right up there with the best of them. I don't keep whole milk on hand much these days, but when I'm craving my Mama's Movin' Fast Fudge, I make an exception. A half-pint is all you'll need from the store to whip up the most amazing dessert.

> 2 cups unsweetened 100% cocoa powder
>
> ¾ cup unsalted butter, softened
>
> 1 cup water
>
> ⅔ cup whole milk
>
> 1 cup 0g net carbs sweetener
>
> 1 teaspoon pure vanilla extract
>
> ¼ teaspoon salt

1 Grease a 9" × 9" baking dish.

2 In the top pan of a double boiler add cocoa powder and butter, and stir to combine.

3 In the bottom pan of the double boiler add water and bring to a boil over medium-high heat. Reduce heat to low and cover with the top pan.

4 Stir cocoa mixture constantly while slowly adding milk, sweetener, vanilla, and salt until fudge is completely blended and creamy, approximately 10 minutes. Fudge will become increasingly more difficult to stir.

5 Transfer fudge to prepared baking dish. Using a spatula, evenly press fudge into all corners of the dish. Cover and refrigerate.

6 Serve cold. Cut into serving-sized squares right before serving.

NET CARBS

2G

SERVES 20

PER SERVING:

CALORIES	90
FAT	8G
PROTEIN	2G
SODIUM	35MG
FIBER	3G
CARBOHYDRATES	10G
NET CARBS	2G
SUGAR	1G
SUGAR ALCOHOL	5G

TIME

PREP TIME:	15 MINUTES
COOK TIME:	10 MINUTES
TOTAL TIME:	25 MINUTES

TIPS & OPTIONS

Take extra precaution while stirring the hot cocoa and butter mixture in the double boiler. Steam is escaping from the bottom pan of the double boiler.

Once cooled, cut fudge into individually sized portions of 2" × 2" squares. (Recipe makes approximately twenty pieces of candy.) Place immediately into snack-sized Ziploc bags or else risk overindulging!

Hide fudge in the very bottom of your freezer, away from yourself and others. Keep for when an emergency chocolate craving occurs.

HIBISCUS TURBO TEA

PER SERVING:
CALORIES	66
FAT	6G
PROTEIN	1G
SODIUM	26MG
FIBER	0G
CARBOHYDRATES	2G
NET CARBS	2G
SUGAR	0G

TIME

PREP TIME:	10 MINUTES
COOK TIME:	0 MINUTES
TOTAL TIME:	10 MINUTES

TIPS & OPTIONS ≫

Adjust the tea, coconut milk, and sweetener levels to suit your tastes.

Trick your friends into believing you just came from Starbucks with a Pink Drink—float slices of strawberry inside your drink and serve in a recycled clear cup with lid.

I was at a work meeting the first time I tried a cup of hibiscus tea. I was feeling jittery from all the coffee I had been drinking that morning, so I decided to try a lighter alternative. Maybe it was due to its gorgeous pink color, but I fell in love with this new brew on the spot. The flavor is somewhat tart, almost like what you'd taste biting into a fresh cranberry. To remedy that sour flavor, I add coconut milk and sugar-free sweetener. The combination makes the most delicious cup of Hibiscus Turbo Tea.

6 cups unsweetened brewed hibiscus tea

¾ cup unsweetened canned coconut milk, Premium 12–14% coconut fat

6 (1-gram) packets 0g net carbs sweetener

2 teaspoons pure vanilla extract

1½ cups ice cubes

¼ cup fresh mint leaves

1   Add tea, coconut milk, sweetener, and vanilla to a pitcher and stir to combine until sweetener is dissolved.

2   Divide evenly among four tall glasses over ice. Top with mint leaves and serve.

CAYENNE CHARGED CHOCOLATE PUDDING

SERVES 2

PER SERVING:

CALORIES	299
FAT	24G
PROTEIN	4G
SODIUM	159MG
FIBER	12G
CARBOHYDRATES	18G
NET CARBS	6G
SUGAR	2G

TIME

PREP TIME:	10 MINUTES
COOK TIME:	0 MINUTES
TOTAL TIME:	10 MINUTES

TIPS & OPTIONS »

If you must, omit the cayenne. Maybe next time you'll be braver.

The avocados MUST be at peak ripeness. This is required for them to blend properly and create the thick "fat" base needed for Cayenne Charged Chocolate Pudding.

I've never met a pudding I didn't like. I'm sure Freud would point back to my toddler days as an explanation, but for me, I just love creamy food on a spoon. Yogurt, soups, or pudding? I love them all. Cayenne Charged Chocolate Pudding is definitely for grown folks, though. There is no kid play when it comes to the kick of cayenne!

3 tablespoons unsweetened canned coconut milk

2 medium avocados, peeled and pitted

½ cup ice cubes

2 tablespoons unsweetened 100% cocoa powder

1 teaspoon pure vanilla extract

1 teaspoon ground cinnamon

2 tablespoons 0g net carbs sweetener

⅛ teaspoon salt

⅛ teaspoon ground cayenne pepper

1 Add all ingredients to a food processor or blender and pulse until even and creamy, 2–3 minutes, stopping midway to scrape down sides with a rubber spatula.

2 Serve immediately.

BREAKNECK SALTY PECAN BARK

Craving chocolate doesn't make you a DLK flunky. Desiring sweets is normal. Instead of flogging yourself for wanting a dessert, figure out how to satisfy your urge (*oooh, that sounds scandalous!*). Some folks find success by keeping a dark chocolate gourmet candy bar (in the freezer) for a nip. Would that work for you—*or would you eat the whole bar?* It's the age-old conundrum of quality versus quantity. Myself, I prefer a few pieces of sugar-free Breakneck Salty Pecan Bark.

> 1 cup sugar-free chocolate chips
>
> 1 tablespoon coconut oil
>
> 1 cup pecan halves
>
> ⅛ teaspoon salt

1 Line a small baking sheet with parchment paper.

2 In a medium microwave-safe bowl, add chocolate chips and oil and microwave on high 30 seconds. Stir and microwave again 30 seconds.

3 Stir in pecans until coated.

4 Spread mixture evenly on prepared baking sheet (one that will fit in your freezer). Sprinkle with salt.

5 Freeze at least 20 minutes to harden.

6 Break into 1"–2" pieces and serve. Store leftovers in a medium resealable container.

NET CARBS

2G

SERVES 6

PER SERVING:

CALORIES	276
FAT	24G
PROTEIN	4G
SODIUM	48MG
FIBER	11G
CARBOHYDRATES	21G
NET CARBS	2G
SUGAR	1G
SUGAR ALCOHOL	8G

TIME

PREP TIME:	25 MINUTES
COOK TIME:	1 MINUTE
TOTAL TIME:	26 MINUTES

TIPS & OPTIONS

Any type of nut can be used in this recipe. Experiment with other low-carb nuts such as hazelnuts, almonds, or macadamia nuts (all 2 grams net carbs per 1-ounce serving).

Double up on this recipe so you have plenty. This tasty and simple dessert won't last long, especially when word gets out.

Dip chunks of Breakneck Salty Pecan Bark into peanut butter. *You're welcome.*

FRENZIED UNICORN FRAP

My teenage children can be bribed to do just about anything with the promise of a trip to Starbucks afterward. I'm always surprised by what they order. It's never on the menu, but the employees know exactly what they want. Apparently, I'm too old to know about the secret menu. I created this low-carb version of their favorite drink, the Unicorn Frappuccino, just so they would stop calling me a "boomer."

- **2 cups ice cubes**
- **1½ cups unsweetened vanilla almond milk**
- **3 tablespoons 0g net carbs sweetener**
- **½ teaspoon pure vanilla extract**
- **½ cup blueberries plus 8 whole fresh berries, divided**
- **¼ cup Swoop Cream (see recipe in this chapter)**
- **1 tablespoon sugar-free strawberry syrup**

1. To a blender add ice, almond milk, sweetener, vanilla, and ½ cup blueberries. Pulse 30–60 seconds to blend.

2. Divide evenly between two tall glasses. Top each glass with 2 tablespoons Swoop Cream. Evenly drizzle strawberry syrup on top of cream.

3. Thread four blueberries onto a cocktail skewer; repeat with remaining blueberries. Garnish drinks with skewers and serve immediately.

NET CARBS

6G

SERVES 2

PER SERVING:

CALORIES	101
FAT	7G
PROTEIN	2G
SODIUM	151MG
FIBER	2G
CARBOHYDRATES	8G
NET CARBS	6G
SUGAR	5G

TIME

PREP TIME:	10 MINUTES
COOK TIME:	0 MINUTES
TOTAL TIME:	10 MINUTES

TIPS & OPTIONS

Fresh or frozen blueberries can be used.

If you are like me and struggle with not being one of the "cool kids," search for upcoming trends using #starbuckssecretmenu on *Instagram*. At the very least, you can name-drop the newest drinks and impress the grandkids. Don't have *Instagram*? Hmmm… Well, maybe I can't help you after all.

BEEP, BEEP, BROWNIE!

NET CARBS

2G

SERVES 1

PER SERVING:
CALORIES   100
FAT   6G
PROTEIN   8G
SODIUM   401MG
FIBER   5G
CARBOHYDRATES   7G
NET CARBS   2G
SUGAR   0G

TIME

PREP TIME: 15 SECONDS
COOK TIME: 45 SECONDS
TOTAL TIME: 1 MINUTE

TIPS & OPTIONS »

Always make sure you have your food covered when heating in the microwave. It has a tendency to splatter and boil all over the place at times.

In moments of weakness, I've convinced myself it's acceptable to double or triple this recipe (don't judge). Let me forewarn you: This never ends well.

I have serious problems when it comes to portion control. It's like my mind sees a pan of brownies and thinks to itself, "One pan equals one serving for me!" If low-carb desserts are in the house, I nibble away at them until they're gone, one bite at a time, every time I pass through the kitchen. Making single-serving-sized desserts like Beep, Beep, Brownie!, cooked in the microwave in just a minute, has truly been a godsend. I enjoy eating this without any guilt or worry about going overboard.

1 large egg

1 tablespoon unsweetened 100% cocoa powder

1 tablespoon 0g net carbs sweetener

1 tablespoon Carbquik baking mix

⅛ teaspoon pure vanilla extract

⅛ teaspoon salt

1 In a well-greased coffee mug, beat egg with a fork.

2 Add remaining ingredients and stir thoroughly to combine.

3 Microwave on high covered 45 seconds. Enjoy warm right from mug.

FRANTIC VANILLA FROSTING

Frosting makes everything tastes better; wouldn't you agree? I created Frantic Vanilla Frosting out of necessity. I desperately wanted something sweet but hadn't been to the grocery store yet that week. I was out of, well, almost everything. With only a few dribs and drabs in every container, I mixed and matched, blended and creamed. The resulting mixture was a frosting recipe worthy of posting in the DLK Hall of Fame. Frantic Vanilla Frosting can be enjoyed on any dessert (or more often than not at my house, simply licked off a spoon).

> 3 tablespoons full-fat cream cheese, softened
>
> 1½ tablespoons heavy whipping cream
>
> 2 tablespoons 0g net carbs sweetener
>
> ¼ teaspoon pure vanilla extract

1 In a small bowl, blend all ingredients until smooth. If desired, use an electric hand mixer to smooth out any lumps.

2 Cover and refrigerate until ready to serve. Eat within four days.

NET CARBS

1G

SERVES 8

PER SERVING:

CALORIES	23
FAT	2G
PROTEIN	0G
SODIUM	20MG
FIBER	0G
CARBOHYDRATES	3G
NET CARBS	1G
SUGAR	0G
SUGAR ALCOHOL	2G

TIME

PREP TIME:	2 MINUTES
COOK TIME:	0 MINUTES
TOTAL TIME:	2 MINUTES

TIPS & OPTIONS

Frantically whisk the frosting by hand and avoid having to get out the mixer. You can do it!

Add a few drops of food coloring to your frosting to magically customize any dessert.

Reboot Frantic Vanilla Frosting with a variety of recipes: Swift Cinnamon Rolls (see Chapter 5), Shortcut Cinnamon Toast Sticks (see Chapter 5), Delivery Donuts (see Chapter 5), or Avocado Bolt Brownies (see recipe in this chapter), just to name a few.

CRASH COURSE CHOCOLATE CHIP COOKIES

NET CARBS

2G

SERVES 8

PER SERVING:
CALORIES	231
FAT	21G
PROTEIN	5G
SODIUM	24MG
FIBER	3G
CARBOHYDRATES	9G
NET CARBS	2G
SUGAR	1G
SUGAR ALCOHOL	4G

TIME

PREP TIME:	10 MINUTES
COOK TIME:	20 MINUTES
TOTAL TIME:	30 MINUTES

TIPS & OPTIONS

If you choose, add a different low-carb nut prior to mixing. Might I suggest walnuts?

Live a little. Fold pieces of Atkins Endulge Chocolate Peanut Candies (which look like M&M's) into the batter prior to baking. They have just 1 gram net carbs per 1 (1.2-ounce) pack serving.

Use room-temperature butter and cream cheese for this recipe (avoid using the microwave, which could oversoften it). This little tip will prevent your cookies from turning into melted pancakes.

My first few attempts at creating these family favorites resulted in a giant mess. My cookies were either too puffy, or worse, melted into one giant puddle. Ironically, my family didn't care one bit. (Truth be told, neither did I!) We were usually so excited to have homemade Crash Course Chocolate Chip Cookies coming out of the oven that we paid little attention to their unique shape.

> 1¼ cups superfine blanched almond flour
> 3½ tablespoons full-fat cream cheese, softened
> ¼ cup unsalted butter, softened
> ¼ cup 0g net carbs sweetener
> ½ teaspoon pure vanilla extract
> ¼ cup whole macadamia nuts
> 2 tablespoons sugar-free chocolate chips

1 Preheat oven to 350°F. Line a baking sheet with parchment paper.

2 In a medium bowl, combine all ingredients except nuts and chocolate chips. Stir until thoroughly mixed and a dough forms.

3 Fold in nuts and chocolate chips until evenly incorporated.

4 Scoop out dough in 1" balls and pat down to no more than ¼" thickness. Place on parchment paper with at least ½" between cookies.

5 Bake 20 minutes until cookies start to brown.

6 Transfer to a plate and serve warm.

INSTANT ICE CREAM

NET CARBS

7G

SERVES 2

PER SERVING:

CALORIES	327
FAT	31G
PROTEIN	2G
SODIUM	34MG
FIBER	1G
CARBOHYDRATES	8G
NET CARBS	7G
SUGAR	5G

TIME

PREP TIME:	5 MINUTES
COOK TIME:	0 MINUTES
TOTAL TIME:	5 MINUTES

TIPS & OPTIONS »

Heavy whipping cream, the key ingredient in keto ice cream, should be enjoyed in moderation. Even though the ingredient has low (or no) carbs per serving, cream is calorie dense. All of that deliciousness is easy to overdo! That's why dairy is toward the top of the DIRTY, LAZY, KETO food pyramid.

My addiction to sweet and salty foods probably started when I was in preschool. I remember dipping French fries into a paper-wrapped ice cream cone and thinking I should call Ronald McDonald to tell him my discovery. Nowadays, I sub zucchini fries or salty green beans for my fry fix, and Instant Ice Cream for the occasional dessert treat.

> ¾ cup frozen sliced unsweetened strawberries
>
> ¾ cup heavy whipping cream, very cold
>
> 6 (1-gram) packets 0g net carbs sweetener

1 In a food processor, add all ingredients and pulse 30–60 seconds until smooth and thick.

2 Divide between two chilled bowls and serve immediately.

BYE-BYE BACON MAPLE CUPCAKES

One of the many things I love about a cupcake is its size—*built-in portion control*. The next time you're craving a salty-sweet treat, whip up a quick batch of these low-carb bacon maple beauties.

Cupcakes

½ cup unsalted butter, softened

1 cup full-fat cream cheese, softened

1 cup 0g net carbs sweetener

1 teaspoon pure vanilla extract

2 tablespoons sugar-free pancake syrup

4 large eggs

1 tablespoon baking powder

½ teaspoon salt

2½ cups superfine blanched almond flour

Maple Frosting

1 cup unsalted butter, softened

1½ cups 0g net carbs confectioners'-style sweetener

3 tablespoons heavy whipping cream

3 tablespoons sugar-free pancake syrup, divided

¼ cup cooked bacon bits

½ cup pecan halves

1. Preheat oven to 375°F. Line twenty cups of two muffin tins with twenty cupcake liners.

2. In the medium bowl of an electric mixer, combine butter, cream cheese, sweetener, vanilla, syrup, and eggs. Beat on high speed until batter is smooth. Add baking powder and salt. Beat again, scraping sides of bowl often.

3. Add almond flour and beat until thoroughly combined.

4. Divide batter equally among prepared muffin cups.

5. Bake 20 minutes until a toothpick inserted into the center of a cupcake comes out clean. Let cool 3 minutes. Remove cupcakes from tins to a cooling rack.

6. In a small bowl, mix butter, confectioners'-style sweetener, cream, and 2 teaspoons syrup and beat 2–3 minutes until thoroughly combined.

7. Place frosting into a piping bag and pipe Maple Frosting onto cupcakes, leaving liners on. Evenly sprinkle bacon bits and pecans on cupcakes. Drizzle with remaining syrup.

8. Serve or store in an airtight container in the refrigerator.

NET CARBS	
2G	

SERVES 20	
PER SERVING:	
CALORIES	299
FAT	28G
PROTEIN	6G
SODIUM	232MG
FIBER	2G
CARBOHYDRATES	15G
NET CARBS	2G
SUGAR	1G
SUGAR ALCOHOL	11G

TIME	
PREP TIME:	10 MINUTES
COOK TIME:	20 MINUTES
TOTAL TIME:	30 MINUTES

TIPS & OPTIONS

You can make your own sugar-free confectioners'-style sweetener by blending the sweetener of your choice in a high-speed blender with just a pinch of cornstarch. (For your reference, cornstarch has 7 grams net carbs per 1-tablespoon serving.)

Instead of a fancy-pants pastry bag, I use a heavy-duty, gallon-sized Ziploc bag with the corner snipped off. The cleanup is much faster this way! Simply toss the bag when finished.

AVOCADO BOLT BROWNIES

Similar to the draw of popcorn at the movie theater, something magical happens when homemade brownies bake in the oven. Granted, I'm assuming your Avocado Bolt Brownies actually make it into the oven! Just this morning as I was making a batch of these gems, my daughter had to pull the pan away from me as I kept sticking my tasting spatula back into the batter. (Oh, don't act like you haven't done that!)

2 medium avocados, peeled, pitted, and mashed

2 large eggs, beaten

⅓ cup unsweetened 100% cocoa powder

⅓ cup superfine blanched almond flour

¾ cup 0g net carbs brown sugar substitute

1 teaspoon pure vanilla extract

1 teaspoon baking powder

¼ teaspoon salt

½ cup sugar-free chocolate chips

1 Preheat oven to 350°F. Grease a 9" × 9" baking dish.

2 In a food processor or blender, add all ingredients except chocolate chips. Blend 2–3 minutes until creamy, scraping batter from the sides often.

3 Fold in chocolate chips and pour into prepared baking dish. Bake 25 minutes until a toothpick inserted in the center comes out clean.

4 Slice into twelve servings. Serve warm.

NET CARBS

3G

SERVES 12

PER SERVING:

CALORIES	109
FAT	9G
PROTEIN	3G
SODIUM	103MG
FIBER	5G
CARBOHYDRATES	22G
NET CARBS	3G
SUGAR	0G
SUGAR ALCOHOL	14G

TIME

PREP TIME:	5 MINUTES
COOK TIME:	25 MINUTES
TOTAL TIME:	30 MINUTES

TIPS & OPTIONS

Make cupcake-style brownies instead by dividing batter equally among twelve muffin cups fitted with cupcake liners.

Substitute ½ cup walnut pieces for chocolate chips.

Note that this recipe creates a thin style of brownie (which bakes faster). Mama can't wait!

Top cooled Avocado Bolt Brownies with a rebooted portion of Frantic Vanilla Frosting (see recipe in this chapter).

Enjoy with a cold glass of "milk." One of my favorites is Silk Unsweet Vanilla Almondmilk with 0 grams net carbs per 1-cup serving.

ADDITIONAL RESOURCES

- For additional free resources, visit www.dirtylazyketo.com
- Want direct support from Stephanie? Join the private, limited-enrollment Premium DIRTY, LAZY, KETO support group for women only (subscription-based) "DIRTY, LAZY, KETO Premium Support Group by Stephanie Laska" at www.facebook.com/dirtylazyketo or wwww.facebook.com/becomesupporter/661359364046718/ through the Premium link at http://bit.ly/SupporterDLK.
- Listen to the author directly on the free podcast *DIRTY, LAZY, Girl* available wherever you listen to podcasts—links available at www.dirtylazyketo.com
- Get involved in the DIRTY, LAZY, KETO community:

   www.facebook.com/dirtylazyketo
   www.facebook.com/groups/DirtyLazyKeto
   www.youtube.com/c/DIRTYLAZYKETOStephanieLaska
   www.instagram.com/dirtylazyketo/
   www.instagram.com/140lost/
   www.pinterest.com/dirtylazyketo/
   www.twitter.com/140lost

RECIPE RESOURCES

CALCULATING RECIPE SERVING SIZES

The exact amount of a serving is clearly spelled out on nutrition labels, but not in recipes. Why is that? There are too many variables involved with cooking to provide an exact amount. The size of eggs you use or the size of your pans directly affects how much food is made. But let's not overcomplicate this. In the spirit of Lazy Keto, put away your food scales and measuring cups when estimating what portion to serve yourself. Follow this simple calculation instead:

Divide the recipe quantity by the *yield* to determine the serving size.

If a lasagna serves eight people and has 9 grams of net carbs per serving, cut your lasagna into eight even pieces and enjoy. Each piece of lasagna is a single serving, meaning each piece will contain 9 grams of net carbs. Easy-peasy!

GLOSSARY

As a courtesy, I've included a glossary of how I am using common keto vocabulary. (Keep in mind that my definitions might be different from what you have heard before.)

KETO AND KETO FACTIONS

Dirty Keto

Dirty Keto is eating whatever foods you choose within your macro goals or limits (which are different for everyone). Unfortunately, there are a lot of misconceptions about Dirty Keto. Critics are horrified about including junk food or processed meats into one's diet. They assume we survive *solely* on hot dogs and sugar-free Red Bull! *That's just not true.* Instead, Dirty Keto empowers you with more flexible options about what to eat. There is no judgment or strict rules about your lifestyle. You might "eat clean" during the work week but then live a little on the weekends. Foods aren't demonized either—artificial sweeteners and low-carb substitutes are fair game. Dirty Keto followers don't limit their food or beverage choices and might even be spotted drinking a Diet Coke (*oh, the horror!*).

DIRTY, LAZY, KETO

DIRTY, LAZY, KETO is not just a diet; it's a lifestyle. As a modern hybrid, it reaps the benefits of losing weight, but without limitations of food choices or the obligation of counting every macro. We eat foods that are higher in fat, moderate in protein, and lower in carbs, but allow for a little fun and flexibility. We are open to the idea of artificial sweeteners (Diet Coke or Splenda for example) and include packaged foods (protein bars, low-carb tortillas) in our meals. Dirty *and* Lazy Keto followers count only net carbs. I am the superhero of this category! I even coined the term. *Somebody make me a T-shirt!*

Keto

Keto is simply a shortened word for *ketogenic.*

Ketogenic diet

The ketogenic diet is a diet of foods high in fat, moderate in protein, and low in carbohydrates, with the goal of putting the body into ketosis.

Keto police

Keto police insist Strict Keto rules must be followed at all times! Though they don't wear a uniform, you can easily spot a member of the keto police by their social media posts that frequently ridicule others, arguing, "but THAT'S NOT KETO!" Keto police believe their purity and high standards make them superior; they constantly feel the need to educate and "correct" dissenting keto disciples.

Ketosis

Ketosis occurs when the body burns ketones from the liver as the main energy source (as opposed to using glucose as the energy source, derived from carbs). Ketosis is often an indicator (but not a requirement) of weight loss.

Lazy Keto

Lazy Keto followers only count their net carbs intake—not fat grams or protein intake. Lazy Keto does *not* mean unwilling to work hard for weight loss. This term refers to just counting a single macro in keto—the net carb—not a relaxed lifestyle or lack of energy. Not tracking doesn't mean overconsumption, though! Common sense is *always* used.

Strict Keto

Strict Keto adheres to a rigid and closely monitored ketogenic diet comsisting of no more than 20 grams of net carbohydrates per day. Followers insist on organic ingredients and avoid all processed foods. The keto prescription for weight loss never deviates: Calories distributed are distributed to a perfect ratio of 75 percent fat, 20 percent protein, and 5 percent carbohydrates.

If you are not sure what keto camp you fall into, try taking the free, short quiz I created on my website at www.dirtylazyketo.com/quiz/.

RELATED KETO TERMS

Calories

Calories are units of heat that food provides to the body. There are no "good" or "bad" calories. You've got to let this one go, people! A calorie is just an innocent unit of measurement, like a cup or a gallon. Our bodies *require* calories to survive. With DIRTY, LAZY, KETO, calories are not the focus (instead, net carbs are). The 1980s are over, my friends, and counting calories of low-fat foods is just as passé as leg warmers.

Carbohydrates/carbs

Carbohydrates, or carbs (for short), are sugars, starches, and fibers found in fruits, grains, vegetables, and milk products. Carbohydrates contain 4 calories per gram.

Chaffle

Chaffle started off as a portmanteau of "cheese waffles," but the term has since evolved to include a variety of recipes made with a waffle maker.

Fat

Fat is the densest form of energy, providing 9 calories per gram. The most obvious example of fat is oil (olive, coconut, sesame, canola, vegetable, and so on). Less clear examples of fats are dairy foods, nuts, avocados, and oily fish. Some fats have a better reputation than others (think about how the media portrays eggs, mayonnaise, Alfredo sauce, or chicken skin). No matter what the quality of the source, *fat is fat is fat*.

Fiber

Fiber is not digested by the body and is removed as waste. There are two types of fiber: soluble and insoluble. Fiber is a complex carbohydrate that does not raise blood sugar. *Fiber is your friend.*

Insoluble fiber

Insoluble fiber does *not* absorb water. Insoluble fiber moves through the intestine mostly intact, adding bulk to the stool and preventing constipation. Low-carb foods that contain notable amounts of insoluble fiber include blueberries, raspberries, strawberries, raw almonds, flaxseed, sesame seeds, walnuts, Brussels sprouts, cooked kale, and soybeans.

Keto flu

Keto flu is an avoidable set of symptoms (headache, lethargy, leg cramps) associated with dehydration, often experienced at the onset of the keto diet. Because the metabolic process of ketosis requires more water, increased hydration is required by the body.

Macronutrients/macros

Macronutrients, or macros, come in three packages: *carbohydrates*, *protein*, and *fat*. All macronutrients are obtained through foods in the diet, as the body cannot produce them. Each macro fulfills vital roles for your health. All macros contain calories but at different densities. Carbohydrates and proteins have 4 calories per gram, and fat has 9 calories per gram.

Net carbs

Net carbs are the unit of measurement tracked in DIRTY, LAZY, KETO. On a nutrition label, net carbs are calculated by subtracting all fiber and sugar alcohol grams from the listed amount of carbohydrates. Total carbs, minus fiber, minus sugar alcohol, equals net carbs. Net carbs are the leftover carbs in this mathematical equation.

Protein

Protein has 4 calories per gram. Proteins take longer to digest because they are long-chain amino acids. Protein is largely found in meats, dairy foods, eggs, legumes, nuts, and seafood.

Soluble fiber

Soluble fiber attracts water. When you eat foods high in soluble fiber, it turns to mush inside your body. Soluble fiber absorbs water quickly and helps to soften stool. It slows down your digestion and helps you to feel full. Examples of low-carb foods with notable amounts of soluble fiber include blackberries, strawberries, flaxseed, psyllium seed husks, artichokes, and soybeans.

Sugar alcohols

Sugar alcohols are reduced-calorie sweeteners. They do not contain alcohol! They are commonly used in sugar-free candy and low-carb desserts and are not digested by the body.

US/METRIC CONVERSION CHARTS

VOLUME CONVERSIONS

US VOLUME MEASURE	METRIC EQUIVALENT
⅛ teaspoon	0.5 milliliter
¼ teaspoon	1 milliliter
½ teaspoon	2 milliliters
1 teaspoon	5 milliliters
½ tablespoon	7 milliliters
1 tablespoon (3 teaspoons)	15 milliliters
2 tablespoons (1 fluid ounce)	30 milliliters
¼ cup (4 tablespoons)	60 milliliters
⅓ cup	90 milliliters
½ cup (4 fluid ounces)	125 milliliters
⅔ cup	160 milliliters
¾ cup (6 fluid ounces)	180 milliliters
1 cup (16 tablespoons)	250 milliliters
1 pint (2 cups)	500 milliliters
1 quart (4 cups)	1 liter (about)

WEIGHT CONVERSIONS

US VOLUME MEASURE	METRIC EQUIVALENT
½ ounce	15 grams
1 ounce	30 grams
2 ounces	60 grams
3 ounces	85 grams
¼ pound (4 ounces)	115 grams
½ pound (8 ounces)	225 grams
¾ pound (12 ounces)	340 grams
1 pound (16 ounces)	454 grams

OVEN TEMPERATURE CONVERSIONS

DEGREES FAHRENHEIT	DEGREES CELSIUS
200 degrees F	95 degrees C
250 degrees F	120 degrees C
275 degrees F	135 degrees C
300 degrees F	150 degrees C
325 degrees F	160 degrees C
350 degrees F	180 degrees C
375 degrees F	190 degrees C
400 degrees F	205 degrees C
425 degrees F	220 degrees C
450 degrees F	230 degrees C

BAKING PAN SIZES

AMERICAN	METRIC
8 × 1½ inch round baking pan	20 × 4 cm cake tin
9 × 1½ inch round baking pan	23 × 3.5 cm cake tin
11 × 7 × 1½ inch baking pan	28 × 18 × 4 cm baking tin
13 × 9 × 2 inch baking pan	30 × 20 × 5 cm baking tin
2 quart rectangular baking dish	30 × 20 × 3 cm baking tin
15 × 10 × 2 inch baking pan	30 × 25 × 2 cm baking tin (Swiss roll tin)
9 inch pie plate	22 × 4 or 23 × 4 cm pie plate
7 or 8 inch springform pan	18 or 20 cm springform or loose bottom cake tin
9 × 5 × 3 inch loaf pan	23 × 13 × 7 cm or 2 lb narrow loaf or pate tin
1½ quart casserole	1.5 liter casserole
2 quart casserole	2 liter casserole

INDEX

CONTENTS

INTRODUCTION

Baking is the perfect blend of art, science, and pleasure. There's something so gratifying about having a sweet indulgence to treat yourself with when you need it. Unfortunately, most recipes for baked goods seem to make enough to feed a small army! What do you do when you just want a small dessert, but every recipe seems designed for twelve or more? The amount of waste that results can be so daunting that it'll have you reaching for packed, processed foods instead of the home-baked treat you're craving.

The Ultimate Baking for One Cookbook is here to help! In this book, you'll find 175 recipes for your favorite treats and baked goods with all the work of scaling down the portions done for you—so you can have your sweets without all the waste! Want to enjoy a pie just for you? You'll find perfectly portioned recipes like Classic Apple Pie, Pecan Pie, and Silky Chocolate Ganache Tart in Chapter 5. Want a freshly baked cookie or brownie but don't want to have to make three dozen of them? Check out Chapter 2 for Chocolate Chip Cookies, Buttery Sugar Cookies, and Minty Mocha Brownies—all made to satisfy your cravings without all the waste. No matter what you prefer, from sweet treats and decadent desserts to savory breads and buttery biscuits, this book has you covered.

But before you preheat your oven, check out Chapter 1, where you will find the basics of baking for one, baking techniques and terms, lists of tools and pans to make baking for one easier, and ingredients to have on hand so you can bake anytime a craving hits. You will also find troubleshooting tips to give you confidence in the kitchen.

This book will be your guide to a world of delicious baking without waste or worry! Whether you live alone, you're a parent who wants to indulge while the kids enjoy their own treats, or you have a partner who travels, it's always fun to indulge in home-baked treats. Just remember, when you are baking for one, you don't have to share—unless you want to! Enjoy!

CHAPTER 1

BAKING FOR ONE MADE EASY

Baking can be a pleasure. You would be hard-pressed to find many people who don't love a freshly baked cupcake, warm cookies, or a pie with sweet fruit and a crisp, buttery crust. However, recipes for baked goods often make more than a single person can consume, which can lead to food waste or overeating. Fortunately, with recipes made specifically for one person you can still have the pleasure of baking and the satisfaction of a delicious treat, but you don't have to worry about throwing food away or the guilt that often comes with indulging too much.

In this chapter, you will learn basic baking techniques so you will be set up for success. You'll also learn about the tools you need to bake for one, what ingredients are good to have on hand and how to store them, and tips and troubleshooting advice to make your baking successful. With the solid base you learn here, you'll be ready to bake with confidence and to enjoy the perfect portion of whatever you desire! With less waste and more fun, baking for one may become your favorite activity!

TIPS FOR BAKING FOR ONE

Baking just for yourself is much less work and stress than baking a full-batch recipe. It takes far less time overall, and cleanup is generally easier too. Planning ahead and keeping a well-stocked pantry and kitchen will help you to be ready to bake when a craving hits.

Tip 1: Stock Up on Staples

Baked goods generally use a lot of the same ingredients. When you are shopping do not shy away from full-sized bags of flour or sugar, and make sure you have some basic spices like cinnamon and ginger. You can store flour and spices in the refrigerator or freezer to prolong their shelf life.

Tip 2: Try Bulk Shopping

Bulk sections of most grocery stores or natural food stores are a great resource for buying smaller amounts of ingredients for recipes that you might not use up otherwise. Most bulk sections sell dried fruits, nuts, various flours, oats, chocolate, sugar, and sometimes different kinds of candy.

Tip 3: Preparation Is Key

Be sure you check your recipe before you start to bake to make sure you have everything you need so you are not disappointed later. Get out all the bowls, pans, and ingredients before you start baking, and let any ingredients come to room temperature as directed.

Tip 4: Use the Right Size Tools and Bowls

Baking for one will not require your largest bowls and pans. Using the right size bowl will ensure all your ingredients are incorporated properly. The same goes for tools. Smaller whisks and spatulas are better for smaller-batch recipes.

Tip 5: Keep an Eye on It

Watch your small-batch and single-serving baked goods as they bake. Every oven is different, and you can go from perfectly baked to burnt in minutes. Always start checking at the minimum time listed on your recipe, and check every minute until your recipe is baked to your liking.

Tip 6: Get Creative

Measured ingredients like flour, sugar, and leavening are developed in a ratio that makes them successful. It is difficult to make swaps for these ingredients, but you can add your own twist in different ways. First, you can swap granulated sugar for brown sugar in most recipes with little difference in texture. Second, add ingredients like chocolate chips, nuts, and fruits. Feel free to swap or omit them as desired. Finally, try different flavors of extracts. Be sure to reduce the volume of other liquid extracts, such as vanilla, and it's best to use just $1/8$ teaspoon of extracts like almond, lemon, butter, peppermint, or fruity extracts like strawberry, banana, and coconut.

BAKING TECHNIQUES

Baking is different from savory cooking in that precision and technique are important. While you may be able to casually toss a little of this and a little of that into your pot of pasta sauce, doing the same with a muffin or cake recipe can lead to disaster. Understanding where you need to adhere to the recipe as written, and where you can add your creative flair, will help you build confidence while baking.

Measuring Dry Ingredients

When measuring any type of flour, you want to employ the scoop-and-sweep method. First, lightly mix your flour so no large clumps are seen. Spoon the flour into your measuring cup until it is slightly heaped. With the blunt side of a butter knife or offset spatula, gently sweep the excess flour back into the container.

When measuring granulated sugar, it is fine to dip your measuring cup into the sugar directly and scoop it out, but light and dark brown sugar must be packed into the cup to avoid air pockets.

For other dry ingredients such as chocolate, nuts, and fruits, first note if the ingredients are measured whole or chopped. It is best to spoon or gently pack measuring cups with these ingredients. You should scoop leavening agents like baking soda and baking powder directly from the container with the measuring spoon so the contents are heaped, then sweep the excess away with a straight edge.

Measuring Wet Ingredients

Always measure at eye level on a flat surface. Looking level at the measurement lines will ensure you do not under- or over-measure your wet ingredients. When measuring thick, wet ingredients, like sour cream or yogurt, spoon them into the cup and tap it gently as you fill, so the amount is level. If you are measuring sticky ingredients, like molasses or honey, give measuring cups or spoons a quick spritz of nonstick cooking spray to help them release more easily, and to ensure you get the full measure of the ingredient.

Preparing Pans for Baking

The gold standard for preparing cake pans, loaf pans, and cookie sheets is nonstick cooking spray. A light, even coating is enough. If you do not have nonstick spray or prefer not to use it, you can use a light coating of butter or vegetable oil and dust it with a thin layer of flour (or cocoa powder for chocolate cakes). For baking sheets or cake pans, you can use baking parchment, which is a type of paper impregnated with silicone to prevent sticking. You can also use a reusable silicone mat for cookie sheets if you want to cut back on waste.

TOOLS AND EQUIPMENT

A baker is only as good as the tools they use, and baking for one requires more specialized equipment. Never fear, most of this equipment is easy to find at your local

home or kitchen stores and can easily be sourced online.

Baking Pans
- ¼ sheet pans
- 6" pie pan
- 8-ounce ramekins
- 4" springform pan
- 4" × 2" round cake pan
- 5" × 3" mini-loaf pan
- 5" × 7" baking dish
- 6" round cake pan
- 8" × 8" cake pan
- 8" loaf pan
- 9" × 5" loaf pan
- Twelve-cup muffin pan
- 4" pie and tart pans
- 6¼" cast iron skillet

Measuring Cups and Spoons
- Dry measuring cups in 1 cup, ½ cup, ⅓ cup, and ¼ cup sizes
- Wet measuring cup with lines for ¼ cup, ⅓ cup, ½ cup, ⅔ cup, ¾ cup, and 1 cup
- Measuring spoons in 1 tablespoon, 1 teaspoon, ½ teaspoon, and ¼ teaspoon sizes

Hand Tools and Knives
- Rubber or silicone heatproof spatula
- Small offset spatula
- Whisk
- Pizza cutter
- Chef's knife
- Paring knife
- Serrated knife

- Strainer or colander
- Fine grater

Small Appliances
- Hand mixer
- Blender
- Food processor

INGREDIENTS AND PANTRY STAPLES

A well-stocked pantry, refrigerator, and freezer will prepare you to be ready to whip up baked treats anytime. The following ingredients will set you up to make many of the recipes in this book and are also useful for other types of cooking and baking.

Refrigerated Ingredients
- Active dry yeast
- Butter, salted and unsalted
- Cheese, shredded
- Cream cheese
- Eggs, large
- Heavy whipping cream
- Jam or jelly
- Maple syrup
- Mayonnaise
- Milk
- Sour cream

Frozen Ingredients
- Frozen fruit
- Puff pastry

Pantry Staples

- All-purpose flour
- Almond extract
- Baking powder
- Baking soda
- Bread flour
- Chocolate chips
- Cornstarch
- Dried fruits
- Dry gelatin
- Granulated sugar
- Honey
- Light brown sugar
- Nonstick cooking spray
- Nut butter
- Nuts—whole or chopped
- Powdered sugar
- Vanilla extract
- Vegetable oil

ADVICE FOR SUCCESS

Experience in baking requires time, effort, and practice. Of course, it helps that you can eat what you make so there is a reward when you are done! This section will offer you tips and advice for successful baking and, in particular, how to bake for one with ease.

How to Read a Recipe

Begin by reading the recipe through at least twice so you are familiar with the ingredients and the order in which they are used. Be on the lookout for divided ingredients that are used in different steps in the recipe. Be sure to note any ingredients or tools that need

to be prepped in advance and ingredients that need to be warmed to room temperature before starting; verify oven preheating instructions and pan sizes; and look for any nonactive prep steps like chilling, cooling, or freezing, and see if you can work on any other parts of the recipe during that time. It is always a good idea to verify you have all the ingredients called for before starting and to check that they are fresh and ready to use. There is nothing worse than getting halfway through a recipe and realizing you are out of eggs or butter.

When Is It Done?

Small-batch baking is like any other baking, and you can rely on a good timer as well as your senses to know when your creations are ready. Here are a few things to watch for as the timer ticks down:

- **Look at color:** Most baked goods like cookies and pastry items should be golden to deep brown. Chocolate baked goods, which will be a little trickier, will often have a dull sheen but are not shiny when they are ready. Custards will also have a slightly dull sheen, as will baked cheesecakes.
- **Check the texture:** Cakes, cupcakes, and muffins will spring back when gently pressed in the center, and cakes will pull away from the sides of the pan. Pie and pastry crust will be firm to the touch and flaky. Custards and puddings baked in the oven will be set around the edges but will jiggle slightly in the center.

- **Use your nose:** Once you can smell a baked item, such as cakes, brownies, and cookies, it is almost ready. It is a good practice to peek at your baked items as you near the end of cooking time, and once the smell is strong.

AVOIDING WASTE

Eggs, butter, and milk are no-brainers for refrigerator storage, but other ingredients may also be refrigerated to help them keep longer. Flour, for example, has a pantry life of about six months, but you can extend that to up to a year by stashing your flour in an airtight container in the refrigerator. For even longer storage you can keep your flour in the freezer for up to eighteen months. Other items you can keep in the refrigerator or freezer include chocolate bars and chips, nuts, oats, active dry yeast, maple syrup, and dried fruits.

Just because a baked item is designed for one does not mean you have to finish it all in one sitting. If you have any leftover cookies or brownies, they can be stored at room temperature in an airtight container for up to three days, or frozen for up to a month. Fruit pies can also be kept at room temperature in an airtight container up to two days, along with breads, rolls, and biscuits. Items with dairy, cream cheese, or cheese should be stored in the refrigerator in an airtight container up to three days.

FOOD SAFETY

Before you begin your baking-for-one adventure, please take note of a few food safety tips.

- Never use the same tools for measuring flour to measure other ingredients without washing them in hot, soapy water first, and be sure to avoid putting ready-to-eat baked items on the same surfaces as raw flour. Flour is just ground raw grain, and during harvesting and processing the grains can become contaminated with harmful bacteria, such as pathogenic *Escherichia coli* and *Salmonella*. Flour, like raw eggs and other raw ingredients, should be cooked thoroughly before eating.
- Check ingredients to ensure they are fresh. Oils, nuts and nut butters, flour, and butter should have a pleasant, neutral smell, so a funky or unpleasant smell means it is likely rancid. Same for milk and other dairy products. They should smell slightly sweet in the case of milk and pleasantly tangy for buttermilk, yogurt, and sour cream. Any other odors mean it has spoiled and should be discarded.
- Finally, crack your eggs into a separate bowl. Eggs stored in the refrigerator that are within their best-by date are usually safe to consume, but occasionally an egg may be bad. Rather than ruin other ingredients with a spoiled egg, crack eggs into a small bowl first to check for smell and color.

CHAPTER 2
SMALL-BATCH COOKIES AND BROWNIES

Is there anything better than cookies or brownies warm from the oven? Just the smell of them is enough to make your mouth water! Cookies and brownies are among the most popular sweet treats for a good reason. They are quick to prepare, fun to make, come in a tantalizing array of flavors, and are versatile enough to make a fun snack, yummy breakfast, or decadent dessert. The ultimate in portable comfort food, cookies and brownies are great as an on-the-go treat or tucked into a lunch box to make your work or school lunches a little more special. Is there anything cookies and brownies can't do?

In this chapter you will discover the joys of small-batch cookie and brownie making! The recipes are designed to yield approximately six generously sized cookies or brownies, so there are no worries about cookies going stale before you eat them. From classics like Chocolate Chip Cookies and Classic Cocoa Brownies to more over-the-top creations like Key Lime Butter Cookies, Peanut Butter Crunch Blondies, and Dulce de Leche Blondies, there should be a recipe for every season and every craving. No matter which recipe you choose you are mere moments away from the perfect portion of sweet, rich comfort!

CHOCOLATE CHIP COOKIES

PREP TIME: 10 MIN | COOK TIME: 12 MIN | YIELDS 6 COOKIES

These are no ordinary chocolate chip cookies! Crisp around the edges, tender in the center, and packed with more chocolate chips than should be legal, these cookies are designed to satisfy! If you like, you can use a blend of different baking chips, such as semisweet, white, or milk.

INGREDIENTS

¼ cup salted butter

¼ cup packed light brown sugar

1 tablespoon granulated sugar

1 large egg yolk

¼ teaspoon pure vanilla extract

½ cup all-purpose flour

¼ teaspoon baking soda

¾ cup semisweet chocolate chips

1. Preheat oven to 350°F and line a baking sheet with parchment.

2. In a medium bowl, use a hand mixer on medium speed to cream together butter, brown sugar, and granulated sugar until creamy, about 1 minute. Add egg yolk and vanilla and beat until well combined, about 30 seconds. Scrape down the sides of the bowl as needed.

3. Add flour and baking soda and mix on low speed for 10 seconds to just combine flour, then fold in chocolate chips with a spatula until evenly distributed and no dry flour remains.

4. Scoop dough into six balls and place on prepared baking sheet about 3" apart. Bake 12–14 minutes or until cookies are golden brown around the edges and just set in the center.

5. Cool on the baking sheet 10 minutes before transferring to a wire rack to cool another 10 minutes. Enjoy warm or at room temperature.

Why Salted Butter?

Most traditional recipes for cookies, cakes, and other baked goods call for unsalted butter—because you will season the batter or dough with salt—but in small-batch baking salted butter works better. It is hard to measure an exact "pinch" of salt, but salted butter takes the guesswork out of how much salt to add and helps to ensure the salt is well distributed throughout the dough or batter.

BUTTERY SUGAR COOKIES

PREP TIME: 10 MIN | COOK TIME: 12 MIN | YIELDS 6 COOKIES

These sugar cookies are rich, buttery, and easy to make. You can make these more festive by rolling them in colored sugar for different times of the year. In springtime think pastels, in fall think orange and black, and for the holidays think red and green or blue and white!

INGREDIENTS

¼ cup salted butter, at room temperature

⅓ cup granulated sugar

1 large egg yolk

¼ teaspoon pure vanilla extract

1 drop (about ¹⁄₁₆ teaspoon) almond extract

½ cup all-purpose flour

¼ teaspoon baking powder

⅓ cup coarse decorating sugar

1. Preheat oven to 350°F and line a baking sheet with parchment.

2. In a medium bowl, use a hand mixer on medium speed to cream butter until smooth, about 30 seconds, then add sugar and beat until creamy and lighter in color, about 1 minute. Add egg yolk, vanilla, and almond extract and beat until well combined, about 30 seconds. Scrape down the sides of the bowl as needed.

3. Add flour and baking powder and mix on low speed for 10 seconds to just combine flour, then increase speed to medium and beat until smooth, about 30 seconds.

4. Scoop dough into six balls. Roll each ball in decorating sugar, then place on prepared baking sheet about 1" apart. Bake 12–14 minutes or until cookies are golden brown around the edges and just set in the center.

5. Cool on the baking sheet 10 minutes before transferring to a wire rack to cool to room temperature.

CLASSIC PEANUT BUTTER COOKIES

PREP TIME: 10 MIN | COOK TIME: 8 MIN | YIELDS 6 COOKIES

You can make some fun changes to these cookies to jazz them up if you like. You can swap smooth peanut butter for chunky if you like a nutty bite, or you can add ½ cup of either peanut butter chips or chocolate chips to the dough after the ingredients are just combined. Use a spatula to fold them in, then scoop and bake as directed.

INGREDIENTS

¼ cup salted butter

⅓ cup smooth peanut butter

¼ cup powdered sugar

2 tablespoons packed light brown sugar

½ teaspoon pure vanilla extract

1 large egg yolk

½ cup all-purpose flour

¼ teaspoon baking soda

1. Preheat oven to 350°F and line a baking sheet with parchment.

2. In a medium bowl, use a hand mixer on medium speed to cream butter until smooth, about 30 seconds, then add peanut butter and beat until well mixed, about 30 seconds. Add powdered sugar and brown sugar and beat until creamy and lighter in color, about 1 minute. Add vanilla and egg yolk and beat until well combined, about 30 seconds. Scrape down the sides of the bowl as needed.

3. Add flour and baking soda and mix on low 10 seconds to just combine flour, then increase speed to medium and beat until smooth, about 30 seconds.

4. Scoop dough into six balls and place on prepared baking sheet about 1" apart. With the tines of a fork press each cookie with a crosshatch pattern.

5. Bake 8–10 minutes or until cookies are golden brown around the edges and set in the center.

6. Cool on the baking sheet 10 minutes before transferring to a wire rack to cool to room temperature.

NO-BAKE COOKIES

PREP TIME: 1 HOUR | COOK TIME: 1 MIN | YIELDS 6 COOKIES

No-bake cookies are great on a warm day or anytime you want a cookie without having to turn on your oven. No-bake does not mean no-cook, however. All the cooking is done on the stove, but it takes almost no time. Feel free to add up to ⅓ cup chopped roasted and unsalted peanuts to these for a little more crunch and texture.

INGREDIENTS

⅓ cup granulated sugar

1 tablespoon cocoa powder

2 tablespoons whole milk

1 tablespoon unsalted butter

3 tablespoons creamy peanut butter

⅓ cup plus 1 tablespoon quick-cooking oats

⅛ teaspoon salt

1. Line a baking sheet with wax paper or parchment.

2. In a small saucepan over medium heat, add sugar, cocoa powder, and milk. Bring to a boil and cook 1 minute.

3. Remove pan from heat and stir in remaining ingredients until well combined.

4. Drop mixture into six mounds on prepared baking sheet. Cool to room temperature, then refrigerate 1 hour before serving.

MONSTER COOKIES

PREP TIME: 1 HOUR | COOK TIME: 10 MIN | YIELDS 6 COOKIES

Monster cookies are peanut butter cookies that are packed with goodies such as oats, candy pieces, and chocolate chips. The fun part of monster cookies is that you can add any extras you like, so if candy pieces are not your thing, you can use chopped-up peanut butter cups or candy bars. You can even add a few tablespoons of chopped nuts!

INGREDIENTS

¼ cup salted butter

⅓ cup smooth peanut butter

3 tablespoons granulated sugar

3 tablespoons packed light brown sugar

½ teaspoon pure vanilla extract

1 large egg yolk

½ cup all-purpose flour

¼ teaspoon baking soda

¼ cup old-fashioned oats

¼ cup chocolate-coated candy pieces (such as M&M's)

¼ cup milk chocolate chips

1. Preheat oven to 350°F and line a baking sheet with parchment.

2. In a medium bowl, use a hand mixer on medium speed to cream butter until smooth, about 30 seconds, then add peanut butter and beat until well mixed, about 30 seconds. Add granulated sugar and brown sugar and beat until creamy and lighter in color, about 1 minute. Add vanilla and egg yolk and beat until well combined, about 30 seconds. Scrape down the sides of the bowl as needed.

3. Add flour and baking soda and mix on low 10 seconds to just combine flour. Add oats, candy pieces, and chocolate chips and fold with a spatula to combine.

4. Cover bowl and chill 1 hour.

5. Scoop dough into six balls and place on prepared baking sheet about 1" apart.

6. Bake 10–12 minutes or until cookies are golden brown around the edges and set in the center.

7. Cool on the baking sheet 10 minutes before transferring to a wire rack to cool to room temperature.

OATMEAL RAISIN COOKIES

PREP TIME: 1 HOUR | COOK TIME: 12 MIN | YIELDS 6 COOKIES

You do not need to chill the dough for these cookies, but if you do you will end up with a thicker, chewier, and more flavorful cookie. The chilling time allows the oats to absorb some of the liquid in the dough, helping them to plump before baking. This results in a chewier texture and relaxes the gluten so the edges of the cookie crisp.

INGREDIENTS

¼ cup salted butter

⅓ cup packed light brown sugar

1 large egg yolk

¼ teaspoon pure vanilla extract

½ cup all-purpose flour

¼ teaspoon ground cinnamon

¼ teaspoon baking soda

½ cup old-fashioned oats

¼ cup raisins

1. Preheat oven to 350°F and line a baking sheet with parchment.

2. In a medium bowl, use a hand mixer on medium speed to cream together butter and brown sugar until creamy, about 1 minute. Add egg yolk and vanilla and beat until well combined, about 30 seconds. Scrape down the sides of the bowl as needed.

3. Add flour, cinnamon, and baking soda and mix on low 10 seconds to just combine flour, then fold in oats and raisins with a spatula until evenly distributed and no dry flour remains. Cover the bowl and chill 1 hour.

4. Scoop dough into six balls and place on prepared baking sheet about 1" apart. Bake 12–14 minutes or until cookies are golden brown around the edges and just set in the center.

5. Cool on the baking sheet 10 minutes before transferring to a wire rack to cool another 10 minutes. Enjoy warm or at room temperature.

SNICKERDOODLES

PREP TIME: 10 MIN | COOK TIME: 9 MIN | YIELDS 6 COOKIES

Snickerdoodles originated in New England and are widely popular across the US. The funny name can't be directly tied to any specific origin, but some believe it is a portmanteau of the word *snicker*, meaning "smothered laugh," and *doodle*, a Germanic word meaning "foolish." Whatever the meaning, these Snickerdoodles are delicious!

INGREDIENTS

⅓ cup salted butter

⅓ cup plus 2 tablespoons granulated sugar, divided

1 tablespoon packed light brown sugar

¼ teaspoon pure vanilla extract

1 large egg yolk

¾ cup all-purpose flour

¼ teaspoon baking soda

¼ teaspoon cream of tartar

1 teaspoon ground cinnamon

1. Preheat oven to 350°F and line a baking sheet with parchment.

2. In a medium bowl, use a hand mixer on medium speed to cream together butter, ⅓ cup granulated sugar, and brown sugar until creamy, about 1 minute. Add vanilla and egg yolk and beat until well combined, about 30 seconds. Scrape down the sides of the bowl as needed.

3. Add flour, baking soda, and cream of tartar and mix on low 10 seconds to just combine flour, then increase speed to medium and beat until dough is smooth, about 30 seconds.

4. In a small bowl, combine remaining 2 tablespoons granulated sugar and cinnamon and mix well.

5. Scoop dough into six balls and roll in cinnamon sugar. Place on prepared baking sheet about 1" apart and gently flatten each ball to ½" thick. Bake 9–12 minutes or until cookies are just starting to turn golden brown around the edges.

6. Cool to room temperature on the baking sheet.

GINGERSNAPS

PREP TIME: 1 HOUR | COOK TIME: 10 MIN | YIELDS 6 COOKIES

These cookies get their name from the snappy kick of ginger and from their crisp texture, which comes from using vegetable oil instead of butter. If you have fresh ginger, you can grate up to ¼ teaspoon into the dough to amp up the ginger flavor.

INGREDIENTS

3 tablespoons vegetable oil

¼ cup packed dark brown sugar

1 large egg yolk

½ cup all-purpose flour

¼ teaspoon baking soda

⅛ teaspoon ground cinnamon

⅛ teaspoon ground ginger

1 pinch (about 1/16 teaspoon) cloves

2 tablespoons granulated sugar

1. Preheat oven to 375°F and line a baking sheet with parchment.

2. In a medium bowl, use a hand mixer on medium speed to cream together oil, brown sugar, and egg yolk. Scrape down the sides of the bowl as needed.

3. Add flour, baking soda, cinnamon, ginger, and cloves and mix on low 10 seconds to just combine flour, then increase speed to medium and beat until dough is smooth, about 30 seconds. Cover bowl and chill 1 hour.

4. In a small bowl, add granulated sugar.

5. Scoop dough into six balls and roll in sugar. Place on prepared baking sheet about 2" apart. Bake 10–12 minutes or until cookies are firm in the center.

6. Cool 10 minutes on the baking sheet before transferring to a wire rack to cool to room temperature.

DOUBLE-CHOCOLATE CHUNK COOKIES

PREP TIME: 1 HOUR | COOK TIME: 12 MIN | YIELDS 6 COOKIES

If you do not have chocolate chunks or a chocolate bar to make into chunks, you can use chocolate chips. While the chunks do make for larger pockets of gooey chocolate, chips will certainly do the job. Feel free to add ¼ cup chopped pecans or walnuts to these if you like!

INGREDIENTS

¼ cup salted butter

¼ cup packed light brown sugar

2 tablespoons granulated sugar

1 large egg yolk

½ teaspoon pure vanilla extract

½ cup all-purpose flour

1 tablespoon Dutch-processed cocoa powder

¼ teaspoon baking soda

¾ cup semisweet chocolate chunks

1. Preheat oven to 350°F and line a baking sheet with parchment.

2. In a medium bowl, use a hand mixer on medium speed to cream together butter, brown sugar, and granulated sugar until creamy, about 1 minute. Add egg yolk and vanilla and beat until well combined, about 30 seconds. Scrape down the sides of the bowl as needed.

3. Add flour, cocoa powder, and baking soda and mix on low 10 seconds to just combine flour, then fold in chocolate chunks with a spatula until evenly distributed and no dry flour remains. Cover bowl and chill 1 hour.

4. Scoop dough into six balls and place on prepared baking sheet about 1" apart. Bake 12–14 minutes or until cookies are firm around the edges and just set in the center.

5. Cool on the baking sheet 10 minutes before transferring to a wire rack to cool another 10 minutes. Enjoy warm or at room temperature.

WHITE CHOCOLATE MACADAMIA NUT COOKIES

PREP TIME: 1 HOUR | COOK TIME: 9 MIN | YIELDS 6 COOKIES

There is no need to spend money on premium macadamia nuts for baking. Unless the recipe calls for whole nuts, it is more cost-effective to buy pieces, often called baking pieces. With pieces, there is no need to chop the nuts. You just measure and add to the recipe.

INGREDIENTS

¼ cup salted butter

¼ cup granulated sugar

2 tablespoons packed light brown sugar

¼ teaspoon pure vanilla extract

1 large egg yolk

½ cup all-purpose flour

¼ teaspoon baking soda

⅓ cup white chocolate chips

¼ cup chopped macadamia nuts

1. Preheat oven to 350°F and line a baking sheet with parchment.

2. In a medium bowl, use a hand mixer on medium speed to cream together butter, granulated sugar, and brown sugar until creamy, about 1 minute. Add vanilla and egg yolk and beat until well combined, about 30 seconds. Scrape down the sides of the bowl as needed.

3. Add flour and baking soda and mix on low 10 seconds to just combine flour, then fold in chocolate chips and macadamia nuts with a spatula until evenly distributed and no dry flour remains. Cover bowl and chill 1 hour.

4. Scoop dough into six balls and place on prepared baking sheet about 1" apart. Bake 9–12 minutes or until cookies are golden brown around the edges and just set in the center.

5. Cool on the baking sheet 10 minutes before transferring to a wire rack to cool another 10 minutes. Enjoy warm or at room temperature.

Chilling Cookie Dough

Chilling dough can allow for a few things to happen. First, as the dough chills it dries out, and that results in a chewier cookie with crisper edges. Second, the flavors will have a chance to develop so your cookies will have a more refined flavor. Finally, chilling the dough controls the spread and results in thicker cookies.

PECAN DATE COOKIES

PREP TIME: 1 HOUR | COOK TIME: 8 MIN | YIELDS 6 COOKIES

Dates give these cookies a caramelly sweet flavor and a chewy texture, making them almost irresistible. Chopped dates are available in most stores, but these cookies taste better with freshly chopped dates. The ready-chopped kind are often dry and less flavorful. Any leftover dates can be stashed in the refrigerator and used in smoothies, chopped and added to salads, or used to make more batches of these cookies!

INGREDIENTS

3 tablespoons salted butter

¼ cup granulated sugar

¼ teaspoon pure vanilla extract

1 large egg yolk

½ cup all-purpose flour

⅛ teaspoon baking soda

⅓ cup chopped pecans

¼ cup chopped dates

1. Preheat oven to 350°F and line a baking sheet with parchment.

2. In a medium bowl, use a hand mixer on medium speed to cream together butter and sugar until creamy, about 30 seconds. Add vanilla and egg yolk and beat until well combined, about 30 seconds. Scrape down the sides of the bowl as needed.

3. Add flour and baking soda and mix on low 10 seconds to just combine flour, then fold in pecans and dates with a spatula until evenly distributed and no dry flour remains. Cover bowl and chill 1 hour.

4. Scoop dough into six balls and place on prepared baking sheet about 1" apart. Bake 8–10 minutes or until cookies are golden brown around the edges and just set in the center.

5. Cool on the baking sheet 10 minutes before transferring to a wire rack to cool another 10 minutes. Enjoy warm or at room temperature.

MOLASSES COOKIES

PREP TIME: 1 HOUR | COOK TIME: 9 MIN | YIELDS 6 COOKIES

Molasses makes these cookies soft and chewy and gives them a rich, unique flavor. If you do not have molasses, swap it for honey, and you'll have a soft and chewy honey cookie instead. For a more sparkly cookie, roll them in coarse sanding sugar instead of granulated sugar.

INGREDIENTS

¼ cup salted butter

⅓ cup plus 2 tablespoons granulated sugar, divided

1 tablespoon molasses

1 large egg yolk

½ cup plus 1 tablespoon all-purpose flour

¼ teaspoon baking soda

¼ teaspoon ground cinnamon

⅛ teaspoon ground ginger

⅛ teaspoon pumpkin pie spice

1. Preheat oven to 350°F and line a baking sheet with parchment.

2. In a medium bowl, use a hand mixer on medium speed to cream together butter, ⅓ cup sugar, and molasses until creamy, about 1 minute. Add egg yolk and beat until well combined, about 30 seconds. Scrape down the sides of the bowl as needed.

3. Add flour, baking soda, cinnamon, ginger, and pumpkin pie spice and mix on low 10 seconds to just combine flour, then increase speed to medium and beat until dough is smooth, about 30 seconds. Cover bowl and chill 1 hour.

4. In a small bowl, add remaining 2 tablespoons sugar.

5. Scoop dough into six balls and roll in sugar. Place on prepared baking sheet about 1" apart. Bake 9–12 minutes or until cookies are firm around the edges and set in the center.

6. Cool 10 minutes on the baking sheet before transferring to a wire rack to cool to room temperature.

CHOCOLATE CHIP SKILLET COOKIE

PREP TIME: 10 MIN | COOK TIME: 14 MIN | YIELDS 1 COOKIE

All you need to make this recipe complete is a scoop of your favorite ice cream and a spoon! This makes a BIG cookie and is enough to share if you like. This recipe calls for a 6¼" cast iron skillet, but if you do not have one you can use a 6" round cake pan or even a 6" casserole dish.

INGREDIENTS

3 tablespoons salted butter

2 tablespoons packed light brown sugar

2 tablespoons granulated sugar

1 large egg yolk

¼ teaspoon pure vanilla extract

¼ cup plus 2 tablespoons all-purpose flour

⅛ teaspoon baking soda

⅓ cup semisweet chocolate chips

⅛ teaspoon flaky sea salt

1. Preheat oven to 350°F and lightly grease a 6¼" cast iron skillet with nonstick cooking spray.

2. In a medium bowl, use a hand mixer on medium speed to cream together butter, brown sugar, and granulated sugar until creamy, about 1 minute. Add egg yolk and vanilla and beat until well combined, about 30 seconds. Scrape down the sides of the bowl as needed.

3. Add flour and baking soda and mix on low 10 seconds to just combine flour, then fold in chocolate chips with a spatula until evenly distributed and no dry flour remains.

4. Press cookie dough into prepared skillet in an even layer and sprinkle with sea salt. Bake 14–16 minutes or until cookie is golden brown and puffed around the edges.

5. Remove from oven and cool 10 minutes. Enjoy warm or at room temperature.

BROWN SUGAR PECAN BREAKFAST COOKIES

PREP TIME: 10 MIN | COOK TIME: 14 MIN | YIELDS 6 COOKIES

These nutty breakfast cookies are made even better with a little semisweet chocolate. If you have a bar of good-quality dark chocolate on hand, you can chop it into pieces and use that in place of the chips.

INGREDIENTS

½ cup creamy peanut butter

1 medium banana, peeled and mashed

3 tablespoons packed light brown sugar

½ teaspoon pure vanilla extract

¼ teaspoon sea salt

½ teaspoon ground cinnamon

1 cup quick-cooking oats

½ cup chopped pecans

¼ cup semisweet chocolate chips

1. Preheat oven to 325°F and line a baking sheet with parchment.

2. In a medium bowl, use a hand mixer on medium speed to combine peanut butter, banana, and brown sugar. Beat until well combined, about 30 seconds, then add vanilla, salt, and cinnamon and mix until well combined, about 30 seconds.

3. With a spatula, fold in oats, pecans, and chocolate chips until evenly combined.

4. Scoop dough into six mounds and place on prepared baking sheet 2" apart. Bake 14–16 minutes or until cookies are brown and soft but not gooey. Cool completely on baking sheet.

Freezing Nuts and Chocolate

Freezing nuts and chocolate is an easy way to extend their shelf life and avoid waste if you decide to buy them in bulk. Bulk buying is cost-effective, and using your freezer is a great way to save money and preserve your food. Nuts will keep up to 6 months in an airtight container in the freezer, and chocolate keeps up to 18 months!

KEY LIME BUTTER COOKIES

PREP TIME: 30 MIN | COOK TIME: 12 MIN | YIELDS 6 COOKIES

Let the flavor of these cookies take you away to sandy beaches and blue seas with the tangy flavor of key lime! If you are not able to find key limes in the produce department, you can use regular limes without losing any of the flavor. To make these cookies more festive you can sprinkle the melted white chocolate with green sprinkles before it sets.

INGREDIENTS

¼ cup salted butter, at room temperature

3 tablespoons powdered sugar

1 teaspoon freshly grated key lime zest

¼ teaspoon key lime juice

½ cup all-purpose flour

⅓ cup white chocolate chips

1. Preheat oven to 325°F and line a baking sheet with parchment.

2. In a medium bowl, use a hand mixer on medium speed to cream butter until smooth, about 30 seconds, then add sugar, lime zest, and lime juice and beat until creamy, about 30 seconds. Scrape down the sides of the bowl as needed.

3. Add flour and mix on low 10 seconds to just combine flour, then increase speed to medium and beat until smooth, about 30 seconds. Dough will be firm.

4. Scoop dough into six balls and place on prepared baking sheet 2" apart. With a glass or palm of your hand, flatten each ball to ¼" thickness. Bake 12–14 minutes or until cookies are just golden brown around the bottom edges and just set in the center. Cool on the baking sheet completely to room temperature.

5. In a small microwave-safe bowl, add chocolate chips. Microwave in 15-second intervals, stirring well between each interval, until chocolate is melted. Drizzle or dip cookies with melted chocolate. Place in refrigerator 20 minutes to harden. Bring back to room temperature before serving.

SHORTBREAD COOKIES

PREP TIME: 10 MIN | **COOK TIME: 12 MIN** | **YIELDS 6 COOKIES**

Buttery shortbread cookies are perfect with a cup of strong tea or a steaming mug of coffee. If you want to make these special you can drizzle them with a little melted chocolate or sprinkle coarse sanding sugar over the tops before baking for a sparkly top.

INGREDIENTS

¼ cup salted butter, at room temperature

3 tablespoons powdered sugar

1 teaspoon whole milk

¼ teaspoon pure vanilla extract

½ cup all-purpose flour

1. Preheat oven to 325°F and line a baking sheet with parchment.

2. In a medium bowl, use a hand mixer on medium speed to cream butter until smooth, about 30 seconds, then add sugar, milk, and vanilla and beat until creamy, about 30 seconds. Scrape down the sides of the bowl as needed.

3. Add flour and mix on low speed 10 seconds to just combine flour, then increase speed to medium and beat until smooth, about 30 seconds. Dough will be firm.

4. Scoop dough into six balls and place on prepared baking sheet 2" apart. With a glass or palm of your hand, flatten each ball to ¼" thickness. Bake 12–14 minutes or until cookies are just golden brown around the bottom edges and just set in the center. Cool on the baking sheet completely to room temperature.

CLASSIC COCOA BROWNIES

PREP TIME: 10 MIN | COOK TIME: 20 MIN | YIELDS 6 BROWNIES

These brownies are your classic, nostalgic, chocolatey brownie. They are perfect as is, or you can dust them with a little powdered sugar, frost them with Chocolate Buttercream (see Chapter 3), or eat them warm with a scoop of vanilla ice cream.

INGREDIENTS

¼ cup salted butter, at room temperature

¼ cup packed light brown sugar

¼ cup granulated sugar

1 large egg

¾ teaspoon pure vanilla extract

¼ cup all-purpose flour

3 tablespoons Dutch-processed cocoa powder

⅛ teaspoon baking powder

1. Preheat oven to 350°F and spray a 9" × 5" loaf pan with nonstick cooking spray.

2. In a medium bowl, use a hand mixer on medium speed to cream butter until smooth, about 30 seconds. Add brown sugar and granulated sugar and mix on medium speed until well combined, about 30 seconds. Add egg and vanilla and mix on low speed to just combine, about 10 seconds.

3. Sift flour, cocoa powder, and baking powder into bowl and mix on low speed until no dry flour remains, about 20 seconds.

4. Pour batter evenly into prepared pan. Bake 20–24 minutes or until edges are firm and center is just set.

5. Cool in pan 20 minutes, then turn out onto a cutting board and cool 20 minutes more before slicing. Serve warm or at room temperature.

TRIPLE-CHOCOLATE BROWNIES

PREP TIME: 10 MIN | COOK TIME: 20 MIN | YIELDS 6 BROWNIES

If you love chocolate then look no further! These ultra-fudgy brownies are packed with white, milk, and semisweet chocolate chips for a decadent brownie sure to please. If you do not have honey, you can use corn syrup or an additional tablespoon of brown sugar.

INGREDIENTS

¼ cup salted butter, at room temperature

⅓ cup semisweet chocolate chips, divided

¼ cup packed light brown sugar

2 tablespoons granulated sugar

1 tablespoon honey

1 large egg

½ teaspoon pure vanilla extract

¼ cup all-purpose flour

3 tablespoons cocoa powder

¼ cup white chocolate chips

¼ cup milk chocolate chips

1. Preheat oven to 350°F and spray a 9" × 5" loaf pan with nonstick cooking spray, then line pan with parchment, making sure there is an overhang of at least 3".

2. In a medium microwave-safe bowl, combine butter and 2 tablespoons semisweet chocolate chips. Microwave in 30-second intervals, stirring well between each interval, until butter and chocolate are melted.

3. To melted butter and chocolate, add brown sugar, granulated sugar, and honey and mix with a spatula until well combined, about twenty strokes. Add egg and vanilla and beat until egg is thoroughly combined, about thirty strokes.

4. Sift flour and cocoa powder into bowl and gently fold six to eight times until the dry ingredients are just incorporated, then add remaining semisweet chips, white chocolate chips, and milk chocolate chips and fold to combine, about five strokes.

5. Pour batter evenly into prepared pan. Bake 20–24 minutes or until edges are firm and center is just set.

6. Cool in pan 20 minutes, then use excess parchment to lift brownies onto a cutting board. Cool 20 minutes more before slicing. Serve warm or at room temperature.

BLONDIES

PREP TIME: 10 MIN | COOK TIME: 20 MIN | YIELDS 6 BLONDIES

Blondies are not always given the credit they deserve! Aside from being just as rich as their chocolatey siblings, they allow the flavors of vanilla and brown sugar to really sing. If you like, you can fold in up to ⅓ cup chopped nuts, chocolate chips, or candy pieces.

INGREDIENTS

¼ cup salted butter, at room temperature

⅓ cup packed light brown sugar

2 tablespoons granulated sugar

1 large egg yolk

¾ teaspoon pure vanilla extract

⅛ teaspoon almond extract

½ cup all-purpose flour

⅛ teaspoon baking powder

1. Preheat oven to 350°F and spray a 9" × 5" loaf pan with nonstick cooking spray.

2. In a medium bowl, use a hand mixer on medium speed to cream butter until smooth, about 30 seconds. Add brown sugar and granulated sugar and mix on medium speed until well combined, about 30 seconds. Add egg yolk, vanilla, and almond extract and mix on low speed to just combine, about 10 seconds.

3. Sift flour and baking powder into bowl and mix on low speed until no dry flour remains, about 20 seconds.

4. Pour batter evenly into prepared pan. Bake 20–24 minutes or until edges are firm and center is just set.

5. Cool in pan 20 minutes, then turn out onto a cutting board and cool 20 minutes more before slicing. Serve warm or at room temperature.

CHERRY OATMEAL BREAKFAST COOKIES

PREP TIME: 10 MIN | COOK TIME: 14 MIN | YIELDS 6 COOKIES

Cookies for breakfast? Yes, please! These cookies are a fun yet healthy way to start your day. While dried cherries are called for, you can easily swap them for any dried fruits you prefer, or omit the fruit and add more pumpkin seeds or use sunflower seeds instead!

INGREDIENTS

½ cup creamy almond butter

1 medium banana, peeled and mashed

2 tablespoons honey

¾ teaspoon pure vanilla extract

¼ teaspoon sea salt

½ teaspoon pumpkin pie spice

1 cup quick-cooking oats

⅓ cup roughly chopped dried cherries

¼ cup chopped almonds

2 tablespoons unsalted pumpkin seeds

1. Preheat oven to 325°F and line a baking sheet with parchment.

2. In a medium bowl, use a hand mixer on medium speed to combine almond butter, banana, and honey. Beat until well combined, about 30 seconds, then add vanilla, salt, and pumpkin pie spice and mix until well combined, about 30 seconds.

3. With a spatula, fold in oats, cherries, almonds, and pumpkin seeds until evenly combined.

4. Scoop dough into six mounds and place on prepared baking sheet 2" apart. Bake 14–16 minutes or until cookies are brown and soft but not gooey. Cool completely on baking sheet. Enjoy warm or at room temperature.

BROOKIES

PREP TIME: 10 MIN | COOK TIME: 22 MIN | YIELDS 6 BROOKIES

Can't decide between cookies or brownies? With these brookies you do not need to choose. If you have ready-prepared cookie dough from the grocery store, you can swap that here if you like. Two to three pieces, or about ¼ cup, will do the trick.

INGREDIENTS

¼ cup salted butter, at room temperature

⅓ cup semisweet chocolate chips, divided

3 tablespoons packed light brown sugar

3 tablespoons granulated sugar

1 tablespoon honey

1 large egg

½ teaspoon pure vanilla extract

¼ cup all-purpose flour

3 tablespoons Dutch-processed cocoa powder

½ batch Chocolate Chip Cookies dough (see recipe in this chapter)

1. Preheat oven to 350°F and spray a 9" × 5" loaf pan with nonstick cooking spray, then line pan with parchment, making sure there is an overhang of at least 3".

2. In a medium microwave-safe bowl, combine butter and 2 tablespoons chocolate chips. Microwave in 30-second intervals, stirring well between each interval, until butter and chocolate are melted.

3. To melted butter and chocolate, add brown sugar, granulated sugar, and honey and mix with a spatula until well combined, about twenty strokes. Add egg and vanilla and beat until egg is thoroughly combined, about thirty strokes.

4. Sift flour and cocoa powder into bowl and gently fold six to eight times until the dry ingredients are well incorporated, about twelve strokes.

5. Pour batter evenly into prepared pan. Spoon Chocolate Chip Cookies dough evenly onto the brownie batter in heaping teaspoons. Gently press the cookie dough into the batter, then sprinkle reserved chocolate chips over top. Bake 22–26 minutes or until edges are firm and center is just set and the cookie dough pieces are golden.

6. Cool in pan 20 minutes, then use excess parchment to lift Brookies onto a cutting board. Cool 20 minutes more before slicing. Serve warm or at room temperature.

CHEESECAKE BROWNIES

Tangy cheesecake is a delightful foil to rich brownies, and the swirled effect of these Cheesecake Brownies makes them look as good as they taste! Leftover cream cheese can be used to make Personal Cheesecakes (see Chapter 3) or Peanut Butter Fluff Pie (see Chapter 5).

INGREDIENTS

¼ cup salted butter, at room temperature

¼ cup packed light brown sugar

¼ cup plus 1 tablespoon granulated sugar, divided

1 large egg

1 teaspoon pure vanilla extract, divided

¼ cup all-purpose flour

3 tablespoons Dutch-processed cocoa powder

⅛ teaspoon baking powder

3 ounces cream cheese, at room temperature

1 large egg yolk

1. Preheat oven to 350°F and spray a 9" × 5" loaf pan with nonstick cooking spray.

2. In a medium bowl, use a hand mixer on medium speed to cream butter until smooth, about 30 seconds. Add brown sugar and ¼ cup granulated sugar and mix on medium speed until well combined, about 30 seconds. Add egg and ½ teaspoon vanilla and mix on low speed to just combine, about 10 seconds.

3. Sift flour, cocoa powder, and baking powder into bowl and mix on low speed until no dry flour remains, about 20 seconds. Pour batter evenly into prepared pan.

4. In a separate medium bowl, add remaining 1 tablespoon granulated sugar, remaining ½ teaspoon vanilla, cream cheese, and egg yolk. Beat on medium speed until smooth and creamy, about 1 minute. Pour cheesecake mixture over brownie batter. Use a butter knife to swirl batter so cheesecake and chocolate are swirled to your liking.

5. Bake 20–24 minutes or until edges are firm and center is just set. Cheesecake should not look wet or jiggly.

6. Cool in pan 20 minutes, then turn out onto a cutting board and cool 20 minutes more before slicing. Serve warm or at room temperature.

TURTLE BROWNIES

PREP TIME: 10 MIN | COOK TIME: 20 MIN | YIELDS 6 BROWNIES

When an item is called "turtle" it means it is a combination of chocolate, caramel, and nuts, such as walnuts or pecans.

INGREDIENTS

¼ cup salted butter, at room temperature

½ cup semisweet chocolate chips, divided

¼ cup packed light brown sugar

2 tablespoons granulated sugar

1 tablespoon honey

1 large egg

½ teaspoon pure vanilla extract

¼ cup all-purpose flour

3 tablespoons Dutch-processed cocoa powder

⅓ cup chopped walnuts, divided

6 individually wrapped caramels, such as Kraft Candy Caramels

1½ teaspoons heavy cream

1. Preheat oven to 350°F. Spray a 9" × 5" loaf pan with nonstick cooking spray and then line pan with parchment, making sure there is an overhang of at least 3".

2. In a medium microwave-safe bowl, combine butter and 2 tablespoons chocolate chips. Microwave in 30-second intervals, stirring well between each interval, until butter and chocolate are melted.

3. To melted butter and chocolate, add brown sugar, granulated sugar, and honey and mix with a spatula until well combined, about twenty strokes. Add egg and vanilla and beat until egg is thoroughly combined, about thirty strokes.

4. Sift flour and cocoa powder into bowl and gently fold six to eight times until the dry ingredients are just incorporated, then add ¼ cup chocolate chips and ¼ cup walnuts and fold to combine, about five strokes.

5. Pour batter evenly into prepared pan. Sprinkle remaining chocolate chips and walnuts over top. Bake 20–24 minutes or until edges are firm and center is just set.

6. Cool in pan 20 minutes, then use excess parchment to lift brownies onto a cutting board to cool.

7. In a small microwave-safe bowl, combine caramels and cream. Microwave in 30-second intervals, stirring well between each interval, until caramels are melted. Drizzle melted caramel over warm brownies. Cool to room temperature before serving.

PEANUT BUTTER CRUNCH BLONDIES

PREP TIME: 10 MIN | COOK TIME: 20 MIN | YIELDS 6 BLONDIES

The crunch in these blondies comes from chopped peanuts and candy-coated peanut butter candies. If you are allergic to peanuts feel free to swap almond butter for peanut butter and use your favorite candies and nuts.

INGREDIENTS

¼ cup peanut butter

⅓ cup packed light brown sugar

2 tablespoons granulated sugar

1 large egg

¾ teaspoon pure vanilla extract

½ cup all-purpose flour

⅛ teaspoon baking powder

¼ cup chopped unsalted peanuts

¼ cup candy-coated peanut butter candies, such as Reese's Pieces

1. Preheat oven to 350°F and spray a 9" × 5" loaf pan with nonstick cooking spray.

2. In a medium bowl, use a hand mixer on medium speed to cream peanut butter until smooth, about 30 seconds. Add brown sugar and granulated sugar and mix on medium speed until well combined, about 30 seconds. Add egg and vanilla and mix on low speed to just combine, about 10 seconds.

3. Sift flour and baking powder into bowl and mix on low speed until no dry flour remains, about 20 seconds. Fold in peanuts and peanut butter candies.

4. Pour batter evenly into prepared pan. Bake 20–24 minutes or until edges are firm and center is just set.

5. Cool in pan 20 minutes, then turn out onto a cutting board and cool 20 minutes more before slicing. Serve warm or at room temperature.

COCOA VANILLA SWIRL BROWNIES

PREP TIME: 10 MIN | COOK TIME: 20 MIN | YIELDS 6 BROWNIES

To get the best-looking swirls in these brownies it is important to remember that less is more. The less you swirl, the more definition there will be between the two batters. One or two passes vertically and horizontally in the pan should do the trick!

INGREDIENTS

¼ cup salted butter, at room temperature

⅓ cup packed light brown sugar

2 tablespoons granulated sugar

1 large egg yolk

¾ teaspoon pure vanilla extract

½ cup all-purpose flour

⅛ teaspoon baking powder

2 teaspoons Dutch-processed cocoa powder

½ teaspoon honey

1. Preheat oven to 350°F and spray a 9" × 5" loaf pan with nonstick cooking spray.

2. In a medium bowl, use a hand mixer on medium speed to cream butter until smooth, about 30 seconds. Add brown sugar and granulated sugar and mix on medium speed until well combined, about 30 seconds. Add egg yolk and vanilla and mix on low speed to just combine, about 10 seconds.

3. Sift flour and baking powder into bowl and mix on low speed until no dry flour remains, about 20 seconds.

4. Divide batter evenly between two medium bowls. To one bowl, add cocoa powder and honey and mix well to combine.

5. Pour chocolate batter evenly into prepared pan. Spoon vanilla batter in dollops over chocolate. Use a butter knife to swirl batter so vanilla and chocolate are swirled to your liking. Bake 20–24 minutes or until edges are firm and center is just set.

6. Cool in pan 20 minutes, then turn out onto a cutting board and cool 20 minutes more before slicing. Serve warm or at room temperature.

MINTY MOCHA BROWNIES

PREP TIME: 10 MIN | COOK TIME: 20 MIN | YIELDS 6 BROWNIES

If you love a peppermint mocha from your favorite coffee shop, then you will love these brownies. Instant coffee powder gives them that mocha kick. Do not freeze or refrigerate leftover instant coffee. Instead, keep it in your pantry in a dark, cool place.

INGREDIENTS

¼ cup salted butter, at room temperature

¼ cup packed light brown sugar

2 tablespoons granulated sugar

2 teaspoons instant coffee

1 large egg

½ teaspoon pure vanilla extract

⅛ teaspoon peppermint extract

¼ cup all-purpose flour

3 tablespoons Dutch-processed cocoa powder

⅛ teaspoon baking powder

1. Preheat oven to 350°F and spray a 9" × 5" loaf pan with nonstick cooking spray.

2. In a medium bowl, use a hand mixer on medium speed to cream butter until smooth, about 30 seconds. Add brown sugar and granulated sugar and mix on medium speed until well combined, about 30 seconds. Add coffee, egg, vanilla, and peppermint extract and mix on low speed to just combine, about 10 seconds.

3. Sift flour, cocoa powder, and baking powder into bowl and mix on low speed until no dry flour remains, about 20 seconds.

4. Pour batter evenly into prepared pan. Bake 20–24 minutes or until edges are firm and center is just set.

5. Cool in pan 20 minutes, then turn out onto a cutting board and cool 20 minutes more before slicing. Serve warm or at room temperature.

Storing Cookies and Brownies

Even with small-batch baking you may have a few cookies or brownies left for the next day. The best way to store them is in an airtight container at room temperature if you plan to eat them within a day or two. For longer storage, you can stash them in the refrigerator up to a week.

FUDGE BROWNIES WITH COFFEE FROSTING

PREP TIME: 10 MIN | COOK TIME: 20 MIN | YIELDS 6 BROWNIES

If you do not have an espresso maker you can use very strong coffee or even instant coffee for the frosting.

INGREDIENTS

¼ cup salted butter, at room temperature

½ cup semisweet chocolate chips, divided

¼ cup packed light brown sugar

2 tablespoons granulated sugar

1 tablespoon honey

1 large egg

½ teaspoon pure vanilla extract

¼ cup all-purpose flour

3 tablespoons cocoa powder

¼ cup chopped pecans

¼ cup unsalted butter

¾ cup powdered sugar

2 tablespoons espresso, cooled to room temperature

⅛ teaspoon salt

1. Preheat oven to 350°F. Spray a 9" × 5" loaf pan with nonstick cooking spray and then line pan with parchment, making sure there is an overhang of at least 3".

2. In a medium microwave-safe bowl, combine salted butter and 2 tablespoons chocolate chips. Microwave in 30-second intervals, stirring well between each interval, until melted.

3. To melted chocolate, add brown sugar, granulated sugar, and honey and mix with a spatula until well combined. Add egg and vanilla and beat until egg is thoroughly combined, about thirty strokes.

4. Sift flour and cocoa powder into bowl and gently fold six to eight times until the dry ingredients are just incorporated, then add remaining chocolate chips and pecans and fold to combine, about five strokes.

5. Pour batter evenly into prepared pan. Bake 20–24 minutes or until edges are firm and center is set.

6. Cool in pan 20 minutes, then use excess parchment to lift brownies onto a cutting board to cool to room temperature.

7. In a small bowl, combine unsalted butter, powdered sugar, espresso, and salt. Beat on low speed for 30 seconds, then increase speed to medium and beat for 1 minute or until well combined and fluffy. Spread frosting over cooled brownies. Serve.

NUTTY BROWNIES

PREP TIME: 10 MIN | COOK TIME: 20 MIN | YIELDS 6 BROWNIES

Nuts are rich in antioxidants and fiber, and they are delicious, so adding a variety of nuts to your diet is always a good idea. With this recipe, you can get your nut fix in the form of a fudgy brownie packed with walnuts, pecans, and hazelnuts!

INGREDIENTS

¼ cup salted butter, at room temperature

⅓ cup packed light brown sugar

3 tablespoons granulated sugar

1 teaspoon corn syrup

1 large egg

½ teaspoon pure vanilla extract

¼ cup all-purpose flour

3 tablespoons cocoa powder

⅛ teaspoon baking soda

⅓ cup chopped pecans, divided

⅓ cup chopped walnuts, divided

⅓ cup chopped hazelnuts, divided

1. Preheat oven to 350°F and spray a 9" × 5" loaf pan with nonstick cooking spray.

2. In a medium bowl, use a hand mixer on medium speed to cream butter until smooth, about 30 seconds. Add brown sugar, granulated sugar, and corn syrup and mix on medium speed until well combined, about 30 seconds. Add egg and vanilla and mix on low speed to just combine, about 10 seconds.

3. Sift flour, cocoa powder, and baking soda into bowl and mix on low speed until no dry flour remains, about 20 seconds. Fold in ¼ cup each pecans, walnuts, and hazelnuts until evenly distributed.

4. Pour batter evenly into prepared pan, then sprinkle remaining nuts evenly over top. Bake 20–24 minutes or until edges are firm and center is just set.

5. Cool in pan 20 minutes, then turn out onto a cutting board and cool 20 minutes more before slicing. Serve warm or at room temperature.

ALMOND BUTTER OATMEAL BLONDIES

PREP TIME: 10 MIN | COOK TIME: 20 MIN | YIELDS 6 BLONDIES

Nut butters make an excellent substitute for dairy butter in many recipes while also adding a lovely, nutty taste. If you don't have almond butter on hand, you can make these with peanut butter, sunflower butter, or cashew butter.

INGREDIENTS

¼ cup creamy almond butter

⅓ cup packed light brown sugar

2 tablespoons maple syrup

1 large egg yolk

¾ teaspoon pure vanilla extract

½ cup all-purpose flour

¼ teaspoon ground cinnamon

⅛ teaspoon baking powder

½ cup old-fashioned oats

¼ cup chopped almonds

1. Preheat oven to 350°F and spray a 9" × 5" loaf pan with nonstick cooking spray.

2. In a medium bowl, use a hand mixer on medium speed to cream almond butter until smooth, about 30 seconds. Add brown sugar and maple syrup and mix on medium speed until well combined, about 30 seconds. Add egg yolk and vanilla and mix on low speed to just combine, about 10 seconds.

3. Sift flour, cinnamon, and baking powder into bowl and mix on low speed until no dry flour remains, about 20 seconds. Fold in oats until well combined.

4. Pour batter evenly into prepared pan. Sprinkle top evenly with almonds. Bake 20–24 minutes or until edges are firm and center is just set.

5. Cool in pan 20 minutes, then turn out onto a cutting board and cool 20 minutes more before slicing. Serve warm or at room temperature.

Homemade Nut Butters

If you need a small amount of nut butter for a recipe and you do not want to buy a whole jar, you can make it at home. Simply toast 1½ cups of raw nuts in a dry skillet over medium-low heat until fragrant, about 10 minutes. Let them cool, then add them to a food processor or high-powered blender and process until smooth, 10–12 minutes. You can add a pinch of salt and a little sugar to your nut butter once it is smooth, then let it cool to room temperature and store it in an airtight container in your pantry.

DULCE DE LECHE BLONDIES

PREP TIME: 10 MIN | COOK TIME: 20 MIN | YIELDS 6 BLONDIES

Dulce de leche, which translates to "candy milk" or "sweet milk," is a Latin American treat made by slowly cooking milk and sugar for hours until the mixture is deeply caramelized and thick. You can find it in cans or squeeze tubes in most grocery stores.

INGREDIENTS

¼ cup salted butter, at room temperature

¼ cup packed light brown sugar

3 tablespoons granulated sugar

1 tablespoon honey

1 large egg yolk

¾ teaspoon pure vanilla extract

½ cup all-purpose flour

¼ teaspoon ground cinnamon

⅛ teaspoon baking powder

⅓ cup prepared dulce de leche

1. Preheat oven to 350°F and spray a 9" × 5" loaf pan with nonstick cooking spray.

2. In a medium bowl, use a hand mixer on medium speed to cream butter until smooth, about 30 seconds. Add brown sugar, granulated sugar, and honey and mix on medium speed until well combined, about 30 seconds. Add egg yolk and vanilla and mix on low speed to just combine, about 10 seconds.

3. Sift flour, cinnamon, and baking powder into bowl and mix on low speed until no dry flour remains, about 20 seconds.

4. Pour batter evenly into prepared pan. Dollop dulce de leche over top of batter, then use a butter knife to swirl into batter. Bake 20–24 minutes or until edges are firm and center is just set.

5. Cool in pan 20 minutes, then turn out onto a cutting board and cool 20 minutes more before slicing. Serve warm or at room temperature.

CHAPTER 3

CAKES AND CHEESECAKES

When you think of a celebration, a party, or a gathering of friends and family you probably think of cake. Whether it is a stacked-up layer cake, creamy cheesecake, or a lightning-fast mug cake, cake makes an ordinary day feel special and a rough day feel not so bad. Cakes have a magical, nostalgic quality to them, and when you are eating cake, it is hard to feel bad. The trouble with most cake recipes is they make more than one person could (or should) eat in one sitting. Thankfully, there is a solution!

In this chapter we will explore a variety of individual or small-batch layer cakes, mug cakes, cupcakes, skillet cakes, and cheesecakes. Before you ask, this chapter also has small-batch frosting recipes perfect for one small layer cake or six cupcakes, because what is cake without frosting? Scaled down to make enough for one, these cakes, cupcakes, mug cakes, and cheesecakes are a great way to celebrate, comfort, or simply indulge. With perfectly portioned cakes, any day of the week can be your personal celebration!

CHOCOLATE LAYER CAKE FOR ONE

PREP TIME: 10 MIN | COOK TIME: 18 MIN | YIELDS 1 (4") ROUND LAYER CAKE

Have you ever wanted a whole layer cake for yourself? Now you can have one, and you do not have to share! This cake is very tender and moist and keeps well at room temperature in a covered container for up to three days. If you find you can't finish the whole cake in one sitting, place a little plastic wrap or parchment against the exposed cake to keep it fresh.

INGREDIENTS

⅔ cup all-purpose flour

¼ cup cocoa powder

½ teaspoon baking soda

¼ teaspoon salt

¼ cup vegetable oil

½ cup granulated sugar

1 large egg yolk

2 tablespoons whole milk

½ teaspoon pure vanilla extract

½ cup boiling water

1. Preheat oven to 350°F and spray two 4" × 2" round cake pans with nonstick cooking spray.

2. In a medium bowl, sift together flour, cocoa powder, baking soda, and salt. Set aside.

3. In a small bowl, whisk together oil, sugar, egg yolk, milk, and vanilla. Pour into flour mixture and stir until just combined. Add boiling water in four additions, stirring until smooth after each addition.

4. Divide batter between prepared cake pans. Bake 18–22 minutes or until cakes spring back when gently pressed in center and edges come away from sides of pan.

5. Cool in pans 10 minutes before turning out onto wire racks to cool to room temperature.

6. Once cakes are cooled frost as desired and serve.

Types of Cocoa Powder

There are two main types of cocoa powder. One is unsweetened cocoa powder, or natural cocoa powder. Natural cocoa powder is acidic and works better with baking soda to enhance leavening. With Dutch-processed cocoa powder, the cocoa beans are washed in an alkaline solution to reduce acidity. You should use Dutch-processed cocoa powder in recipes that call for baking powder, as it has an acid included and does not rely on the cocoa powder for that additional boost.

CHOCOLATE BUTTERCREAM

PREP TIME: 10 MIN | COOK TIME: 0 MIN | YIELDS ABOUT 1 CUP

This frosting is a no-cook buttercream, so it is guaranteed to be quick, easy, and luscious. This recipe yields enough frosting for one 4" round layer cake or six cupcakes.

INGREDIENTS

4 tablespoons unsalted butter, at room temperature

1 cup powdered sugar

¼ cup cocoa powder

⅛ teaspoon salt

1 tablespoon whole milk

¼ teaspoon pure vanilla extract

1. In a medium bowl, use a hand mixer on medium speed to cream butter until smooth.

2. Add sugar, cocoa powder, and salt and mix on low speed until just combined, about 30 seconds.

3. Add milk and vanilla and beat on medium speed until smooth and fluffy, about 1 minute.

VANILLA BUTTERCREAM

PREP TIME: 10 MIN | COOK TIME: 0 MIN | YIELDS ABOUT 1 CUP

The combination of vanilla extract, almond extract, and butter extract gives this frosting a rich and complex flavor like the frosting from a bakery. This recipe yields enough frosting for one 4" round layer cake or six cupcakes.

INGREDIENTS

4 tablespoons unsalted butter, at room temperature

1 cup powdered sugar

⅛ teaspoon salt

1 tablespoon heavy cream

¼ teaspoon pure vanilla extract

⅛ teaspoon butter-flavored extract

1 drop (about 1/16 teaspoon) almond extract

1. In a medium bowl, use a hand mixer on medium speed to cream butter until smooth.

2. Add sugar and salt to bowl. Mix on low speed until just combined, about 10 seconds.

3. Add cream, vanilla, butter extract, and almond extract. Increase speed to medium and beat until smooth and fluffy, about 1 minute.

GOLDEN BUTTER CAKE FOR ONE

PREP TIME: 10 MIN | COOK TIME: 18 MIN | YIELDS 1 (4") ROUND LAYER CAKE

Butter cake can go from perfectly moist to dry and crumbly in no time, so be sure not to overbake it, or it could turn out dry. Start checking early. The cake is ready when the edges are just pulling back from the sides of the pan and it springs back when you touch the center.

INGREDIENTS

1 cup all-purpose flour

½ teaspoon baking powder

⅛ teaspoon salt

⅔ cup granulated sugar

6 tablespoons unsalted butter, at room temperature

1 large egg

½ teaspoon pure vanilla extract

⅛ teaspoon almond extract

⅓ cup whole milk, at room temperature

1. Preheat oven to 350°F and spray two 4" × 2" round cake pans with nonstick cooking spray.

2. In a medium bowl, sift together flour, baking powder, and salt. Set aside.

3. In a separate medium bowl, add sugar and butter. Use a hand mixer on medium speed to cream until smooth, about 1 minute, then add egg, vanilla, and almond extract and blend until well combined and fluffy, about 1 minute.

4. Add flour mixture to wet ingredients alternately with milk, beating on low speed after each addition until just combined, about 10 seconds.

5. Divide batter between prepared pans. Bake 18–22 minutes or until cakes spring back when gently pressed in center and edges come away from sides of pan. Cool in pans 10 minutes before turning out onto wire racks to cool to room temperature.

6. Once cakes are cooled frost as desired and serve.

MOLTEN CHOCOLATE CAKE

PREP TIME: 10 MIN | COOK TIME: 20 MIN | SERVES 1

Molten Chocolate Cake, with its flowing chocolate center, is easier to make than most people think. It a fun dessert to treat yourself with any time of the day. A scoop of vanilla ice cream or sweetened whipped cream is the perfect accompaniment to this cake.

INGREDIENTS

2 ounces chopped dark chocolate

2 ounces salted butter, at room temperature

1 large egg

2 tablespoons granulated sugar

¼ teaspoon pure vanilla extract

1 tablespoon plus 1 teaspoon all-purpose flour

1. Preheat oven to 350°F. Spray an 8-ounce ramekin with nonstick cooking spray.

2. In the top of a simmering double-boiler, add chocolate. Heat until melted. Remove chocolate from heat and stir in butter until melted. Set aside.

3. In a medium bowl, combine egg and sugar. Use a hand mixer to beat on medium speed until light and fluffy, about 1 minute. Stir in vanilla and chocolate mixture until well combined, then add flour and mix on low speed until no lumps remain, about 30 seconds.

4. Transfer batter to prepared ramekin. Bake 20–25 minutes or until edges of cake are firm and coming away from ramekin but center is soft when gently pressed.

5. Cool cake in ramekin 1 minute before serving. You can serve directly in ramekin or run a thin knife around the edge of the ramekin and carefully turn cake out onto a small plate. Enjoy immediately.

CONFETTI MUG CAKE

PREP TIME: 5 MIN | COOK TIME: 1 MIN | SERVES 1

Need cake in a hurry? A mug cake is the perfect solution. Ready in minutes, a mug cake is the perfect single-serving cake for any time of day or night. Be sure your mug is microwave-safe; otherwise, the handle may become very hot while cooking.

INGREDIENTS

¼ cup all-purpose flour

¼ teaspoon baking powder

1 tablespoon plus 1 teaspoon granulated sugar

3 tablespoons whole milk

1 tablespoon vegetable oil

¼ teaspoon pure vanilla extract

2 tablespoons rainbow sprinkles, divided

2 tablespoons whipped cream

1. In an 8-ounce microwave-safe mug, add flour, baking powder, sugar, milk, oil, and vanilla. Mix with a fork until smooth, then stir in 1½ tablespoons sprinkles.

2. Microwave on high 60–90 seconds or until cake is puffed and cooked through and the top is no longer shiny.

3. Let cake rest in microwave 1 minute, then carefully remove and top with whipped cream and remaining ½ tablespoon sprinkles. Serve immediately.

BOSTON CREAM PIE

PREP TIME: 2¼ HOURS | COOK TIME: 23 MIN | YIELDS 1 (4") ROUND LAYER CAKE

Invented in Boston in the nineteenth century, Bostin Cream Pie is actually a cake made of soft sponge cake layers filled with vanilla custard and topped with chocolate frosting. You can speed up this recipe by swapping the custard for ready-made pudding from the grocery store!

INGREDIENTS

1 cup all-purpose flour

½ teaspoon baking powder

⅛ teaspoon salt

½ cup plus 2 tablespoons granulated sugar, divided

¼ cup vegetable oil

1 large egg

1 teaspoon pure vanilla extract, divided

⅓ cup plus ½ cup whole milk, at room temperature, divided

1 large egg yolk, at room temperature

2 teaspoons cornstarch

1 tablespoon salted butter

2 tablespoons heavy cream

1 tablespoon corn syrup

1 ounce chopped bittersweet chocolate

1. Preheat oven to 350°F and spray two 4" × 2" round cake pans with nonstick cooking spray.

2. In a medium bowl, sift together flour, baking powder, and salt. Set aside.

3. In a separate medium bowl, add ½ cup sugar, oil, egg, and ½ teaspoon vanilla and use a hand mixer to beat on medium speed until well combined, about 1 minute.

4. Add flour mixture alternately with ⅓ cup milk, beating on low speed after each addition until just combined, about 10 seconds.

5. Divide batter between prepared pans. Bake 18–22 minutes or until cakes spring back when gently pressed in center and edges come away from sides of pan. Cool in pans 10 minutes before turning out onto wire racks to cool to room temperature.

6 While cakes cool, prepare filling. In a small sauce-pan over medium heat, warm the remaining ½ cup milk until it just simmers. In a small bowl, whisk 2 tablespoons warm milk into egg yolk to temper, then add to warm milk in pan along with remaining 2 tablespoons sugar and cornstarch. Whisking con-stantly, bring to a boil, about 4 minutes, and then cook 15 seconds. Turn off heat and whisk in butter and remaining ½ teaspoon vanilla. Transfer custard to a bowl, cover surface of custard with plastic, and refrigerate 2 hours or until well chilled.

7 While custard cools, prepare frosting. In a small saucepan, add cream and corn syrup. Heat until it just simmers, then pour into a heatproof bowl and add chocolate. Let stand 1 minute, then stir until chocolate is melted and frosting is smooth.

8 To assemble, place cake layer top-side down on a large plate. Spread cooled custard over cake, top with second cake top-side down, and spread frost-ing over top. Serve immediately, or refrigerate up to three days in an airtight container.

CHOCOLATE MUG CAKE

PREP TIME: 5 MIN | COOK TIME: 1 MIN | SERVES 1

The secret to making this Chocolate Mug Cake moist and flavorful is mayonnaise. It replaces oil and egg in this recipe, as well as salt.

INGREDIENTS

3 tablespoons all-purpose flour

3 tablespoons light brown sugar

3 tablespoons Dutch-processed cocoa powder

⅛ teaspoon baking powder

2 tablespoons mayonnaise

2 tablespoons heavy cream

1 tablespoon water

¼ teaspoon pure vanilla extract

1. In an 8-ounce microwave-safe mug, add flour, brown sugar, cocoa powder, and baking powder. Whisk well to combine, then add the remaining ingredients and stir until mixture is smooth. Be careful not to overmix. Use a small spatula to scrape batter from the edges of the mug.

2. Microwave on high 60–90 seconds or until cake rises and center is firm.

3. Cool 30 seconds before removing from microwave and enjoying.

VANILLA MUG CAKE

PREP TIME: 5 MIN | COOK TIME: 1 MIN | SERVES 1

Vanilla beans offer a bright, rich vanilla flavor with a hint of fruitiness. They add a robust vanilla flavor to this quick and easy cake!

INGREDIENTS

1 tablespoon salted butter

¼ cup all-purpose flour

¼ teaspoon baking powder

1 tablespoon plus 1 teaspoon granulated sugar

3 tablespoons whole milk

½ teaspoon vanilla beans scraped from 1 vanilla pod

2 tablespoons whipped cream

1. In an 8-ounce microwave-safe mug, add butter. Microwave on high 20–30 seconds or until melted.

2. To mug, add flour, baking powder, sugar, milk, and vanilla beans. Mix with a fork until smooth.

3. Microwave on high 60–90 seconds or until cake is puffed and the top is no longer shiny.

4. Let cake rest in microwave 1 minute, then remove and top with whipped cream. Serve immediately.

GERMAN CHOCOLATE CUPCAKES

PREP TIME: 30 MIN | COOK TIME: 26 MIN | YIELDS 6 CUPCAKES

The German Chocolate Cake we know today was created in 1852 when baker Samuel German wanted to develop a recipe for his brand of sweet baking chocolate. This interpretation transforms the traditional layer cake into cupcakes!

INGREDIENTS

½ cup all-purpose flour

2 tablespoons cocoa powder

½ teaspoon baking powder

¼ teaspoon baking soda

¼ teaspoon salt

½ cup granulated sugar

3 tablespoons vegetable oil

2 tablespoons sour cream

2 large egg yolks, divided

½ teaspoon pure vanilla extract, divided

½ cup boiling water

¼ cup evaporated milk

¼ cup packed light brown sugar

2 tablespoons salted butter

½ cup shredded sweetened coconut

⅓ cup chopped pecans

1 recipe Chocolate Buttercream (see recipe in this chapter)

1. Preheat oven to 350°F and line six cups of a muffin pan with paper liners.

2. In a medium bowl, sift together flour, cocoa powder, baking powder, baking soda, and salt. Set aside.

3. In a small bowl, whisk together granulated sugar, oil, sour cream, 1 egg yolk, and ¼ teaspoon vanilla. Pour into flour mixture and stir until just combined. Add boiling water in two additions, stirring until smooth after each addition.

4. Divide batter between cupcake liners. Bake 16–18 minutes or until cakes spring back in center when gently pressed. Cool in pans 5 minutes before turning out onto wire racks to cool to room temperature.

5. Next, prepare the coconut pecan topping. In a small saucepan over medium heat, add milk, remaining egg yolk, brown sugar, and butter and mix until egg yolk is completely incorporated. Stir constantly until mixture comes to a boil and thickens, 10–12 minutes. Stir in remaining ¼ teaspoon vanilla, coconut, and pecans. Cool to room temperature.

6. To assemble, pipe a thick ring of Chocolate Buttercream around the edge of each cupcake. Spoon coconut pecan filling into the center. Serve or store cupcakes in the refrigerator in an airtight container up to 3 days.

JAPANESE-STYLE STRAWBERRY CAKE

PREP TIME: 10 MIN | COOK TIME: 18 MIN | YIELDS 1 (4") ROUND LAYER CAKE

This refreshing cake is called "strawberry shortcake" in Japan. It is a popular celebration cake there, and is often served for birthdays and anniversaries and during the holiday season. It is frosted with whipped cream and is best eaten the day it is made.

INGREDIENTS

1 cup all-purpose flour

½ teaspoon baking powder

⅛ teaspoon salt

1 large egg, yolk and white separated

⅔ cup granulated sugar, divided

⅓ cup unsalted butter, at room temperature

¾ teaspoon pure vanilla extract, divided

⅓ cup whole milk, at room temperature

⅓ heavy whipping cream

1 tablespoon powdered sugar

6 medium strawberries, tops removed and cut in half

1. Preheat oven to 350°F and spray two 4" × 2" round cake pans with nonstick cooking spray.

2. In a medium bowl, sift together flour, baking powder, and salt. Set aside.

3. In a separate medium bowl, add egg white. Use a hand mixer to beat on medium speed until frothy, about 20 seconds. While continuing to beat, slowly add 2 tablespoons granulated sugar. Once sugar is added, continue to beat until egg white forms firm peaks, 20–40 seconds. Set aside.

4. In a third medium bowl, use hand mixer on medium speed to cream butter until smooth, then add egg yolk, remaining granulated sugar, and ½ teaspoon vanilla. Beat until well combined and fluffy, about 1 minute.

5. Add flour mixture to wet ingredients alternately with milk, beating on low speed after each addition until just combined, about 10 seconds each. Fold in beaten egg white in two additions, folding until no streaks of egg white remain.

6. Divide batter between prepared pans. Bake 18–22 minutes or until cakes spring back when gently pressed in center and edges come away from sides of pan. Cool in pans 10 minutes before turning out onto wire racks to cool to room temperature.

7. Once cakes are cooled, prepare the filling. In a medium bowl, combine whipping cream, powdered sugar, and remaining ¼ teaspoon vanilla. Use a hand mixer to beat on low speed until sugar is dissolved, about 20 seconds, then beat on medium-high speed until the cream forms soft peaks, about 1 minute.

8. To assemble, place one cake layer top-side down on a large plate. Spread 2 tablespoons whipped cream over cake. Top with 6 strawberry halves, then 2 more tablespoons cream. Place second cake layer top-side down over cream, then frost top of cake with remaining cream. Decorate top with remaining strawberries. Enjoy immediately or refrigerate in an airtight container up to 4 hours.

STRAWBERRY SHORTCAKE

PREP TIME: 10 MIN | COOK TIME: 12 MIN | SERVES 1

This recipe takes the humble strawberry shortcake to the next level! This sweet version adds extra flavor to every bite with a hint of cinnamon and vanilla and a crunchy sugar topping. Fresh strawberries are traditional, but you can make this with blueberries, raspberries, or blackberries. You can even use sliced bananas if you want!

INGREDIENTS

¼ cup plus 1 teaspoon all-purpose flour

¼ teaspoon baking powder

1 teaspoon granulated sugar

⅛ teaspoon ground cinnamon

1 tablespoon cubed salted butter, chilled

2 tablespoons buttermilk

⅛ teaspoon pure vanilla extract

1 teaspoon coarse sanding sugar

½ cup whipped cream

3 medium-sized fresh strawberries, hulled and chopped

1. Preheat oven to 350°F and line a baking sheet with parchment or reusable silicone baking mat.

2. In a medium bowl, combine flour, baking powder, granulated sugar, and cinnamon. Whisk well to combine. Add butter and use your fingers to rub mixture until it resembles coarse sand.

3. Make a well in dry ingredients and add buttermilk and vanilla. Gently stir until a shaggy dough forms and no dry flour remains.

4. Transfer dough onto prepared baking sheet in one heaped mound and sprinkle sanding sugar over top. Bake 12–15 minutes or until biscuit is puffed and golden brown. Cool on the baking sheet 5 minutes before transferring to a large plate.

5. To serve, split biscuit in half horizontally. Spoon ¾ of whipped cream onto bottom biscuit. Sprinkle ¾ of strawberries on cream. Top with biscuit half and garnish with remaining cream and strawberries. Serve immediately.

Tart Strawberries?

If you have berries that are not as sweet as you would like, you can cheat the sweetness by adding ¼ teaspoon sugar for every two chopped or sliced strawberries. The sugar will draw out some of the berries' liquid and will add the sweetness they are missing. Let the berries and sugar stand for 5 minutes, then drain off any excess liquid before using the mixture. This method will make the berries a little softer, but that is a small price to pay for sweet perfection.

CREAM-FILLED CUPCAKES

These Cream-Filled Cupcakes are the elevated version of the classic store-bought treat. You can make this filling for any kind of cupcake, and you can even use it to fill sandwich cookies.

INGREDIENTS

½ cup all-purpose flour

2 tablespoons cocoa powder

½ teaspoon baking powder

¼ teaspoon baking soda

3/8 teaspoon salt, divided

½ cup granulated sugar

3 tablespoons vegetable oil

2 tablespoons sour cream

1 large egg yolk

¾ teaspoon pure vanilla extract, divided

½ cup boiling water

1 teaspoon hot water

3.5 ounces (about ½ jar) marshmallow cream

¼ cup vegetable shortening

3 tablespoons powdered sugar

1 recipe Chocolate Buttercream (see recipe in this chapter)

1. Preheat oven to 350°F and line six cups of a muffin pan with paper liners.

2. In a medium bowl, sift together flour, cocoa powder, baking powder, baking soda, and ¼ teaspoon salt. Set aside.

3. In a small bowl, whisk together granulated sugar, oil, sour cream, egg yolk, and ½ teaspoon vanilla. Pour into flour mixture and stir until just combined. Add boiling water in two additions, stirring until smooth after each addition.

4. Divide batter between cupcake liners. Bake 16–18 minutes or until cakes spring back in center when gently pressed. Cool in pans 5 minutes before turning out onto wire racks to cool to room temperature.

5. Next, prepare the cupcake filling. In a medium bowl, combine hot water and remaining ⅛ teaspoon salt. Mix until salt is dissolved, then add remaining ¼ teaspoon vanilla, marshmallow cream, shortening, and powdered sugar and beat on medium speed until mixture is light and fluffy, about 2 minutes. Transfer mixture to a piping bag fitted with a round tip.

6. To assemble, use a paring knife to cut an X into the top of each cupcake. Pipe cream filling into X until it just starts to come out of the top of the cupcake. Frost tops of cupcakes with Chocolate Buttercream. Serve or store cupcakes at room temperature in an airtight container up to 3 days.

STICKY TOFFEE MUG PUDDING

You can use ready-chopped dates for this recipe, but you will need to chop them until they are quite fine so they melt into the cake. Adding a small scoop of vanilla ice cream will make this cake more like the versions served in restaurants.

INGREDIENTS

2 medium dates, finely chopped

2 tablespoons boiling water

⅛ teaspoon baking soda

1 tablespoon salted butter, melted

2 tablespoons packed light brown sugar

1 large egg yolk

1 tablespoon plus 2 teaspoons all-purpose flour

⅛ teaspoon baking powder

2 tablespoons caramel sauce

1. In an 8-ounce microwave-safe mug, add dates, water, and baking soda. Stir well, then microwave 30 seconds.

2. To mug, add butter, brown sugar, egg yolk, flour, and baking powder and mix well.

3. Microwave 1 minute 20 seconds or until cake is puffed and cooked through and the top is no longer shiny. Let cake rest in microwave 1 minute before removing.

4. Top with caramel sauce before serving. Enjoy immediately.

PUMPKIN SPICE MUG CAKE

PREP TIME: 5 MIN | COOK TIME: 1 MIN | SERVES 1

Fans of the PSL (Pumpkin Spice Latte) will enjoy this easy-to-make treat! Any leftover pumpkin purée can be refrigerated up to a week and used to make Pumpkin Spice Cheesecake (see recipe in this chapter) and Pumpkin Pie (see Chapter 5).

INGREDIENTS

¼ cup all-purpose flour

¼ teaspoon baking powder

¼ teaspoon pumpkin pie spice

1 tablespoon plus 1 teaspoon granulated sugar

2 tablespoons pumpkin purée

1 tablespoon whole milk

1 tablespoon vegetable oil

¼ teaspoon pure vanilla extract

2 tablespoons whipped cream

1 tablespoon caramel sauce

1. In an 8-ounce microwave-safe mug, add flour, baking powder, pumpkin pie spice, sugar, pumpkin purée, milk, oil, and vanilla. Mix with a fork until smooth.

2. Microwave on high 60–90 seconds or until cake is puffed and cooked through and the top is no longer shiny.

3. Let cake rest in microwave 1 minute, then carefully remove and top with whipped cream and caramel sauce. Serve immediately.

Mug Cake Tips

Here are some tips to help you become a master mug cake maker. First, don't fill your mug more than halfway with batter, or it may spill over while cooking. Second, mug cakes will puff a lot when cooking then sink back down. That is normal and to be expected. Third, mug cakes do not brown, so expect cakes to be pale (unless they are chocolate, of course). Finally, use the lowest cooking time to start, and add time as needed. Your first few cakes may need tweaking, but once you understand your microwave and how it cooks the cakes you will be able to nail the timing.

PERSONAL CHEESECAKES

PREP TIME: 4¼ HOURS | COOK TIME: 26 MIN | YIELDS 6 CHEESECAKES

Ready-crushed graham crackers are available in the baking section of most grocery stores, and leftover crumbs can be kept in the freezer for up to a year. If you have other kinds of crisp cookies, you can use them in place of the graham crackers; just be sure they are finely crushed.

INGREDIENTS

½ cup plus 2 tablespoons graham cracker crumbs

3 tablespoons granulated sugar, divided

3 tablespoons unsalted butter, melted and cooled

4 ounces cream cheese, at room temperature

¼ teaspoon freshly grated lemon zest

¼ teaspoon cornstarch

1 large egg yolk

2 tablespoons sour cream

2 teaspoons heavy cream

¼ teaspoon pure vanilla extract

1. Preheat oven to 350°F and line six cups of a muffin pan with paper liners.

2. In a small bowl, combine cracker crumbs, 1 tablespoon sugar, and butter. Mix until all crumbs are well coated in butter, then divide crumb mixture between prepared muffin cups and press down to form a crust. Bake 8–10 minutes or until crusts are firm, then remove from oven.

3. While crusts are cooling, prepare filling. In a medium bowl, add cream cheese, remaining 2 tablespoons sugar, and lemon zest. Use a hand mixer to beat on medium speed until smooth and creamy, about 2 minutes. Add cornstarch, egg yolk, and sour cream. Beat until well combined, about 30 seconds, then add heavy cream and vanilla and mix on low speed until well incorporated, about 15 seconds.

4. Divide filling between prepared crusts, then gently rap pan on counter three times to level mixture. Bake 18–20 minutes or until cheesecakes are set around edges but centers are still slightly jiggly.

5. Cool in pan to room temperature, then transfer to an airtight container and refrigerate 4 hours before serving.

CHOCOLATE MINI-CHEESECAKES

PREP TIME: 4¼ HOURS | COOK TIME: 26 MIN | YIELDS 6 CHEESECAKES

Using melted chocolate along with cocoa powder will take the chocolate flavor of these mini-cheesecakes to the next level. If you would like to add a little warm spice to these cheesecakes, swap the chocolate cookies for cinnamon graham cracker crumbs in the crust.

INGREDIENTS

½ cup plus 2 tablespoons crushed chocolate cookies

3 tablespoons packed light brown sugar, divided

3 tablespoons unsalted butter, melted and cooled

4 ounces cream cheese, at room temperature

2 tablespoons semisweet chocolate, melted and cooled

1 teaspoon Dutch-processed cocoa powder

¼ teaspoon cornstarch

1 large egg yolk

2 tablespoons sour cream

2 teaspoons heavy cream

¼ teaspoon pure vanilla extract

1. Preheat oven to 350°F and line six cups of a muffin pan with paper liners.

2. In a small bowl, combine cookie crumbs, 1 tablespoon brown sugar, and butter. Mix until all crumbs are well coated in butter, then divide crumb mixture between prepared muffin cups and press down to form a crust. Bake 8–10 minutes or until crusts are firm, then remove from oven.

3. While crusts are cooling, prepare filling. In a medium bowl, add cream cheese, melted chocolate, remaining 2 tablespoons brown sugar, and cocoa powder. Use a hand mixer to beat on medium speed until smooth and creamy, about 2 minutes. Add cornstarch, egg yolk, and sour cream. Beat until well combined, about 30 seconds, then add heavy cream and vanilla and mix on low speed until well incorporated, about 15 seconds.

4. Divide filling between prepared crusts, then gently rap pan on counter three times to level mixture. Bake 18–20 minutes or until cheesecakes are set around edges but centers are still slightly jiggly.

5. Cool in pan to room temperature, then transfer to an airtight container and refrigerate 4 hours before serving.

TEXAS SKILLET SHEET CAKE

PREP TIME: 10 MIN | COOK TIME: 25 MIN | SERVES 1

The origins of this cake are murky at best, but what we do know is that this cake is a staple of potlucks and buffets across Texas and most of America. If you have sour cream on hand, you can substitute it in equal amounts for buttermilk to make the cake even more tender and soft.

INGREDIENTS

¼ cup all-purpose flour

¼ cup granulated sugar

½ teaspoon baking powder

⅛ teaspoon ground cinnamon

4 tablespoons salted butter, divided

5 tablespoons cocoa powder, divided

3 tablespoons water

¼ cup buttermilk

1 large egg

½ teaspoon pure vanilla extract

2 tablespoons whole milk

½ cup powdered sugar

3 tablespoons chopped toasted pecans

1. Preheat oven to 350°F and lightly spray a 6¼" cast iron skillet with nonstick cooking spray.

2. In a medium bowl, add flour, granulated sugar, baking powder, and cinnamon. Whisk to combine, then set aside.

3. In a small saucepan, add 3 tablespoons butter, 3 tablespoons cocoa powder, and water. Heat over medium-low heat, stirring constantly, until butter is melted and cocoa is dissolved, about 5 minutes. Remove from heat and cool slightly, about 3 minutes then add buttermilk, egg, and vanilla and whisk until well combined.

4. Pour wet ingredients into dry and stir until combined, about twelve strokes. Pour batter into prepared skillet and bake 18–22 minutes or until cake springs back when gently pressed in center and edges come away from sides of pan. Remove from oven.

5. While cake cools, prepare frosting. In a small saucepan over medium-low heat, add remaining 1 tablespoon butter, remaining 2 tablespoons cocoa powder, and milk. Once butter has melted and cocoa powder has dissolved, remove from heat and add powdered sugar. Mix until smooth, then add pecans. Pour frosting over warm cake, then allow to cool to room temperature before serving.

LEMON POUND CAKE

PREP TIME: 15 MIN | COOK TIME: 28 MIN | SERVES 1

When it comes to a refreshingly sweet snack to liven up a dull afternoon, you can't go wrong with this tart yet sweet Lemon Pound Cake! Use freshly squeezed lemon juice in the cake and in the glaze for the best flavor.

INGREDIENTS

½ cup all-purpose flour

½ teaspoon baking powder

¼ cup salted butter, at room temperature

½ cup granulated sugar

1 large egg, at room temperature

3½ teaspoons freshly squeezed lemon juice, divided

1 teaspoon freshly grated lemon zest

¼ teaspoon pure vanilla extract

2 tablespoons whole milk

¼ cup powdered sugar

1. Preheat oven to 350°F and spray a 5" × 3" mini-loaf pan with nonstick cooking spray.

2. In a small bowl, add flour and baking powder. Whisk well to incorporate. Set aside.

3. In a medium bowl, add butter and granulated sugar. Use a hand mixer on low speed to cream until sugar is just dissolved, about 10 seconds, then increase speed to medium and beat until light and fluffy, about 2 minutes. Add egg, 2 teaspoons lemon juice, lemon zest, and vanilla and beat until well combined, about 20 seconds.

4. Add flour mixture alternately with milk in three additions, mixing until just combined and no dry flour remains.

5. Transfer batter to prepared pan. Bake 28–30 minutes or until cake springs back when gently pressed in center and edges come away from sides of pan. Cool cake completely in pan before turning out.

6. Once cake is cooled, prepare glaze. In a small bowl, combine remaining 1½ teaspoons lemon juice with powdered sugar and whisk until smooth. Spoon glaze over cooled cake. Serve immediately or cover and store at room temperature up to 3 days.

TURTLE CHEESECAKE

PREP TIME: 2¼ HOURS | COOK TIME: 30 MIN | SERVES 1

Caramel ice cream topping is an easy way to add rich caramel flavor to most desserts like this one, and it will keep in the refrigerator up to a year. If you prefer, you can make the caramel topping by melting three wrapped soft caramels with 1 teaspoon heavy cream in a microwave until smooth.

INGREDIENTS

¼ cup graham cracker crumbs

2 tablespoons granulated sugar, divided

1 tablespoon unsalted butter, melted and cooled

2 ounces cream cheese, at room temperature

¼ teaspoon cornstarch

1 large egg yolk

1 tablespoon sour cream

1 teaspoon heavy cream

¼ teaspoon pure vanilla extract

3 tablespoons caramel sauce

2 tablespoons chopped toasted pecans

2 tablespoons semisweet chocolate, melted

1. Preheat oven to 350°F and spray the bottom of a 4" springform pan with nonstick cooking spray.

2. In a small bowl, combine cracker crumbs, 1 tablespoon sugar, and butter. Mix until all crumbs are well coated in butter, then transfer crumb mixture to prepared pan and press down to form a crust. Bake 8–10 minutes or until crust is firm, then remove from oven.

3. While crust is cooling, prepare filling. In a medium bowl, add cream cheese and remaining 1 tablespoon sugar. Use a hand mixer to beat on medium speed until smooth and creamy, about 2 minutes. Add cornstarch, egg yolk, and sour cream. Beat until well combined, about 30 seconds, then add heavy cream and vanilla and mix on low speed until well incorporated, about 15 seconds.

4. Spread filling onto crust, then gently rap pan on counter three times to level mixture. Bake 22–25 minutes or until cheesecake is set around edges but still slightly jiggly in center. Cool in pan to room temperature, then transfer to an airtight container and refrigerate 2 hours.

5. To assemble, spread caramel sauce over top of cheesecake. Sprinkle pecans over caramel, then drizzle melted chocolate over top. Serve immediately or cover and chill up to 5 days.

CARROT CAKE WITH CREAM CHEESE FROSTING

PREP TIME: 10 MIN | COOK TIME: 18 MIN | YIELDS 1 (4") ROUND LAYER CAKE

The trick to keeping this Carrot Cake extra-moist and tender is swapping vegetable oil for butter.

INGREDIENTS

1 cup all-purpose flour

½ teaspoon baking powder

¾ teaspoon ground cinnamon, divided

⅛ teaspoon ground nutmeg

⅛ teaspoon ground cloves

⅛ teaspoon salt

⅔ cup granulated sugar

6 tablespoons vegetable oil

1 large egg

¾ teaspoon pure vanilla extract, divided

⅓ cup whole milk, at room temperature

¼ cup finely grated carrot

1 ounce cream cheese, at room temperature

2 tablespoons unsalted butter, at room temperature

½ cup powdered sugar

1. Preheat oven to 350°F and spray two 4" × 2" round cake pans with nonstick cooking spray.

2. In a medium bowl, sift together flour, baking powder, ½ teaspoon cinnamon, nutmeg, cloves, and salt. Set aside.

3. In a large bowl, add granulated sugar, oil, egg, and ½ teaspoon vanilla. Use a hand mixer to blend on low speed until well combined, about 1 minute.

4. Add flour mixture alternately with milk, beating on low speed after each addition until just combined, about 10 seconds per addition. Fold in grated carrot.

5. Divide batter between prepared pans. Bake 18–22 minutes or until cakes spring back when gently pressed in center and edges come away from sides of pan. Cool in pans 10 minutes before turning out onto wire racks to cool to room temperature.

6. Once cakes are cooled, prepare frosting. In a medium bowl, combine cream cheese and butter. Use a hand mixer to beat on low speed until smooth, about 1 minute. Add powdered sugar, remaining cinnamon, and remaining vanilla and beat until smooth and fluffy, about 1 minute.

7. To assemble, place one cake layer top-side down on a large plate. Add half of frosting and spread in an even layer. Top with second cake layer top-side down and spread remaining frosting over top. Enjoy immediately or refrigerate up to 3 days.

VANILLA BEAN CHEESECAKE WITH CHERRY TOPPING

PREP TIME: 4¼ HOURS | COOK TIME: 33 MIN | SERVES 1

Dark sweet cherries are available in the freezer section year-round and are always sweet and tasty.

INGREDIENTS

¼ cup vanilla wafer cookie crumbs

2 tablespoons granulated sugar, divided

1 tablespoon unsalted butter, melted and cooled

2 ounces cream cheese, at room temperature

¼ teaspoon cornstarch

1 large egg yolk

1 tablespoon sour cream

1 teaspoon heavy cream

¼ teaspoon vanilla bean paste

¼ cup frozen chopped dark sweet cherries, thawed

1 tablespoon powdered sugar

⅛ teaspoon almond extract

1. Preheat oven to 350°F and spray the bottom of a 4" springform pan with nonstick cooking spray.

2. In a small bowl, combine vanilla wafer crumbs, 1 tablespoon granulated sugar, and butter. Mix until all crumbs are well coated in butter, then transfer crumb mixture to prepared pan and press down to form a crust. Bake 8–10 minutes or until crust is firm, then remove from oven.

3. While crust is cooling, prepare filling. In a medium bowl, add cream cheese and remaining 1 tablespoon sugar. Use a hand mixer to beat on medium speed until smooth and creamy, about 2 minutes. Add cornstarch, egg yolk, and sour cream. Beat until well combined, about 30 seconds, then add heavy cream and vanilla bean paste and mix on low speed until well incorporated, about 15 seconds.

4. Spread filling onto crust, then gently rap pan on counter three times to level mixture. Bake 22–25 minutes or until cheesecake is set around edges but still slightly jiggly in center. Cool in pan, then put in an airtight container and refrigerate 2 hours.

5. To prepare the topping, in a small saucepan over medium-low heat, add cherries and powdered sugar. Bring to a simmer, about 2 minutes, then reduce heat to low and cook, stirring constantly, until cherries are thick, about 1 minute. Remove from heat and stir in almond extract. Cool completely before spooning over cheesecake. Serve immediately.

BUTTER RUM MUG CAKE

PREP TIME: 5 MIN | COOK TIME: 3 MIN | SERVES 1

If you prefer not to use rum or do not have it, you can stir in ⅛ teaspoon of rum extract after melting the butter and brown sugar, or you can leave it out and add an additional ⅛ teaspoon of vanilla.

INGREDIENTS

1 tablespoon salted butter

1 teaspoon dark rum

1 tablespoon plus 3 teaspoons packed light brown sugar, divided

¼ cup all-purpose flour

¼ teaspoon baking powder

3 tablespoons whole milk

1 tablespoon vegetable oil

¼ teaspoon pure vanilla extract

1. In a small microwave-safe bowl, combine butter, rum, and 2 teaspoons brown sugar. Microwave 30 seconds, stir, then heat for 15-second bursts until butter is melted and bubbling and sugar is dissolved. Set aside.

2. In an 8-ounce microwave-safe mug, add flour, baking powder, remaining 1 tablespoon plus 1 teaspoon brown sugar, milk, oil, and vanilla. Mix with a fork until smooth.

3. Microwave on high 60–90 seconds or until cake is puffed and cooked through and the top is no longer shiny.

4. Let cake rest in microwave 1 minute, then carefully remove. With a toothpick poke a few holes into cake, then pour butter rum mixture over it. Serve immediately.

PUMPKIN SPICE CHEESECAKE

PREP TIME: 4¼ HOURS | COOK TIME: 30 MIN | SERVES 1

This cheesecake is delicious all on its own, but if you want to add a little extra decadence you can top it with sweetened whipped cream, dust with a sprinkle of ground cinnamon, and drizzle all of that with a tablespoon of caramel sauce. A few chopped and toasted pecans would also be nice!

INGREDIENTS

¼ cup cinnamon graham cracker crumbs

1 tablespoon granulated sugar

1 tablespoon unsalted butter, melted and cooled

2 ounces cream cheese, at room temperature

2 tablespoons pumpkin purée

1 tablespoon packed light brown sugar

¼ teaspoon cornstarch

¼ teaspoon pumpkin pie spice

1 large egg yolk

1 tablespoon sour cream

1 teaspoon heavy cream

¼ teaspoon pure vanilla extract

1. Preheat oven to 350°F and spray the bottom of a 4" springform pan with nonstick cooking spray.

2. In a small bowl, combine cracker crumbs, granulated sugar, and butter. Mix until all crumbs are well coated in butter, then transfer crumb mixture into prepared pan and press down to form a crust. Bake 8–10 minutes or until crust is firm, then remove from oven.

3. While crust is cooling, prepare filling. In a medium bowl, add cream cheese, pumpkin purée, and brown sugar. Use a hand mixer to beat on medium speed until smooth and creamy, about 2 minutes. Add cornstarch, pumpkin pie spice, egg yolk, and sour cream. Beat until well combined, about 30 seconds. Add heavy cream and vanilla and mix on low speed until well incorporated, about 15 seconds.

4. Spread filling onto crust, then gently rap pan on counter three times to level mixture. Bake 22–25 minutes or until cheesecake is set around edges but still slightly jiggly in center. Cool in pan to room temperature, then transfer to an airtight container and refrigerate 2 hours before serving.

COCONUT MUG CAKE

PREP TIME: 5 MIN | COOK TIME: 1 MIN | SERVES 1

The southern holiday classic coconut cake is made quick, easy, and perfectly portioned in this mug cake adaptation. For a toasted coconut version, place coconut in a dry skillet over medium-low heat. Cook, stirring constantly, until golden brown, 5–8 minutes.

INGREDIENTS

¼ cup all-purpose flour

3 tablespoons shredded sweetened coconut, divided

1 tablespoon plus 2 teaspoons granulated sugar

¼ teaspoon baking powder

3 tablespoons whole milk

1 tablespoon vegetable oil

⅛ teaspoon pure vanilla extract

⅛ teaspoon coconut extract

2 tablespoons whipped cream

1 In an 8-ounce microwave-safe mug, add flour, 2 tablespoons coconut, sugar, baking powder, milk, oil, vanilla, and coconut extract. Mix with a fork until smooth.

2 Microwave on high 60–90 seconds or until cake is puffed and cooked through and the top is no longer shiny.

3 Let cake rest in microwave 1 minute, then carefully remove and top with whipped cream and remaining 1 tablespoon coconut. Serve immediately.

MINTY MINI-CHEESECAKES

PREP TIME: 4¼ HOURS | COOK TIME: 26 MIN | YIELDS 6 CHEESECAKES

Crushed crème de menthe candy is available around the holidays in most grocery stores, but if you can't find it, you can roughly chop whole crème de menthe candies.

INGREDIENTS

½ cup plus 2 tablespoons chocolate cookie crumbs

3 tablespoons granulated sugar, divided

3 tablespoons unsalted butter, melted and cooled

4 ounces cream cheese, at room temperature

1 tablespoon crème de menthe liqueur or ¼ teaspoon mint extract

¼ teaspoon cornstarch

1 large egg yolk

2 tablespoons sour cream

2 teaspoons heavy cream

¼ teaspoon pure vanilla extract

⅔ cup crème de menthe candy bits, divided

1. Preheat oven to 350°F and line six cups of a muffin pan with paper liners.

2. In a small bowl, combine cookie crumbs, 1 tablespoon sugar, and butter. Mix until all crumbs are well coated in butter, then divide crumb mixture between prepared muffin cups and press down to form a crust. Bake 8–10 minutes or until crusts are firm, then remove from oven.

3. While crusts are cooling, prepare filling. In a medium bowl, add cream cheese, crème de menthe liqueur or mint extract, and remaining 2 tablespoons sugar. Beat on medium speed until smooth and creamy, about 2 minutes. Add cornstarch, egg yolk, and sour cream. Beat until well combined, about 30 seconds. Add heavy cream and vanilla and mix on low speed until well incorporated, about 15 seconds. Fold in ½ cup crème de menthe candy pieces.

4. Divide filling between prepared crusts, then gently rap pan on counter three times to level mixture. Sprinkle remaining crème de menthe candy pieces on tops of cheesecakes. Bake 18–20 minutes or until cheesecakes are set around edges but still slightly jiggly in centers. Cool in pan to room temperature, then transfer to an airtight container and refrigerate 4 hours before serving.

CHOCOLATE COCONUT CUPCAKES

PREP TIME: 30 MIN | COOK TIME: 16 MIN | YIELDS 6 CUPCAKES

Chocolate and coconut are a delicious combination, and when you add luscious Vanilla Buttercream (see recipe in this chapter) to the mix you have a cupcake that coconut lovers will swoon for.

INGREDIENTS

½ cup all-purpose flour

2 tablespoons Dutch-processed cocoa powder

½ teaspoon baking powder

¼ teaspoon baking soda

¼ teaspoon salt

½ cup granulated sugar

3 tablespoons melted butter

¼ cup sour cream

1 large egg yolk

½ teaspoon pure vanilla extract

⅛ teaspoon coconut extract

¼ cup boiling water

½ cup shredded sweetened coconut

1 recipe Vanilla Buttercream (see recipe in this chapter)

1. Preheat oven to 350°F and line six cups of a muffin pan with paper liners.

2. In a medium bowl, sift together flour, cocoa powder, baking powder, baking soda, and salt. Set aside.

3. In a small bowl, whisk together sugar, butter, sour cream, egg yolk, vanilla, and coconut extract. Pour into flour mixture and stir until just combined. Add boiling water, stirring until smooth. Fold in shredded coconut.

4. Divide batter between cupcake liners. Bake 16–18 minutes or until cakes spring back in center when gently pressed. Cool in pans 5 minutes before turning out onto wire racks to cool to room temperature.

5. To assemble, frost each cupcake with Vanilla Buttercream. Store cupcakes in the refrigerator in an airtight container up to 3 days.

JELLY ROLL FOR ONE

PREP TIME: 10 MIN | COOK TIME: 8 MIN | SERVES 1

A jelly roll may seem complex, but it is really about timing. The cake must be hot when you roll it the first time to avoid cracks. If you prefer to avoid that step, cook the cake on a wire rack, cut it in half, spread the jelly on one half, top it with the second half, and enjoy!

INGREDIENTS

3 tablespoons powdered sugar, divided

¼ cup all-purpose flour

¼ teaspoon baking powder

1 large egg

⅓ cup granulated sugar

1 tablespoon water

¼ teaspoon pure vanilla extract

3 tablespoons seedless raspberry jam

1. Preheat oven to 375°F and spray a 9" × 5" loaf pan with nonstick cooking spray. Line pan with strips of parchment, allowing paper to hang over sides of pan. Spray parchment lightly with nonstick cooking spray.

2. Sprinkle a clean towel with 2 tablespoons powdered sugar. Set aside.

3. In a small bowl, sift together flour and baking powder. Set aside.

4. In a medium bowl, use a hand mixer to beat egg on high speed for 3 minutes or until pale yellow and thick. Gradually beat in granulated sugar until egg forms a ribbon when beaters are lifted from the mixture that takes a second to flatten out.

5. Reduce speed to low and beat in water and vanilla, then add flour mixture in three additions, mixing until batter is smooth between each addition.

6. Spread batter in prepared pan. Bake 8–10 minutes or until cake springs back when gently pressed in center and edges come away from sides of pan.

7. Using parchment remove cake from pan and turn out onto prepared towel. While cake is hot roll cake in towel from narrow end. Cool on a wire rack to room temperature.

8. Once cool, carefully unroll cake. Spread jam onto cake and roll up cake. Sprinkle top with remaining 1 tablespoon powdered sugar.

CRANBERRY COFFEE CAKE

PREP TIME: 10 MIN | COOK TIME: 18 MIN | SERVES 1

Cranberry Coffee Cake is the perfect treat to use up cranberry sauce around the holidays. It goes well with a cup of hot coffee or a mug of black tea. This cake uses whole-berry cranberry sauce from a can, but you can swap it for jellied cranberry sauce. You can also eliminate the cranberry sauce in place of any jam you like, so feel free to experiment!

INGREDIENTS

½ cup all-purpose flour

¼ teaspoon baking powder

¼ cup salted butter, at room temperature

¼ cup granulated sugar

1 large egg white

½ teaspoon pure vanilla extract

⅛ teaspoon almond extract

2 tablespoons sour cream

¼ cup chopped walnuts, divided

⅓ cup whole-berry cranberry sauce

1. Preheat oven to 350°F and spray a 6¼" cast iron skillet with nonstick cooking spray.

2. In a medium bowl, sift together flour and baking powder. Set aside.

3. In a separate medium bowl, add butter and sugar. Use a hand mixer on medium speed to cream until smooth, about 1 minute, then add egg white, vanilla, and almond extract and blend until well combined and fluffy, about 1 minute.

4. Add flour mixture alternately with sour cream, beating on low speed for 10 seconds after each addition until just combined.

5. Add half of batter to pan and spread until smooth. Sprinkle 2 tablespoons walnuts over top and add dollops of cranberry sauce. Spread remaining batter over top and sprinkle with remaining 2 tablespoons nuts. Bake 18–22 minutes or until a toothpick inserted into center of cake comes out clean. Cool 1 hour before serving.

What Is Coffee Cake?

Coffee cake is designed to be enjoyed with coffee—hence the name. It is usually a slightly dense cake flavored with fruit, nuts, and spices. It is less sweet than other types of cake and often has sour cream or buttermilk added for a little tanginess. Coffee cakes can be unadorned or topped with a streusel or crumble topping. Thrifty home bakers of the past made coffee cakes to use up leftover fruits, nuts, and jams, so they were reducing waste and adding flavor!

COOKIE BUTTER CHEESECAKE

PREP TIME: 2¼ HOURS | COOK TIME: 30 MIN | SERVES 1

Cookie butter, a spread made from ground Belgian spice cookies called *speculoos*, has a devoted following. The creamy spread can be found in a variety of textures from creamy to crunchy and should be available in your grocery store where nut butters are sold.

INGREDIENTS

¼ cup plus 2 tablespoons *speculoos* cookie crumbs, divided

1 tablespoon granulated sugar

1 tablespoon unsalted butter, melted and cooled

2 ounces cream cheese, at room temperature

2 tablespoons creamy cookie butter

1 tablespoon packed light brown sugar

¼ teaspoon cornstarch

1 large egg yolk

1 tablespoon sour cream

1 teaspoon heavy cream

½ teaspoon pure vanilla extract

1. Preheat oven to 350°F and spray the bottom of a 4" springform pan with nonstick cooking spray.

2. In a small bowl, combine ¼ cup cookie crumbs, sugar, and butter. Mix until all crumbs are well coated in butter, then transfer crumb mixture to prepared pan and press to form a crust. Bake 8–10 minutes or until crust is firm, then remove from oven.

3. While crust is cooling, prepare filling. In a medium bowl, add cream cheese, cookie butter, and brown sugar. Use a hand mixer to beat on medium speed until smooth and creamy, about 2 minutes. Add cornstarch, egg yolk, and sour cream. Beat on medium speed until well combined, about 30 seconds. Add heavy cream and vanilla and mix on low speed until well incorporated, about 15 seconds.

4. Spread filling onto crust, then gently rap pan on counter three times to level mixture. Bake 22–25 minutes or until cheesecake is set around edges but still slightly jiggly in center. Cool in pan to room temperature, then transfer to an airtight container and refrigerate 2 hours. Garnish with remaining 2 tablespoons cookie crumbs before serving.

BLACK FOREST CAKE

PREP TIME: 10 MIN | COOK TIME: 23 MIN | YIELDS 1 (4") ROUND LAYER CAKE

If you have a can of cherry pie filling on hand, you can use ½ cup of it in this recipe in place of the cooked cherry filling.

INGREDIENTS

⅔ cup all-purpose flour

¼ cup Dutch-processed cocoa powder

½ teaspoon baking powder

¼ teaspoon salt

¼ cup salted butter, melted and cooled

½ cup granulated sugar

1 large egg yolk

2 tablespoons whole milk

¾ teaspoon pure vanilla extract, divided

½ cup boiling water

½ cup frozen dark sweet cherries, thawed, juices reserved

½ teaspoon cornstarch

½ cup heavy whipping cream

1 tablespoon powdered sugar

1 tablespoon kirsch liqueur, divided

1 tablespoon roughly grated dark chocolate

1. Preheat oven to 350°F and spray two 4" × 2" round cake pans with nonstick cooking spray.

2. In a medium bowl, sift together flour, cocoa powder, baking powder, and salt. Set aside.

3. In a small bowl, whisk together butter, granulated sugar, egg yolk, milk, and ½ teaspoon vanilla. Pour into flour mixture and stir until combined. Add boiling water in four additions, stirring after each addition.

4. Divide batter between prepared cake pans. Bake 18–22 minutes or until cakes spring back in center when gently pressed and edges come away from sides. Cool in pans 10 minutes before turning out onto wire racks to cool to room temperature.

5. In a small saucepan, add cherries with their juices and cornstarch. Heat over medium-low heat until cherry mixture is thick, about 5 minutes. Turn off heat and cool to room temperature.

6. In a medium bowl, add whipping cream, powdered sugar, and remaining ¼ teaspoon vanilla. Use a hand mixer to beat on low speed, about 10 seconds, then increase speed to medium and beat until cream forms soft peaks, about 1 minute.

7. To assemble, place one cake layer top-side down on a large plate. Brush cake with ½ tablespoon kirsch. Spread half of whipped cream on cake, top with cherries, then place second cake layer on top and brush with remaining kirsch. Spread remaining cream on top and garnish with chocolate. Serve immediately or refrigerate until ready.

CHAPTER 4
BREADS, ROLLS, AND BISCUITS

The smell of freshly baked bread makes the mouth water and evokes a feeling of comfort. Humans have been baking bread, in one form or another, for over thirty thousand years; bread is one of the earliest ways humans consumed grains. Rich in complex carbohydrates, bread is a significant form of energy and nutrition. It can be sliced and used for sandwiches, made into rolls, or rolled flat for wraps and tortillas. It is as versatile as it is delicious!

This chapter is all about the world of small-batch bread making. From crusty dinner rolls to flaky biscuits and petite loaves, this chapter offers you recipes for fresh bread without the worry of it going stale before you can enjoy it. From sweet breads like Small-Batch Cinnamon Rolls and Sticky Buns to savory staples like Cheesy Garlic Pull-Apart Bread and Ham and Cheddar Scones, and even more unusual breads like savory meat-stuffed Bierrocks with Beer Cheese Sauce and Korean Egg Bread (Gyeran Bbang), you can enjoy freshly baked breads for breakfast, lunch, and dinner in portions that are perfect for one.

SMALL-BATCH DINNER ROLLS

PREP TIME: 2 HOURS | COOK TIME: 19 MIN | YIELDS 4 ROLLS

These dinner rolls are soft, lightly sweet, and perfect as an addition to any meal. If you do not have bread flour, you can use only all-purpose flour.

INGREDIENTS

¼ cup whole milk

1 tablespoon granulated sugar

½ teaspoon dry active yeast

1 large egg yolk

2 tablespoons unsalted butter, melted and cooled

¼ teaspoon salt

½ cup all-purpose flour

½ cup bread flour

1. In a small microwave-safe bowl, heat milk on high for 20 seconds or until it reaches 110°F. Stir in sugar and yeast and allow to stand until yeast is bubbling and foamy, about 10 minutes.

2. To the work bowl of a stand mixer fitted with a dough hook, or in a large bowl using a wooden spoon, add yeast mixture, egg yolk, and butter. Mix on medium speed until well combined, then add salt and both flours and mix on low speed 1 minute. Increase speed to medium and knead 4 minutes or until dough is smooth. If mixing by hand, use the spoon to stir in the flour until it forms a shaggy ball, then knead in the bowl by hand until dough is smooth, about 10 minutes.

3. Form dough into a smooth ball, then cover bowl with a damp towel and let rise in a draft-free spot 1 hour or until doubled in bulk.

4. Preheat oven to 375°F and line a ¼ sheet pan or 8" × 8" cake pan with parchment.

5. Turn dough out onto a lightly floured surface. Press out any air bubbles with your palm. Divide the dough into four pieces and roll each into a smooth ball. Place dough balls on prepared pan. Cover with a damp towel and allow to rise 30 minutes.

6. Bake 18–20 minutes or until rolls are golden brown on top and bottom. Cool in pan 10 minutes before serving.

WHOLE-WHEAT CLOVERLEAF ROLLS

PREP TIME: 2 HOURS | COOK TIME: 19 MIN | YIELDS 4 ROLLS

If you do not want to make these into a cloverleaf shape you can divide the dough into four balls and make four regular rolls. Bake them in a 6" round cake pan so you can pull them apart and enjoy the soft edges!

INGREDIENTS

¼ cup whole milk

1 tablespoon honey

½ teaspoon dry active yeast

1 large egg yolk

2 tablespoons unsalted butter, melted and cooled

¼ teaspoon salt

¾ cup all-purpose flour

¼ cup whole-wheat flour

1. In a small microwave-safe bowl, heat milk on high for 20 seconds or until it reaches 110°F. Stir in honey and yeast and allow to stand until yeast is bubbling and foamy, about 10 minutes.

2. To the work bowl of a stand mixer fitted with a dough hook, or in a large bowl using a wooden spoon, add yeast mixture, egg yolk, and butter. Mix on medium speed until well combined, about 1 minute, then add salt and both flours and mix on low speed for 1 minute. Increase speed to medium and knead 4 minutes or until dough is smooth. If mixing by hand, use the spoon to stir in the flour until it forms a shaggy ball, then knead in the bowl by hand until dough is smooth, about 10 minutes.

3. Form dough into a smooth ball, then cover bowl with a damp towel and let rise in a draft-free spot 1 hour or until doubled in bulk.

4. Preheat oven to 375°F and spray four cups of a muffin pan with nonstick cooking spray.

5. Turn dough out onto a lightly floured surface. Press out any air bubbles with your palm. Divide the dough into twelve pieces and roll each into a smooth ball. Place three dough balls in each prepared cup. Cover with a damp towel and allow to rise 30 minutes or until rolls are puffy and a finger pressed into the side leaves a mark.

6. Bake 18–20 minutes or until rolls are golden brown on top and firm to the touch. Cool in pan 10 minutes before serving.

SMALL-BATCH SOFT PRETZELS

PREP TIME: 2 HOURS | COOK TIME: 14 MIN | YIELDS 2 PRETZELS

A quick dip into simmering baking soda water is what gives these pretzels their distinctive flavor and color. These are wonderful with the Beer Cheese Sauce from the Bierrocks recipe in this chapter. If you want, you can make these sweet by omitting the salt and brushing the hot pretzels with butter, then dusting them with cinnamon sugar.

INGREDIENTS

⅓ cup whole milk

1 tablespoon granulated sugar

½ teaspoon dry active yeast

1 large egg yolk

3 tablespoons unsalted butter, melted and cooled, divided

¼ teaspoon salt

1 cup all-purpose flour

6 cups water

⅓ cup baking soda

1 teaspoon coarse salt

1. In a small microwave-safe bowl, heat milk 20 seconds or until it reaches 110°F. Stir in sugar and yeast and allow to stand until yeast is bubbling and foamy, about 10 minutes.

2. To the work bowl of a stand mixer fitted with a dough hook, or a large bowl using a wooden spoon, add yeast mixture, egg yolk, and 2 tablespoons butter. Mix on medium speed until well combined, about 1 minute, then add salt and flour and mix on low speed for 1 minute. Increase speed to medium and knead 4 minutes or until dough is smooth. If mixing by hand, use the spoon to stir in the flour until it forms a shaggy ball, then knead in the bowl by hand until dough is smooth, about 10 minutes.

3. Form dough into a smooth ball, then cover bowl with a damp towel and let rise in a draft-free spot 1 hour or until doubled in bulk.

4. Preheat oven to 450°F and line a ¼ sheet pan with parchment. Spray parchment with nonstick cooking spray.

5. In a medium pot, add water and baking soda. Bring to a boil over high heat, about 10 minutes.

Continued on next page ▶

6. Turn dough out onto a lightly floured surface. Press out any air bubbles with your palm. Divide the dough into two pieces and roll each into a 25" rope. Form rope into a U shape, twist the two ends of the rope in the center, then press the ends down onto the bottom of the U to form a pretzel shape.

7. Carefully lower formed pretzels one at a time into boiling water and baking soda. Boil 40 seconds, then transfer to prepared baking pan. Sprinkle pretzels with coarse salt.

8. Bake 12–15 minutes or until pretzels are deeply golden brown on top and bottom. Brush with remaining 1 tablespoon butter and serve hot.

Pretzel Dogs

If you want to make these pretzels a complete meal you can transform them into pretzel dogs! Divide the dough into four pieces, roll each piece into a 10" rope, then wrap each rope around a hot dog that has been patted dry with a towel so the dough will stick. Be sure to pinch the end of the dough to the dough wrapped around the dog to prevent unraveling. Proceed with the recipe as directed and enjoy with yellow mustard!

SMALL-BATCH FRENCH BREAD

PREP TIME: 3 HOURS | COOK TIME: 21 MIN | YIELDS 1 (10") LOAF

Because French bread contains no fat, it does not keep well and is best eaten the day it is baked. If you have any left over, you can cube it, toss in a little olive oil, and bake in a 350°F oven for 10–12 minutes to make some spectacular croutons.

INGREDIENTS

⅓ cup water

¼ teaspoon granulated sugar

½ teaspoon dry active yeast

¼ teaspoon salt

¾ cup bread flour

1. In a small microwave-safe bowl, heat water on high for 20 seconds or until it reaches 110°F. Stir in sugar and yeast and allow to stand until yeast is bubbling and foamy, about 10 minutes.

2. To the work bowl of a stand mixer fitted with a dough hook, or in a large bowl using a wooden spoon, add yeast mixture, salt, and flour. Mix on low speed for 1 minute, then increase speed to medium and knead for 4 minutes or until dough is smooth. If mixing by hand, use the spoon to stir in the flour until it forms a shaggy ball, then knead in the bowl by hand until dough is smooth, about 10 minutes.

3. Form dough into a smooth ball, then cover bowl with a damp towel and let rise in a draft-free spot 1½ hours or until doubled in bulk.

4. Preheat oven to 425°F and line a ¼ sheet pan with parchment.

5. Turn dough out onto a lightly floured surface. Press out any air bubbles with your palm. Stretch dough into a 10"-long rectangle, then roll into a loaf shape. Tuck ends under, then roll gently to even loaf. Cover with a damp towel and let rise 1 hour.

6. With a sharp knife or razor blade, make three diagonal slashes down the loaf. Put loaf on prepared sheet pan and bake 20–25 minutes or until bread is deeply golden and sounds hollow when gently thumped on the side. Turn off oven, crack door 1", and let loaf cool fully in oven. Enjoy the same day as it is baked.

SMALL-BATCH HAMBURGER BUNS

PREP TIME: 2 HOURS | COOK TIME: 19 MIN | YIELDS 4 BUNS

These buns are big and fluffy, and they toast beautifully. You can also use these for breakfast sandwiches with egg, cheese, and your favorite meat or meat alternative, or use them for grilled chicken or fried fish sandwiches!

INGREDIENTS

⅓ cup water

2 teaspoons granulated sugar

½ teaspoon dry active yeast

1 large egg, beaten, divided

1 tablespoon unsalted butter, melted and cooled

½ teaspoon salt

1 cup bread flour

½ cup all-purpose flour

1 tablespoon sesame seeds

1. In a small microwave-safe bowl, heat water on high for 20 seconds or until it reaches 110°F. Stir in sugar and yeast and allow to stand until yeast is bubbling and foamy, about 10 minutes.

2. To the work bowl of a stand mixer fitted with a dough hook, add yeast mixture, half beaten egg, and butter. Mix on medium speed until well combined, about 1 minute, then add salt and both flours and mix on low speed for 1 minute. Increase speed to medium and knead 4 minutes or until dough is smooth.

3. Form dough into a smooth ball, then cover bowl with a damp towel and let rise in a draft-free spot 1 hour or until doubled in bulk.

4. Preheat oven to 375°F and line a ¼ sheet pan or 8" × 8" cake pan with parchment.

5. Turn dough out onto a lightly floured surface. Press out any air bubbles with your palm. Divide the dough into four pieces and roll each into a smooth ball. Place dough balls on prepared pan. Cover with a damp towel and allow to rise 45 minutes.

6. Brush tops of rolls with remaining half egg, then sprinkle sesame seeds over top. Bake 18–22 minutes or until buns are deeply golden brown on top and bottom and are firm to the touch. Cool to room temperature on pan before slicing in half and serving.

BIERROCKS WITH BEER CHEESE SAUCE

PREP TIME: 2½ HOURS | COOK TIME: 32 MIN | YIELDS 4 BUNS AND ¾ CUP SAUCE

Bierrocks are a German stuffed bun typically filled with ground beef, sauerkraut, and onion. They are also known as *runza* or *krautburger*. This recipe combines them with a beer cheese dipping sauce to make them extra fun to eat!

INGREDIENTS

¼ pound ground beef

¼ medium yellow onion, peeled and finely diced

¼ cup finely chopped prepared sauerkraut

½ cup whole milk

2 teaspoons granulated sugar

½ teaspoon dry active yeast

1 large egg, beaten, divided

½ teaspoon salt

1½ cups plus 1 teaspoon all-purpose flour, divided

1 tablespoon unsalted butter

⅛ teaspoon smoked paprika

½ cup lager beer

2 tablespoons heavy cream

¼ cup shredded sharp Cheddar cheese

1. In a medium nonstick skillet over medium heat, combine ground beef and onion. Cook until beef is browned and onion is soft, about 10 minutes. Remove from heat and drain excess grease. Stir in sauerkraut and set aside to cool.

2. In a small microwave-safe bowl, heat milk on high for 20 seconds or until it reaches 110°F. Stir in sugar and yeast and allow to stand until yeast is bubbling and foamy, about 10 minutes.

3. To the work bowl of a stand mixer fitted with a dough hook, or in a large bowl using a wooden spoon, add yeast mixture, half beaten egg, salt, and 1 cup flour. Mix on low speed for 1 minute, then increase speed to medium and knead for 4 minutes or until dough is smooth. If mixing by hand, use the spoon to stir in the flour until it forms a shaggy ball, then knead in the bowl by hand until dough is smooth, about 10 minutes.

4. Form dough into a smooth ball, then cover bowl with a damp towel and let rise in a draft-free spot 1 hour or until doubled in bulk.

5. Preheat oven to 375°F and line a ¼ sheet pan with parchment.

6 Turn dough out onto a lightly floured surface. Press out any air bubbles with your palm. Divide the dough into four pieces and flatten into a rough circle. Divide filling into the center of each piece of dough. Pull edges toward the center and pinch to seal. Place dough balls seam-side down on prepared pan. Cover with a damp towel and allow to rise 45 minutes or until buns are puffy and a finger pressed into the side leaves a mark.

7 Brush tops of rolls with remaining half egg. Bake 18–22 minutes or until buns are deeply golden brown on top and bottom and are firm to the touch. Cool 10 minutes before serving.

8 While buns bake, prepare cheese sauce. In a medium saucepan over medium-low heat, add butter. Once melted and foaming add remaining ½ cup plus 1 teaspoon flour and smoked paprika. Cook 1 minute or until flour is just golden brown. Slowly whisk in beer, making sure to whisk out any lumps, and cook until sauce starts to thicken, about 2 minutes. Add cream and whisk to combine, then remove from heat and whisk in cheese. If sauce is too thick add more cream to thin it out. Serve buns with cheese sauce for dipping.

CHEESY GARLIC PULL-APART BREAD

PREP TIME: 2 HOURS | COOK TIME: 16 MIN | YIELDS 8 ROLLS

These cheese-stuffed garlic rolls are a delicious snack while watching the big game, while enjoying Italian food, or anytime you need some cheese-stuffed comfort food. Serve these with a warm marinara sauce for dipping!

INGREDIENTS

¼ cup whole milk

1 teaspoon granulated sugar

½ teaspoon dry active yeast

1 large egg yolk

4 tablespoons unsalted butter, melted and cooled, divided

¼ teaspoon salt

½ cup all-purpose flour

½ cup bread flour

¼ teaspoon garlic powder

2 sticks mozzarella string cheese, each cut into four pieces

1 medium clove garlic, peeled and minced

1. In a small microwave-safe bowl, heat milk on high for 20 seconds or until it reaches 110°F. Stir in sugar and yeast and allow to stand until yeast is bubbling and foamy, about 10 minutes.

2. To the work bowl of a stand mixer fitted with a dough hook, or in a large bowl using a wooden spoon, add yeast mixture, egg yolk, and 2 table-spoons butter. Mix on medium speed until well combined, about 1 minute, then add salt, both flours, and garlic powder and mix on low speed for 1 minute. Increase speed to medium and knead 4 minutes or until dough is smooth. If mixing by hand, use the spoon to stir in the flour until it forms a shaggy ball, then knead in the bowl by hand until dough is smooth, about 10 minutes.

3. Form dough into a smooth ball, then cover bowl with a damp towel and let rise in a draft-free spot 1 hour or until doubled in bulk.

4. Preheat oven to 375°F and spray a 6" round cake pan with nonstick cooking spray.

5. Turn dough out onto a lightly floured surface. Press out any air bubbles with your palm. Divide the dough into eight pieces. Flatten each piece into a rough circle, place a piece of mozzarella

in the center, then tuck the edges over cheese. Roll each piece of dough-wrapped cheese into a smooth ball and place in prepared pan. Cover with a damp towel and allow to rise 30 minutes or until rolls are puffy and a finger pressed into the side leaves a mark.

6 While rolls rise, prepare garlic butter. In a small microwave-safe bowl, add remaining 2 tablespoons butter and garlic. Microwave 30 seconds or until butter is sizzling and garlic is fragrant. Set aside.

7 Bake rolls 14–16 minutes or until they are golden brown on top and feel firm to the touch. While still hot, brush with garlic butter. Cool 10 minutes before serving.

Pizza and Nacho Rolls

If you want to make these into a pizza-flavored treat add your favorite pizza toppings into each dough ball before shaping. Some ideas include a slice or two of pepperoni, some crumbled cooked Italian sausage, finely chopped onions and peppers, sliced olives, or chopped ham and pineapple. If you are adding raw vegetables, be sure to chop them very finely so they will be cooked through. For a more Tex-Mex flair, swap the mozzarella for cubed Cheddar and add a slice of pickled jalapeño for a spicy kick, and dip it in salsa!

STICKY BUNS

PREP TIME: 2 HOURS | COOK TIME: 23 MIN | YIELDS 4 ROLLS

Feel free to swap the nuts in the topping to any you have on hand that you like. Walnuts or even peanuts would be a fun twist. You can also add up to ¼ cup of raisins, dried cranberries, or chopped dried cherries to the cinnamon filling for bursts of fruity flavor.

INGREDIENTS

¼ cup whole milk

2 tablespoons granulated sugar

½ teaspoon dry active yeast

1 large egg yolk

7 tablespoons unsalted butter, melted and cooled, divided

¼ teaspoon salt

½ cup all-purpose flour

½ cup bread flour

2 teaspoons dry milk powder

½ cup packed light brown sugar, divided

1 teaspoon ground cinnamon

1 tablespoon honey

⅔ cup chopped pecans

1. In a small microwave-safe bowl, heat milk 20 seconds or until it reaches 110°F. Stir in granulated sugar and yeast and allow to stand until yeast is bubbling and foamy, about 10 minutes.

2. To the work bowl of a stand mixer fitted with a dough hook, or in a large bowl using a wooden spoon, add yeast mixture, egg yolk, and 3 table-spoons butter. Mix on medium speed until well combined, about 1 minute, then add salt, both flours, and milk powder. Mix on low speed for 1 minute, then increase speed to medium and knead 4 minutes or until dough is smooth. If mixing by hand, use the spoon to stir in the flour until it forms a shaggy ball, then knead in the bowl by hand until dough is smooth, about 10 minutes.

3. Form dough into a smooth ball, then cover bowl with a damp towel and let rise in a draft-free spot 1 hour or until doubled in bulk.

4. In a small bowl, combine 1 tablespoon butter, ¼ cup brown sugar, and cinnamon. Mix until well combined. Set aside.

5. In a small saucepan, add remaining ¼ cup brown sugar, remaining 3 tablespoons butter, honey, and pecans. Heat over medium heat until brown sugar is melted and starting to simmer around the edges, about 4 minutes.

6. Preheat oven to 375°F and spray a 6" round cake pan with nonstick cooking spray. Pour pecan mixture into prepared pan and spread to edges. Set aside.

7. Turn dough out onto a lightly floured surface. Press out any air bubbles with your palm. Roll dough out into a ½"-thick rectangle approximately 4" × 6". Spread cinnamon mixture over dough, then roll dough along the long edge into a spiral. Slice into four rolls and place in prepared pan on top of pecan mixture. Cover with a damp towel and allow to rise 30 minutes or until rolls are puffy and a finger pressed into the side leaves a mark.

8. Bake 18–20 minutes or until rolls are golden brown on top and feel firm to the touch. Immediately, but carefully, turn buns onto a serving plate. Cool 15 minutes before serving.

GARLIC KNOTS

PREP TIME: 2 HOURS | COOK TIME: 25 MIN | YIELDS 4 ROLLS

These Garlic Knots are the perfect accompaniment to Italian food, steak dinners, or a hearty bowl of soup. If you prefer not to buy a whole bulb of garlic for this recipe, you can find chunky garlic paste in most produce departments. It keeps for weeks in the refrigerator and tastes better than ready-chopped garlic from a jar.

INGREDIENTS

¼ cup whole milk

1 teaspoon granulated sugar

½ teaspoon dry active yeast

1 large egg yolk

4 tablespoons unsalted butter, melted and cooled, divided

¼ teaspoon salt

½ cup all-purpose flour

½ cup bread flour

2 medium cloves garlic, chopped (about 1 tablespoon)

1 teaspoon dried basil

1 tablespoon freshly grated Parmesan cheese

1. In a small microwave-safe bowl, heat milk on high for 20 seconds or until it reaches 110°F. Stir in sugar and yeast and allow to stand until yeast is bubbling and foamy, about 10 minutes.

2. To the work bowl of a stand mixer fitted with a dough hook, or in a large bowl using a wooden spoon, add yeast mixture, egg yolk, and 2 tablespoons butter. Mix on medium speed until well combined, about 1 minute, then add salt and both flours and mix on low speed for 1 minute. Increase speed to medium and knead 4 minutes or until dough is smooth. If mixing by hand, use the spoon to stir in the flour until it forms a shaggy ball, then knead in the bowl by hand until dough is smooth, about 10 minutes.

3. Form dough into a smooth ball, then cover bowl with a damp towel and let rise in a draft-free spot 1 hour or until doubled in bulk.

4. Preheat oven to 375°F and line a ¼ sheet pan or 8" × 8" cake pan with parchment.

5. Turn dough out onto a lightly floured surface. Press out any air bubbles with your palm. Divide the dough into four pieces and roll each into a 6"-long rope. Tie each rope into a simple knot, then place on prepared pan. Cover with a damp towel and allow to rise 30 minutes or until rolls are puffy and a finger pressed into the side leaves a mark.

6. While knots rise, prepare garlic butter topping. In a small saucepan, add remaining 2 tablespoons butter and garlic. Heat over low heat until garlic is fragrant, about 5 minutes. Turn off heat and stir in basil. Set aside.

7. Bake rolls 18–20 minutes or until they are golden brown on top and bottom. Take knots out of oven and brush with garlic butter. Sprinkle each knot with Parmesan. Serve hot.

SMALL-BATCH CINNAMON ROLLS

PREP TIME: 2 HOURS | COOK TIME: 19 MIN | YIELDS 4 ROLLS

You can prepare these rolls the night before serving, cover them with plastic wrap or reusable beeswax paper, and place them in the refrigerator overnight to rise. Pull them out to stand at room temperature 1 hour before you plan to bake them so the yeast has a chance to wake up.

INGREDIENTS

¼ cup whole milk

2 tablespoons granulated sugar

½ teaspoon dry active yeast

1 large egg yolk

5 tablespoons unsalted butter, melted and cooled, divided

¼ teaspoon salt

½ cup all-purpose flour

½ cup bread flour

2 teaspoons dry milk powder

¼ cup packed light brown sugar

1 teaspoon ground cinnamon

1. In a small microwave-safe bowl, heat milk 20 seconds or until it reaches 110°F. Stir in granulated sugar and yeast and allow to stand until yeast is bubbling and foamy, about 10 minutes.

2. To the work bowl of a stand mixer fitted with a dough hook, or a large bowl using a wooden spoon, add yeast mixture, egg yolk, and 2 tablespoons butter. Mix on medium speed until well combined, then add salt, both flours, and milk powder. Mix on low speed 1 minute, then increase speed to medium and knead 4 minutes or until dough is smooth. If mixing by hand, use the spoon to stir in the flour until it forms a shaggy ball, then knead in the bowl by hand until dough is smooth, about 10 minutes.

3. Form dough into a smooth ball, then cover bowl with a damp towel and let rise in a draft-free spot 1 hour or until doubled in bulk.

4. In a small bowl, combine remaining 3 tablespoons butter, brown sugar, and cinnamon. Mix until well combined. Set aside.

5. Preheat oven to 375°F and spray an 8" round cake pan with nonstick cooking spray.

Continued on next page ▶

6. Turn dough out onto a lightly floured surface. Press out any air bubbles with your palm. Roll dough out into a ½"-thick rectangle approximately 10" × 12". Spread cinnamon mixture over dough, then roll dough along the long edge into a log. Slice into four rolls and place 1" apart in prepared pan. Cover with a damp towel and allow to rise 30 minutes or until rolls are puffy and a finger pressed into the side leaves a mark.

7. Bake 18–20 minutes or until rolls are golden brown on top and bottom. Cool in pan 5 minutes before serving.

Cinnamon Roll Frosting

If you like creamy frosting on your cinnamon rolls you should try this recipe. Mix 1 tablespoon melted butter, 2 teaspoons milk, and ¼ teaspoon vanilla with ¾ cup powdered sugar. Whisk until it forms a smooth glaze that is thick but pourable, like pancake batter. If you like your glaze a little thinner, add a little extra milk ½ teaspoon at a time. This spreads best over warm, not hot, cinnamon rolls, and the frosting will melt a little into the rolls, adding more sweetness in each bite, so let the cinnamon rolls cool at least 15 minutes before frosting.

SMALL-BATCH FLOUR TORTILLAS

Nothing beats the flavor of a freshly griddled flour tortilla. These tortillas make excellent breakfast tacos, soft tacos, quesadillas, or sandwich wraps. If you have lard, use that instead of shortening to give these tortillas a more authentic flavor.

INGREDIENTS

½ cup all-purpose flour

⅛ teaspoon salt

⅛ teaspoon baking powder

1 tablespoon vegetable shortening

¼ cup warm milk

1. In a medium bowl, add flour, salt, and baking powder. Whisk to combine.

2. Add shortening and use your fingers to rub it into the flour until flour resembles coarse sand. Stir in milk and knead until dough forms a smooth ball, 8–10 minutes.

3. Turn dough out onto a lightly floured surface and divide into four balls. Cover dough balls with a damp cloth and let rest 30 minutes.

4. Once rested, roll dough balls into 6" circles. Cover with a damp towel.

5. While dough is resting, place a griddle or cast iron skillet over medium heat. Once hot, add one to two tortillas, depending on the size of the griddle. Cook until tortillas start to puff and the bottoms have dark brown spots, 1–2 minutes. Flip and cook until the second side is golden brown and the tortillas are steaming hot, 1–2 minutes more. Transfer to a large plate and cover with a dry towel while you repeat with remaining dough. Serve warm.

CHINESE-STYLE STEAMED BUNS

PREP TIME: 6½ HOURS | COOK TIME: 25 MIN | YIELDS 4 BUNS

Char siu sauce is a Chinese-style barbecue sauce found in most grocery stores in the Asian food section. It is a sweet, sticky sauce flavored with white pepper, five-spice, and hoisin sauce. If you can't find it, you can use 2 tablespoons of hoisin sauce with ¼ teaspoon five-spice powder.

INGREDIENTS

3 teaspoons vegetable oil, divided

⅓ pound ground pork

1 teaspoon minced garlic

1 medium green onion, green part only, chopped

2 tablespoons char siu sauce

5 tablespoons water, heated to 100°F, divided

¼ cup plus 3 tablespoons all-purpose flour

1 teaspoon active dry yeast

2 teaspoons granulated sugar, divided

¼ cup cake flour

½ teaspoon baking powder

¼ teaspoon salt

1. In a medium skillet over medium heat, add 2 teaspoons oil. Once hot, add pork, garlic, and onion and cook until pork is cooked through, about 10 minutes. Add char siu sauce and stir to combine. Cook until pork mixture is thick and sticky, about 5 minutes. Turn off heat and cool to room temperature before refrigerating until ready to use.

2. In a medium bowl, combine 3 tablespoons hot water, 3 tablespoons all-purpose flour, yeast, and 1 teaspoon sugar. Mix until smooth, cover with a damp towel, and let stand at room temperature 1 hour or until very bubbly.

3. To mixture, add remaining 1 teaspoon oil, remaining 2 tablespoons hot water, remaining ¼ cup all-purpose flour, remaining 1 teaspoon sugar, cake flour, baking powder, and salt and mix until a smooth ball of dough forms. Cover bowl with a damp towel and let rise 4 hours.

4. Turn dough out onto a lightly floured surface and use your palm to gently press out air bubbles. Divide dough into four pieces and shape each into a circle that is thick in the center and thinner around the edges. Divide pork mixture between

dough pieces, then wrap dough around filling and pinch to close. Place dough pinched-side down and use a cupped palm to roll with a circular motion to shape into a smooth ball.

5   Place buns on small squares of parchment, cover with a damp towel, and let rise 1 hour.

6   While buns rise, prepare steamer. Place a steamer basket and lid over a pot filled with water and bring to a boil.

7   Carefully place buns with their parchment into prepared steamer. Cover and let steam 10 minutes or until buns are puffed, shiny, and firm to the touch. Serve hot.

Optional Steamed Bun Fillings

Steamed buns can be filled with any number of delicious things and can be used as a main dish, side dish, or snack. Some different filling options include prepared sweet red bean paste, stir-fried cabbage with minced chicken and hoisin sauce, chopped shrimp, stir-fried green onion with garlic, or roasted and mashed Korean yam. You can also leave them unfilled and serve with roasted pork, duck, or your favorite stir-fry.

EASY SKILLET FLATBREAD

PREP TIME: 10 MIN | COOK TIME: 2 MIN | YIELDS 2 FLATBREADS

These flatbreads work best with full-fat Greek yogurt, but if you do not have any, you can use low-fat yogurt and stir in 1 teaspoon of olive oil. If you have self-rising flour, you can use ½ cup of that in place of the dry ingredients.

INGREDIENTS

½ cup all-purpose flour

½ teaspoon baking powder

¼ teaspoon baking soda

¼ teaspoon salt

½ cup full-fat plain Greek yogurt

1. In a medium bowl, add flour, baking powder, baking soda, and salt. Whisk to combine.

2. Add yogurt and mix until mixture just forms a ball.

3. Turn dough out onto a lightly floured surface and divide into two balls. Cover dough balls with a damp cloth and let rest 10 minutes.

4. Once rested, roll dough balls into 8" circles.

5. Place a griddle or cast iron skillet over medium heat. Once hot, add one to two flatbreads, depending on the size of the griddle, and cook until puffed and browned, 1–2 minutes. Flip and cook until the second side is golden brown and the flatbread is steaming hot, 1–2 minutes more. Transfer to a large plate and cover with a dry towel while you repeat with remaining dough. Serve warm.

DOUGHNUT HOLES

PREP TIME: 10 MIN | COOK TIME: 4 MIN | YIELDS 6 DOUGHNUT HOLES

Fresh, homemade doughnuts are a wonderful treat, and this recipe makes just the right amount for one person to enjoy! If you like, you can swap the whole milk for buttermilk for a tangier doughnut. If you do, also add a pinch of nutmeg to add even more flavor!

INGREDIENTS

Oil, for frying

½ cup powdered sugar

¼ teaspoon ground cinnamon

½ cup all-purpose flour

1 tablespoon granulated sugar

¼ teaspoon baking powder

⅛ teaspoon salt

1 large egg yolk

¼ cup whole milk

1 teaspoon unsalted butter, melted

¼ teaspoon pure vanilla extract

1. In a large heavy-bottom pot with deep sides, add 2" oil over medium-high heat until it reaches 350°F.

2. In a medium bowl, add powdered sugar and cinnamon. Stir to combine then set aside.

3. In a separate medium bowl, add flour, granulated sugar, baking powder, and salt. Whisk to combine.

4. In a small bowl, whisk together egg yolk, milk, butter, and vanilla. Pour wet ingredients into dry and mix until batter is smooth.

5. Using a cookie scoop or two spoons, carefully drop 1" balls of batter into heated oil. Fry 2 minutes per side or until golden brown all over. Remove from oil and drain on a paper towel–lined plate 1 minute, then toss in powdered sugar mixture. Enjoy warm.

Filled Doughnut Holes

If you like, you can add filling to your doughnut holes. You will need a piping bag or heavy-duty freezer bag and a round metal piping tip. Snip the tip off the end of the bag, or one corner of a freezer bag, and add the metal tip. All you need to do now is load the filling of your choice into the bag, press the tip into the doughnut hole, and squeeze the filling until it just starts to come out from around the piping tip. Seedless strawberry or raspberry jam is a popular choice, but you could also fill your doughnuts with prepared chocolate or vanilla pudding, prepared lemon curd, or dulce de leche!

BAKED CINNAMON SUGAR DOUGHNUTS

PREP TIME: 10 MIN | COOK TIME: 9 MIN | YIELDS 2 DOUGHNUTS

Baked doughnuts are best the day they are made, so most recipes will make far too many for one person to enjoy before they go stale. This recipe solves that problem by making two fluffy, cinnamon sugar–coated doughnuts perfect for one person to enjoy!

INGREDIENTS

¼ cup all-purpose flour

¼ teaspoon baking powder

⅛ teaspoon baking soda

⅛ teaspoon salt

1 large egg yolk

1 tablespoon plus 2 teaspoons packed light brown sugar

2 tablespoons sour cream

1 tablespoon plus 1½ teaspoons unsalted butter, melted, divided

¼ teaspoon pure vanilla extract

¼ cup granulated sugar

¼ teaspoon ground cinnamon

1. Preheat oven to 350°F and spray two cups of a doughnut pan with nonstick cooking spray.

2. In a medium bowl, combine flour, baking powder, baking soda, and salt. Whisk to combine and set aside.

3. In a small bowl, combine egg yolk, brown sugar, sour cream, 1½ teaspoons butter, and vanilla. Whisk to combine, then add to dry ingredients and mix until batter is smooth.

4. Divide batter between prepared doughnut cups, making sure to smooth batter on top. Bake 9–11 minutes or until edges are golden brown and doughnut springs back when gently pressed in the center. Cool in pan 2 minutes, then turn out onto a wire rack and let stand until cool enough to touch.

5. In a shallow bowl, combine granulated sugar and cinnamon and mix well. Brush warm doughnuts with remaining 1 tablespoon butter, then dredge doughnuts in cinnamon sugar. Enjoy warm.

FLAKY BISCUITS

PREP TIME: 30 MIN | COOK TIME: 18 MIN | YIELDS 4 BISCUITS

Flaky biscuits are a thing of beauty. The trick to a perfectly flaky biscuit is to fold and press your dough instead of traditional kneading. Folding and pressing will give you the delicious layers you desire! If you do not have bread flour, you can swap it with all-purpose flour.

INGREDIENTS

¼ cup plus 1 teaspoon all-purpose flour

¼ cup plus 1 teaspoon bread flour

½ teaspoon baking powder

½ teaspoon granulated sugar

¼ teaspoon salt

3 tablespoons cubed salted butter, chilled

3 tablespoons cold buttermilk

1. Preheat oven to 350°F and line a baking sheet with parchment or a reusable silicone baking mat.

2. In a medium bowl, combine flours, baking powder, sugar, and salt. Whisk well to combine. Add butter and use your fingers to rub mixture until butter is in pea-sized pieces and flour resembles coarse sand. Cover and chill 10 minutes.

3. Make a well in dry ingredients and add buttermilk. Gently stir until it just forms a shaggy ball. Turn out onto a lightly floured surface and press dough into a ½"-thick rectangle, then fold dough in half. Turn the dough a quarter turn and repeat this process four more times. You may need to use a spatula or bench scraper the first few times, as dough will be shaggy. Cover dough and chill 10 minutes.

4. Once the dough is chilled, use your hands to form dough into a 5" × 3" rectangle approximately ½" thick. Use a sharp chef's knife to cut dough into four squares by pressing straight down and lifting straight up. This will help your layers to stay separate. Transfer biscuits to prepared baking sheet.

5. Bake 18–20 minutes or until biscuits are puffed and golden brown. Cool on the baking sheet 5 minutes before enjoying.

GARLIC CHEESE BISCUITS

If you are a fan of the garlic cheese biscuits served by a popular seafood chain restaurant, you are going to love these! Packed with plenty of sharp cheddar and topped with an herb and garlic butter glaze, these biscuits are perfect with seafood, steaks, or chicken.

INGREDIENTS

½ cup plus 1 tablespoon all-purpose flour

¼ teaspoon baking powder

⅛ teaspoon baking soda

¼ teaspoon granulated sugar

⅛ teaspoon garlic powder

⅛ teaspoon onion powder

3 tablespoons cubed salted butter, chilled

3 tablespoons buttermilk

⅓ cup finely shredded sharp Cheddar cheese

2 tablespoons salted butter, at room temperature

1 teaspoon minced garlic

½ teaspoon dried chives

1. Preheat oven to 350°F and line a baking sheet with parchment or a reusable silicone baking mat.

2. In a medium bowl, combine flour, baking powder, baking soda, sugar, garlic powder, and onion powder. Whisk well to combine. Add cubed butter and use your fingers to rub mixture until it resembles coarse sand.

3. Make a well in dry ingredients and add buttermilk. Gently stir two times, then add cheese and stir until a shaggy batter forms and no dry flour remains.

4. Scoop batter onto prepared baking sheet in four equal mounds. Bake 12–15 minutes or until biscuits are puffed and golden brown.

5. While biscuits bake, add butter, garlic, and chives to a small saucepan. Heat over medium-low heat until butter is melted and garlic is fragrant, 2–3 minutes. Remove from heat and let cool.

6. Once biscuits come out of oven, brush with garlic butter mixture. Cool on the baking sheet 5 minutes before serving.

CINNAMON PULL-APART BREAD

PREP TIME: 20 MIN | COOK TIME: 15 MIN | SERVES 1

This personal-sized version of the classic monkey bread is made with biscuit dough rather than yeast dough, so it is easier and faster than the classic.

INGREDIENTS

⅓ cup all-purpose flour

1 tablespoon granulated sugar

¼ teaspoon baking powder

1½ tablespoons cubed salted butter, chilled

2 tablespoons cold buttermilk

2 tablespoons salted butter, melted

¼ teaspoon pure vanilla extract

2 tablespoons packed light brown sugar

¼ teaspoon ground cinnamon

1. Preheat oven to 350°F and spray an 8-ounce ramekin with nonstick cooking spray.

2. In a medium bowl, combine flour, granulated sugar, and baking powder. Whisk well to combine. Add cubed butter and use your fingers to rub mixture until butter is in pea-sized pieces and flour resembles coarse sand.

3. Make a well in dry ingredients and add buttermilk. Gently stir until it just forms a shaggy ball. Turn out onto a lightly floured surface and press dough into a ¼"-thick rectangle, then fold dough in half. Turn the dough a quarter turn and repeat this process four more times. You may need to use a spatula the first few times, as the dough will be shaggy. Cover dough and chill 10 minutes.

4. Once the dough is chilled, use a sharp chef's knife to cut dough into twelve small pieces by pressing straight down and lifting straight up. This will help your layers to stay separate.

5. In a small bowl, combine melted butter and vanilla. In a separate small bowl, combine brown sugar and cinnamon. Mix well.

6. Dip biscuit pieces into butter, then roll in cinnamon sugar. Place into ramekin. Top with any remaining butter and cinnamon sugar.

7. Bake 15–17 minutes or until biscuits are puffed and sides are bubbling. Cool 3 minutes, then run a knife around edge to loosen and turn out onto a medium plate. Enjoy warm.

IRISH SODA BREAD

PREP TIME: 10 MIN | COOK TIME: 20 MIN | YIELDS 1 LOAF

Soda bread is traditionally just flour, baking soda, salt, and buttermilk. This version adds a little sugar and an egg yolk for extra richness. The raisins are totally optional and can be left out or replaced with any dried fruit you enjoy. You can also swap them for chocolate chips for a sweeter version.

INGREDIENTS

½ cup all-purpose flour

1 tablespoon granulated sugar

¼ teaspoon baking powder

⅛ teaspoon baking soda

2 tablespoons cubed salted butter, chilled

¼ cup raisins

¼ cup buttermilk

1 large egg yolk

1. Preheat oven to 425°F and line a baking sheet with parchment or a reusable silicone baking mat.

2. In a medium bowl, combine flour, sugar, baking powder, and baking soda. Whisk to combine. Add cubed butter and use your fingers to rub mixture until butter is in pea-sized pieces and flour resembles coarse sand. Toss in raisins.

3. In a small bowl, whisk together buttermilk and egg yolk. Add to dry ingredients and mix until a shaggy dough forms. Turn dough out onto a lightly floured surface and gently knead three to five times or until dough is smooth.

4. Shape dough into a 4" ball and place on prepared baking sheet. Use a sharp knife to cut a cross pattern into top of dough about ½" deep.

5. Bake 20–25 minutes or until bread is golden brown and a toothpick or wooden skewer inserted into the center of loaf comes out clean. Cool on the baking sheet 10 minutes, then transfer to a rack to cool until just warm. Serve warm or at room temperature.

HAM AND CHEDDAR SCONES

PREP TIME: 30 MIN | COOK TIME: 15 MIN | YIELDS 4 SCONES

Scones are a bit denser and crumblier than biscuits, so they are perfect for slathering with soft butter, clotted cream, or whipped cream cheese! These savory scones are perfect for breakfast, served as a midday snack, or enjoyed with a warm bowl of soup or stew!

INGREDIENTS

$\frac{2}{3}$ cup all-purpose flour

$\frac{1}{2}$ teaspoon baking powder

$\frac{1}{2}$ teaspoon granulated sugar

$\frac{1}{8}$ teaspoon salt

2 tablespoons cubed salted butter, chilled

$\frac{1}{4}$ cup shredded sharp Cheddar cheese

$\frac{1}{4}$ cup chopped smoked ham

$\frac{1}{4}$ cup cold heavy cream

1 large egg yolk

1. Preheat oven to 350°F and line a baking sheet with parchment or a reusable silicone baking mat.

2. In a medium bowl, combine flour, baking powder, sugar, and salt. Whisk well to combine. Add butter and use your fingers to rub mixture until butter is in pea-sized pieces and flour resembles coarse sand. Toss in cheese and ham and mix well. Cover and chill 10 minutes.

3. Make a well in dry ingredients and add cream and egg yolk. Gently whisk egg yolk with cream, then stir in flour until it just forms a shaggy ball. Turn out onto a lightly floured surface and press dough into a ½"-thick rectangle, then fold dough in half. Turn the dough a quarter turn and repeat this process four more times. You may need to use a spatula or bench scraper the first few times, as the dough will be shaggy. Cover dough and chill 10 minutes.

4. Once the dough is chilled, use your hands to form dough into a ¾"-thick circle. Use a sharp chef's knife to cut dough into four wedges by pressing straight down and lifting straight up. Transfer wedges to prepared baking sheet.

5. Bake 15–18 minutes or until scones are puffed and golden brown. Cool on the baking sheet 5 minutes before enjoying.

MINI-JAPANESE MILK BREAD

PREP TIME: 3 HOURS | COOK TIME: 25 MIN | YIELDS 6 (½") SLICES

This recipe super-hydrates a portion of the flour with milk so the bread ends up staying fresher longer. This loaf of soft and chewy bread is just the right size for one person to enjoy over a couple of days for making sandwiches, toasting, or to make Classic Bread Pudding (see Chapter 6).

INGREDIENTS

¼ cup heavy cream, divided

¼ cup water, divided

½ cup all-purpose flour, divided

½ cup bread flour, divided

1 teaspoon active dry yeast

1 tablespoon granulated sugar, divided

1 teaspoon dry milk powder

½ teaspoon salt

1 large egg white

1 tablespoon unsalted butter, melted and cooled

1. In a small saucepan, add 2 tablespoons cream, 2 tablespoons water, 2 tablespoons all-purpose flour, and 2 tablespoons bread flour. Whisk until smooth, then cook, stirring constantly, over medium heat until mixture becomes very thick and forms a ball around the spatula. Remove from heat and cool 20 minutes.

2. In a small microwave-safe bowl, heat remaining 2 tablespoons water on high in 20-second intervals until it reaches 100°F. Stir in yeast and 1 teaspoon sugar and mix well. Let stand 10 minutes or until foamy and bubbling.

3. Place cooked flour mixture into work bowl of a stand mixer fitted with the dough hook. Add remaining ingredients along with yeast mixture. Mix on low speed for 2 minutes, then increase speed to medium and mix 4 minutes or until dough forms a smooth ball around the hook. The dough should be a little sticky but not wet to the touch. If it clings to your fingers add more all-purpose flour a teaspoon at a time until the proper texture is reached.

4. Turn dough out onto a work surface dusted with flour. Gently knead dough, adding flour to keep it from sticking, 3 minutes, then form into a smooth ball and place in a lightly greased bowl. Cover with a damp towel and allow to rise until doubled in bulk, about 1½ hours.

5. Preheat oven to 350°F and spray an 8" loaf pan with nonstick cooking spray.

6. Once risen, turn dough out onto a lightly floured surface and use your palm to press dough flat. Once flat, use your fingertips to poke holes in dough to make sure it is thoroughly degassed. You do not want any large gas bubbles to remain.

7. Divide dough into two equal pieces. Form each piece into an 11"-long log. Twist the logs together to form a loaf and transfer to prepared loaf pan. Cover with a damp towel and allow to proof until dough is puffy and a finger pressed into dough leaves an imprint, about 45 minutes.

8. Bake 20–25 minutes or until bread is golden brown all over and sounds hollow when gently thumped on the side. Cool in pan 10 minutes before turning out onto a wire rack to cool to room temperature.

HONEY BUTTER BISCUITS

These biscuits are light and fluffy and provide the perfect accompaniment to a savory dinner by adding a sweet touch to help cleanse the palate. Because they are drenched in honey butter as they come out of the oven there is no need to add any extra butter when serving—unless you want to!

INGREDIENTS

½ cup plus 1 tablespoon all-purpose flour

¼ teaspoon baking powder

⅛ teaspoon baking soda

⅛ teaspoon salt

3 tablespoons cubed salted butter, chilled, divided

3 tablespoons buttermilk

2 tablespoons honey, divided

1. Preheat oven to 350°F and line a baking sheet with parchment or a reusable silicone baking mat.

2. In a medium bowl, combine flour, baking powder, baking soda, and salt. Whisk well to combine. Add 2 tablespoons butter and use your fingers to rub mixture until it resembles coarse sand.

3. Make a well in dry ingredients and add buttermilk and 1 tablespoon honey. Gently stir until a shaggy batter forms and no dry flour remains.

4. Scoop batter onto prepared baking sheet in four equal mounds. Bake 12–15 minutes or until biscuits are puffed and golden brown.

5. While biscuits bake, prepare honey butter. In a small microwave-safe bowl, add remaining 1 tablespoon butter and remaining 1 tablespoon honey and heat in 20-second intervals, stirring well between each interval, until melted. Set aside.

6. When biscuits come out of oven brush them with honey butter. Cool on the baking sheet 5 minutes before enjoying.

KOREAN EGG BREAD (GYERAN BBANG)

PREP TIME: 10 MIN | COOK TIME: 20 MIN | YIELDS 2 BREADS

Korean egg bread is a popular street food in South Korea during the cooler months. It is essentially a sweet pancake that is grilled in an oval-shaped mold with a whole egg inside. Think of it as an all-in-one breakfast! Enjoy these warm for the best flavor.

INGREDIENTS

1 large egg white

2 tablespoons salted butter, melted

1 tablespoon granulated sugar

2 teaspoons whole milk

⅛ teaspoon pure vanilla extract

3 tablespoons all-purpose flour

¼ teaspoon baking powder

2 large eggs

1. Preheat oven to 350°F and spray two cups of a muffin pan with nonstick cooking spray.

2. In a small bowl, combine egg white, butter, sugar, milk, and vanilla. Mix well.

3. In a medium bowl, combine flour and baking powder. Whisk to combine, then pour egg mixture into dry ingredients and mix until a smooth batter forms.

4. Fill each prepared muffin cup ¼ full with batter. Crack 1 egg into each cup, then top with remaining batter. Make sure egg is mostly covered.

5. Bake 20–25 minutes or until muffins are golden brown and a toothpick inserted into the center comes out clean. Cool in pan 5 minutes before turning out onto a large plate. Serve warm.

PERSONAL PIZZA CRUST

PREP TIME: 1½ HOURS | COOK TIME: 9 MIN | YIELDS 1 CRUST

The beauty of a personal pizza is you can top it any way you want! From red sauce to pesto, and pepperoni to mushroom, the only limits are your imagination. If you are going to use a pizza stone, be sure to add it to the oven before heating so it warms evenly, making the crust even crisper on the outside and fluffy on the inside.

INGREDIENTS

¼ cup water

1 tablespoon granulated sugar

½ teaspoon dry active yeast

½ cup bread flour

⅛ teaspoon salt

¼ teaspoon olive oil

1. In a small microwave-safe bowl, heat water 20 seconds or until it reaches 110°F. Stir in sugar and yeast and allow to stand until yeast is bubbling and foamy, about 10 minutes.

2. To the work bowl of a stand mixer fitted with a dough hook, or in a large bowl using a wooden spoon, add yeast mixture with remaining ingredients. Mix on low speed until just combined, about 1 minute, then increase speed to medium and knead 4 minutes or until dough is smooth. If mixing by hand, use the spoon to stir in flour until it forms a shaggy ball, then knead in the bowl by hand until dough is smooth, about 10 minutes.

3. Form dough into a smooth ball, then cover bowl with a damp towel and let rise in a draft-free spot 1 hour or until doubled in bulk.

4. Preheat oven to 450°F.

5. Turn dough out onto a lightly floured surface. Press out any air bubbles with your palm. Stretch dough into a circle 8"–10" wide. Transfer dough to a baking sheet or pizza pan.

6. Bake 3–4 minutes or until crust is par-baked and starting to bubble. Remove from oven and add your preferred pizza toppings, then return to oven 5–8 minutes or until toppings are heated to your preference.

BROWN SUGAR SCONES WITH FRESH BERRIES

PREP TIME: 30 MIN | COOK TIME: 15 MIN | YIELDS 4 SCONES

Dark brown sugar gives these scones a rich, almost molasses flavor, which pairs well with fresh berries. If fresh berries are not in season feel free to use unsweetened frozen berries that have been thawed and drained of excess juices.

INGREDIENTS

⅔ cup all-purpose flour

½ teaspoon baking powder

3 tablespoons dark brown sugar, divided

⅛ teaspoon salt

2 tablespoons cubed salted butter, chilled

⅓ cup fresh blueberries

¼ cup cold heavy cream

1 large egg yolk

1. Preheat oven to 350°F and line a baking sheet with parchment or a reusable silicone baking mat.

2. In a medium bowl, combine flour, baking powder, 2 tablespoons brown sugar, and salt. Whisk well to combine. Add butter and use your fingers to rub mixture until butter is in pea-sized pieces and flour resembles coarse sand. Toss in blueberries and mix well. Cover and chill 10 minutes.

3. Make a well in dry ingredients and add cream and egg yolk. Gently whisk egg yolk with cream, then stir in flour until it just forms a shaggy ball. Turn out onto a lightly floured surface and press dough into a ½"-thick rectangle, then fold dough in half. Turn dough a quarter turn and repeat this process three more times. You may need to use a spatula or bench scraper the first few times, as the dough will be shaggy. Cover dough and chill 10 minutes.

4. Once chilled, use your hands to form dough into a ¾"-thick circle. Use a sharp chef's knife to cut dough into four wedges by pressing straight down and lifting straight up. Transfer wedges to prepared baking sheet. Top each with a sprinkle of remaining 1 tablespoon brown sugar.

5. Bake 15–18 minutes or until scones are puffed and golden brown. Cool on the baking sheet 5 minutes before enjoying.

PIGS IN BISCUITS

This variation of the traditional pigs in a blanket uses fluffy biscuit dough in place of the traditional yeast dough and is a great meal or snack (think the big game). Make these up the evening before, and you can cook them straight from the refrigerator for breakfast the next day. You can also make these with hot dogs for a lunch-sized meal!

INGREDIENTS

¼ cup all-purpose flour

¼ teaspoon baking powder

¼ teaspoon granulated sugar

2 tablespoons cubed salted butter, chilled

1 tablespoon plus 1 teaspoon cold buttermilk

6 cocktail-sized sausages, dried well

1. Preheat oven to 350°F and line a baking sheet with parchment or a reusable silicone baking mat.

2. In a medium bowl, combine flour, baking powder, and sugar. Whisk well to combine. Add butter and use your fingers to rub mixture until butter is in pea-sized pieces and flour resembles coarse sand. Cover and chill 10 minutes.

3. Make a well in dry ingredients and add buttermilk. Gently stir until it just forms a shaggy ball. Turn out onto a lightly floured surface and press dough into a ¼"-thick rectangle, then fold dough in half. Turn dough a quarter turn and repeat this process four more times. You may need to use a spatula or bench scraper the first few times, as the dough will be shaggy. Cover dough and chill 10 minutes.

4. Once chilled, use your hands to form dough into a ¼"-thick rectangle. Use a sharp chef's knife to cut dough into six strips by pressing straight down and lifting straight up.

5. Wrap each biscuit strip around a sausage and place them seam-side down on prepared baking sheet.

6. Bake 8–11 minutes or until biscuits are puffed and golden brown and sausages are hot. Cool on the baking sheet 5 minutes before enjoying.

SMALL-BATCH PAIN AU CHOCOLAT

PREP TIME: 3 HOURS | COOK TIME: 13 MIN | YIELDS 4 ROLLS

Translating to "chocolate bread," *pain au chocolat* is a popular French pastry that combines a buttery, flaky roll with rich, semisweet chocolate. This recipe takes a few shortcuts from the more complicated original, but the results are just as delicious! If you are making these on a warm day you may want to chill them a little longer between folds to keep your butter cold.

INGREDIENTS

¼ cup water

1 tablespoon granulated sugar

½ teaspoon dry active yeast

1 large egg yolk

2 tablespoons unsalted butter, melted and cooled

¼ teaspoon salt

½ cup all-purpose flour

½ cup bread flour

¼ cup unsalted butter, at room temperature

2 ounces coarsely chopped semisweet chocolate

1 tablespoon heavy cream

1. In a small microwave-safe bowl, heat water 20 seconds or until it reaches 110°F. Stir in sugar and yeast and allow to stand until yeast is bubbling and foamy, about 10 minutes.

2. To the work bowl of a stand mixer fitted with a dough hook, or in a large bowl using a wooden spoon, add yeast mixture, egg yolk, and melted butter. Mix on medium speed until well combined, then add salt and both flours and mix on low speed for 1 minute. Increase speed to medium and knead 4 minutes or until dough is smooth. If mixing by hand, use the spoon to stir in flour until it forms a shaggy ball, then knead in the bowl by hand until dough is smooth, about 10 minutes.

3. Form dough into a smooth ball, then cover bowl with a damp towel and let rise in a draft-free spot 1 hour or until doubled in bulk.

4. Line a ¼ sheet pan or 8" × 8" cake pan with parchment.

5. Turn dough out onto a lightly floured surface. Press out any air bubbles with your palm. Roll dough into a ¼"-thick 6" × 3" rectangle. Spread room-temperature butter over dough, then fold the short sides of the dough into the center like folding a letter, wrap in plastic, and chill 30 minutes.

6. After 30 minutes, remove dough from refrigerator to a lightly floured surface with the long side facing you. Roll dough out to a ¼"-thick 6" × 3" rectangle and repeat the folds as before. Cover and return to refrigerator 15 minutes.

7. Once chilled, roll dough out into a ¼"-thick 6" × 3" rectangle. Cut dough into four rectangles, divide chocolate along short side of rectangles, then roll dough over chocolate. Transfer to prepared sheet pan, cover with a damp towel, and allow to rise 30 minutes or until rolls are puffy and a finger pressed into the side leaves a mark.

8. Preheat oven to 400°F.

9. Once risen, brush rolls with cream, then bake 12–15 minutes or until rolls are golden brown on top and bottom and puffed. Cool on the baking sheet 10 minutes before serving.

EASY BUTTERMILK DROP BISCUITS

PREP TIME: 10 MIN | COOK TIME: 18 MIN | YIELDS 4 BISCUITS

Drop biscuits are among the easiest biscuits going. Simply mix, scoop, and bake, and in less than 30 minutes you have hot biscuits ready for whatever meal you are making. To make these extra rich, brush them with a little melted butter when they are fresh from the oven!

INGREDIENTS

½ cup all-purpose flour

¼ teaspoon baking powder

⅛ teaspoon baking soda

½ teaspoon granulated sugar

⅛ teaspoon salt

2 tablespoons cubed salted butter, chilled

¼ cup plus 1 tablespoon buttermilk

1. Preheat oven to 350°F and line a baking sheet with parchment or a reusable silicone baking mat.

2. In a medium bowl, combine flour, baking powder, baking soda, sugar, and salt. Whisk well to combine. Add butter and use your fingers to rub mixture until it resembles coarse sand.

3. Make a well in dry ingredients and add buttermilk. Gently stir until a shaggy dough forms and no dry flour remains.

4. Scoop dough onto prepared baking sheet in four equal mounds. Bake 18–20 minutes or until biscuits are puffed and golden brown. Cool on the baking sheet 3 minutes before enjoying.

Drop Biscuit Variations

Drop biscuits are versatile. You can make them into beer cheese biscuits by swapping 2 tablespoons of buttermilk for a lager-style beer, and adding ⅓ cup coarsely shredded sharp Cheddar with the wet ingredients. You can also make sweet blueberry maple biscuits by swapping 1 tablespoon buttermilk for 1 tablespoon maple syrup and folding in ⅓ cup fresh or frozen blueberries. Use your imagination and enjoy!

EASY BISCUIT CINNAMON ROLLS

PREP TIME: 30 MIN | COOK TIME: 15 MIN | YIELDS 2 ROLLS

These cinnamon rolls are tender and sweet, and they satisfy any cinnamon roll craving without having to wait for yeast to activate, dough to proof, and rolls to rise.

INGREDIENTS

¼ cup plus 1 teaspoon all-purpose flour

¼ cup plus 1 teaspoon bread flour

½ teaspoon baking powder

1 teaspoon granulated sugar

3 tablespoons cubed salted butter, chilled

¼ cup cold buttermilk

¼ teaspoon pure vanilla extract

2 tablespoons salted butter, at room temperature

2 tablespoons packed light brown sugar

¼ teaspoon ground cinnamon

1. Preheat oven to 350°F and line a baking sheet with parchment or a reusable silicone baking mat.

2. In a medium bowl, combine flours, baking powder, and granulated sugar. Whisk well to combine. Add chilled butter and use your fingers to rub mixture until butter is in pea-sized pieces and flour resembles coarse sand. Cover and chill 10 minutes.

3. Make a well in dry ingredients and add buttermilk and vanilla. Gently stir until it just forms a shaggy ball. Turn out onto a lightly floured surface and press dough into a ½"-thick rectangle, then fold dough in half. Turn dough a quarter turn and repeat this process four more times. You may need to use a spatula the first few times, as dough will be shaggy. Cover dough and chill 10 minutes.

4. In a small bowl, combine room-temperature butter, brown sugar, and cinnamon. Mix until smooth.

5. Once chilled, use your hands to form dough into a ½"-thick rectangle. Spread cinnamon filling over dough, then roll dough along the short side into a log. Use a sharp chef's knife to cut dough in half by pressing straight down and lifting straight up. This will help your layers to stay separate. Transfer rolls to prepared baking sheet.

6. Bake 15–18 minutes or until rolls are puffed and golden brown and cinnamon filling is bubbling. Cool on the baking sheet 5 minutes before enjoying.

CHAPTER 5
PIES, TARTS, AND COBBLERS

Pies, tarts, and cobblers are some of the most beloved comfort foods. They can be sweet or savory, they can be enjoyed at almost any occasion, and they can right the wrongs of the day. The only problem with them is they are best when they are fresh, meaning the day they are made. No one wants soggy pie or stale cobbler, but a full-sized recipe will leave you with just that. The solution can be found ahead!

In this chapter you will find recipes to make petite versions of the classics sized just right for one person to enjoy. You will also find recipes to make pastry and cookie crusts, so your pies will have the perfect homemade base. You will find seasonal favorites like Classic Apple Pie and Pecan Pie, savory pies like Ham and Cheddar Quiche for One, and unique recipes like Chocolate Cobbler and Peanut Butter Fluff Pie. Throughout the chapter, there are additional tips and tricks to help you bake with success and less waste. So, enjoy your pie, cobbler, or tart—and enjoy all of it too!

PERSONAL-SIZED PASTRY CRUST

PREP TIME: 40 MIN | COOK TIME: 0 MIN | YIELDS 1 (6") CRUST

Pastry pie crusts are a classic, and are what most people think of when pie is mentioned. This crust can easily be doubled for a double-crust pie. It is extremely versatile and can be used for sweet and savory dishes, so you can use the same recipe for fruit pies, cream pies, pot pies, and quiche!

INGREDIENTS

½ cup all-purpose flour

½ teaspoon granulated sugar

3 tablespoons cubed salted butter, chilled

1 tablespoon ice water

1. In a medium bowl, combine flour and sugar. Whisk well to combine.

2. Add butter to flour and use your fingers to work butter into flour until it resembles coarse sand with a few pea-sized pieces.

3. Add water and mix with your fingers until dough starts to clump. If needed, add more water 1 teaspoon at a time until dough comes together and no dry flour remains.

4. Turn dough out onto a lightly floured surface and flatten dough with your palm into a fat disk. Fold dough in half and press dough out again. Rotate dough a quarter turn and repeat folding and pressing twice more. Wrap dough in plastic and chill 30 minutes or up to overnight.

5. When ready to use, pull dough from refrigerator and let it warm up 10 minutes before rolling it out on a lightly floured surface as directed for your recipe.

Blind Baking

If your recipe calls for a baked pastry crust you will need to do the following. First, slip crust into a pie or tart pan. Be sure to let the crust slip into the pan; do not tug or pull. Next, line the inside of the crust with aluminum foil, then fill with uncooked rice or dried beans. Bake at 350°F for 10 minutes, then carefully remove foil and beans or rice. Return to the oven and bake 10–15 minutes more or until crust is golden brown all over and crisp. Cool completely before filling.

COOKIE CRUST FOR ONE

PREP TIME: 10 MIN | COOK TIME: 8 MIN | YIELDS 1 (6") CRUST

You can make this crust with any kind of crisp cookies or graham crackers that you like. You can also make this with finely crushed pretzels for a sweet and savory twist on a traditional crust perfect for cream and mousse pies.

INGREDIENTS

½ cup finely ground cookie crumbs

2 tablespoons salted butter, melted

1 tablespoon granulated sugar

1. Preheat oven to 350°F.
2. In a medium bowl, combine all ingredients and mix until crumbs are evenly coated in butter.
3. Transfer crumbs to a 6" pie or tart pan and press crumbs into pan so bottom and sides are packed in evenly and firmly.
4. Bake 8 minutes or until crust is golden brown and smelling toasty. Cool to room temperature before filling.

KEY LIME PIE

PREP TIME: 4½ HOURS | COOK TIME: 10 MIN | YIELDS 1 (6") PIE

Key limes are small, so it takes quite a few to get a substantial amount of juice, but the work is worth it. If you want a shortcut, you can purchase bottled key lime juice in most grocery stores.

INGREDIENTS

2 large egg yolks

3 tablespoons key lime juice

¼ cup sweetened condensed milk

⅛ teaspoon pure vanilla extract

1 Cookie Crust for One, baked and cooled (see recipe in this chapter)

1. Preheat oven to 350°F.
2. In a medium bowl, whisk egg yolks to break, then add lime juice, condensed milk, and vanilla. Mix until smooth.
3. Pour filling into prepared Cookie Crust for One. Bake 10 minutes. Remove from oven and cool 20 minutes at room temperature before refrigerating 4 hours. Serve chilled.

CLASSIC APPLE PIE

PREP TIME: 30 MIN | COOK TIME: 46 MIN | YIELDS 1 (6") PIE

Firm apples are best for baked apple pies. Granny Smith apples make a tarter pie filling, while Fuji and Pink Lady are more balanced in flavor.

INGREDIENTS

2 Personal-Sized Pastry Crusts, unbaked, divided (see recipe in this chapter)

2 medium-sized firm baking apples, peeled, cored, and sliced

1 tablespoon granulated sugar

½ tablespoon unsalted butter

¼ teaspoon ground cinnamon

⅛ teaspoon allspice

1 teaspoon water

½ teaspoon cornstarch

½ teaspoon lemon juice

1 tablespoon whole milk

1. Roll out half Personal-Sized Pastry Crust on a lightly floured surface until it forms an 8" circle. Slide dough into a 6" pie pan. Cover with plastic wrap and refrigerate until ready to use.

2. Roll out remaining half crust on a lightly floured surface until it forms a 7" circle. Slide crust onto a large plate. Cover with plastic wrap and refrigerate.

3. Preheat oven to 400°F and place a baking sheet on bottom rack of oven.

4. In a medium skillet, add apples, sugar, butter, cinnamon, and allspice. Heat over medium heat until butter melts, then cook, stirring often, until apples are tender, about 5 minutes.

5. Reduce heat to low. In a small bowl, add water and cornstarch and mix to form a slurry. Add slurry to apples and mix well. Cook until mixture thickens, about 1 minute. Add lemon juice and stir well. Remove from heat and cool 10 minutes.

6. Remove pie crusts from refrigerator. Spread apple mixture evenly into pastry-lined pie pan. Place top crust over apples. Trim dough to ½" of pan's edge. Tuck edge of top crust under edge of bottom crust. Crimp dough using your fingers or a fork.

7. Cut four ½" vents into pie. Brush with milk, then bake 5 minutes. Reduce heat to 350°F and bake 35–40 minutes or until crust is golden brown.

8. Remove pie from oven and let cool 1 hour before enjoying.

FRESH STRAWBERRY PIE

PREP TIME: 1½ HOURS | COOK TIME: 2 MIN | YIELDS 1 (6") PIE

When strawberries are in season this pie is the perfect way to celebrate them. The traditional strawberry pie is often made with strawberry gelatin, but for this dish, fresh berries are puréed and then thickened with cornstarch so the flavor of the fresh berries is allowed to shine.

INGREDIENTS

1 cup hulled fresh strawberries, sliced in half, divided

¼ cup granulated sugar

¼ cup water, divided

1 tablespoon cornstarch

½ teaspoon pure vanilla extract, divided

1 Personal-Sized Pastry Crust, baked and cooled (see recipe in this chapter)

¼ cup heavy whipping cream

1 tablespoon powdered sugar

1. In a blender, add ¼ cup strawberries, granulated sugar, and 2 tablespoons water. Purée until smooth, then strain mixture through a fine-mesh strainer into a medium saucepan.

2. Place the saucepan over medium heat and cook puréed strawberry mixture until sugar dissolves, about 1 minute.

3. In a small bowl, add remaining 2 tablespoons water and cornstarch and stir to make a slurry. Pour slurry into strawberry purée and stir to mix. Cook until mixture thickens, about 30 seconds. Remove from heat and stir in ¼ teaspoon vanilla. Stir in remaining ¾ cup berries.

4. Pour strawberries into Personal-Sized Pastry Crust. Place in refrigerator at least 1 hour or until filling is chilled thoroughly.

5. Once pie is chilled, in a medium bowl, add cream, powdered sugar, and remaining ¼ teaspoon vanilla. Whip on medium speed until soft peaks form, about 2 minutes. Spread whipped cream over pie. Serve immediately.

Hulling Strawberries

To hull fresh strawberries, insert the tip of a sharp paring knife into the top of the strawberry next to the stem cap at a 45-degree angle toward the center of the berry. Cut around the green top and gently lift the top from the berry; discard.

TOASTED COCONUT CREAM PIE

PREP TIME: 4½ HOURS | COOK TIME: 15 MIN | YIELDS 1 (6") PIE

Full-fat coconut milk provides an additional layer of coconut flavor to this pie, but if you do not have any, you can use 1 full cup of half-and-half. Toasting the coconut adds a special touch to this pie but is unnecessary if you prefer to skip this step. Graham cracker crumbs are perfect for the crust of this pie.

INGREDIENTS

⅓ cup shredded sweetened coconut, divided

½ cup full-fat canned coconut milk

½ cup half-and-half

3 tablespoons granulated sugar

1 tablespoon cornstarch

1 large egg yolk

1 tablespoon unsalted butter

½ teaspoon pure vanilla extract, divided

1 Cookie Crust for One, baked and cooled (see recipe in this chapter)

¼ cup heavy whipping cream

1 tablespoon powdered sugar

1. In a small skillet over medium-low heat, add coconut. Cook, stirring constantly, until coconut just starts to turn golden, 4–6 minutes. Remove skillet from heat and continue to stir 1 minute to prevent burning. Set aside.

2. In a medium saucepan over medium-low heat, whisk together coconut milk, half-and-half, sugar, cornstarch, and egg yolk. Whisk until mixture starts to steam, about 4 minutes. Continue to whisk constantly until mixture thickens and starts to simmer, about 6 minutes. Cook 15 seconds, then remove from heat and stir in ¼ cup toasted coconut, butter, and ¼ teaspoon vanilla. Mix well.

3. Pour mixture into prepared Cookie Crust for One. Place a layer of plastic wrap directly on filling and chill 4 hours or overnight.

4. Once chilled, in medium bowl, add cream, powdered sugar, and remaining ¼ teaspoon vanilla. Whip on medium speed until soft peaks form, about 2 minutes.

5. Spread cream over pie and garnish with remaining toasted coconut. Serve immediately or chill up to 1 hour.

CARAMEL APPLE PIE

PREP TIME: 30 MIN | COOK TIME: 46 MIN | YIELDS 1 (6") PIE

This crumble-topped pie has all the best flavors of a caramel apple baked into an irresistible pie. This is at its most delicious when served warm with a scoop of cool vanilla ice cream!

INGREDIENTS

1 Personal-Sized Pastry Crust, unbaked (see recipe in this chapter)

2 tablespoons all-purpose flour

2 tablespoons packed light brown sugar

1½ tablespoons unsalted butter, divided

2 medium-sized firm baking apples, peeled, cored, and sliced

1 tablespoon granulated sugar

¼ teaspoon ground cinnamon

1 teaspoon water

½ teaspoon cornstarch

4 caramel candies, cut in half

1. Roll out Personal-Sized Pastry Crust on a lightly floured surface until it forms an 8" circle. Slide dough into a 6" pie pan, making sure not to stretch or tug. Cover with plastic wrap and refrigerate.

2. In a small bowl, combine flour and brown sugar. Mix well, then add 1 tablespoon butter and use your fingers to rub butter into flour until it forms a crumble. Cover with plastic wrap and refrigerate.

3. Preheat oven to 400°F and place a baking sheet on bottom rack of oven.

4. In a medium skillet, add apples, granulated sugar, remaining ½ tablespoon butter, and cinnamon. Heat over medium heat until butter melts, then cook, stirring often, until apples are tender, about 5 minutes.

5. Reduce heat to low. In a small bowl, add water and cornstarch and mix to form a slurry. Add to apples and mix. Cook until mixture thickens, about 1 minute. Remove from heat and cool 10 minutes.

6. Remove pie crust and crumble from refrigerator. Spread half of the apple mixture evenly into pastry-lined pie pan and top with caramels. Cover with remaining apples, then top with crumble.

7. Bake on heated baking sheet 5 minutes, then reduce heat to 350°F and bake another 35–40 minutes or until crumble is golden brown.

8. Let cool 1 hour before enjoying.

PUMPKIN PIE

PREP TIME: 10 MIN | COOK TIME: 35 MIN | YIELDS 1 (6") PIE

Pumpkin pie is a fall classic and is perfect when there is a chill in the air. For this recipe, be sure you purchase pure pumpkin purée, not pumpkin pie filling, which has sugar and spices added. Leftover pumpkin purée can be used in smoothies, soups, or made into Pumpkin Bread (see Chapter 7).

INGREDIENTS

1 Personal-Sized Pastry Crust, unbaked (see recipe in this chapter)

3 tablespoons granulated sugar

¼ teaspoon ground cinnamon

⅛ teaspoon ground allspice

⅛ teaspoon ground cloves

1 pinch (about 1/16 teaspoon) ground nutmeg

1 large egg yolk

¾ cup pumpkin purée

¼ cup heavy cream

1 Preheat oven to 400°F.

2 Roll out Personal-Sized Pastry Crust on a lightly floured surface until it forms an 8" circle. Slide dough into a 6" pie pan, making sure not to stretch or tug. Cover with plastic wrap and refrigerate until ready to use.

3 In a medium bowl, whisk together sugar, cinnamon, allspice, cloves, and nutmeg until well combined.

4 Add egg yolk, pumpkin, and cream and whisk until smooth.

5 Pour mixture into prepared crust and place on a baking sheet. Bake in lower third of oven 10 minutes, then reduce heat to 350°F and bake an additional 25–30 minutes or until filling is set at the edges and slightly wobbly in the center.

6 Cool 3 hours on a wire rack before enjoying.

Quick Pumpkin Bisque

You can use leftover pumpkin purée to make a delicious soup. In a medium saucepan over medium heat, add 1 tablespoon salted butter. Once melted, about 20 seconds, add ¼ chopped onion and cook until soft, about 2 minutes. Add ¼ teaspoon ground cinnamon and ⅛ teaspoon each ground cumin and ground coriander. Sauté for 30 seconds, then add 1 cup vegetable broth and 1 cup pumpkin purée. Mix until well combined, then simmer for 20 minutes. Transfer mixture to a blender and purée until smooth, then stir in 3 tablespoons heavy cream. Serve hot.

VERY BERRY POCKET PIE

PREP TIME: 10 MIN | **COOK TIME: 20 MIN** | **YIELDS 1 (5") PIE**

Pocket pies are also called hand pies because they can be eaten out of hand, no plates or forks required. It may feel decadent, but this pie makes an excellent breakfast when you are looking for a fun treat to start your day. Use any mix of berries that are freshest in the market.

INGREDIENTS

½ cup mixed fresh berries

2 tablespoons granulated sugar

2 teaspoons cornstarch

½ teaspoon freshly grated lemon zest

1 Personal-Sized Pastry Crust, unbaked (see recipe in this chapter)

1 tablespoon whole milk

1. Preheat oven to 350°F and line a baking sheet with parchment or a reusable silicone baking mat.

2. In a medium bowl, combine berries, sugar, cornstarch, and lemon zest. Toss to combine. Set aside.

3. Roll out Personal-Sized Pastry Crust on a lightly floured surface until it forms an 8" circle and place on prepared baking sheet.

4. Add berry mixture to center of crust. Brush milk around edge of crust, fold in half, then crimp dough with your fingers or the tines of a fork. With a paring knife, cut two small slits into top of pie, then brush lightly with milk.

5. Bake 20–25 minutes or until pie is golden brown and filling is bubbling. Cool on the baking sheet at least 20 minutes before serving.

PEANUT BUTTER FLUFF PIE

PREP TIME: 2½ HOURS | COOK TIME: 0 MIN | YIELDS 1 (6") PIE

This pie is sweet and tangy with a rich peanut butter flavor. It pairs well with a cup of strong coffee or a shot of espresso. To ramp up the peanut butter flavor you can use finely crushed peanut butter cookies for the crust, such as the Classic Peanut Butter Cookies in Chapter 2.

INGREDIENTS

3 tablespoons creamy peanut butter

1 ounce cream cheese, at room temperature

¼ cup powdered sugar, divided

¼ cup heavy whipping cream

¼ teaspoon pure vanilla extract

1 Cookie Crust for One, baked and cooled (see recipe in this chapter)

2 tablespoons hot fudge sauce

1 tablespoon peanut pieces

1. In a medium bowl, combine peanut butter and cream cheese. Use a hand mixer on low speed to cream together until smooth, about 30 seconds. Add 2 tablespoons powdered sugar and beat on low speed for 10 seconds, then increase speed to high and beat until light and fluffy, about 2 minutes. Set aside.

2. In a separate medium bowl, add 2 tablespoons powdered sugar, cream, and vanilla. Beat on low speed 30 seconds, then increase speed to high and beat until cream forms soft peaks, about 1 minute.

3. Add whipped cream to peanut butter mixture and beat on medium speed until thoroughly mixed and fluffy, about 20 seconds.

4. Spread filling inside prepared Cookie Crust for One. Cover loosely with plastic wrap and refrigerate 2 hours.

5. To serve, garnish with hot fudge sauce and peanuts and serve immediately.

Hot Fudge Sauce for One

Homemade hot fudge sauce is easy to make, and it tastes so much better than store-bought. To make enough for one, combine 3 tablespoons heavy cream, 2 tablespoons granulated sugar, 1 tablespoon unsalted butter, and 1 teaspoon corn syrup in a small saucepan. Bring to a boil over medium heat and stir to melt butter and sugar. Allow to boil for 1 minute, then remove from heat and stir in 1½ ounces chopped semisweet chocolate and ¼ teaspoon vanilla extract until smooth. Use immediately or store in the refrigerator and reheat in the microwave before serving.

APPLE CINNAMON POCKET PIE

PREP TIME: 10 MIN | COOK TIME: 20 MIN | YIELDS 1 (5") PIE

For a sparkly decorative flourish you can sprinkle the top of this pie with a little coarse sanding sugar and a pinch of additional cinnamon. The coarse sugar will not fully melt, leaving the crust with a pretty, glittery finish.

INGREDIENTS

½ cup chopped apple

2 tablespoons packed light brown sugar

2 teaspoons cornstarch

¼ teaspoon ground cinnamon

1 Personal-Sized Pastry Crust, unbaked (see recipe in this chapter)

1 tablespoon whole milk

1. Preheat oven to 350°F and line a baking sheet with parchment or a reusable silicone baking mat.

2. In a medium bowl, combine apples, brown sugar, cornstarch, and cinnamon. Toss to combine. Set aside.

3. Roll out Personal-Sized Pastry Crust on a lightly floured surface until it forms an 8" circle and place on prepared baking sheet.

4. Add apple mixture to center of crust. Brush milk around edge of crust, fold in half, then crimp dough with your fingers or the tines of a fork. With a paring knife, cut two small slits into top of pie, then brush lightly with milk.

5. Bake 20–25 minutes or until pie is golden brown and filling is bubbling. Cool on the baking sheet at least 20 minutes before serving.

Store-Bought Pastry Crust

Sometimes you want a pie without the hassle of making a crust from scratch. When that happens, you can use ready-made pastry crusts from the refrigerated section of the grocery store. One-third of a crust should be enough for most single-serving recipes. Simply fold the corners into the center of the wedge, then roll on a lightly floured surface until crust is 8" in diameter. The leftover crust can be chilled up to a week, and the unused crust can be frozen, then thawed overnight for use another time.

CHERRY ALMOND POCKET PIE

PREP TIME: 10 MIN | COOK TIME: 23 MIN | YIELDS 1 (5") PIE

Almond extract is powerful stuff, and just a little will go a long way, so while ⅛ teaspoon may not seem like much, it is more than enough to flavor this pie. If you also want the crunch of almond in the pie you can add 2 tablespoons of toasted slivered almonds to the filling along with the vanilla and almond extracts.

INGREDIENTS

½ cup frozen dark sweet cherries, thawed, juices reserved

2 tablespoons packed light brown sugar

2 teaspoons cornstarch

⅛ teaspoon ground cinnamon

¼ teaspoon pure vanilla extract

⅛ teaspoon almond extract

1 Personal-Sized Pastry Crust, unbaked (see recipe in this chapter)

1 tablespoon whole milk

1. In a medium saucepan, combine cherries with their juice, brown sugar, cornstarch, and cinnamon. Cook over medium heat until mixture thickens, about 3 minutes. Remove from heat and stir in vanilla and almond extract. Cool to room temperature.

2. Preheat oven to 350°F and line a baking sheet with parchment or a reusable silicone baking mat.

3. Roll out Personal-Sized Pastry Crust on a lightly floured surface until it forms an 8" circle and place on prepared baking sheet.

4. Add cherry mixture to center of crust. Brush milk around edge of crust, fold in half, then crimp dough with your fingers or the tines of a fork. With a paring knife, cut two small slits into top of pie, then brush lightly with milk.

5. Bake 20–25 minutes or until pie is golden brown and filling is bubbling. Cool on the baking sheet at least 20 minutes before serving.

CARAMEL CUSTARD PIE

PREP TIME: 15 MIN | **COOK TIME: 45 MIN** | **YIELDS 1 (6") PIE**

The caramel flavor in this pie comes from boiling the butter and light brown sugar. While this mixture cooks, the butterfat will brown, adding a rich layer of additional flavor to the filling. This step may seem a little fussy, but it is worth it, so don't skip it!

INGREDIENTS

1 Personal-Sized Pastry Crust, unbaked (see recipe in this chapter)

¼ cup packed light brown sugar

3 tablespoons salted butter

1 large egg

⅓ cup evaporated milk

2 teaspoons all-purpose flour

¼ teaspoon pure vanilla extract

1. Preheat oven to 400°F.

2. Roll out Personal-Sized Pastry Crust on a lightly floured surface until it forms an 8" circle. Slide dough into a 6" pie pan, making sure not to stretch or tug. Cover with plastic wrap and refrigerate until ready to use.

3. In a medium saucepan over medium heat, combine brown sugar and butter. Bring to a boil and cook, stirring frequently, 5 minutes or until butter smells nutty. Cool 2 minutes.

4. In a medium bowl, add egg, milk, flour, and vanilla. Whisk until smooth. Slowly whisk in the cooled sugar mixture and whisk until smooth.

5. Pour pie filling into prepared crust and tap gently to release any air bubbles.

6. Bake 5 minutes, then turn oven down to 325°F and bake 35–40 minutes or until pie is golden brown and set throughout.

7. Cool completely before serving.

CHOCOLATE CHIP COOKIE PIE

PREP TIME: 10 MIN | COOK TIME: 35 MIN | YIELDS 1 (6") PIE

If you enjoy ooey-gooey chocolate chip cookies then you will love this pie. It has all the flavors found in traditional chocolate chip cookies baked into a decadent pie. This pie is delicious when it is still slightly warm and served with ice cream or whipped cream.

INGREDIENTS

1 Personal-Sized Pastry Crust, unbaked (see recipe in this chapter)

1 large egg

1 tablespoon all-purpose flour

1 tablespoon granulated sugar

3 tablespoons packed light brown sugar

3 tablespoons salted butter, melted and cooled

¼ teaspoon pure vanilla extract

½ cup semisweet chocolate chips

1. Preheat oven to 325°F.

2. Roll out Personal-Sized Pastry Crust on a lightly floured surface until it forms an 8" circle. Slide dough into a 6" pie pan, making sure not to stretch or tug. Cover with plastic wrap and refrigerate until ready to use.

3. In a medium bowl, add egg, flour, granulated sugar, brown sugar, butter, and vanilla. Whisk to combine. Add chocolate chips and stir to mix.

4. Pour pie filling into prepared crust and tap gently to release any air bubbles.

5. Bake 35–40 minutes or until pie is golden brown and puffed around edges but still slightly wobbly in center.

6. Cool completely before serving.

BLUEBERRY CRUMBLE PIE

PREP TIME: 15 MIN | COOK TIME: 40 MIN | YIELDS 1 (6") PIE

If you are using frozen blueberries for this pie, it is best to thaw them and drain off the excess juices so the pie won't be too watery. This is a good idea when using any frozen fruits for pies, tarts, and crumbles. Save the juices for smoothies!

INGREDIENTS

1 Personal-Sized Pastry Crust, unbaked (see recipe in this chapter)

2 tablespoons all-purpose flour

2 tablespoons packed light brown sugar

1 tablespoon unsalted butter

1¼ cups fresh blueberries

1 tablespoon plus 2 teaspoons granulated sugar

1 tablespoon cornstarch

½ teaspoon freshly grated lemon zest

1. Preheat oven to 400°F and place a baking sheet on bottom rack of oven.

2. Roll out Personal-Sized Pastry Crust on a lightly floured surface until it forms an 8" circle. Slide dough into a 6" pie pan, making sure not to stretch or tug. Cover with plastic wrap and refrigerate until ready to use.

3. In a small bowl, combine flour and brown sugar. Mix well, then add butter and use your fingers to rub butter into flour until it forms a crumble. Cover with plastic wrap and refrigerate until ready to use.

4. In a medium bowl, combine blueberries, granulated sugar, cornstarch, and lemon zest. Mix well. Pour blueberry mixture into prepared crust. Sprinkle crumble topping over top.

5. Bake on heated baking sheet 5 minutes, then reduce heat to 350°F and bake another 35–40 minutes or until crumble is golden brown and filling is bubbling.

6. Remove pie from oven and let cool 1 hour before enjoying.

Streusel, Crumble, and Crisp

Ever wondered what the difference is between a crumble, crisp, and streusel? Streusel can be either a crisp or a crumble; it is any topping made with butter, flour, sugar, and other ingredients. A crisp is a bit denser and is simply butter, flour, and sugar mixed until clumps form. A crisp contains the same ingredients but adds old-fashioned oats, which get crisp while baking.

CHESS PIE

PREP TIME: 15 MIN | COOK TIME: 35 MIN | YIELDS 1 (6") PIE

This pie, thought to have English origins, is now a staple of the American South. Don't be deceived by the simple ingredients. The rich custard filling is sweet and a little gooey, much like a pecan pie, and this version is flavored with vanilla and lemon.

INGREDIENTS

1 Personal-Sized Pastry Crust, unbaked (see recipe in this chapter)

1 large egg

2 tablespoons salted butter, melted and cooled

¼ cup granulated sugar

1 teaspoon yellow cornmeal

2 tablespoons whole milk

1 teaspoon lemon juice

¼ teaspoon pure vanilla extract

1. Preheat oven to 350°F.

2. Roll out Personal-Sized Pastry Crust on a lightly floured surface until it forms an 8" circle. Slide dough into a 6" pie pan, making sure not to stretch or tug. Cover with plastic wrap and refrigerate until ready to use.

3. In a medium bowl, add egg, butter, sugar, cornmeal, milk, lemon juice, and vanilla. Whisk until smooth.

4. Pour pie filling into prepared crust and tap gently to release any air bubbles.

5. Bake 35–40 minutes or until pie is golden brown and set throughout.

6. Cool completely before serving.

FRESH PEACH GALETTE

PREP TIME: 20 MIN | COOK TIME: 20 MIN | YIELDS 1 (5") TART

A galette is a rustic tart that does not require any special baking tools or skills. This galette will become a summer favorite when peach season is at its peak. The galette is simply begging to be topped with a scoop of vanilla or peach ice cream.

INGREDIENTS

1 Personal-Sized Pastry Crust, unbaked (see recipe in this chapter)

1 large yellow peach, peeled, pitted, and sliced into eight wedges

2 teaspoons packed light brown sugar

1 teaspoon cornstarch

⅛ teaspoon ground cinnamon

1. Preheat oven to 375°F and line a baking sheet with parchment or a reusable silicone baking mat.

2. Roll out Personal-Sized Pastry Crust on a lightly floured surface until it forms an 8" circle and place on prepared baking sheet.

3. In a medium bowl, add peach slices, brown sugar, cornstarch, and cinnamon. Toss to coat peach slices evenly.

4. Arrange peach slices in center of pastry crust, leaving a 1" border around the edge of peaches. Fold pastry crust over the edges of peach slices.

5. Bake 20–25 minutes or until peaches are tender and crust is golden brown. Cool 10 minutes before serving.

SINGLE-SERVING PEACH COBBLER

PREP TIME: 15 MIN | COOK TIME: 35 MIN | YIELDS 1 (6") COBBLER

Peach cobbler traditionally has a sweet drop biscuit topping that, when baked, resembles cobblestones. This version adds a little cinnamon to the biscuits to enhance the flavor of the peaches, and to make every bite even more delicious!

INGREDIENTS

¼ cup all-purpose flour

2 tablespoons granulated sugar, divided

¼ teaspoon baking powder

⅛ teaspoon ground cinnamon

1 tablespoon cubed salted butter, chilled

2 tablespoons whole milk

2 medium peaches, peeled, pitted, and sliced

2 tablespoons packed light brown sugar

1 tablespoon cornstarch

¼ teaspoon pure vanilla extract

1. Preheat oven to 350°F and place a baking sheet on bottom rack of oven.

2. In a medium bowl, combine flour, 1 tablespoon granulated sugar, baking powder, and cinnamon. Whisk well to combine. Add butter and use your fingers to rub mixture until it resembles coarse sand.

3. Make a well in dry ingredients and add milk. Gently stir until a shaggy batter forms and no dry flour remains. Set aside.

4. In a medium bowl, add peaches, brown sugar, cornstarch, and vanilla. Toss well to coat. Transfer mixture to a 6" pie pan.

5. Dollop biscuit mixture evenly over peaches by heaping teaspoons. Sprinkle with remaining 1 tablespoon granulated sugar.

6. Bake on heated baking sheet 35–40 minutes or until topping is golden brown and filling is bubbling.

7. Remove cobbler from oven and let cool 30 minutes before enjoying.

CHOCOLATE CREAM PIE

PREP TIME: 4½ HOURS | **COOK TIME: 11 MIN** | **YIELDS 1 (6") PIE**

If you love chocolate and want to pack in as much chocolate as you can, make this pie with a chocolate cookie crust rather than graham cracker. Dutch-processed cocoa powder makes the flavor of this pie a little more bitter than natural cocoa powder, so if you prefer a sweeter flavor, you can make the switch.

INGREDIENTS

1 cup half-and-half

3 tablespoons granulated sugar

1 tablespoon Dutch-processed cocoa powder

1 tablespoon cornstarch

1 large egg yolk

1 tablespoon unsalted butter

1 tablespoon chopped semisweet chocolate

½ teaspoon pure vanilla extract, divided

1 Cookie Crust for One, baked and cooled (see recipe in this chapter)

¼ cup heavy whipping cream

1 tablespoon powdered sugar

1. In a medium saucepan, whisk together half-and-half, granulated sugar, cocoa powder, cornstarch, and egg yolk. Place pan over medium-low heat and whisk until mixture starts to steam, about 4 minutes. Whisk constantly until mixture thickens and starts to simmer, about 6 minutes. Cook 15 seconds, then remove from heat and stir in butter, chocolate, and ¼ teaspoon vanilla. Mix well.

2. Pour mixture into prepared Cookie Crust for One. Place a layer of plastic wrap directly on filling and chill 4 hours or overnight.

3. Once chilled, in a medium bowl, add cream, powdered sugar, and remaining ¼ teaspoon vanilla. Whip on medium speed until soft peaks form, about 2 minutes.

4. Spread cream over pie. Serve immediately or chill up to 1 hour.

BERRY APPLE CRISP

PREP TIME: 15 MIN | COOK TIME: 35 MIN | YIELDS 1 (6") CRISP

The oats in this topping add a chewy texture, but if you do not have oats, you can omit them or replace them with a tablespoon of finely chopped raw pecans, almonds, or walnuts. A little bit of ground cinnamon—about ⅛ teaspoon—would also be a lovely addition.

INGREDIENTS

2 tablespoons all-purpose flour

1 tablespoon old-fashioned oats

2 tablespoons packed light brown sugar

2 tablespoons unsalted butter

1 cup hulled fresh strawberries, quartered

1 medium-sized firm baking apple, peeled, cored, and cut into ½" pieces

1 tablespoon granulated sugar

1 tablespoon cornstarch

½ teaspoon freshly grated lemon zest

¼ teaspoon pure vanilla extract

1. Preheat oven to 350°F and place a baking sheet on bottom rack of oven.

2. In a small bowl, combine flour, oats, and brown sugar. Mix well, then add butter and use your fingers to rub butter into flour until it forms a crumble. Cover with plastic wrap and refrigerate until ready to use.

3. In a medium bowl, combine strawberries, apple, granulated sugar, cornstarch, lemon zest, and vanilla. Toss until evenly mixed. Transfer to a 6" pie pan and sprinkle crisp topping over top.

4. Bake on heated baking sheet 35–40 minutes or until crisp topping is golden brown and filling is bubbling.

5. Remove crisp from oven and let cool 1 hour before enjoying.

PECAN PIE

PREP TIME: 15 MIN | COOK TIME: 40 MIN | YIELDS 1 (6") PIE

The first printed recipes for pecan pie came out of Texas in the 1870s, but the dish quickly spread across the American South and Midwest, where it became a staple throughout the year, particularly during the fall and winter holidays.

INGREDIENTS

1 Personal-Sized Pastry Crust, unbaked (see recipe in this chapter)

2 tablespoons packed light brown sugar

¼ cup corn syrup

1 large egg

2 teaspoons unsalted butter, melted and cooled

2 teaspoons all-purpose flour

¼ teaspoon pure vanilla extract

¼ cup plus 1 tablespoon chopped pecans

1. Preheat oven to 400°F and place a baking sheet on bottom rack of oven.

2. Roll out Personal-Sized Pastry Crust on a lightly floured surface until it forms an 8" circle. Slide dough into a 6" pie pan, making sure not to stretch or tug. Cover with plastic wrap and refrigerate until ready to use.

3. In a medium bowl, combine brown sugar, corn syrup, egg, butter, flour, and vanilla. Whisk until well incorporated and smooth. Stir in pecans and transfer mixture to prepared crust.

4. Bake on heated baking sheet 5 minutes, then reduce heat to 350°F and bake another 35–40 minutes or until pie has puffed all over and crust is golden brown.

5. Remove pie from oven and let cool completely to room temperature before enjoying.

Pie Crust Browning Too Fast?

If you find your pie crust edges are perfectly cooked before your pie's filling is done, you can wrap the crust edges with a strip of aluminum foil. A single layer is usually enough, but you can use a double layer to provide added shielding. The same applies to a crumble, crisp, or top crust. A layer of foil laid on top will stop excess browning but allow for continued cooking.

HAM AND CHEDDAR QUICHE FOR ONE

PREP TIME: 15 MIN | COOK TIME: 48 MIN | YIELDS 1 (6") QUICHE

Quiche is perfect for breakfast, lunch, or dinner, and pairs well with a mixed green salad or a cup of fresh fruit. You can bake this quiche in advance and reheat it in your oven for 10 minutes at 350°F.

INGREDIENTS

1 Personal-Sized Pastry Crust, unbaked (see recipe in this chapter)

2 large eggs

¼ cup whole milk

3 tablespoons heavy cream

⅛ teaspoon salt

⅛ teaspoon ground nutmeg

¼ cup finely chopped ham

¼ cup shredded Cheddar cheese

1. Preheat oven to 350°F.

2. Roll out Personal-Sized Pastry Crust on a lightly floured surface until it forms an 8" circle. Slide dough into a 6" pie pan, making sure not to stretch or tug.

3. Line inside of crust with baking parchment or aluminum foil, fill with uncooked rice or dried beans, and bake 10 minutes. Remove weights and lining, prick bottom of crust four or five times with a fork, then return to oven another 3 minutes. Remove from oven and cool to room temperature.

4. In a medium bowl, add eggs, milk, cream, salt, and nutmeg. Whisk until well combined.

5. Layer ham and cheese in bottom of par-baked pastry crust. Pour egg mixture over top.

6. Bake 35–40 minutes or until filling is golden brown and puffed all over. Cool 30 minutes before serving. Enjoy warm or at room temperature.

PEACH PIE

PREP TIME: 30 MIN | COOK TIME: 41 MIN | YIELDS 1 (6") PIE

Fruit pies that are first cooked on the stove will yield a thicker filling and will not cause an air gap between the filling and the top crust of the pie. The top crust of this Peach Pie is made into a lattice, but you can make it a double-crust pie if that makes your life easier.

INGREDIENTS

2 Personal-Sized Pastry Crusts, unbaked, divided (see recipe in this chapter)

2 medium peaches, peeled, pitted, and sliced

1 tablespoon packed light brown sugar

½ tablespoon unsalted butter

¼ teaspoon ground cardamom

1 teaspoon water

½ teaspoon cornstarch

¼ teaspoon pure vanilla extract

1 tablespoon whole milk

1. Roll out half of Personal-Sized Pastry Crust on a lightly floured surface until it forms an 8" circle. Slide dough into a 6" pie pan, making sure not to stretch or tug. Cover with plastic wrap and refrigerate until ready to use.

2. Roll out remaining half crust on a lightly floured surface until it forms a 7" circle. Cut circle into seven strips. Slide strips onto a large plate. Cover with plastic wrap and refrigerate until ready to use.

3. Preheat oven to 400°F and place a baking sheet on bottom rack of oven.

4. In a medium skillet, add peaches, brown sugar, butter, and cardamom. Heat over medium heat until butter melts, about 20 seconds, then cook, stirring often, until peaches are tender, about 5 minutes.

5. Reduce heat to low. In a small bowl, add water and cornstarch and mix to form a slurry. Add slurry to peaches and mix well. Cook until mixture thickens, about 1 minute. Turn off heat and add vanilla and stir well. Cool 10 minutes.

6. Remove pie crusts from refrigerator. Spread peach mixture evenly in pastry-lined pie pan. Place four crust strips evenly across top of pie. Pull middle strip toward center and lay one reserved strip across bottom ⅓ of pie. Pull two outside strips down pie and lay another reserved strip across center of pie. Pull outside strips back into place. Pull top of middle strip down and lay final strip across pie. Replace strip.

7. Trim dough to ½" of pan's edge. Tuck edge of top crust under edge of bottom crust. Crimp dough with your fingers or the tines of a fork.

8. Brush pastry lattice with milk, then bake on heated baking sheet 5 minutes. Reduce heat to 350°F and bake another 30–35 minutes or until crust is golden brown and filling is bubbling.

9. Remove pie from oven and let cool 1 hour before enjoying.

SILKY CHOCOLATE GANACHE TART

PREP TIME: 1¼ HOURS | COOK TIME: 11 MIN | YIELDS 1 (6") TART

You can grind whole almonds for this tart in a food processor by pulsing them to fine crumbs. Alternatively, you can use ready-ground almond flour and store any excess in your freezer, where it will keep up to a year.

INGREDIENTS

⅓ cup finely ground almonds

2 tablespoons graham cracker crumbs

2 tablespoons unsalted butter, melted and cooled

1 tablespoon granulated sugar

½ cup heavy cream

3 ounces finely chopped semisweet chocolate

2 tablespoons unsalted butter, at room temperature

¼ teaspoon pure vanilla extract

⅛ teaspoon flaky sea salt

1. Preheat oven to 350°F.

2. In a small bowl, combine almonds, cracker crumbs, melted butter, and sugar. Mix until nuts and cracker crumbs are evenly coated in butter. Transfer to a 6" pie pan and press into pan so bottom and sides are packed in evenly and firmly.

3. Bake 8–10 minutes or until crust is golden brown. Set aside to cool to room temperature.

4. In a small saucepan over medium heat, add cream. Once it just comes to a simmer, about 3 minutes, remove from heat and add chocolate and room-temperature butter. Let stand 1 minute, then whisk until mixture is smooth. Stir in vanilla.

5. Pour ganache into prepared crust. Chill uncovered 1 hour. Garnish with sea salt before serving.

CHOCOLATE FUDGE PIE

PREP TIME: 15 MIN | COOK TIME: 38 MIN | YIELDS 1 (6") PIE

Baked custard pies are a bit richer than other kinds of pies. This chocolate pie is definitely rich and is perfect for people who love chocolate desserts that pack a punch. If you want a mocha fudge pie add ¼ teaspoon of instant espresso powder with the cocoa powder.

INGREDIENTS

1 Personal-Sized Pastry Crust, unbaked (see recipe in this chapter)

1 ounce chopped unsweetened chocolate

1 tablespoon unsalted butter

1 large egg

3 tablespoons packed light brown sugar

¼ cup corn syrup

1 teaspoon cocoa powder

¼ teaspoon pure vanilla extract

1. Preheat oven to 375°F.

2. Roll out Personal-Sized Pastry Crust on a lightly floured surface until it forms an 8" circle. Slide dough into a 6" pie pan, making sure not to stretch or tug.

3. In a small microwave-safe bowl, add chocolate and butter. Heat 30 seconds, stir well, then heat in 15-second intervals, stirring well between each interval, until melted and smooth.

4. In a medium bowl, add melted chocolate mixture along with remaining ingredients. Mix until smooth and fully incorporated.

5. Pour filling mixture into prepared crust. Bake 35–40 minutes or until filling is puffed all over and crust is golden brown. Cool completely to room temperature before serving.

BUTTERSCOTCH PIE

PREP TIME: 4½ HOURS | COOK TIME: 11 MIN | YIELDS 1 (6") PIE

Most people think of the hard candy when they think of butterscotch, but for this recipe the butterscotch flavor comes from the brown sugar used to flavor the custard. If you have some good scotch on hand, you can add a teaspoon at the end of simmering to flavor the custard.

INGREDIENTS

1 cup half-and-half

¼ cup packed light brown sugar

1 tablespoon cornstarch

1 large egg yolk

1 tablespoon unsalted butter

½ teaspoon pure vanilla extract, divided

1 Cookie Crust for One, baked and cooled (see recipe in this chapter)

¼ cup heavy whipping cream

1 tablespoon powdered sugar

1. In a medium saucepan, whisk together half-and-half, brown sugar, cornstarch, and egg yolk. Place pan over medium-low heat and whisk until mixture starts to steam, about 4 minutes. Whisk constantly until mixture thickens and starts to simmer, about 6 minutes. Cook 15 seconds, then remove from heat and stir in butter and ¼ teaspoon vanilla. Mix well.

2. Pour mixture into prepared Cookie Crust for One. Place a layer of plastic wrap directly on filling and chill 4 hours or overnight.

3. Once chilled, in a medium bowl, add cream, powdered sugar, and remaining ¼ teaspoon vanilla. Use a hand mixer to whip on medium speed until soft peaks form, about 2 minutes.

4. Spread cream over pie. Serve immediately or chill up to 1 hour.

PERSONAL SPINACH AND GRUYÈRE QUICHE

PREP TIME: 30 MIN | COOK TIME: 53 MIN | YIELDS 1 (6") QUICHE

Gruyère cheese is a Swiss-style cheese with a nutty flavor and creamy texture. It is often used for making fondue and has a pleasant earthy flavor when warm. If you are unable to find Gruyère cheese, you can use baby Swiss in its place.

INGREDIENTS

1 Personal-Sized Pastry Crust, unbaked (see recipe in this chapter)

2 teaspoons butter

1 cup baby spinach

2 large eggs

¼ cup whole milk

3 tablespoons heavy cream

⅛ teaspoon salt

⅛ teaspoon ground nutmeg

¼ cup shredded Gruyère cheese

1. Preheat oven to 350°F.

2. Roll out Personal-Sized Pastry Crust on a lightly floured surface until it forms an 8" circle. Slide dough into a 6" pie pan, making sure not to stretch or tug.

3. Line inside of crust with baking parchment or aluminum foil, fill with uncooked rice or dried beans, and bake 10 minutes. Remove weights and lining, prick bottom of crust four or five times with a fork, then return to oven another 3 minutes. Remove from oven and cool to room temperature.

4. In a medium skillet over medium heat, add butter. Once melted add spinach and cook, stirring often, until wilted, about 5 minutes. Remove from heat and transfer spinach to a colander. Press to release liquid. Transfer to a cutting board and finely chop. Set aside.

5. In a medium bowl, add eggs, milk, cream, salt, and nutmeg. Whisk until well combined.

6. Layer chopped spinach and cheese in bottom of par-baked pastry crust. Pour egg mixture over top.

7. Bake 35–40 minutes or until filling is golden brown and puffed all over. Cool 30 minutes before serving. Enjoy warm or at room temperature.

MINI APPLE BLUEBERRY COBBLER

PREP TIME: 30 MIN | **COOK TIME: 30 MIN** | **YIELDS 1 (6") COBBLER**

This cobbler is a celebration of fresh fruit and is wonderful on a warm summer day. Just a pinch of allspice in the topping and almond extract in the filling will add a little oomph to the flavors of the apples and blueberries.

INGREDIENTS

¼ cup all-purpose flour

¼ cup granulated sugar, divided

¼ teaspoon baking powder

⅛ teaspoon allspice

1 tablespoon cubed salted, butter, chilled

2 tablespoons whole milk

1 medium-sized firm baking apple, peeled, cored, and sliced

1 cup fresh blueberries

1 tablespoon cornstarch

¼ teaspoon pure vanilla extract

⅛ teaspoon almond extract

1. Preheat oven to 350°F and place a baking sheet on bottom rack of oven.

2. In a medium bowl, combine flour, 1 tablespoon sugar, baking powder, and allspice. Whisk well to combine. Add butter and use your fingers to rub mixture until it resembles coarse sand.

3. Make a well in dry ingredients and add milk. Gently stir until a shaggy batter forms and no dry flour remains. Set aside.

4. In a medium bowl, add apple, blueberries, 2 tablespoons sugar, cornstarch, vanilla, and almond extract. Toss well to coat. Transfer mixture to a 6" pie pan.

5. Dollop biscuit mixture evenly over fruit by heaping teaspoons. Sprinkle with remaining 1 tablespoon sugar.

6. Bake on heated baking sheet 30–35 minutes or until topping is golden brown and filling is bubbling.

7. Remove cobbler from oven and let cool 30 minutes before enjoying.

CHOCOLATE COBBLER

Chocolate cobbler is a magical dish. You layer melted butter, a stiff cake batter, cocoa, sugar, and boiling water into a pan, and after baking, you end up with a cake-like top with a rich fudgy sauce underneath! Be sure to bake this on a foil-lined baking sheet, as the sauce can sometimes bubble over a little.

INGREDIENTS

1 tablespoon salted butter

½ cup granulated sugar, divided

4 teaspoons cocoa powder, divided

⅓ cup all-purpose flour

⅛ teaspoon baking powder

⅛ teaspoon baking soda

2 tablespoons whole milk

¼ teaspoon pure vanilla extract

⅓ cup boiling water

1. Preheat oven to 350°F.

2. Add butter to a 5" × 7" baking dish and place on a baking sheet lined with aluminum foil. Place in oven and bake until melted, about 5 minutes. Remove from oven and set aside.

3. In a medium bowl, add ¼ cup sugar, 2 teaspoons cocoa powder, flour, baking powder, and baking soda. Whisk to combine. Add milk and vanilla and stir to mix, then spread over melted butter. Add remaining ¼ cup sugar and remaining 2 teaspoons cocoa powder over top, then pour boiling water over it. Do not mix.

4. Bake 25–30 minutes or until top is set but the whole cobbler jiggles slightly when moved. Cool 20 minutes before serving.

CHAPTER 6

PUDDINGS AND CUSTARDS

When you think of elegant desserts, what comes to mind? Like many people, you probably think of things like a crème brûlée topped with a caramelized sugar crust, silky and rich chocolate pot de crème, and crisp chocolate éclairs stuffed with vanilla pastry cream. These desserts make you feel like you are having a special treat. If you have ever made any of these desserts at home, you know the recipes yield six, eight, or even twelve portions, and they do not keep all that well.

This chapter will help you to enjoy your favorite custard and pudding desserts in portions better suited to one person. From custard-filled Orange Cream Puffs and Chocolate Chip Croissant Bread Pudding to simple Flan for One and citrusy Crema Catalana, this chapter will offer you recipes as well as tips and tricks to make your single-serving desserts a success! While these recipes do take a little more time, they are absolutely worth it. The reward is the pleasure you will find while dipping your spoon into a perfectly baked custard, or sinking your teeth into a velvety bread pudding. Nothing is stopping you from indulging in an elegant dessert, and remember—you deserve it!

ORANGE CREAM PUFFS

These crisp puffs have a bright orange flavor and are perfect when filled with traditional pastry cream, whipped cream, or even vanilla ice cream. If you choose ice cream, be sure to add a drizzle of chocolate over the top!

INGREDIENTS

3 tablespoons water

2 tablespoons orange juice

3 tablespoons salted butter

⅓ cup all-purpose flour

1 teaspoon granulated sugar

½ teaspoon freshly grated orange zest

1 large egg

¼ teaspoon pure vanilla extract

1 recipe Vanilla Pastry Cream (see recipe in this chapter)

2 tablespoons powdered sugar

1. Preheat oven to 400°F and line a baking sheet with parchment or a reusable silicone baking mat.

2. In a medium saucepan over medium heat, add water, orange juice, and butter. Bring mixture to a boil, then add flour, granulated sugar, and orange zest and cook, stirring constantly, until the mixture forms a smooth ball and a film develops on bottom of the pan, about 1 minute.

3. Remove pan from heat and transfer dough to a medium bowl. Let dough cool 10 minutes or until it is cool enough to touch.

4. Add egg and vanilla. Use a hand mixer on medium speed to beat until batter is smooth and glossy, about 30 seconds. Spoon dough onto the prepared baking sheet with two spoons into four mounds about 2" apart.

5. Bake 10 minutes, then reduce oven to 325°F and bake 25–30 minutes or until puffs are golden brown and puffed. Transfer to a rack and allow to cool to room temperature.

6. Once cool, slice each shell in half horizontally. Transfer Vanilla Pastry Cream into a piping bag fitted with a medium round tip. Pipe cream onto one half of each shell and top with second half.

7. Dust tops of puffs generously with powdered sugar before enjoying.

CHOCOLATE ÉCLAIRS

PREP TIME: 20 MIN | COOK TIME: 39 MIN | YIELDS 4 (4") ÉCLAIRS

A chocolate éclair is an elegant dessert that is easier to make than you think.

INGREDIENTS

⅓ cup water

3 tablespoons salted butter

⅓ cup all-purpose flour

1 teaspoon granulated sugar

1 large egg

¼ teaspoon pure vanilla extract

1 recipe Vanilla Pastry Cream (see recipe in this chapter)

2 tablespoons heavy whipping cream

¼ cup semisweet chocolate chips

1. Preheat oven to 400°F and line a baking sheet with parchment or a reusable silicone baking mat.

2. In a medium saucepan over medium heat, add water and butter. Bring to a boil, then add flour and sugar and cook, stirring constantly, until the mixture forms a smooth ball and a film develops on bottom of the pan, about 1 minute.

3. Remove pan from heat and transfer dough to a medium bowl. Let dough cool 10 minutes or until it is cool enough to touch.

4. Add egg and vanilla. Use a hand mixer on medium speed to beat until batter is smooth and glossy, about 30 seconds. Transfer mixture to a piping bag fitted with a large round (#9) tube. Pipe dough into six equal lines on baking sheet about 2" apart.

5. Bake 10 minutes, then reduce oven to 325°F and bake 25–30 minutes or until éclairs are golden brown and puffed. Transfer to a rack, gently poke a paring knife into the side of each éclair shell, and allow to cool to room temperature.

6. Once cool, slice each shell in half horizontally. Pipe Vanilla Pastry Cream into bottom of each shell.

7. In a small microwave-safe bowl, add cream and heat 30 seconds. Stir in chocolate chips and heat in 15-second intervals until chocolate is melted.

8. Dip top shell into chocolate, then place on top of filling. Refrigerate uncovered 10 minutes to set chocolate.

VANILLA PASTRY CREAM

Pastry cream can be used to fill cakes and cupcakes, spread into a baked pastry crust and topped with fresh fruit, piped into cream puffs, or simply eaten with a spoon. If you want to make this cream even richer, use heavy cream in place of half-and-half. To make a chocolate version, add 1 teaspoon of cocoa powder.

INGREDIENTS

¾ cup half-and-half

3 tablespoons granulated sugar

1 tablespoon cornstarch

1 large egg yolk

¼ teaspoon pure vanilla extract

1 teaspoon unsalted butter

1. In a blender, combine half-and-half, sugar, cornstarch, and egg yolk. Purée until smooth, about 20 seconds.

2. Transfer mixture to a small saucepan and place over medium-low heat. Cook, whisking constantly, until mixture comes to a boil and thickens, about 8 minutes.

3. Remove from heat and whisk in vanilla and butter. Once smooth, pour mixture through a strainer into a medium bowl. Place a layer of plastic wrap directly on pastry cream and chill at least 4 hours before using.

BAKED EGG CUSTARD

PREP TIME: 4 HOURS | COOK TIME: 40 MIN | SERVES 1

Mace is the lacy coating outside of the nutmeg seed and is considered its sister spice. The flavor is very similar to nutmeg but lighter and blended with spicy cinnamon. If you do not have any mace, you can use nutmeg, preferably freshly grated, in its place.

INGREDIENTS

½ cup half-and-half

1 large egg yolk

1 tablespoon granulated sugar

⅛ teaspoon cornstarch

1 pinch (about ¹⁄₁₆ teaspoon) ground mace

1. Preheat oven to 325°F.

2. In a small bowl, combine half-and-half, egg yolk, sugar, and cornstarch. Whisk until smooth. Transfer mixture to a 7-ounce ramekin and dust top with mace.

3. Place ramekin in a small baking dish. Add recently boiled water until it reaches halfway up the side of the ramekin.

4. Bake 40–45 minutes or until custard is set around the edges but still a little jiggly in the center. Transfer ramekin to a wire rack and cool to room temperature, then chill at least 4 hours before enjoying.

Baked Custards

A baked custard, properly prepared, is silky and rich but not too heavy. You can't rush a baked custard, as it needs time to gently bake in a water bath and then needs some time to chill thoroughly. The water bath is key to gently cooking the custard, which will prevent it from curdling or splitting while baking, so don't skip that step.

CHOCOLATE CUSTARD

PREP TIME: 6 HOURS | COOK TIME: 38 MIN | SERVES 1

If you would like to make this into a Mexican hot chocolate–flavored treat, add ⅛ teaspoon cinnamon and a fat pinch of nutmeg to the sugar and cocoa powder, then proceed with the recipe as written.

INGREDIENTS

1 tablespoon granulated sugar

1 tablespoon cocoa powder

½ cup half-and-half

2 tablespoons semisweet chocolate chips

2 teaspoons unsalted butter

1 large egg yolk

¼ teaspoon pure vanilla extract

1. In a medium saucepan, add sugar and cocoa powder and whisk until well combined. Slowly whisk in half-and-half and heat over medium heat until sugar has melted and the mixture comes to a simmer, about 3 minutes. Remove from heat and whisk in chocolate chips and butter until smooth.

2. In a small bowl, whisk together egg yolk and vanilla. While whisking, ladle a few tablespoons of hot half-and-half mixture into the egg yolk, then whisk egg yolk mixture into half-and-half in pan.

3. Transfer mixture to a 7-ounce ramekin and chill 2 hours.

4. Preheat oven to 325°F.

5. Once chilled, place ramekin in a small baking dish. Add recently boiled water until it reaches halfway up the side of the ramekin.

6. Bake 35–40 minutes or until custard is set around edges but slightly jiggly in center. Transfer ramekin to a wire rack and cool to room temperature, then chill at least 4 hours before enjoying.

Custard Baking Tips

Baked custards should always be baked in a water bath unless otherwise noted. That gentle baking keeps the texture smooth. Watch the time carefully. Check early and test your custard by shaking the pan gently. Once ready, the edges should be set and the center should jiggle slightly. If you pull it too soon the custard will not set or it will be watery. If it overbakes, it will become grainy, similar to scrambled eggs.

PERSONAL BANANA PUDDING

This version of banana pudding has a toasted meringue topping that is popular in the American South. It is generally served slightly warm, but if you wish to enjoy it chilled, simply cool to room temperature before refrigerating uncovered at least 2 hours.

INGREDIENTS

3 tablespoons plus 1 teaspoon granulated sugar, divided

1 tablespoon all-purpose flour

¾ cup half-and-half

1 large egg, yolk and white separated

¼ teaspoon pure vanilla extract

1 teaspoon salted butter

½ medium-sized ripe banana, peeled and sliced

6 vanilla wafer cookies

1 pinch (about ⅟₁₆ teaspoon) cream of tartar

1. Preheat oven to 400°F.

2. In a small saucepan, combine 3 tablespoons sugar and flour. Whisk to combine, then add half-and-half and egg yolk. Whisk until smooth.

3. Heat mixture over medium-low heat, whisking constantly, until it just comes to a boil and thickens, about 5 minutes. Remove pan from heat and whisk in vanilla and butter.

4. Spread ⅓ of custard mixture in bottom of a 7-ounce ramekin. Top with half of banana slices and 3 vanilla wafers. Repeat with remaining custard, bananas, and wafers, ending with a layer of custard.

5. In a medium bowl, add egg white and cream of tartar. Use a hand mixer on medium-low speed to beat egg white until foamy, then gradually add remaining 1 teaspoon sugar and continue to beat on high speed until stiff peaks form.

6. Spoon meringue over top of pudding, making sure meringue covers edges of ramekin. Bake 8–10 minutes or until meringue is golden brown. Remove from oven and cool 20 minutes before serving.

FLAN FOR ONE

If you do not want to make the caramel for the top of the flan you can use 1 tablespoon of prepared caramel sauce in its place. A good-quality caramel ice cream topping will work just as well as the homemade caramel, but the added cream gives it a creamier flavor.

INGREDIENTS

¼ cup granulated sugar, divided

1 teaspoon water

½ cup half-and-half

1 large egg yolk

¼ teaspoon pure vanilla extract

⅛ teaspoon cornstarch

1 pinch (about ¹⁄₁₆ teaspoon) ground cinnamon

1. Preheat oven to 325°F.

2. In a small saucepan, add 2 tablespoons sugar and water. Heat over medium heat until sugar melts and starts to turn golden brown, about 5 minutes. Immediately pour caramel into a 7-ounce ramekin and swirl so it covers bottom completely. Set aside.

3. In a small bowl, combine remaining 2 tablespoons sugar, half-and-half, egg yolk, vanilla, and cornstarch. Whisk until smooth, then add cinnamon and whisk until fully incorporated. Transfer mixture to ramekin.

4. Place ramekin in a small baking dish. Add recently boiled water until it reaches halfway up the side of the ramekin.

5. Bake 40–45 minutes or until custard is set around the edges but still a little jiggly in the center. Transfer ramekin to a wire rack and cool to room temperature. Run a thin knife around the edge of the custard to loosen, then place a small plate on ramekin and turn over until flan releases. Enjoy at room temperature or chilled.

RICE PUDDING

PREP TIME: 10 MIN | COOK TIME: 35 MIN | SERVES 1

Rice pudding is an excellent way to use leftover rice. This recipe calls for white rice, but you can use brown rice if that is what you have on hand. Feel free to use any dried fruits you like if raisins are not to your taste. Dried cranberries are lovely in this pudding!

INGREDIENTS

1 large egg

2 tablespoons whole milk

2 tablespoons granulated sugar

¼ teaspoon pure vanilla extract

⅛ teaspoon ground cinnamon

½ cup cooked white rice

2 tablespoons raisins

1. Preheat oven to 350°F and lightly spray a 7-ounce ramekin with nonstick cooking spray.

2. In a medium bowl, combine egg and milk. Whisk until fully incorporated, then add sugar, vanilla, and cinnamon and whisk well.

3. Add rice and raisins and stir to combine, then transfer to prepared ramekin. Place ramekin in a small baking dish. Add recently boiled water until it reaches halfway up the side of the ramekin.

4. Bake 35–40 minutes or until custard is set around the edges but still a little jiggly in the center. Transfer ramekin to a wire rack and cool 15 minutes before serving. Enjoy warm or at room temperature.

Making Small Batches of Rice

Making a single portion of rice can be tricky if you're using the traditional methods. An easier, if unconventional, way to get perfect rice in small portions is to boil it like pasta. Use three times the water to uncooked white rice, boil for 11 minutes, drain, then return to the pot. Cover and let stand 5 minutes. The rice will be fluffy and ready to enjoy.

ORANGE CRANBERRY BREAD PUDDING

PREP TIME: 30 MIN | COOK TIME: 30 MIN | SERVES 1

Rubbing the orange zest and sugar together helps to release more of the orange oil in the zest, which will infuse more of the custard with citrus flavor. If you want to add an extra special touch you can garnish the hot bread pudding with a tablespoon of white chocolate chips.

INGREDIENTS

1½ cups cubed bread, left out for 3 hours to dry out slightly

2 tablespoons dried cranberries

3 tablespoons granulated sugar

½ teaspoon freshly grated orange zest

1 large egg yolk

½ cup whole milk

¼ teaspoon pure vanilla extract

¼ teaspoon ground cinnamon

1 tablespoon unsalted butter, at room temperature

1. Preheat oven to 350°F and spray a 6" pie pan with nonstick cooking spray.

2. In a medium bowl, combine bread cubes and cranberries. Set aside.

3. In a small bowl, add sugar and orange zest. With your fingers, rub sugar and zest together until very fragrant. Whisk in egg yolk until smooth, then add milk, vanilla, and cinnamon and whisk until smooth.

4. Pour milk mixture over bread cubes and mix to combine. Let stand 10 minutes, stir again, then allow to stand 10 minutes more.

5. Transfer soaked bread and custard to prepared pan. Dot top with butter. Bake 30–35 minutes or until pudding is puffed all over and golden brown. Remove from oven and transfer to wire rack. Cool 15 minutes before serving. Enjoy warm.

CLASSIC BREAD PUDDING

PREP TIME: 30 MIN | COOK TIME: 30 MIN | SERVES 1

This bread pudding is simple to prepare and is satisfying but not too rich. If you would like to enjoy this for breakfast, you can prepare it the evening before, cover, and refrigerate overnight. The next morning, uncover and bake it straight from the refrigerator, adding 1 extra minute to the cooking time.

INGREDIENTS

1½ cups cubed bread, left out 3 hours to dry out slightly

2 tablespoons raisins

3 tablespoons packed light brown sugar

1 large egg yolk

½ cup whole milk

¼ teaspoon pure vanilla extract

¼ teaspoon ground cinnamon

1 tablespoon unsalted butter, at room temperature

1. Preheat oven to 350°F and spray a 6¼" cast iron skillet with nonstick cooking spray.

2. In a medium bowl, add bread cubes and raisins. Set aside.

3. In a small bowl, whisk together brown sugar and egg yolk. Add milk, vanilla, and cinnamon and whisk until smooth.

4. Pour milk mixture over bread cubes and mix to combine. Let stand 10 minutes, stir again, then allow to stand more 10 minutes.

5. Transfer soaked bread and custard to prepared skillet. Dot top with butter. Bake 30–35 minutes or until pudding is puffed all over and golden brown. Remove from oven and transfer to wire rack. Cool 15 minutes before serving. Enjoy warm.

Bread for Bread Pudding

Most crusty or sandwich bread works well for bread pudding. It is an excellent way to use up heels and stale slices that no one wants. You can stash leftover pieces of bread in an airtight container in the freezer to use for bread pudding later. Cube it up before freezing, then thaw it 1 hour before proceeding with your recipe.

CRÈME BRÛLÉE

PREP TIME: 2½ HOURS | COOK TIME: 23 MIN | SERVES 1

Perhaps one of the most elegant desserts out there, crème brûlée is exceptionally creamy and rich with a crisp candy sugar topping. If you do not have a kitchen torch, heat your broiler, place a rack near the top of the oven, and broil the sugar until it melts. It only takes a few minutes, so keep an eye on it to prevent scorching.

INGREDIENTS

½ cup heavy cream

¼ teaspoon vanilla bean paste

2 large egg yolks

¼ cup granulated sugar, divided

1. Preheat oven to 300°F.

2. In a small saucepan, add cream and vanilla bean paste. Heat over medium heat until cream simmers, about 3 minutes. Set aside.

3. In a small bowl, combine egg yolks and 3 tablespoons sugar. Whisk until smooth, then slowly whisk in hot cream. Transfer mixture to a 7-ounce ramekin.

4. Place ramekin in a small baking dish. Add recently boiled water until it reaches halfway up the side of the ramekin.

5. Bake 20–25 minutes or until custard is set around the edges but still a little jiggly in the center. Transfer ramekin to a wire rack and cool to room temperature, then chill at least 2 hours.

6. To serve, sprinkle remaining 1 tablespoon sugar evenly over top of custard. With a small torch, or under a heated broiler, melt sugar until caramelized. Cool 2 minutes to allow sugar to harden before enjoying.

SPICED CARDAMOM CUSTARD

PREP TIME: 4½ HOURS | COOK TIME: 40 MIN | SERVES 1

Cardamom is a member of the ginger family and is a pod containing many fragrant seeds. It is popular in Indian cuisine, features prominently in chai tea, and pairs well with cinnamon and chocolate.

INGREDIENTS

½ cup half-and-half

1 large egg yolk

1 tablespoon packed dark brown sugar

½ teaspoon freshly grated orange zest

⅛ teaspoon ground cardamom

⅛ teaspoon ground cinnamon

⅛ teaspoon pure vanilla extract

1. Preheat oven to 325°F.

2. In a small bowl, combine half-and-half, egg yolk, and brown sugar. Whisk until smooth, then add orange zest, cardamom, cinnamon, and vanilla and whisk until fully incorporated. Transfer mixture to a 7-ounce ramekin.

3. Place ramekin in a small baking dish. Add recently boiled water until it reaches halfway up the side of the ramekin.

4. Bake 40–45 minutes or until custard is set around the edges but still a little jiggly in the center. Transfer ramekin to a wire rack and cool to room temperature, then chill at least 4 hours before enjoying.

CHOCOLATE CHIP CROISSANT BREAD PUDDING

PREP TIME: 30 MIN | COOK TIME: 30 MIN | SERVES 1

If you are looking for an extra-buttery dessert studded with chocolate, then you have hit the jackpot with this recipe! Croissants make for an extra-decadent bread pudding, due to the butter used to puff the layers. If you are using fresh croissants you will want to let the cubes stand uncovered for at least a few hours to dry out so the custard absorbs better.

INGREDIENTS

1½ cups cubed stale croissants

3 tablespoons semisweet chocolate chips, divided

3 tablespoons granulated sugar

1 large egg yolk

½ cup half-and-half

1 teaspoon bourbon

¼ teaspoon pure vanilla extract

1 tablespoon unsalted butter, at room temperature

1. Preheat oven to 350°F and spray a 6" pie pan with nonstick cooking spray.

2. In a medium bowl, add croissant cubes and 2 tablespoons chocolate chips. Set aside.

3. In a small bowl whisk, together sugar and egg yolk until smooth. Add half-and-half, bourbon, and vanilla and whisk until smooth.

4. Pour custard mixture over bread cubes and mix to combine. Let stand 10 minutes, stir again, then allow to stand 10 minutes more.

5. Transfer soaked bread and custard to prepared pan. Dot top with butter. Bake 30–35 minutes or until pudding is puffed all over and golden brown. Remove from oven, transfer to wire rack, and garnish with remaining 1 tablespoon chocolate chips. Cool 15 minutes before serving. Enjoy warm.

Why Stale Bread?

Stale bread is generally used for things like bread pudding and French toast because it absorbs liquids better. Fresh bread will result in an uneven texture since the custard will not fully absorb into it. You can use your oven to speed up the process. Place your bread on a baking sheet and bake at 225°F until dry and crusty, about 30 minutes.

MICROWAVE BREAD PUDDING

PREP TIME: 10 MIN | COOK TIME: 3 MIN | SERVES 1

What happens when you are short on time but really need some bread pudding? You turn to the microwave! This version is ready in a flash and will satisfy any bread pudding craving. Enjoy this warm because it is somewhat less charming when eaten cold.

INGREDIENTS

1 cup cubed sandwich bread

1 tablespoon golden raisins

1 large egg

¼ cup half-and-half

2 tablespoons whole milk

2 tablespoons granulated sugar

¼ teaspoon pure vanilla extract

⅛ teaspoon ground nutmeg

1 teaspoon powdered sugar

1. In a microwave-safe 10-ounce dish, place bread and raisins.

2. In a small bowl, combine egg, half-and-half, milk, granulated sugar, and vanilla. Whisk well, then pour mixture over bread. Sprinkle top with nutmeg.

3. Microwave 1 minute, then check to see if there is any liquid remaining in dish. Continue to microwave in 30-second intervals until no liquid remains.

4. Remove from microwave and cool 2 minutes. Dust with powdered sugar and enjoy warm.

CREMA CATALANA

PREP TIME: 4½ HOURS | COOK TIME: 6 MIN | SERVES 1

This Spanish custard is similar to crème brûlée with a caramelized sugar topping and creamy custard, but where crème brûlée is slowly baked in a water bath, Crema Catalana is cooked entirely on the stove. It is flavored with orange, lemon, and cinnamon, popular flavors in Spain, which is known for growing citrus.

INGREDIENTS

½ cup plus 1 tablespoon whole milk

2 tablespoons granulated sugar, divided

1½ teaspoons cornstarch

1" strip fresh orange zest

1" strip fresh lemon zest

½ cinnamon stick

1 large egg yolk, beaten

¼ teaspoon pure vanilla extract

1. In a small saucepan, add milk, 1 tablespoon plus 2 teaspoons sugar, and cornstarch. Whisk until smooth, then add orange zest, lemon zest, and cinnamon stick. Heat over medium-low heat and cook, whisking constantly, until mixture comes to a simmer, about 3 minutes.

2. In a small bowl, add egg yolk and vanilla. Whisk 3 tablespoons of hot milk mixture into egg yolk, then whisk yolk mixture back into milk in pan. Continue to cook until custard is bubbling and thick, about 3 minutes.

3. Strain custard into a 7-ounce ramekin and smooth top. Place a layer of plastic wrap directly on custard, then refrigerate 4 hours or until fully chilled.

4. To serve, sprinkle top with remaining 1 teaspoon sugar. With a small torch, or under a heated broiler, melt sugar until caramelized. Cool 2 minutes to allow sugar to harden before enjoying.

How to Make Citrus Zest Strips

To make strips of fresh citrus zest you only need a vegetable peeler. Take your citrus and pull the vegetable peeler down the fruit to slice off a strip of zest. Do not press too hard, or you will get too much of the pith, which can make your mixture bitter. Be sure to cover the citrus with plastic wrap and refrigerate so the fruit does not dry out before you can eat it.

BREAD AND BUTTER PUDDING

PREP TIME: 1½ HOURS | COOK TIME: 32 MIN | SERVES 1

Bread and butter pudding is popular in British cuisine. You can use standard sandwich bread, or, if you have brioche or challah in your bread box you can use either one to add extra richness. The amaretto can be omitted if you do not have it on hand.

INGREDIENTS

3 tablespoons boiling water

2 tablespoons golden raisins

1 teaspoon amaretto

2 tablespoons unsalted butter, at room temperature

3 slices white bread, crusts removed

2 large egg yolks

3 tablespoons plus 1 teaspoon granulated sugar, divided

6 tablespoons heavy cream

2 tablespoons half-and-half

¼ teaspoon vanilla bean paste

1. In a small bowl, add water and raisins. Let stand 1 hour, then drain and add amaretto. Set aside.

2. Preheat oven to 350°F and spray a 6" pie pan with nonstick cooking spray.

3. Butter bread slices on both sides. Cut 1 slice into ½" cubes. Cut remaining slices into four triangles. Set aside.

4. In a small bowl, whisk together egg yolks and 3 tablespoons sugar until smooth. Set aside.

5. In a small saucepan, add cream and half-and-half. Heat over medium heat until milk just comes to a simmer, about 2 minutes. Add 2 tablespoons hot cream mixture to egg yolks and whisk well, then whisk mixture back into saucepan. Immediately remove from heat and stir in vanilla bean paste.

6. Lay cubed bread on base of prepared pie pan. Top with raisins, then place bread triangles over top. Pour custard over bread, making sure each slice is evenly coated. Let stand 10 minutes at room temperature to soak.

7. Place pie pan in a larger baking dish and add recently boiled water until it reaches halfway up the pan. Bake 30 minutes or until filling is set. Remove from oven and transfer to wire rack.

8. Sprinkle remaining 1 teaspoon sugar over top and torch or broil until sugar is caramelized. Serve warm or at room temperature.

PAN DE CALATRAVA

This recipe is a variation of a Spanish custard bread pudding. The texture is thick and creamy, but not too heavy because of the French bread. There is also a hint of citrus, which adds a refreshing taste. This pudding can be made with stale cake cubes, crusty bread cubes, or even leftover hard cookies like biscotti.

INGREDIENTS

½ cup cubed French bread, left out 4 hours to dry out slightly

½ cup plus 2 tablespoons whole milk

3 tablespoons granulated sugar

1" strip fresh lemon zest

1 large egg yolk

¼ teaspoon pure vanilla extract

1 pinch (about ¹⁄₁₆ teaspoon) ground cinnamon

1. Preheat oven to 325°F.

2. Lightly spray an 8-ounce ramekin with nonstick cooking spray. Arrange bread cubes in ramekin. Set aside.

3. In a small saucepan, add milk, sugar, and lemon zest. Heat over medium-low heat and cook, whisking constantly, until mixture comes to a simmer, about 3 minutes.

4. In a small bowl, add egg yolk and vanilla. Whisk 3 tablespoons of hot milk mixture into egg yolk, then whisk yolk mixture back into milk in pan. Remove pan from heat and strain mixture into prepared ramekin. Sprinkle cinnamon over top.

5. Place ramekin in a small baking dish. Add recently boiled water until it reaches halfway up the side of the ramekin.

6. Bake 35–40 minutes or until custard is set around the edges but still a little jiggly in the center. Transfer ramekin to a wire rack and cool to room temperature, then chill 2 hours.

7. To serve, run a thin knife around the edge of the custard to loosen, then place a small plate on ramekin and turn over until custard releases. Enjoy at room temperature or chilled.

BUTTERSCOTCH CUSTARD

PREP TIME: 6½ HOURS | COOK TIME: 38 MIN | SERVES 1

Butterscotch is similar to caramel, but it has a richer flavor because it starts with brown sugar rather than white sugar. It is thought to have originated in Yorkshire in the nineteenth century. Butterscotch can be made into a sauce for pouring over cakes and ice cream, or it can be whisked into custards like the one you find here!

INGREDIENTS

3 tablespoons packed dark brown sugar

2 teaspoons unsalted butter

½ cup half-and-half

1 large egg yolk

¼ teaspoon pure vanilla extract

⅛ teaspoon cornstarch

1. In a medium saucepan, add brown sugar and butter. Heat over medium heat until sugar has melted. Whisk in half-and-half until smooth, then allow mixture to come to a simmer, about 3 minutes. Remove from heat.

2. In a small bowl, whisk together egg yolk, vanilla, and cornstarch. While whisking, ladle a few tablespoons of hot half-and-half mixture into the egg yolk, then whisk egg yolk mixture into half-and-half in the pan.

3. Transfer mixture to a 7-ounce ramekin and chill 2 hours.

4. Preheat oven to 325°F.

5. Once chilled, cover ramekin with aluminum foil, poke a few holes into foil to release steam, and place ramekin in a small baking dish. Add recently boiled water until it reaches halfway up the side of the ramekin.

6. Bake 35–40 minutes or until custard is set around edges but slightly jiggly in center. Transfer ramekin to a wire rack and cool to room temperature, then chill at least 4 hours before enjoying.

BAKED COFFEE CUSTARD

PREP TIME: 4½ HOURS | COOK TIME: 35 MIN | SERVES 1

This custard is the dessert form of a coffee shop classic—iced vanilla latte. Instant espresso powder can be found in the coffee aisle along with instant coffee, and it offers the richest flavor here. If you do not use espresso powder often, you can store it in your freezer up to a year.

INGREDIENTS

½ cup half-and-half

1 large egg yolk

1 tablespoon granulated sugar

¼ teaspoon instant espresso powder

¼ teaspoon cocoa powder

⅛ teaspoon pure vanilla extract

1. Preheat oven to 325°F.

2. In a small bowl, combine half-and-half, egg yolk, sugar, espresso powder, cocoa powder, and vanilla. Whisk until smooth. Transfer mixture to a 7-ounce ramekin.

3. Place ramekin in a small baking dish. Add recently boiled water until it reaches halfway up the side of the ramekin.

4. Bake 35–40 minutes or until custard is set around the edges but still a little jiggly in the center. Transfer ramekin to a wire rack and cool to room temperature, then chill at least 4 hours before enjoying.

EGGNOG CUSTARD

Around the holiday season eggnog is a popular treat, often spiked with a little whiskey or rum. Here the delicious flavors of eggnog are baked into an ultra-rich custard dessert. The whiskey called for is totally optional. It can be replaced with spiced rum or ⅛ teaspoon rum extract if desired.

INGREDIENTS

¼ cup half-and-half

¼ cup heavy cream

1 large egg yolk

1 tablespoon granulated sugar

1 teaspoon whiskey

¼ teaspoon pure vanilla extract

⅛ teaspoon ground cinnamon

1 pinch (about 1⁄16 teaspoon) ground nutmeg

1. Preheat oven to 325°F.

2. In a small bowl, combine half-and-half, cream, egg yolk, sugar, whiskey, vanilla, cinnamon, and nutmeg. Whisk until smooth. Transfer mixture to a 7-ounce ramekin.

3. Place ramekin in a small baking dish. Add recently boiled water until it reaches halfway up the side of the ramekin.

4. Bake 35–40 minutes or until custard is set around the edges but still a little jiggly in the center. Transfer ramekin to a wire rack and cool to room temperature, then chill at least 4 hours before enjoying.

CINNAMON DULCE DE LECHE FLAN

PREP TIME: 10 MIN | COOK TIME: 45 MIN | SERVES 1

Dulce de leche can be purchased in a resealable squeeze bottle in most well-stocked grocery stores either in the ice cream toppings aisle or with Latin American foods. It is a caramelized condensed milk and is often used in coffee and desserts. It keeps for months in the refrigerator.

INGREDIENTS

3 tablespoons granulated sugar, divided

1 teaspoon water

¼ cup half-and-half

¼ cup dulce de leche

1 large egg yolk

¼ teaspoon pure vanilla extract

⅛ teaspoon cornstarch

⅛ teaspoon ground cinnamon

1. Preheat oven to 325°F.

2. In a small saucepan, add 2 tablespoons sugar and water. Heat over medium heat until sugar melts and starts to turn golden brown, about 5 minutes. Immediately pour resulting caramel into a 7-ounce ramekin and swirl so it covers bottom completely. Set aside.

3. In a small bowl, combine remaining 1 tablespoon sugar, half-and-half, dulce de leche, egg yolk, vanilla, and cornstarch. Whisk until smooth, then add cinnamon and whisk until fully incorporated. Transfer mixture to ramekin.

4. Place ramekin in a small baking dish. Add recently boiled water until it reaches halfway up the side of the ramekin.

5. Bake 40–45 minutes or until custard is set around the edges but still a little jiggly in the center. Transfer ramekin to a wire rack and cool to room temperature. Run a thin knife around the edge of the custard to loosen, then place a small plate on ramekin and turn over until flan releases. Enjoy at room temperature or chilled.

RASPBERRY CUSTARD CAKE

PREP TIME: 10 MIN | COOK TIME: 30 MIN | SERVES 1

This dish is a personal-sized take on raspberry custard kuchen, a popular German dessert. It is a hybrid of cake and custard studded with tangy raspberries. This is best when made with fresh berries, so if raspberries are not available feel free to use fresh blackberries, blueberries, cherries, or diced strawberries.

INGREDIENTS

2 tablespoons all-purpose flour, divided

1½ teaspoons cubed salted butter

1 tablespoon plus ½ teaspoon heavy cream, divided

1 tablespoon plus ½ teaspoon granulated sugar, divided

¼ cup fresh raspberries

1 large egg yolk

¼ teaspoon cornstarch

¼ teaspoon pure vanilla extract

1. Preheat oven to 350°F and lightly spray a 7-ounce ramekin with nonstick cooking spray. Set aside.

2. In a small bowl, combine 1 tablespoon plus 2 teaspoons all-purpose flour and butter. Use your fingers to rub butter into flour until well combined. Add ½ teaspoon cream and mix to combine.

3. Press dough into prepared ramekin and sprinkle remaining 1 teaspoon flour and ½ teaspoon sugar on top, then arrange raspberries over top. Set aside.

4. In a small bowl, whisk together remaining 1 tablespoon sugar, remaining 1 tablespoon cream, egg yolk, cornstarch, and vanilla. Pour over raspberries.

5. Bake 30–35 minutes or until custard is puffed and just golden brown around the edges. Cool to room temperature before enjoying.

Is the Custard Really Done?

If you are new to custard making you may want to double-check your shake test with another method until you become more confident. You can use a thin paring knife dipped in just off center of the custard. If it comes out clean, then your custard is ready. If it has any custard clinging to the blade, add another few minutes to the cooking time.

CHOCOLATE POT DE CRÈME

PREP TIME: 4½ HOURS | COOK TIME: 53 MIN | SERVES 1

This French dessert is originally from the seventeenth century and is called *pot de crème*, meaning "pot of custard." It is subtly sweet and richly chocolatey, and is the perfect treat for people who love a more sophisticated chocolate dessert. Use the best-quality chocolate you can find because the chocolate is really the star flavor.

INGREDIENTS

⅓ cup heavy cream

2 tablespoons whole milk

1 ounce finely chopped bittersweet chocolate

1 large egg yolk

2 teaspoons granulated sugar

⅛ teaspoon pure vanilla extract

1. Preheat oven to 325°F.

2. In a small saucepan over medium heat, heat cream and milk to a bare simmer, about 3 minutes. Remove from heat and add chocolate. Whisk until smooth, then add egg yolk, sugar, and vanilla. Whisk until smooth.

3. Pour mixture into a 7-ounce ramekin and cover tightly with aluminum foil. Place ramekin into a small baking dish. Add recently boiled water until it reaches halfway up the side of the ramekin.

4. Bake 50–55 minutes or until custard is set around the edges but still a little jiggly in the center. Transfer ramekin to a wire rack and cool to room temperature, then chill at least 4 hours before enjoying.

BAKED CHOCOLATE PUDDING CAKE

PREP TIME: 15 MIN | COOK TIME: 33 MIN | SERVES 1

This baked dessert is similar to a flourless chocolate cake but is lighter in texture. When cooled to room temperature it is like a rich mousse, but you can chill it and enjoy it cold. When cold, the texture is more dense and fudgy. This recipe calls for the best-quality bittersweet chocolate—the darker the better!

INGREDIENTS

1½ tablespoons salted butter, at room temperature

2 ounces finely chopped bittersweet chocolate

1 large egg, yolk and white separated

1 pinch (about 1/16 teaspoon) cream of tartar

2 tablespoons granulated sugar, divided

1. Preheat oven to 350°F.

2. In a small microwave-safe bowl, add butter and chocolate. Microwave 30 seconds, stir well, then microwave in 15-second intervals until fully melted. Set aside.

3. In a medium bowl, add egg white and cream of tartar. Use a hand mixer to beat egg white on medium speed until foamy, about 30 seconds, then gradually add 1 tablespoon sugar and beat on high speed until stiff peaks form, about 1 minute. Set aside.

4. In a small bowl, beat together egg yolk and remaining 1 tablespoon sugar until light in color, about 2 minutes. Add chocolate mixture to egg yolk mixture and mix to combine, about 20 seconds.

5. Fold half of egg white into chocolate mixture until just combined, then add remaining egg white and fold until no streaks remain.

6. Spoon batter into an 8-ounce ramekin. Bake 30–35 minutes or until puffed yet still jiggly in the center. Transfer to a wire rack to cool to room temperature before serving.

BAKED LEMON PUDDING

PREP TIME: 15 MIN | COOK TIME: 30 MIN | SERVES 1

Part silky pudding; part cake; and all warm, comforting deliciousness! The magic of this pudding happens while baking. It splits into two layers, forming a custardy pudding on the bottom and a rich, cake-like layer on the top. If you want more lemon flavor, feel free to add up to ½ teaspoon more lemon zest.

INGREDIENTS

1 large egg, yolk and white separated

1 pinch (about ⅟16 teaspoon) cream of tartar

2 tablespoons granulated sugar, divided

1½ tablespoons salted butter, at room temperature

2 teaspoons lemon juice

½ teaspoon freshly grated lemon zest

2 teaspoons all-purpose flour

2 tablespoons whole milk

1. Preheat oven to 350°F.

2. In a medium bowl, add egg white and cream of tartar. Use a hand mixer to beat egg white on medium speed until foamy, about 20 seconds, then gradually add 1 tablespoon sugar and beat on high speed until stiff peaks form, about 1 minute. Set aside.

3. In a small bowl, beat together butter and remaining 1 tablespoon sugar until light in color, about 2 minutes. Add egg yolk, lemon juice, and lemon zest and beat 1 minute or until well combined and lighter in color.

4. Add flour and milk and mix on low speed until incorporated and smooth, about 15 seconds. Fold half of egg white into yolk mixture until just combined, then add remaining egg white and fold until no streaks remain.

5. Spoon batter into an 8-ounce ramekin. Place ramekin in a small baking dish. Add recently boiled water until it reaches halfway up the side of the ramekin.

6. Bake 30–35 minutes or until pudding is golden brown and set on the top. Transfer ramekin to a wire rack and cool 10 minutes before enjoying.

CREAM CHEESE CUSTARD

PREP TIME: 4½ HOURS | COOK TIME: 35 MIN | SERVES 1

Cream cheese adds a subtle tang to this extra-rich and creamy custard, and the brown sugar adds a delicate caramel sweetness. If you would like to make this more like flan de queso (cheese flan), add a tablespoon of caramel sauce to the bottom of the ramekin before adding the custard.

INGREDIENTS

1 ounce cream cheese, at room temperature

2 tablespoons packed light brown sugar

1 large egg yolk

⅓ cup half-and-half

¼ teaspoon pure vanilla extract

1. Preheat oven to 325°F.

2. In a medium bowl, add cream cheese and brown sugar. Use a hand mixer on medium speed to beat until smooth and creamy, about 30 seconds.

3. Add egg yolk and beat until completely incorporated, then slowly beat in half-and-half until smooth. Stir in vanilla.

4. Transfer mixture to a 7-ounce ramekin. Place ramekin in a small baking dish. Add recently boiled water until it reaches halfway up the side of the ramekin.

5. Bake 35–40 minutes or until custard is set around edges but slightly jiggly in center. Transfer ramekin to a wire rack and cool to room temperature, then chill at least 4 hours before enjoying.

QUICK MICROWAVE CUSTARD PUDDING

PREP TIME: 2¼ HOURS | COOK TIME: 8 MIN | SERVES 1

You might be surprised, but yes, you can make custard in the microwave! This microwave custard recipe does not require cooking on the stove or water baths, making it simple and quick to make. Drizzle the top of the custard with caramel sauce, or serve it with whipped cream and raspberries.

INGREDIENTS

¾ cup whole milk

1 large egg

1 tablespoon granulated sugar

⅛ teaspoon pure vanilla extract

1 pinch (about ¹⁄₁₆ teaspoon) ground cinnamon

1. In a small bowl, combine milk, egg, sugar, and vanilla. Whisk until smooth. Transfer mixture to a 10-ounce microwave-safe ramekin. Sprinkle cinnamon over top.

2. Microwave at 50 percent power 6 minutes, then check if custard is set. If not, continue to microwave in 30-second intervals until custard is set fully.

3. Remove from microwave and refrigerate 2 hours before serving. Enjoy cold.

CHOCOLATE PECAN BREAD PUDDING

PREP TIME: 30 MIN | COOK TIME: 30 MIN | SERVES 1

Brioche is a very rich bread made with more eggs and butter than most sweet bread recipes. Brioche rolls are usually available in the bakery section of most grocery stores, and they can be frozen up to three months, thawed, and eaten as is, or used in recipes like this one. Because this bread is so rich, it takes a little longer to go stale, so leave it out at least 6 hours.

INGREDIENTS

1½ cups cubed brioche bread, left out 6 hours to dry out slightly

2 tablespoons chopped pecans

⅓ cup semisweet chocolate chips, divided

3 tablespoons granulated sugar

1 large egg yolk

1½ teaspoons cocoa powder

½ cup whole milk

¼ teaspoon pure vanilla extract

1 tablespoon unsalted butter, at room temperature

1. Preheat oven to 350°F and spray a 6" pie pan with nonstick cooking spray.

2. In a medium bowl, add bread cubes, pecans, and ¼ cup chocolate chips. Set aside.

3. In a small bowl, add sugar, egg yolk, and cocoa powder and whisk until smooth, then add milk and vanilla. Whisk until smooth.

4. Pour milk mixture over bread cubes and mix to combine. Let stand 10 minutes, stir again, then allow to stand 10 minutes more.

5. Transfer soaked bread and custard to prepared pie pan. Dot top with butter. Bake 30–35 minutes or until pudding is puffed all over and golden brown. Remove from oven and transfer to wire rack. Top with remaining chocolate chips. Cool 15 minutes before serving. Enjoy warm.

CHAPTER 7

MUFFINS AND QUICK BREADS

Muffins and quick breads are incredibly versatile and easy to make. Need breakfast on the go? Muffins have you covered, often in less than 30 minutes from start to finish. Want a sweet snack with a cup of afternoon tea? A loaf or quick bread for one is there to help. Want a bread side for your dinner? A small batch of savory muffins has your back and can be made at a moment's notice. Taking just a few moments to prepare and often requiring nothing more than a bowl, spatula, and pan, muffins and quick breads are some of the easiest yet most satisfying baked goods going.

For muffins and quick breads freshness is key. You certainly can freeze leftover muffins and slices of quick bread, but they are always better fresh. This chapter is packed with small-batch muffin recipes and individual quick bread recipes that are mouthwatering, easy, and ready in a snap so you never have to worry about dry muffins or stale quick bread. You will find classics like Blueberry Muffins and Pumpkin Bread along with more savory options like Jalapeño Corn Muffins and Savory Cheddar Ale Muffins. So, from grab-and-go snacks to break-time treats, you always have time for fresh and fabulous treats made just for you!

BLUEBERRY MUFFINS

PREP TIME: 10 MIN | COOK TIME: 18 MIN | YIELDS 4 MUFFINS

Blueberry Muffins are an excellent way to use frozen blueberries, so you can enjoy these muffins any time of year, even when berries are not in season or not their most flavorful. If you like you can use any sort of berry here, but if you use raspberries or blackberries, select fresh instead of frozen, as the frozen berries can be watery.

INGREDIENTS

½ cup all-purpose flour, divided

¼ cup blueberries

¼ cup granulated sugar

¼ teaspoon baking powder

⅛ teaspoon ground cinnamon

⅛ teaspoon baking soda

⅛ teaspoon salt

¼ cup whole milk

1 large egg, at room temperature

1 tablespoon unsalted butter, melted and cooled

¼ teaspoon pure vanilla extract

⅛ teaspoon almond extract

1. Preheat oven to 350°F and line four cups of a muffin pan with paper liners.

2. In a small bowl, add 1 teaspoon flour and blueberries. Gently toss until berries are coated in flour. Set aside.

3. In a medium bowl, add remaining flour, sugar, baking powder, cinnamon, baking soda, and salt. Whisk to combine. Set aside.

4. In a small bowl, combine milk, egg, butter, vanilla, and almond extract and whisk to combine. Pour wet ingredients into dry ingredients and use a spatula to mix until just combined, about six strokes, then add blueberries and fold to combine, four to six strokes. Do not overmix.

5. Divide batter between prepared muffin cups. Bake 18–20 minutes or until muffins spring back when gently pressed in the center and tops are golden brown. Cool in pan 3 minutes, then transfer to a wire rack to cool to room temperature.

Mix-In Ingredients

If your mixed-in ingredients like berries, chips, or nuts tend to sink, there is a quick trick that will help keep them suspended in the batter. Simply add 1 teaspoon flour to your mix-ins and toss until evenly coated. The flour will help suspend the mix-ins in the batter while they bake and keep them from sinking to the bottom.

CHOCOLATE BANANA BREAD

PREP TIME: 10 MIN | COOK TIME: 30 MIN | SERVES 1

Bananas with mostly black skins are perfect for making banana bread. They have the most potent banana flavor. If you keep bananas in the freezer for making smoothies and shakes, you can use them for banana bread too. Let the banana thaw in the refrigerator until soft enough to mash, then use it as directed in the recipe.

INGREDIENTS

⅓ cup all-purpose flour

¼ cup packed light brown sugar

1 tablespoon Dutch-processed cocoa powder

¼ teaspoon baking powder

¼ teaspoon ground cinnamon

⅛ teaspoon baking soda

⅛ teaspoon salt

¼ cup mashed very ripe banana (about ½ medium banana)

2 tablespoons buttermilk

1 large egg, at room temperature

1 tablespoon unsalted butter, melted and cooled

¼ teaspoon pure vanilla extract

2 tablespoons semisweet chocolate chips

3 tablespoons chopped walnuts, divided

1. Preheat oven to 350°F and spray a 5" × 3" mini-loaf pan with nonstick cooking spray.

2. In a medium bowl, add flour, brown sugar, cocoa powder, baking powder, cinnamon, baking soda, and salt. Whisk to combine. Set aside.

3. In a small bowl, combine banana, buttermilk, egg, butter, and vanilla. Whisk to combine. Pour wet ingredients into dry ingredients and use a spatula to mix until just combined, about six strokes, then add chocolate chips and 2 tablespoons walnuts and fold to combine, four to six strokes. Do not overmix.

4. Transfer batter to prepared pan and top with remaining 1 tablespoon walnuts. Bake 30–35 minutes or until bread springs back when gently pressed in the center and top is golden brown. Cool in pan 3 minutes, then transfer to a wire rack to cool to room temperature.

CHOCOLATE CHIP MUFFINS

PREP TIME: 10 MIN | COOK TIME: 18 MIN | YIELDS 4 MUFFINS

These muffins have a flavor that is reminiscent of chocolate chip cookies, so if you enjoy chocolate chip cookies then you will love these. If you want the chocolate to be more evenly spread throughout the muffins, you can swap the regular-sized chips for miniature chips. You can also use milk, white, or even butterscotch chips if you like.

INGREDIENTS

½ cup plus 2 tablespoons all-purpose flour, divided

2 tablespoons granulated sugar

1 tablespoon cubed unsalted butter, chilled

⅓ cup semisweet chocolate chips

¼ cup packed light brown sugar

¼ teaspoon baking powder

⅛ teaspoon baking soda

⅛ teaspoon salt

¼ cup whole milk

1 large egg, at room temperature

1 tablespoon unsalted butter, melted and cooled

¼ teaspoon pure vanilla extract

1. Preheat oven to 350°F and line four cups of a muffin pan with paper liners.

2. In a small bowl, combine 2 tablespoons flour, granulated sugar, and chilled butter. Use your fingers to mix until mixture clumps together and is crumbly. Chill until ready to use.

3. In a second small bowl, add 1 teaspoon flour and chocolate chips. Gently toss until chips are coated in flour. Set aside.

4. In a medium bowl, add remaining flour, brown sugar, baking powder, baking soda, and salt. Whisk to combine. Set aside.

5. In a third small bowl, combine milk, egg, melted butter, and vanilla and whisk to combine. Pour wet ingredients into dry ingredients and use a spatula to mix until just combined, about six strokes, then add chocolate chips and fold to combine, four to six strokes. Do not overmix.

6. Divide batter between prepared muffin cups. Sprinkle chilled topping evenly over muffins. Bake 18–20 minutes or until muffins spring back when gently pressed in the center and tops are golden brown. Cool in pan 3 minutes, then transfer to a wire rack to cool to room temperature.

CORN BREAD HONEY MUFFINS

PREP TIME: 10 MIN | COOK TIME: 18 MIN | YIELDS 4 MUFFINS

These lightly sweet Corn Bread Honey Muffins are perfect served with savory meals like spicy chili, smoked meats, or fried chicken. If you would like a little kick of spice, feel free to add a couple of fat pinches of cayenne pepper along with the dry ingredients. It will add a little tingle of heat with each bite.

INGREDIENTS

¼ cup all-purpose flour

¼ cup yellow cornmeal

2 teaspoons granulated sugar

¼ teaspoon baking powder

¼ teaspoon baking soda

⅛ teaspoon salt

¼ cup buttermilk

1 large egg, at room temperature

1 tablespoon honey

1 tablespoon vegetable oil

1. Preheat oven to 350°F and line four cups of a muffin pan with paper liners.

2. In a medium bowl, add flour, cornmeal, sugar, baking powder, baking soda, and salt. Whisk to combine. Set aside.

3. In a small bowl, combine buttermilk, egg, honey, and oil and whisk to combine. Pour wet ingredients into dry ingredients and use a spatula to mix until just combined, about ten strokes. Do not overmix.

4. Divide batter between prepared muffin cups. Bake 18–20 minutes or until muffins spring back when gently pressed in the center and tops are golden brown. Cool in pan 3 minutes, then transfer to a wire rack to cool to room temperature.

Honey Butter Spread

Honey butter is delicious on muffins, corn bread, and biscuits, and it is easy to make! In a small bowl, add 4 tablespoons salted butter at room temperature. Use a hand mixer to cream on low speed until smooth, about 30 seconds. Add 2 tablespoons honey, preferably dark honey, and mix on low speed until smooth, about 30 seconds. Transfer to a serving dish and chill well. Serve at room temperature.

LEMON POPPY SEED MUFFINS

The bright flavor of lemon plays well with the deeper, earthier flavor of poppy seeds. The glaze, spooned over the muffins once cool, adds an extra layer of tangy lemon flavor, but if you prefer you can replace the lemon juice with ¾ teaspoon milk and ¼ teaspoon vanilla for a milder flavor.

INGREDIENTS

½ cup all-purpose flour

¼ cup granulated sugar

¼ teaspoon baking powder

⅛ teaspoon baking soda

⅛ teaspoon salt

3 tablespoons buttermilk

1 tablespoon plus 1 teaspoon lemon juice, divided

1 large egg, at room temperature

1 tablespoon vegetable oil

1 teaspoon freshly grated lemon zest

¼ teaspoon pure vanilla extract

1 tablespoon poppy seeds

3 tablespoons powdered sugar

1. Preheat oven to 350°F and line four cups of a muffin pan with paper liners.

2. In a medium bowl, add flour, granulated sugar, baking powder, baking soda, and salt. Whisk to combine. Set aside.

3. In a small bowl, combine buttermilk, 1 tablespoon lemon juice, egg, oil, lemon zest, and vanilla. Whisk to combine. Pour wet ingredients into dry ingredients and use a spatula to mix until just combined, about six strokes, then add poppy seeds and fold to combine, four to six strokes. Do not overmix.

4. Divide batter between prepared muffin cups. Bake 18–20 minutes or until muffins spring back when gently pressed in the center and tops are golden brown. Cool in pan 3 minutes, then transfer to a wire rack to cool to room temperature.

5. Once cool, prepare glaze. In a second small bowl, add powdered sugar and remaining 1 teaspoon lemon juice and mix until smooth. Spoon over cooled muffins, then let stand 30 minutes to set before enjoying.

SAVORY CHEDDAR ALE MUFFINS

PREP TIME: 10 MIN | COOK TIME: 18 MIN | YIELDS 4 MUFFINS

These muffins blend the hoppy flavor of beer with the heat of dry mustard and the sharpness of Cheddar cheese to create a deeply savory muffin. Whip up a batch of these muffins for dipping into beer cheese soup, serving alongside roast beef or stew, or just slathering with plenty of salted butter!

INGREDIENTS

½ cup all-purpose flour

¼ teaspoon baking powder

⅛ teaspoon baking soda

⅛ teaspoon dry mustard powder

⅛ teaspoon salt

2 tablespoons ale-style beer

1 large egg, at room temperature

1 tablespoon unsalted butter, melted and cooled

¼ cup shredded sharp Cheddar cheese

1. Preheat oven to 350°F and line four cups of a muffin pan with paper liners.

2. In a medium bowl, add flour, baking powder, baking soda, mustard, and salt. Whisk to combine. Set aside.

3. In a small bowl, combine beer, egg, and butter. Whisk to combine. Pour wet ingredients into dry ingredients and use a spatula to mix until just combined, about six strokes, then add Cheddar cheese and fold to combine, four to six strokes. Do not overmix.

4. Divide batter between prepared muffin cups. Bake 18–20 minutes or until muffins spring back when gently pressed in the center and tops are golden brown. Cool in pan 3 minutes, then transfer to a wire rack to cool to room temperature.

CHERRY ALMOND COFFEE CAKE

PREP TIME: 10 MIN | COOK TIME: 20 MIN | SERVES 1

Cherry and almond are a classic combination, and here they feature in a tender coffee cake. This version uses cherry pie filling layered in the middle of the cake to add a tart yet sweet edge, perfect with coffee. If you do not want to use pie filling you can use frozen tart-sweet cherries that have been thawed and drained.

INGREDIENTS

½ cup all-purpose flour

¼ cup plus 1 tablespoon granulated sugar, divided

¼ teaspoon baking powder

⅛ teaspoon baking soda

⅛ teaspoon ground cinnamon

⅛ teaspoon salt

¼ cup sour cream

1 large egg, at room temperature

1 tablespoon vegetable oil

¼ teaspoon pure vanilla extract

⅛ teaspoon almond extract

¼ cup cherry pie filling

3 tablespoons sliced almonds, divided

1. Preheat oven to 350°F and spray a 5" × 3" mini-loaf pan with nonstick cooking spray.

2. In a medium bowl, add flour, ¼ cup sugar, baking powder, baking soda, cinnamon, and salt. Whisk to combine. Set aside.

3. In a small bowl, combine sour cream, egg, oil, vanilla, and almond extract. Whisk to combine. Pour wet ingredients into dry ingredients and use a spatula to mix until just combined, about six strokes, then add 2 tablespoons almonds and fold to combine, four to six strokes. Do not overmix.

4. Transfer half of batter to prepared pan and top with cherry filling, then cover with remaining batter and top with remaining 1 tablespoon sugar and remaining 1 tablespoon almonds. Bake 20–22 minutes or until bread springs back when gently pressed in the center and top is golden brown. Cool in pan 5 minutes, then transfer to a wire rack to cool to room temperature.

JALAPEÑO CORN MUFFINS

PREP TIME: 10 MIN | COOK TIME: 18 MIN | YIELDS 4 MUFFINS

Pickled jalapeños add a zesty kick to these corn muffins. Pickling reduces the heat in jalapeños, so if you like things extra spicy you can add ⅛ teaspoon cayenne pepper to these muffins to make up for the heat lost during the pickling process.

INGREDIENTS

¼ cup all-purpose flour

¼ cup yellow cornmeal

¼ teaspoon chili powder

¼ teaspoon baking powder

¼ teaspoon baking soda

⅛ teaspoon salt

¼ cup buttermilk

1 large egg, at room temperature

1 tablespoon vegetable oil

2 tablespoons minced pickled jalapeños

1. Preheat oven to 350°F and line four cups of a muffin pan with paper liners.

2. In a medium bowl, add flour, cornmeal, chili powder, baking powder, baking soda, and salt. Whisk to combine. Set aside.

3. In a small bowl, combine buttermilk, egg, and oil and whisk to combine. Pour wet ingredients into dry ingredients and use a spatula to mix until just combined, about six strokes, then add jalapeños and fold to combine, four to six strokes. Do not overmix.

4. Divide batter between prepared muffin cups. Bake 18–20 minutes or until muffins spring back when gently pressed in the center and tops are golden brown. Cool in pan 3 minutes, then transfer to a wire rack to cool to room temperature.

Small-Batch Jalapeño Popper Spread

For an easy spread perfect for these savory muffins, in a medium bowl, combine 1 ounce cream cheese at room temperature, ¼ cup finely shredded Cheddar cheese, 1 tablespoon mayonnaise, 1 tablespoon minced pickled jalapeño, 1 tablespoon crumbled cooked bacon, and ¼ teaspoon taco seasoning. Mix until smooth, then serve immediately or refrigerate up to one week. This is best served at room temperature to make it easier to spread.

BANANA BREAD FOR ONE

Banana dessert recipes became popular in the US in the 1930s when banana bread became a standard recipe in many cookbooks. Today banana bread is a staple in coffee shops and bakeries. It is simple, but its simplicity is what helps the banana flavor to shine! For a special flourish, top the unbaked bread with a slice or two of fresh banana before baking.

INGREDIENTS

½ cup all-purpose flour

¼ cup packed dark brown sugar

¼ teaspoon baking powder

¼ teaspoon pumpkin pie spice

⅛ teaspoon baking soda

⅛ teaspoon salt

¼ cup mashed very ripe banana (about ½ medium banana)

2 tablespoons buttermilk

1 large egg, at room temperature

1 tablespoon unsalted butter, melted and cooled

¼ teaspoon pure vanilla extract

1 Preheat oven to 350°F and spray a 5" × 3" mini-loaf pan with nonstick cooking spray.

2 In a medium bowl, add flour, brown sugar, baking powder, pumpkin pie spice, baking soda, and salt. Whisk to combine. Set aside.

3 In a small bowl, combine banana, buttermilk, egg, butter, and vanilla. Whisk to combine. Pour wet ingredients into dry ingredients and use a spatula to mix until just combined, about ten strokes. Do not overmix.

4 Transfer batter to prepared pan. Bake 30–35 minutes or until bread springs back when gently pressed in the center and top is golden brown. Cool in pan 3 minutes, then transfer to a wire rack to cool to room temperature.

BLUEBERRY YOGURT BREAD

PREP TIME: 10 MIN | COOK TIME: 30 MIN | SERVES 1

This version of blueberry coffee cake is the perfect mix of sweet and tangy, thanks to the Greek yogurt. This recipe calls for plain-flavored yogurt, but you can use blueberry yogurt for extra flavor—just reduce the sugar by 2 teaspoons. If you are using frozen berries do not thaw them before folding them into the batter.

INGREDIENTS

½ cup all-purpose flour, divided

¼ cup blueberries

¼ cup granulated sugar

¼ teaspoon baking powder

⅛ teaspoon ground cinnamon

⅛ teaspoon baking soda

⅛ teaspoon salt

¼ cup full-fat plain Greek yogurt

2 tablespoons buttermilk

1 large egg, at room temperature

1 tablespoon vegetable oil

¼ teaspoon pure vanilla extract

⅛ teaspoon almond extract

1. Preheat oven to 350°F and spray a 5" × 3" mini-loaf pan with nonstick cooking spray.

2. In a small bowl, add 1 teaspoon flour and blueberries. Toss gently until blueberries are coated in flour. Set aside.

3. In a medium bowl, add remaining flour, sugar, baking powder, cinnamon, baking soda, and salt. Whisk to combine. Set aside.

4. In a second small bowl, combine yogurt, buttermilk, egg, oil, vanilla, and almond extract. Whisk to combine. Pour wet ingredients into dry ingredients and use a spatula to mix until just combined, about six strokes, then add blueberries and fold to mix, three to four strokes. Do not overmix.

5. Transfer batter to prepared pan. Bake 30–35 minutes or until bread springs back when gently pressed in the center and top is golden brown. Cool in pan 3 minutes, then transfer to a wire rack to cool to room temperature.

Using Yogurt in Baking

Full-fat yogurt can be added to quick breads, muffins, or cakes when you want a soft and tender crumb and a slightly tangy taste. Greek-style yogurt, a strained yogurt that is very thick, can't be swapped 1:1 for milk. It is best to thin it with a little milk or, to retain the full tangy flavor, buttermilk in a ratio of three parts Greek yogurt to one part milk or buttermilk. If you do decide to use a lower-fat yogurt do not use anything less than 2 percent.

CHERRY MUFFINS

PREP TIME: 1¼ HOURS | COOK TIME: 18 MIN | YIELDS 4 MUFFINS

Rehydrating dried fruit before using in recipes for lower-fat baked goods will help to keep your baked items moist. The dried fruit will naturally absorb moisture while baking, and in recipes with less fat, like muffins, you will want to preserve all the moisture you can so your baked goods do not become dry. You can also use orange juice to rehydrate fruit for extra flavor.

INGREDIENTS

¼ cup dried cherries

½ cup boiling water

½ cup plus 2 tablespoons all-purpose flour, divided

¼ cup plus 2 tablespoons granulated sugar, divided

1 tablespoon unsalted butter, chilled

¼ teaspoon baking powder

⅛ teaspoon baking soda

⅛ teaspoon salt

¼ cup whole milk

1 large egg, at room temperature

1 tablespoon vegetable oil

¼ teaspoon pure vanilla extract

1. In a small heat-safe bowl, combine cherries and boiling water. Let stand 1 hour until cherries are soft, then drain. Set aside.

2. Preheat oven to 350°F and line four cups of a muffin pan with paper liners.

3. In a second small bowl, combine 2 tablespoons flour, 2 tablespoons sugar, and butter. Use your fingers to mix until mixture clumps together and is crumbly. Chill until ready to use.

4. In a medium bowl, add remaining ½ cup flour, remaining ¼ cup sugar, baking powder, baking soda, and salt. Whisk to combine. Set aside.

5. In a third small bowl, combine milk, egg, oil, and vanilla and whisk to combine. Pour wet ingredients into dry ingredients and use a spatula to mix until just combined, about six strokes, then add cherries and fold to combine, three to four strokes. Do not overmix.

6. Divide batter between prepared muffin cups. Sprinkle chilled topping evenly over muffins. Bake 18–20 minutes or until muffins spring back when gently pressed in the center and tops are golden brown. Cool in pan 3 minutes, then transfer to a wire rack to cool to room temperature.

CRANBERRY ORANGE MUFFINS

These muffins are sweet and refreshing, and the textures of crisp topping and chewy fruit make them very special. If you want to have the cranberries more evenly distributed throughout the muffins, you can roughly chop them before soaking them in the orange juice. Feel free to add up to 2 tablespoons chopped pecans if you like.

INGREDIENTS

¼ cup dried cranberries

½ cup orange juice

½ cup plus 2 tablespoons all-purpose flour, divided

¼ cup plus 2 tablespoons granulated sugar, divided

⅛ teaspoon ground cinnamon

1 tablespoon unsalted butter, chilled

¼ teaspoon baking powder

⅛ teaspoon baking soda

⅛ teaspoon salt

¼ cup whole milk

1 large egg, at room temperature

1 tablespoon vegetable oil

½ teaspoon freshly grated orange zest

¼ teaspoon pure vanilla extract

1. In a small microwave-safe bowl, combine cranberries and orange juice. Microwave 1 minute, then let stand 1 hour until cranberries are soft. Drain and set aside.

2. Preheat oven to 350°F and line four cups of a muffin pan with paper liners.

3. In a small bowl, combine 2 tablespoons flour, 2 tablespoons sugar, cinnamon, and butter. Use your fingers to mix until mixture clumps together and is crumbly. Chill until ready to use.

4. In a medium bowl, add remaining ½ cup flour, remaining ¼ cup sugar, baking powder, baking soda, and salt. Whisk to combine. Set aside.

5. In a second small bowl, combine milk, egg, oil, orange zest, and vanilla and whisk to combine. Pour wet ingredients into dry ingredients and use a spatula to mix until just combined, about six strokes. Add cranberries and fold to combine, three to four strokes. Do not overmix.

6. Divide batter between prepared muffin cups. Sprinkle chilled topping evenly over muffins. Bake 18–20 minutes or until muffins spring back when gently pressed in the center and tops are golden brown. Cool in pan 3 minutes, then transfer to a wire rack to cool to room temperature.

COCONUT LIME MUFFINS

PREP TIME: 10 MIN | COOK TIME: 18 MIN | YIELDS 4 MUFFINS

You can use refrigerated coconut milk for this recipe if you have it, but for the best flavor you should use full-fat canned coconut milk. Be sure to shake it well before using, as the fat can separate. Leftover coconut milk can be used in coffee, added to oatmeal, or mixed into smoothies.

INGREDIENTS

½ cup all-purpose flour

¼ cup granulated sugar

¼ teaspoon baking powder

⅛ teaspoon baking soda

⅛ teaspoon salt

3 tablespoons plus 2 teaspoons full-fat canned coconut milk, divided

1 tablespoon plus 1 teaspoon lime juice, divided

1 large egg, at room temperature

1 tablespoon vegetable oil

1 teaspoon freshly grated lime zest

¼ teaspoon pure vanilla extract

¼ cup shredded sweetened coconut

¼ cup powdered sugar

1 tablespoon unsalted butter, melted and cooled

1. Preheat oven to 350°F and line four cups of a muffin pan with paper liners.

2. In a medium bowl, add flour, granulated sugar, baking powder, baking soda, and salt. Whisk to combine. Set aside.

3. In a small bowl, combine 3 tablespoons coconut milk, 1 tablespoon lime juice, egg, oil, lime zest, and vanilla. Whisk to combine. Pour wet ingredients into dry ingredients and use a spatula to mix until just combined, about six strokes, then add shredded coconut and fold to combine, four to six strokes. Do not overmix.

4. Divide batter between prepared muffin cups. Bake 18–20 minutes or until muffins spring back when gently pressed in the center and tops are golden brown. Cool in pan 3 minutes, then transfer to a wire rack to cool to room temperature.

5. In a second small bowl, combine remaining 2 teaspoons coconut milk, remaining 1 teaspoon lime juice, powdered sugar, and butter. Mix until smooth, then spoon over cooled muffins. Let stand 30 minutes so glaze can set.

FRESH PEACH MUFFINS

PREP TIME: 10 MIN | COOK TIME: 18 MIN | YIELDS 4 MUFFINS

If you would like to add more peach flavor to these muffins, you can purée the remaining peach until smooth and use 2 tablespoons of that purée in place of half the buttermilk. Some buttermilk is required to help activate the baking powder, so don't eliminate all of it.

INGREDIENTS

½ cup all-purpose flour

¼ cup packed light brown sugar

¼ teaspoon baking powder

⅛ teaspoon ground cardamom

⅛ teaspoon baking soda

⅛ teaspoon salt

¼ cup buttermilk

1 large egg, at room temperature

1 tablespoon unsalted butter, melted and cooled

1 teaspoon honey

¼ teaspoon pure vanilla extract

⅛ teaspoon almond extract

¼ cup peeled and finely chopped peach (about ⅓ large peach)

1. Preheat oven to 350°F and line four cups of a muffin pan with paper liners.

2. In a medium bowl, add flour, brown sugar, baking powder, cardamom, baking soda, and salt. Whisk to combine. Set aside.

3. In a small bowl, combine buttermilk, egg, butter, honey, vanilla, and almond extract and whisk to combine. Pour wet ingredients into dry ingredients and use a spatula to mix until just combined, about six strokes, then add peach and fold to combine, four to six strokes. Do not overmix.

4. Divide batter between prepared muffin cups. Bake 18–20 minutes or until muffins spring back when gently pressed in the center and tops are golden brown. Cool in pan 3 minutes, then transfer to a wire rack to cool to room temperature.

PUMPKIN BREAD

PREP TIME: 10 MIN | COOK TIME: 30 MIN | SERVES 1

Pumpkin bread is often considered a fall treat; however, most coffee shops and bakeries carry it year-round. Even so, making it at home is quick and simple. Pumpkin purée can easily be frozen, so any purée you have left after making your personal loaf of Pumpkin Bread won't go bad. Freeze leftovers in ¼-cup portions to make future baking easier!

INGREDIENTS

½ cup all-purpose flour

¼ cup packed light brown sugar

¼ teaspoon baking powder

¼ teaspoon pumpkin pie spice

⅛ teaspoon baking soda

⅛ teaspoon salt

¼ cup pumpkin purée

2 tablespoons buttermilk

1 large egg, at room temperature

2 tablespoons vegetable oil

¼ teaspoon pure vanilla extract

1. Preheat oven to 350°F and spray a 5" × 3" mini-loaf pan with nonstick cooking spray.

2. In a medium bowl, add flour, brown sugar, baking powder, pumpkin pie spice, baking soda, and salt. Whisk to combine. Set aside.

3. In a small bowl, combine pumpkin, buttermilk, egg, oil, and vanilla. Whisk to combine. Pour wet ingredients into dry ingredients and use a spatula to mix until just combined, about ten strokes. Do not overmix.

4. Transfer batter to prepared pan. Bake 30–35 minutes or until bread springs back when gently pressed in the center and top is golden brown. Cool in pan 3 minutes, then transfer to a wire rack to cool to room temperature.

Cinnamon Cream Cheese Spread

This simple spread for Pumpkin Bread, or any sweet muffins, can be made from 2 ounces softened cream cheese, 2 tablespoons powdered sugar, 1 tablespoon unsalted butter at room temperature, ¼ teaspoon ground cinnamon, and ¼ teaspoon vanilla extract. Combine all the ingredients in a small bowl and mix until smooth. You can use this spread at once or chill it and use it later. It is best served at room temperature.

PECAN DATE BREAD

PREP TIME: 10 MIN | COOK TIME: 30 MIN | SERVES 1

When shopping for dates it is better to purchase them in the produce department rather than the dried fruit aisle. Dates should be plump to the touch and feel firm but not hard. The skins can be smooth or wrinkled and should be a little glossy. Avoid dates with any crystals of sugar on the outside, as they are not fresh.

INGREDIENTS

⅓ cup all-purpose flour

¼ cup packed light brown sugar

2 tablespoons whole-wheat flour

¼ teaspoon baking powder

¼ teaspoon ground cinnamon

⅛ teaspoon baking soda

⅛ teaspoon salt

1 pinch (about ¹⁄₁₆ teaspoon) ground cardamom

¼ cup buttermilk

2 teaspoons honey

1 large egg, at room temperature

1 tablespoon vegetable oil

¼ teaspoon pure vanilla extract

¼ cup chopped dates

2 tablespoons chopped pecans

1. Preheat oven to 350°F and spray a 5" × 3" mini-loaf pan with nonstick cooking spray.

2. In a medium bowl, add all-purpose flour, brown sugar, whole-wheat flour, baking powder, cinnamon, baking soda, salt, and cardamom. Whisk to combine. Set aside.

3. In a small bowl, combine buttermilk, honey, egg, oil, and vanilla. Whisk to combine. Pour wet ingredients into dry ingredients and use a spatula to mix until just combined, about six strokes. Add dates and pecans and fold to combine, three to four strokes. Do not overmix.

4. Transfer batter to prepared pan. Bake 30–35 minutes or until bread springs back when gently pressed in the center and top is golden brown. Cool in pan 3 minutes, then transfer to a wire rack to cool to room temperature.

CARROT MUFFINS

PREP TIME: 10 MIN | COOK TIME: 18 MIN | YIELDS 4 MUFFINS

These muffins are packed with carrots, pecans, and raisins, and have a flavor and texture similar to carrot cake but with less fat and sugar. For the 3 tablespoons shredded carrot, use a small, peeled carrot and grate it with a fine grater. Don't use ready-grated carrot from the store. It is often dry and less flavorful.

INGREDIENTS

- ½ cup all-purpose flour
- ¼ cup packed dark brown sugar
- ¼ teaspoon baking powder
- ⅛ teaspoon pumpkin pie spice
- ⅛ teaspoon baking soda
- ⅛ teaspoon salt
- ¼ cup whole milk
- 1 large egg, at room temperature
- 1 tablespoon vegetable oil
- ¼ teaspoon pure vanilla extract
- 3 tablespoons finely shredded carrot
- 2 tablespoons chopped pecans
- 2 tablespoons roughly chopped raisins

1. Preheat oven to 350°F and line four cups of a muffin pan with paper liners.

2. In a medium bowl, add flour, brown sugar, baking powder, pumpkin pie spice, baking soda, and salt. Whisk to combine. Set aside.

3. In a small bowl, combine milk, egg, oil, and vanilla and whisk to combine. Pour wet ingredients into dry ingredients and use a spatula to mix until just combined, about six strokes, then add carrot, pecans, and raisins and fold to combine, four to six strokes. Do not overmix.

4. Divide batter between prepared muffin cups. Bake 18–20 minutes or until muffins spring back when gently pressed in the center and tops are golden brown. Cool in pan 3 minutes, then transfer to a wire rack to cool to room temperature.

CINNAMON SWIRL BREAD

While this bread bakes, the cinnamon sugar filling will swirl naturally throughout the small loaf. If you want to add a little texture to this bread, you can add 2 tablespoons chopped almonds or walnuts to the batter along with the cinnamon sugar for a nutty Cinnamon Swirl Bread. You can use all sour cream or all buttermilk, depending on what you have on hand.

INGREDIENTS

½ cup plus 2 tablespoons all-purpose flour, divided

¼ cup plus 3 tablespoons granulated sugar, divided

1 tablespoon unsalted butter, chilled

¼ teaspoon baking powder

⅛ teaspoon baking soda

⅛ teaspoon salt

2 tablespoons sour cream

2 tablespoons buttermilk

1 large egg, at room temperature

1 tablespoon vegetable oil

¼ teaspoon pure vanilla extract

¼ teaspoon ground cinnamon

1. Preheat oven to 350°F and spray a 5" × 3" mini-loaf pan with nonstick cooking spray.

2. In a small bowl, combine 2 tablespoons flour, 2 tablespoons sugar, and butter. Use your fingers to mix until mixture clumps together and is crumbly. Chill until ready to use.

3. In a medium bowl, add remaining ½ cup flour, ¼ cup sugar, baking powder, baking soda, and salt. Whisk to combine. Set aside.

4. In a second small bowl, combine sour cream, buttermilk, egg, oil, and vanilla. Whisk to combine. Pour wet ingredients into dry ingredients and use a spatula to mix until just combined, about ten strokes. Do not overmix.

5. In a third small bowl, combine remaining 1 tablespoon sugar and cinnamon.

6. Transfer half of batter to prepared pan and top with cinnamon sugar mixture, then cover with remaining batter and top with chilled crumble.

7. Bake 20–22 minutes or until bread springs back when gently pressed in the center and top is golden brown. Cool in pan 5 minutes, then transfer to a wire rack to cool to room temperature.

GINGERBREAD CRUMB MUFFINS

PREP TIME: 10 MIN | COOK TIME: 18 MIN | YIELDS 4 MUFFINS

Fresh gingerbread is a popular winter treat in either cake or cookie form. These muffins take all the best flavors of gingerbread cake and make them into a crumble-topped muffin. You can enjoy these warm with a little soft butter or a bit of whipped cream cheese, and a cup of coffee. If you do not have molasses, you can swap it for honey.

INGREDIENTS

½ cup plus 2 tablespoons all-purpose flour, divided

2 tablespoons granulated sugar

¼ teaspoon plus ⅛ teaspoon ground cinnamon, divided

1 tablespoon unsalted butter, chilled

3 tablespoons packed dark brown sugar

¼ teaspoon baking powder

¼ teaspoon ground ginger

⅛ teaspoon baking soda

⅛ teaspoon salt

1 pinch (about 1/16 teaspoon) ground cloves

¼ cup whole milk

1 tablespoon molasses

1 large egg, at room temperature

1 tablespoon vegetable oil

1. Preheat oven to 350°F and line four cups of a muffin pan with paper liners.

2. In a small bowl, combine 2 tablespoons flour, granulated sugar, ⅛ teaspoon cinnamon, and butter. Use your fingers to mix until mixture clumps together and is crumbly. Chill until ready to use.

3. In a medium bowl, add remaining ½ cup flour, remaining ¼ teaspoon cinnamon, brown sugar, baking powder, ginger, baking soda, salt, and cloves. Whisk to combine. Set aside.

4. In a second small bowl, combine milk, molasses, egg, and oil and whisk to combine. Pour wet ingredients into dry ingredients and use a spatula to mix until just combined, about ten strokes. Do not overmix.

5. Divide batter between prepared muffin cups. Sprinkle chilled topping evenly over muffins. Bake 18–20 minutes or until muffins spring back when gently pressed in the center and tops are golden brown. Cool in pan 3 minutes, then transfer to a wire rack to cool to room temperature.

GLAZED LEMON LOAF

PREP TIME: 10 MIN | COOK TIME: 20 MIN | SERVES 1

A little butter mixed into the glaze makes it richer in flavor and gives it a silky texture. You can make this an orange or lime loaf simply by swapping the zest and juice for the citrus fruit you prefer. You could also make a grapefruit loaf, but you should add an extra ½ teaspoon sugar to counter the sourness of the juice.

INGREDIENTS

½ cup all-purpose flour

¼ cup granulated sugar

¼ teaspoon baking powder

⅛ teaspoon baking soda

⅛ teaspoon salt

3 tablespoons buttermilk

1 tablespoon plus 1 teaspoon lemon juice, divided

1 large egg, at room temperature

1 tablespoon vegetable oil

1 teaspoon freshly grated lemon zest

¼ teaspoon pure vanilla extract

¼ cup powdered sugar

1 teaspoon melted unsalted butter

1. Preheat oven to 350°F and spray a 5" × 3" mini-loaf pan with nonstick cooking spray.

2. In a medium bowl, add flour, granulated sugar, baking powder, baking soda, and salt. Whisk to combine. Set aside.

3. In a small bowl, combine buttermilk, 1 tablespoon lemon juice, egg, oil, lemon zest, and vanilla. Whisk to combine. Pour wet ingredients into dry ingredients and use a spatula to mix until just combined, about ten strokes. Do not overmix.

4. Transfer batter to prepared pan. Bake 20–22 minutes or until bread springs back when gently pressed in the center and top is golden brown. Cool in pan 5 minutes, then transfer to a wire rack to cool until just warm.

5. Once loaf is slightly warm, prepare glaze. In a second small bowl, add powdered sugar, melted butter, and remaining 1 teaspoon lemon juice and mix until smooth. Spoon over loaf, letting glaze drip down the sides. Let stand until fully cool before serving.

Oil versus Butter

Ever wondered why a recipe might call for oil instead of butter and whether you could use them interchangeably? The short answer is yes, you can swap them, and your recipe will turn out just fine. Oil is often used to create a more tender, moist crumb in cakes and muffins. Butter adds a richer flavor, but the crumb will be a little firmer when the cake or muffin is cooled.

ZUCCHINI MUFFINS

PREP TIME: 10 MIN | COOK TIME: 18 MIN | YIELDS 4 MUFFINS

Grated zucchini makes these muffins delightfully moist and tender. They are also hearty and make a great breakfast or midday snack. If you want to make this recipe into a loaf, you can use a 5" × 3" mini-loaf pan sprayed with nonstick spray and add an extra 2–3 minutes to the cooking time.

INGREDIENTS

6 tablespoons all-purpose flour

¼ cup granulated sugar

2 tablespoons whole-wheat flour

¼ teaspoon baking powder

⅛ teaspoon ground cinnamon

⅛ teaspoon baking soda

⅛ teaspoon salt

¼ cup whole milk

1 large egg, at room temperature

1 tablespoon vegetable oil

3 tablespoons grated zucchini

2 tablespoons chopped walnuts

1. Preheat oven to 350°F and line four cups of a muffin pan with paper liners.

2. In a medium bowl, add all-purpose flour, granulated sugar, whole-wheat flour, baking powder, cinnamon, baking soda, and salt. Whisk to combine. Set aside.

3. In a small bowl, combine milk, egg, and oil and whisk to combine. Pour wet ingredients into dry ingredients and use a spatula to mix until just combined, about six strokes, then add shredded zucchini and fold to combine, four to six strokes. Do not overmix.

4. Divide batter between prepared muffin cups and sprinkle tops with walnuts. Bake 18–20 minutes or until muffins spring back when gently pressed in the center and tops are golden brown. Cool in pan 3 minutes, then transfer to a wire rack to cool to room temperature.

STRAWBERRY PECAN BREAD

PREP TIME: 10 MIN | COOK TIME: 30 MIN | SERVES 1

Most strawberry breads have a bright pink color that is boosted by adding a few drops of red food coloring to the batter. This recipe does not include food coloring, so the color of the finished loaf will not be so robustly pink. We eat with our eyes first, and if that pink color will help you enjoy the bread more, feel free to add one drop of red coloring.

INGREDIENTS

½ cup all-purpose flour

¼ cup packed light brown sugar

¼ teaspoon baking powder

⅛ teaspoon baking soda

⅛ teaspoon salt

2 tablespoons buttermilk

2 tablespoons mashed strawberries

1 large egg, at room temperature

1 tablespoon vegetable oil

¼ teaspoon pure vanilla extract

3 tablespoons diced strawberries

2 tablespoons chopped pecans

1. Preheat oven to 350°F and spray a 5" × 3" mini-loaf pan with nonstick cooking spray.

2. In a medium bowl, add flour, brown sugar, baking powder, baking soda, and salt. Whisk to combine. Set aside.

3. In a small bowl, combine buttermilk, mashed strawberries, egg, oil, and vanilla. Whisk to combine. Pour wet ingredients into dry ingredients and use a spatula to mix until just combined, about six strokes, then add diced strawberries and pecans and fold to combine, four to six strokes. Do not overmix.

4. Transfer batter to prepared pan. Bake 30–35 minutes or until bread springs back when gently pressed in the center and top is golden brown. Cool in pan 3 minutes, then transfer to a wire rack to cool to room temperature.

What Is a Stroke?

For muffin and quick bread recipes in this book, the directions say to mix the batter using a specific number of strokes. In this context, a stroke is one turn around the bowl with a spatula. Be sure to pull any dry ingredients from the bottom of the bowl up so each stroke around the bowl is as efficient as possible. The fewer strokes you make, the less gluten you develop, and the more tender the finished result.

DOUBLE CHOCOLATE CHIP BREAD

PREP TIME: 10 MIN | COOK TIME: 30 MIN | SERVES 1

This loaf cake made with Dutch-processed cocoa powder has an earthy, mellow chocolate taste that helps the flavor of the semisweet chips to really pop. You can use regular unsweetened cocoa powder if that is what you have on hand. The flavor will be more robustly chocolatey, which is never a bad thing if you love chocolate.

INGREDIENTS

½ cup all-purpose flour

¼ cup packed light brown sugar

1 tablespoon Dutch-processed cocoa powder

¼ teaspoon baking powder

⅛ teaspoon baking soda

⅛ teaspoon salt

¼ cup buttermilk

1 large egg, at room temperature

1 tablespoon unsalted butter, melted and cooled

¼ teaspoon pure vanilla extract

3 tablespoons semisweet chocolate chips

1. Preheat oven to 350°F and spray a 5" × 3" mini-loaf pan with nonstick cooking spray.

2. In a medium bowl, add flour, brown sugar, cocoa powder, baking powder, baking soda, and salt. Whisk to combine. Set aside.

3. In a small bowl, combine buttermilk, egg, butter, and vanilla. Whisk to combine. Pour wet ingredients into dry ingredients and use a spatula to mix until just combined, about six strokes, then add chocolate chips and fold to combine, four to six strokes. Do not overmix.

4. Transfer batter to prepared pan. Bake 30–35 minutes or until bread springs back when gently pressed in the center and top is golden brown. Cool in pan 3 minutes, then transfer to a wire rack to cool to room temperature.

TOASTED COCONUT BREAD

PREP TIME: 10 MIN | COOK TIME: 35 MIN | SERVES 1

You can toast coconut in large batches and store it in the refrigerator up to a month or in the freezer up to six months. Toasted coconut makes a lovely garnish on cakes and glazed muffins; it can be folded into puddings and custards or added to oatmeal, rice pudding, or bread pudding.

INGREDIENTS

⅓ cup shredded sweetened coconut

½ cup all-purpose flour

¼ cup packed light brown sugar

¼ teaspoon baking powder

⅛ teaspoon baking soda

⅛ teaspoon salt

¼ cup full-fat canned coconut milk

1 large egg, at room temperature

1 tablespoon vegetable oil

¼ teaspoon pure vanilla extract

⅛ teaspoon coconut extract

2 teaspoons powdered sugar

1. Preheat oven to 350°F and spray a 5" × 3" mini-loaf pan with nonstick cooking spray.

2. In a small sauté pan over medium-low heat, add coconut. Cook, stirring constantly, until coconut just turns golden brown, about 5 minutes. Remove pan from heat and cool coconut, stirring constantly for 30 seconds. Set aside.

3. In a medium bowl, add flour, brown sugar, baking powder, baking soda, and salt. Whisk to combine. Set aside.

4. In a small bowl, combine milk, egg, oil, vanilla, and coconut extract. Whisk to combine. Pour wet ingredients into dry ingredients and use a spatula to mix until just combined, about six strokes, then add toasted coconut and fold to combine, four to six strokes. Do not overmix.

5. Transfer batter to prepared pan. Bake 30–35 minutes or until bread springs back when gently pressed in the center and top is golden brown. Cool in pan 3 minutes, then transfer to a wire rack to cool to room temperature. Dust top of loaf with powdered sugar before serving.

PIÑA COLADA BREAD

The refreshing combination of coconut, lime, and pineapple echoes the flavor of the popular piña colada cocktail. If you like, you can soak the cake in a little white rum. When the loaf is hot in the pan, poke it with a toothpick twenty times, then spoon over 2 teaspoons of white rum, letting it soak into the holes. Cool in pan completely before you enjoy!

INGREDIENTS

½ cup all-purpose flour

¼ cup granulated sugar

¼ teaspoon baking powder

⅛ teaspoon baking soda

⅛ teaspoon salt

3 tablespoons full-fat canned coconut milk

1 tablespoon lime juice

1 large egg, at room temperature

1 tablespoon vegetable oil

½ teaspoon freshly grated lime zest

¼ teaspoon pure vanilla extract

⅛ teaspoon coconut extract

¼ cup drained crushed pineapple

2 tablespoons shredded sweetened coconut

2 teaspoons powdered sugar

1. Preheat oven to 350°F and spray a 5" × 3" mini-loaf pan with nonstick cooking spray.

2. In a medium bowl, add flour, granulated sugar, baking powder, baking soda, and salt. Whisk to combine. Set aside.

3. In a small bowl, combine milk, lime juice, egg, oil, lime zest, vanilla, and coconut extract. Whisk to combine. Pour wet ingredients into dry ingredients and use a spatula to mix until just combined, about six strokes, then add pineapple and shredded coconut and fold to combine, four to six strokes. Do not overmix.

4. Transfer batter to prepared pan. Bake 30–35 minutes or until bread springs back when gently pressed in the center and top is golden brown. Cool in pan 3 minutes, then transfer to a wire rack to cool to room temperature. Dust top of loaf with powdered sugar before serving.

FRUITCAKE

PREP TIME: 1¼ HOURS | COOK TIME: 35 MIN | SERVES 1

Commercially prepared fruitcakes are often made with dyed candied fruits and have a dense texture. This version replaces candied fruits with dried fruit hydrated in bourbon, then folded into a molasses-flavored batter. If you do not have bourbon, you can use an equal amount of orange juice.

INGREDIENTS

1 tablespoon chopped dried cherries

1 tablespoon chopped golden raisins

1 tablespoon chopped dates

⅓ cup bourbon

½ cup all-purpose flour

¼ cup packed dark brown sugar

¼ teaspoon baking powder

¼ teaspoon ground cinnamon

⅛ teaspoon baking soda

⅛ teaspoon salt

1 pinch (about 1⁄16 teaspoon) ground cloves

¼ cup buttermilk

2 teaspoons molasses

1 large egg, at room temperature

1 tablespoon vegetable oil

¼ teaspoon pure vanilla extract

2 tablespoons chopped walnuts

1. In a small saucepan, add cherries, raisins, dates, and bourbon. Heat over low heat until liquid simmers, about 5 minutes. Turn off heat and let fruit stand 1 hour, then drain and set aside.

2. Preheat oven to 350°F and spray a 5" × 3" mini-loaf pan with nonstick cooking spray.

3. In a medium bowl, add flour, brown sugar, baking powder, cinnamon, baking soda, salt, and cloves. Whisk to combine. Set aside.

4. In a small bowl, combine buttermilk, molasses, egg, oil, and vanilla. Whisk to combine. Pour wet ingredients into dry ingredients and use a spatula to mix until just combined, about six strokes. Add reserved fruit and walnuts and fold to combine, three to four strokes. Do not overmix.

5. Transfer batter to prepared pan. Bake 30–35 minutes or until bread springs back when gently pressed in the center and top is golden brown. Cool in pan 3 minutes, then transfer to a wire rack to cool to room temperature.

GRANOLA MUFFINS

Granola is a tasty breakfast or snack and so are muffins, so it makes sense to combine them! This recipe makes a handheld granola muffin treat that you can grab on the run or enjoy in a quiet moment. Feel free to use any kind of granola you like, including granola made with dried fruit, nuts, coconut, seeds, and chocolate.

INGREDIENTS

½ cup all-purpose flour

¼ cup granulated sugar

¼ teaspoon baking powder

⅛ teaspoon ground cinnamon

⅛ teaspoon baking soda

⅛ teaspoon salt

¼ cup whole milk

1 large egg, at room temperature

1 tablespoon unsalted butter, melted and cooled

¼ teaspoon pure vanilla extract

⅛ teaspoon almond extract

½ cup granola cereal, divided

1. Preheat oven to 350°F and line four cups of a muffin pan with paper liners.

2. In a medium bowl, add flour, sugar, baking powder, cinnamon, baking soda, and salt. Whisk to combine. Set aside.

3. In a small bowl, combine milk, egg, butter, vanilla, and almond extract and whisk to combine. Pour wet ingredients into dry ingredients and use a spatula to mix until just combined, about six strokes, then add ⅓ cup granola and fold to combine, four to six strokes. Do not overmix.

4. Divide batter between prepared muffin cups and sprinkle remaining granola on top. Bake 18–20 minutes or until muffins spring back when gently pressed in the center and tops are golden brown. Cool in pan 3 minutes, then transfer to a wire rack to cool to room temperature.

CINNAMON CRUNCH MUFFINS

PREP TIME: 10 MIN | COOK TIME: 18 MIN | YIELDS 4 MUFFINS

The crunch in these muffins comes from the crumble topping that is sprinkled on top of the muffins before baking. Be sure to let the topping chill in the refrigerator while you make the muffin batter. If you would like to add 3 tablespoons of finely chopped pecans to this recipe, you can fold them in at the end, and they will add even more texture and flavor.

INGREDIENTS

½ cup plus 2 tablespoons all-purpose flour, divided

¼ cup plus 2 tablespoons granulated sugar, divided

1 tablespoon unsalted butter, chilled

¼ teaspoon baking powder

¼ teaspoon ground cinnamon

⅛ teaspoon baking soda

⅛ teaspoon salt

¼ cup whole milk

1 large egg, at room temperature

1 tablespoon vegetable oil

¼ teaspoon pure vanilla extract

1. Preheat oven to 350°F and line four cups of a muffin pan with paper liners.

2. In a small bowl, combine 2 tablespoons flour, 2 tablespoons sugar, and butter. Use your fingers to mix until mixture clumps together and is crumbly. Chill until ready to use.

3. In a medium bowl, add remaining ½ cup flour, remaining ¼ cup sugar, baking powder, cinnamon, baking soda, and salt. Whisk to combine. Set aside.

4. In a small bowl, combine milk, egg, oil, and vanilla and whisk to combine. Pour wet ingredients into dry ingredients and use a spatula to mix until just combined, about ten strokes. Do not overmix.

5. Divide batter between prepared muffin cups. Sprinkle chilled topping evenly over muffins. Bake 18–20 minutes or until muffins spring back when gently pressed in the center and tops are golden brown. Cool in pan 3 minutes, then transfer to a wire rack to cool to room temperature.

US/METRIC CONVERSION CHARTS

OVEN TEMP CONVERSIONS

Degrees Fahrenheit	Degrees Celsius
200 degrees F	95 degrees C
250 degrees F	120 degrees C
275 degrees F	135 degrees C
300 degrees F	150 degrees C
325 degrees F	160 degrees C
350 degrees F	180 degrees C
375 degrees F	190 degrees C
400 degrees F	205 degrees C
425 degrees F	220 degrees C
450 degrees F	230 degrees C

VOLUME CONVERSIONS

US Volume Measure	Metric Equivalent
⅛ teaspoon	0.5 milliliter
¼ teaspoon	1 milliliter
½ teaspoon	2 milliliters
1 teaspoon	5 milliliters
½ tablespoon	7 milliliters
1 tablespoon (3 teaspoons)	15 milliliters
2 tablespoons (1 fluid ounce)	30 milliliters
¼ cup (4 tablespoons)	60 milliliters
⅓ cup	90 milliliters
½ cup (4 fluid ounces)	125 milliliters
⅔ cup	160 milliliters
¾ cup (6 fluid ounces)	180 milliliters
1 cup (16 tablespoons)	250 milliliters
1 pint (2 cups)	500 milliliters
1 quart (4 cups)	1 liter (about)

WEIGHT CONVERSIONS

US Weight Measure	Metric Equivalent
½ ounce	15 grams
1 ounce	30 grams
2 ounce	60 grams
3 ounce	85 grams
¼ pound (4 ounces)	115 grams
½ pound (8 ounces)	225 grams
¾ pound (12 ounces)	340 grams
1 pound (16 ounces)	454 grams

BAKING PAN SIZES

American	Metric
8 x 1½ inch round baking pan	20 x 4 cm cake tin
9 x 1½ inch round baking pan	23 x 3.5 cm cake tin
11 x 7 x 1½ inch baking pan	28 x 18 x 4 cm baking tin
13 x 9 x 2 inch baking pan	30 x 20 x 5 cm baking tin
2 quart rectangular baking dish	30 x 20 x 3 cm baking tin
15 x 10 x 2 inch baking pan	30 x 25 x 2 cm baking tin (Swiss roll tin)
9 inch pie plate	22 x 4 or 23 x 4 cm pie plate
7 or 8 inch springform pan	18 or 20 cm springform or loose bottom cake tin
9 x 5 x 3 inch loaf pan	23 x 13 x 7 cm or 2 lb narrow loaf or pâté tin
1½ quart casserole	1.5 liter casserole
2 quart casserole	2 liter casserole

HOW TO REDUCE A RECIPE

Original Amount	Half the Amount	One-Third the Amount
1 cup	½ cup	⅓ cup
3/4 cup	6 tablespoons	¼ cup
2/3 cup	⅓ cup	3 tablespoons + 1½ teaspoons
½ cup	¼ cup	2 tablespoons + 2 teaspoons
⅓ cup	2 tablespoons + 2 teaspoons	1 tablespoon + 1¼ teaspoons
¼ cup	2 tablespoons	1 tablespoon + 1 teaspoon
1 tablespoon	1½ teaspoons	1 teaspoon
1 teaspoon	½ teaspoon	¼ teaspoon
½ teaspoon	¼ teaspoon	⅛ teaspoon
¼ teaspoon	⅛ teaspoon	dash

INDEX

Note: Page numbers in **bold** indicate recipe category lists and category overviews.

ABOUT THE AUTHOR

Kelly Jaggers is a cookbook author, recipe developer, food photographer, food stylist, and founder of the recipe blog *Evil Shenanigans* (EvilShenanigans .com). She is the author of *The Everything® Pie Cookbook, Not-So-Humble Pies, Moufflet, The Everything® Easy Asian Cookbook, The Everything® Dutch Oven Cookbook, The Everything® Easy Instant Pot® Cookbook, The Everything® Mediterranean Instant Pot® Cookbook,* and *The "I Love My Instant Pot®" Soup, Stews, and Chilis Recipe Book.* Kelly is also a cooking instructor, personal chef, and caterer. She lives in Dallas with her husband and rescue dogs.

COOKING SOLO
never needs to be boring again!

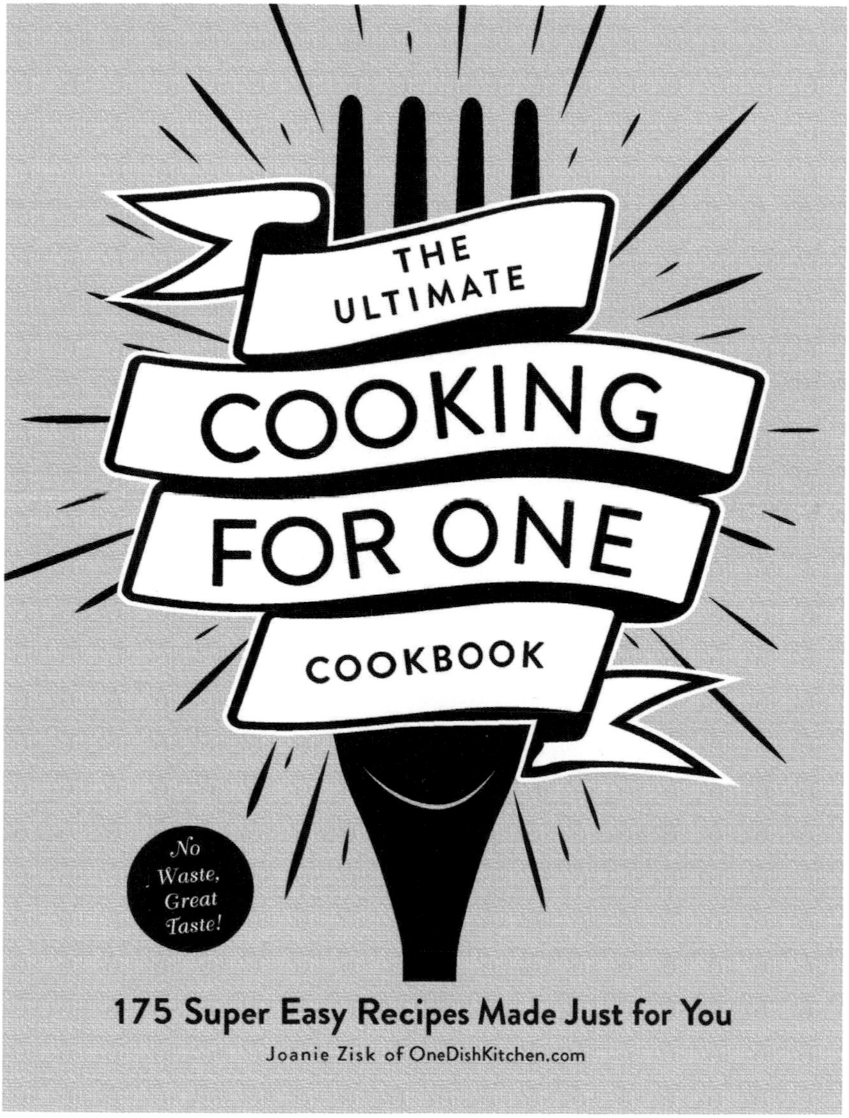

THE ULTIMATE

COOKING FOR ONE COOKBOOK

No Waste, Great Taste!

175 Super Easy Recipes Made Just for You

Joanie Zisk of OneDishKitchen.com

Pick up or download your copy today!

adamsmedia
An Imprint of Simon & Schuster
A ViacomCBS COMPANY

DEDICATION

To my mother, Carol. I miss you every day.

Adams Media
An Imprint of Simon & Schuster, LLC
100 Technology Center Drive
Stoughton, Massachusetts 02072

Copyright © 2021 by Simon & Schuster, LLC

All rights reserved, including the right to reproduce this book or portions thereof in any form whatsoever. For information address Adams Media Subsidiary Rights Department, 1230 Avenue of the Americas, New York, NY 10020.

First Adams Media trade paperback edition November 2021

ADAMS MEDIA and colophon are trademarks of Simon & Schuster.

For information about special discounts for bulk purchases, please contact Simon & Schuster Special Sales at 1-866-506-1949 or business@simonandschuster.com.

The Simon & Schuster Speakers Bureau can bring authors to your live event. For more information or to book an event contact the Simon & Schuster Speakers Bureau at 1-866-248-3049 or visit our website at www.simonspeakers.com.

Interior design by Sylvia McArdle
Interior images © 123RF/Katsiaryna Pleshakova, chelovector
Photographs by Kelly Jaggers

Manufactured in the United States of America

10 9 8 7 6 5 4 3 2

Library of Congress Cataloging-in-Publication Data
Names: Jaggers, Kelly, author.
Title: The ultimate baking for one cookbook / Kelly Jaggers.
Description: Stoughton, MA: Adams Media, 2021. | Series: Ultimate for one | Includes index.
Identifiers: LCCN 2021032929 | ISBN 9781507217337 (pb) | ISBN 9781507217344 (ebook)
Subjects: LCSH: Baking. | Cooking for one. | LCGFT: Cookbooks.
Classification: LCC TX763 .J34 1996 | DDC 641.8/15--dc23
LC record available at https://lccn.loc.gov/2021032929

ISBN 978-1-5072-1733-7
ISBN 978-1-5072-1734-4 (ebook)

Many of the designations used by manufacturers and sellers to distinguish their products are claimed as trademarks. Where those designations appear in this book and Simon & Schuster, LLC, was aware of a trademark claim, the designations have been printed with initial capital letters.

Always follow safety and commonsense cooking protocols while using kitchen utensils, operating ovens and stoves, and handling uncooked food. If children are assisting in the preparation of any recipe, they should always be supervised by an adult.

THE ULTIMATE BAKING FOR ONE COOKBOOK

175 Super Easy Recipes Made Just for You

Kelly Jaggers

ADAMS MEDIA

NEW YORK LONDON TORONTO SYDNEY NEW DELHI

Chapter 1

UNDERSTANDING INFLAMMATION

Throughout your life, your body is bombarded by toxins, chemicals, viruses, bacteria, and other potentially damaging factors. Fortunately, your body naturally responds to these adverse circumstances by initiating an inflammatory response. During this response, the potentially harmful threats are dealt with promptly and completely. But sometimes that response does not turn off, and you are left with chronic inflammation in your body. A silent enemy, inflammation damages your body and can lead to several debilitating diseases. This chapter will discuss inflammation and some changes you can make to keep it at bay.

What Is Inflammation?

The inflammatory response is completely normal and is the cornerstone of the body's healing response. It is simply the way the body supplies nourishment and enhanced immune activity to areas experiencing injury or infection.

Whenever you are exposed to an infectious agent or experience tissue injury or damage, your immune system mounts an inflammatory response. For example, when you cut your finger and it becomes red and swollen, inflammation goes to work, and it's a lifesaver. Blood flow increases to places that require healing. Pain intensifies as a signal that something is wrong within the body. And compounds such as eicosanoids (also known as *prostaglandins*, *prostacyclins*, *thromboxanes*, and *leukotrienes*) are released to attack unwelcome foreign invaders such as bacteria while tending to harmed tissue. Under normal circumstances, once the threat is under control, anti-inflammatory substances are released to turn off the immune response.

The Effects of Chronic Inflammation on the Body

Sometimes, however, inflammation gets the upper hand and continues to operate chronically. This causes continual secretion of pro-inflammatory chemicals in the body. The chronic release and circulation of these chemicals results in an attack on healthy cells, blood vessels, and tissues.

Chronic inflammation generates a wide range of symptoms, including:

- Frequent body aches and pains
- Intermittent infections
- Chronic stiffness
- Loss of joint function
- Recurrent swelling
- Continual congestion
- Persistent indigestion
- Regular bouts of diarrhea
- Unrelenting skin outbreaks

Over time, chronic inflammation acts like a slow but deadly poison, causing overzealous inflammatory chemicals to damage your body as you innocently go about your normal daily activities. The negative consequences associated with out-of-control pro-inflammatory chemicals do not end here. Other diseases and conditions thought to be associated with chronic inflammation include, but are not limited to:

- Allergies
- Anemia
- Asthma
- Cancer
- Crohn's disease
- Congestive heart failure
- Fibromyalgia
- Inflammatory bowel disease (IBD)
- Heart disease
- Kidney failure
- Lupus
- Obesity
- Pancreatitis
- Psoriasis
- Rheumatoid arthritis (RA)
- Stroke

Foods That Increase Inflammation

Research shows that one of the main culprits contributing to chronic inflammation is the food you eat. Certain foods have the ability to trigger inflammation in the body, and when you eat those foods daily, it causes chronic inflammation. It's just as important to stay away from inflammatory foods as it is to add anti-inflammatory foods to your diet. The first step is knowing which foods cause inflammation so you can avoid them!

Advanced Glycation End Products (AGEs)

Researchers have identified chemical reactions that occur in the body that lead to the production of pro-inflammatory substances called *advanced glycation end products* (AGEs). AGEs do not exist in nature but are produced during food processing. Regardless of their source, all AGEs have been shown to exacerbate inflammation.

In a nutshell, the foods high in AGEs are highly processed, refined foods such as:

- Frankfurters, bacon, and powdered egg whites
- Fast foods such as French fries, hamburgers, and fried chicken
- Prepackaged foods that have been preserved, pasteurized, homogenized, or refined, such as white flour, cake mixes, processed cereals, dried milk, dried eggs, pasteurized milk, and canned or frozen precooked meals
- Cream cheese, butter, margarine, and mayonnaise

AGE production is most significant when a mixture of carbohydrates, fats, and proteins is exposed to prolonged thermal processing such as heating, sterilizing, or microwaving. Therefore, foods that have been fried, barbecued, broiled, or cooked in the microwave are more susceptible to higher levels of AGEs.

Trans Fats

Nothing could be more inflammation-promoting than trans fats. These fats lead to the synthesis of pro-inflammatory prostaglandins. Studies have linked high trans fat consumption with high blood levels of CRP (C-reactive protein), the protein linked to inflammation in the body. Foods that tend to be high in trans fats include:

- Fried and deep-fried foods (these are usually cooked in hydrogenated shortening)
- Margarine
- Nondairy creamers
- Shortening
- Baked goods such as cakes, pie crusts, and cookies (especially those with frosting)
- Biscuits
- Frozen breakfast sandwiches
- Doughnuts
- Crackers, chips, and other snack foods that contain the word *hydrogenated* in the ingredient list
- Microwave popcorn

Saturated Fats

Saturated fats are nonessential fats commonly found in meats, high-fat dairy products, and eggs. Although these foods provide important vitamins and minerals, saturated fats can promote inflammation, which is demonstrated by their ability to increase the fibrinogen and CRP inflammatory biomarkers in the blood.

Omega-6 Fatty Acids

Omega-6 fatty acids are a member of the polyunsaturated-fat family. Although they are unsaturated and considered essential in small quantities, excessive intake of omega-6 fatty acids promotes inflammation, encourages blood clotting, and can cause cells in the body to proliferate uncontrollably. The modern diet is weighed down by omega-6 fatty acids because of overconsumption of meats and vegetable oils such as corn, safflower, soybean, and cottonseed that are commonly found in processed foods and fast foods.

Nightshades

Although fruits and vegetables are extremely beneficial to your health, there are certain vegetables that are members of the nightshade family of plants that many claim exacerbate inflammation. These fruits and vegetables include:

- Potatoes
- Tomatoes
- Eggplants
- Sweet and hot peppers (including paprika, cayenne pepper, and Tabasco sauce)
- Ground cherries
- Tomatillos
- Pepinos
- Pimientos

These plants contain a chemical called *solanine*. Anecdotal evidence suggests that solanine may trigger pain and inflammation in some people, but currently there is no research to support the negative claims linked to nightshade vegetables. Individuals with inflammatory conditions can experiment with limiting nightshade vegetables to see if they get any relief from pain and inflammation.

Foods That Fight Inflammation

Now that you know exactly which inflammation-triggering foods you should avoid, what about the good foods? Are there foods that can help control inflammation? Thankfully, there are a myriad of foods that can help your body fight inflammation. In fact, the most powerful inflammation fighters can be found in the grocery store, not the pharmacy! Your best bet is to shop mostly the perimeter of the supermarket where you find fresh, unprocessed foods. Look for a wide variety of brightly colored fruits and vegetables, herbs and spices, and foods with healthy fats. Let's take a closer look at all the inflammation-fighting foods you should be filling your grocery cart up with!

Fruits and Vegetables

Fruits and vegetables are major storehouses of phytochemicals and antioxidants, both of which have anti-inflammatory powers. Phytochemicals are chemicals found in plants, and although they are not essential for life, their benefits are far-reaching, such as helping to reduce the risk of cancer, heart disease, and diabetes. Plants rely on phytochemicals for their own protection and survival. These potent chemicals help plants resist the attacks of bacteria and fungi, the potential havoc brought on by free radicals, and the constant exposure to ultraviolet light from the sun. Fortunately, when we consume plants, the plants' chemicals infuse into our body's tissues and provide ammunition against disease.

In a similar manner to phytochemicals, antioxidants halt and repair free radical damage throughout the body. The most potent antioxidants include vitamin A, vitamin C, vitamin E, and selenium. In addition to fruits and vegetables, these free radical squelchers inhabit whole grains, vegetable oils, nuts, and seeds.

To get the most bang for your buck in the produce section of your local grocery store, choose brightly colored fruits and veggies such as strawberries; blueberries; cantaloupes; spinach; and red, green, and yellow bell peppers. Aim to eat fruits and vegetables that represent each color of the rainbow. It's pretty simple: the more color, the more health benefits. When it comes to fruits, variety is important to ensure you are receiving all the beneficial phytochemicals, antioxidants, vitamins, and minerals while minimizing exposure to any single type of pesticide.

Omega-3 Fatty Acids

Omega-3 fatty acids—polyunsaturated relatives of the omega-6 fatty acid family—have an anti-inflammatory effect in the body. These fatty acids are converted into hormone-like substances called *eicosanoids*. The two most potent omega-3 eicosanoids are eicosapentaenoic acid (EPA) and docosahexaenoic acid (DHA). EPA and DHA have the overall effect of dilating blood vessels, minimizing blood clotting, and reducing inflammation.

Foods high in omega-3s include:

- Fatty fish such as albacore tuna, anchovy, Atlantic herring, halibut, lake trout, mackerel, sardine, stripped sea bass, and wild salmon
- Flaxseeds and flaxseed oils
- Walnuts
- Soybeans
- Tofu

Probiotics

All humans have millions and millions of naturally occurring bacteria in their bodies. Normally, bacteria get a bad rap, but the right types of bacteria, specifically lactobacilli and bifidobacteria, can keep you healthy and even prevent disease. More specifically, these bacteria support the immune system, keeping it strong and better able to fend off disease and illness. They also have anti-inflammatory effects in the gut that can be helpful in treating constipation, diarrhea, inflammatory bowel disease, and irritable bowel syndrome.

You can help good bacteria flourish by consuming foods that contain high concentrations of healthy probiotics (the term *probiotics* means "for life") such as Lactobacillus acidophilus. Fermented milk products such as yogurt, kefir, and some soy-based beverages will increase the probiotic bacteria within your body. Look on the label for the "live and active cultures" statement to ensure that you are increasing your consumption of probiotics.

Lean Protein

Dietary protein is responsible for the growth, maintenance, and repair of the body, but can also contribute to chronic disease development if not chosen properly and in the correct amounts. Lean meats; white-meat poultry; and eggs, on the other hand, will give you clean protein without excessive amounts of pro-inflammatory fats. Cold-water fish offer plenty of quality protein with a kick of anti-inflammatory omega-3 fatty acids.

Vegetable proteins, such as soy foods, beans, lentils, whole grains, seeds, and nuts, will further reduce the presence of pro-inflammatory agents in the body while giving you a blast of phytochemicals and antioxidants.

Garlic

Garlic is a potent anti-inflammatory power food. It contains chemicals that crush the inflammation-promoting substances in the body. As a result, regular garlic consumption can help minimize the side effects of asthma and reduce the pain and inflammation associated with osteoarthritis and rheumatoid arthritis. Garlic can even reduce the production of cancer-causing chemicals that can result when protein is subject to high temperatures through various cooking methods such as grilling.

Curcumin

Curcumin is a substance found in the yellow curry spice turmeric. Curcumin is touted as having antioxidant powers, anti-inflammatory qualities, and possibly even anticancer effects. This spice is popular in India, and some researchers believe there is a link between higher curcumin intake and a lower incidence of Alzheimer's disease. Preliminary findings from animal studies suggest that curcumin may actually possess anti-inflammatory and anticancer properties, but currently very little research exists that evaluates the actual effects of curcumin supplementation on disease risk in humans.

Ginger

Ginger is a tropical plant and a relative of turmeric. Certain constituents of ginger, referred to as *gingerols*, are touted to inhibit numerous biochemicals that promote inflammation, especially in cases of osteoarthritis and rheumatoid arthritis. Again, these claims are unsubstantiated, but one thing that ginger has been found to help with is pregnancy-induced nausea and vomiting. Fresh ginger adds a light spiciness and mellow sweetness to dishes and is a wonderful spice to incorporate into stir-fries and dipping sauces.

Lifestyle Choices That Combat and Reduce Inflammation

There are a number of other simple dietary and lifestyle interventions that can keep inflammation from establishing a foothold over the body. Beating inflammation is not just about changing your diet. Your best defensive mode is to combine dietary and lifestyle interventions to ensure that your body is protected.

- **Stay properly hydrated:** Women should aim for 90 ounces of fluids daily, and men should get 125 ounces.
- **Get enough sleep:** Aim for at least seven to nine hours per night.
- **Exercise regularly:** Exercise at least five days per week, including the three essential components of an exercise program: cardiovascular, strengthening, and flexibility.
- **Manage stress:** Take time for yourself every day to chill out and smell the roses. Schedule regular breathing breaks. Research has shown that taking just one large, deep breath can help alleviate stress and its negative effects on the body.
- **Try supplements:** Supplement your diet every day with 1,000 IUs of vitamin D_3 and 1,000 mg of DHA and EPA from fish oils. Be sure to check with your physician before you begin taking a fish oil supplement, especially if you are currently taking any medications.

Chapter 2
SMOOTHIES

Smoothies bring a big nutritional advantage to the table. When you blend whole foods, you get all of the nutrients, from the fiber to the vitamins and minerals. Nothing gets left out! Aptly named, smoothies are smooth, sometimes creamy, and quick and simple to prepare.

Smoothies are the easiest, most versatile way to add anti-inflammatory nutrients to your day. Whether they replace a meal or become your go-to snack, smoothies take minimal effort to blend and are one of the most delicious ways to incorporate a wide variety of anti-inflammatory foods into your diet.

You can, of course, drink a smoothie at any time during the day, but smoothies are especially popular for breakfast. If you have busy mornings, you can prepare all of the ingredients the night before. Then all you have to do in the morning is blend and go!

Since sugar can be inflammatory, I like to keep my smoothies naturally sweetened with fruit. Sometimes I'll add stevia, a natural sweetener made from the stevia plant, if I need to enhance the sweetness a little more. Enjoy the natural sweetness nature provides in these smoothie recipes!

THE PURPLE MACHINE SMOOTHIE

Serves 1

INGREDIENTS

3 large red kale leaves
1 cup unsweetened almond milk
1 cup frozen blueberries
½ medium banana
¼ teaspoon pure stevia powder

1 Tear the kale leaves away from the tough vein in the center. Discard the vein and place the leaves in a large blender with the almond milk.

2 Blend kale leaves and almond milk on high until the kale is completely broken down.

3 Add frozen blueberries, banana, and stevia and blend on high until thoroughly combined and smooth.

4 Consume immediately.

KEY INGREDIENT: Red Kale

Red kale (as well as the blueberries) gives this smoothie a deep purple color, and both are powerful anti-inflammatory agents. Typically, the more color a food has, the more anti-oxidants it contains. The deep color of the kale and blueberries comes from the antioxidants present in these potent foods. Kale is high in vitamin C and beta-carotene, and these antioxidant vitamins are known to fight damage caused by free radicals. Oxidative stress can lead to inflammation, so those nutrients are helping keep inflammation at bay. Kale has a number of different flavonoids in its leaves, which also come into play in fighting inflammation. In addition, kale is a good source of omega-3 fatty acids and has an ideal ratio of omega-3 fatty acids to omega-6 fatty acids, which is important for fighting inflammation. Omega-3 fatty acids have also been shown to inhibit key inflammatory pathways.

When paired with blueberries, banana, and pure stevia powder, the natural bitter flavor of kale is masked, making this anti-inflammatory smoothie an easy way to get more of the powerhouse leafy green into your diet.

Per Serving
Calories: 184 | Fat: 4.0 g | Protein: 4.4 g | Sodium: 199 mg
Fiber: 8.5 g | Carbohydrates: 38.5 g | Sugar: 21.8 g

STRAWBERRY BEET SMOOTHIE

Serves 1

INGREDIENTS

1 cup whole strawberries, frozen or fresh

1 small beet, peeled and cut into chunks

1 medium banana, peeled and frozen

3 tablespoons chia seeds

2 pitted dates

¼ cup old-fashioned oats

1 cup cold water

1 cup ice

Stevia, to taste (optional)

1 Place all ingredients except stevia in a large blender.

2 Blend the ingredients on high until thoroughly combined and smooth.

3 Taste your smoothie and add stevia if desired.

4 Consume immediately or store in an airtight container in the refrigerator up to 24 hours.

KEY INGREDIENT: Strawberries

This is a vibrant smoothie with a deep pink hue. Deeply pigmented fruits and vegetables are typically high in antioxidants, and indeed, strawberries are an excellent source of antioxidant phytochemicals. The antioxidants in strawberries help rid the body of free radicals that promote inflammation. Eating strawberries every week has been shown to lower levels of C-reactive protein, an inflammation marker that is associated with chronic inflammation. Strawberries have also been associated with reducing pain in arthritis patients.

Don't be scared off by the beet in this smoothie. When paired with sweet strawberries and the banana, the beet is mellow and delicious.

Per Serving

Calories: 535 | Fat: 12.1 g | Protein: 15.8 g | Sodium: 69 mg Fiber: 24.7 g | Carbohydrates: 97.2 g | Sugar: 37.1 g

WILD BLUEBERRY POWER SMOOTHIE

Serves 2

INGREDIENTS

1 cup frozen wild blueberries
1 medium banana
1 tablespoon ground flaxseed meal
½ cup chopped parsley
1½ tablespoons peeled, chopped
   ginger
1 cup cold water
2 tablespoons almond butter

1 Place all ingredients in a large
   blender.

2 Blend the ingredients on high
   until thoroughly combined and
   smooth.

3 Consume immediately or store
   in an airtight container in the
   refrigerator up to 24 hours.

KEY INGREDIENT: Wild Blueberries

Wild blueberries contain more of the powerful antioxidant anthocyanin than cultivated blueberries do, so it's worth seeking them out and adding them to your rotation. Most well-stocked supermarkets will have wild blueberries in their frozen fruit section. In addition to the anti-inflammatory properties wild blueberries possess, anthocyanin is thought to play a role in brain and eye health. Wild blueberries also have 30 percent less (natural) sugar than cultivated blueberries have.

Although the starring role in this smoothie goes to the wild blueberries, that isn't the only ingredient working to reduce inflammation for you. This smoothie brings additional anti-inflammatory goodness through flaxseeds, parsley, ginger, and almonds. It's aptly named a *power smoothie*!

Per Serving
Calories: 216 | Fat: 9.7 g | Protein: 5.6 g | Sodium: 10 mg
Fiber: 6.6 g | Carbohydrates: 28.7 g | Sugar: 14.7 g

CHOCOLATE CHERRY SMOOTHIE

Serves 1

INGREDIENTS

¾ cup unsweetened almond milk, frozen
¾ cup unsweetened almond milk
1 cup cherries, pitted and frozen
1 tablespoon raw cacao powder
¼ teaspoon pure stevia powder

1 Place all ingredients in a large blender.

2 Blend the ingredients on high until thoroughly combined and smooth.

3 For ultimate thickness, consume immediately. Smoothie may also be stored in an airtight container in the refrigerator up to 24 hours.

KEY INGREDIENT: Cherries

Frozen pitted cherries are readily available in many supermarkets year-round. Cherries contain the antioxidants anthocyanin and cyanidin, which have anti-inflammatory effects. Cyanidin is regarded as one of the strongest antioxidants, and it quickly neutralizes reactive oxygen species. Thus, it has a powerful anti-inflammatory effect. It has been found to be especially helpful in dealing with inflammation associated with arthritis. In addition, cherries are a good source of fiber, potassium, calcium, vitamin A, and folic acid.

This is a thick and creamy smoothie that tastes more indulgent than it actually is. Freezing half of the almond milk helps create a thicker, more shake-like smoothie. You can do this easily in ice cube trays.

If you have trouble finding raw cacao powder, unsweetened cocoa powder is a good substitute. Although the antioxidants are diminished, it still has some anti-inflammatory properties.

Per Serving
Calories: 136 | Fat: 5.1 g | Protein: 3.7 g | Sodium: 270 mg
Fiber: 4.9 g | Carbohydrates: 24.5 g | Sugar: 15.4 g

TURMERIC SMOOTHIE

Serves 1

INGREDIENTS

For the Turmeric Paste
¼ cup turmeric powder
½ cup water
¾ teaspoon black pepper

For the Smoothie
1 cup frozen pineapple chunks
1 cup frozen mango chunks
1–1½ cups cold water
1 teaspoon coconut oil
1 teaspoon peeled, chopped fresh
　ginger
1 teaspoon prepared turmeric paste

---

1 First, prepare the Turmeric Paste: Mix the turmeric powder and water in a small saucepan over low heat, stirring until a paste is formed.

2 Once you have a paste, stir in the black pepper. This recipe provides more than you'll need for this smoothie, so cool and store in a glass jar in the refrigerator up to 2 weeks.

3 Next, place all smoothie ingredients in a large blender.

4 Blend the ingredients on high until thoroughly combined and smooth.

5 Consume immediately or store in an airtight container in the refrigerator up to 24 hours.

KEY INGREDIENT: Turmeric

Turmeric is the all-star that gives this anti-inflammatory smoothie its gorgeous golden hue. Turmeric has over two dozen anti-inflammatory compounds, making it a very powerful ingredient to include in your diet. Turmeric has six different compounds that inhibit the COX-2 enzyme (a known promoter of inflammation). Curcumin is the most-noted compound in turmeric and is well known for its ability to ease arthritis pain. In fact, it has been shown to outperform many pharmaceuticals! In addition to the turmeric, you'll also get anti-inflammatory effects from the pineapple and fresh ginger in this smoothie. This is a sweet and spicy smoothie that is irresistible!

Turmeric is best absorbed when paired with black pepper, which is why pepper is included in the paste recipe. And you can use this turmeric paste in more than just this smoothie—try adding it to your scrambled eggs or favorite stir-fry as well!

Per Serving
Calories: 227 | Fat: 4.9 g | Protein: 2.6 g | Sodium: 2 mg
Fiber: 5.6 g | Carbohydrates: 48.5 g | Sugar: 38.8 g

AVOCADO-LADA SMOOTHIE

Serves 1

INGREDIENTS

1½ cups frozen pineapple chunks
½ medium avocado, peeled and
   pitted
2 cups baby spinach
3 tablespoons flaxseeds
1½ cups cold water

1 Place all ingredients in a large
   blender.

2 Blend the ingredients on high
   until thoroughly combined and
   smooth.

3 Consume immediately.

KEY INGREDIENT: Avocado

What could be better than enjoying the flavors of a piña colada in the health-promoting form of a smoothie? The avocado is one of the most nutrient-dense foods on the planet. Avocados have a very low glycemic index and are a great source of pantothenic acid; fiber; copper; folate; and vitamins K, B_6, E, and C. Their anti-inflammatory benefit comes from their fat content. They are a great source of omega-9 fatty acids (heart-healthy monounsaturated fats), which have been shown to improve insulin sensitivity and decrease inflammation.

Spinach, pineapple, and flaxseeds are also working in your favor with their anti-inflammatory compounds. This smoothie is excellent with plain water, or you could add a little extra natural sweetness with hydrating coconut water.

Per Serving
Calories: 414 | Fat: 22.0 g | Protein: 10.0 g | Sodium: 63 mg
Fiber: 17.8 g | Carbohydrates: 49.5 g | Sugar: 25.3 g

ALMOND FLAX SMOOTHIE

Serves 1

INGREDIENTS

1 large banana
⅓ cup ground flaxseed meal
1 cup unsweetened vanilla almond milk
1 tablespoon unsalted almond butter
¼ teaspoon ground cinnamon
1 cup ice

1 Place all ingredients in a large blender.

2 Blend the ingredients on high until thoroughly combined and smooth.

3 Consume immediately or store in an airtight container in the refrigerator up to 24 hours.

KEY INGREDIENT: Flaxseeds

Flaxseeds are an excellent source of the omega-3 fatty acid alpha-linolenic acid (ALA). ALA helps fight the damage in your body from free radicals and is also thought to improve insulin sensitivity. Studies have shown that people with chronic inflammation, especially those who are overweight, who supplement their diet with flaxseeds significantly lower the inflammation marker C-reactive protein.

Almonds, flaxseeds, and cinnamon all have anti-inflammatory properties. These ingredients just so happen to taste fantastic together as well! If you don't have almond butter on hand, you can easily make your own by blending whole almonds in a powerful blender or food processor. You may need to add a little oil to create a smooth butter.

Per Serving
Calories: 419 | Fat: 23.3 g | Protein: 13.6 g | Sodium: 182 mg
Fiber: 13.7 g | Carbohydrates: 42.6 g | Sugar: 15.5 g

VITAMIN C POWER SMOOTHIE

Serves 1

INGREDIENTS

½ medium banana, peeled and frozen
1 medium orange, peeled and cut into segments
1 medium kiwifruit, peeled and cut into quarters
2 cups baby spinach
¾ cup lite canned coconut milk
1 cup ice

1 Place all ingredients in a large blender.

2 Blend the ingredients on high until thoroughly combined and smooth.

3 Consume immediately.

KEY INGREDIENT: Kiwifruit

Kiwifruit contains enzymes that help break down inflammatory complexes in the body. In addition, kiwifruit has an antioxidant peptide, kissper, which is shown to effectively counteract oxidative stress and inflammatory responses in the body. Kiwifruit is also high in vitamin C, an immune boosting vitamin. In fact, you are getting a triple dose of vitamin C from the orange, kiwifruit, and spinach, making this a great smoothie to consume during the cold and flu season! The coconut milk gives this smoothie a creamy, tropical feel. Canned coconut milk is used here, and the lite variety helps keep calories in check.

Per Serving
Calories: 288 | Fat: 10.8 g | Protein: 4.2 g | Sodium: 60 mg
Fiber: 8.6 g | Carbohydrates: 45.4 g | Sugar: 27.5 g

AVOCADO CHOCOLATE SMOOTHIE

Serves 1

INGREDIENTS

½ medium banana
¼ medium avocado, peeled and
  pitted
1 cup vanilla almond milk
1 tablespoon unsalted almond butter
1 tablespoon raw cacao powder
¼ teaspoon pure stevia powder
½ cup ice

---

1 Place all ingredients in a large
   blender.

2 Blend the ingredients on high
   until thoroughly combined and
   smooth.

3 Consume immediately.

KEY INGREDIENT: Raw Cacao Powder

Cacao powder is made from unroasted cacao beans. It's easy to get cacao powder confused with cocoa powder, often used in baking, but they are different. While cocoa powder and cacao powder both start from the cacao bean, the difference is in the processing. The sharpest contrast is that cocoa powder is heated to very high temperatures. While this gives cocoa powder a less bitter taste, it also degrades its nutritional value. Cacao powder is processed at a very low heat, which helps it retain its enzymes, vitamins, and nutrients.

Cacao is rich in antioxidants. In fact, it ranks in the top twenty of all antioxidant foods, based on its Oxygen Radical Absorbance Capacity (ORAC) Scale—a test developed to measure the antioxidant capacity of foods. The powerful antioxidants in cacao, known as *flavonols*, are responsible for the anti-inflammatory effects it possesses. Flavonols can increase nitric oxide bioavailability and also activate nitric oxide synthase, an enzyme that helps the body produce nitric oxide. Nitric oxide is a signaling molecule that provides an anti-inflammatory effect in our bodies. This is why dark chocolate is known to be so healthful!

The banana, avocado, and almond butter also contribute to the nutrition of this smoothie. The best part, though, is that this smoothie gets the most amazing creamy texture from the avocado, and it tastes like a dreamy dessert!

Per Serving
Calories: 317 | Fat: 15.3 g | Protein: 6.7 g | Sodium: 154 mg
Fiber: 7.5 g | Carbohydrates: 38.2 g | Sugar: 23.0 g

BLUEBERRY GINGER SMOOTHIE

Serves 2

INGREDIENTS

1 cup fresh blueberries
1 teaspoon peeled, chopped fresh
  ginger
1 cup unsweetened vanilla almond
  milk
1 cup sliced frozen banana
1 cup ice

1 Place all ingredients in a large
  blender.

2 Blend the ingredients on high
  until thoroughly combined and
  smooth.

3 Consume immediately or store
  in an airtight container in the
  refrigerator up to 24 hours.

KEY INGREDIENT: Blueberries

Blueberries are low in calories and high in antioxidants, and they give this smoothie a vibrant indigo color! Blueberries get their bright blue pigment from a class of antioxidants called *anthocyanins*, which fight inflammation. Anthocyanins have a positive effect on inflammation by inhibiting the expression and biological activity of some pro-inflammatory cytokines. Not only are blueberries going to help you fight inflammation, but they also have been linked to brain and heart health. They are powerful little berries!

The banana in this smoothie lends its natural sweetness. Frozen bananas give this smoothie extra creaminess, so make an effort to freeze the banana ahead of time. Simply slice your banana and freeze it in a freezer-safe container overnight. The fresh ginger adds zing, and ginger is another potent inflammation fighter!

Per Serving
Calories: 124 | Fat: 1.8 g | Protein: 1.9 g | Sodium: 91 mg
Fiber: 4.3 g | Carbohydrates: 29.0 g | Sugar: 16.8 g

CHOCOLATE ALMOND BUTTER SMOOTHIE

Serves 1

INGREDIENTS

1½ medium bananas, peeled and frozen
3 tablespoons unsweetened raw cacao powder
1 tablespoon unsalted almond butter
2 cups baby spinach
2 tablespoons ground flaxseed meal
1 cup unsweetened vanilla almond milk
1 cup ice

1 Place all ingredients in a large blender.

2 Blend the ingredients on high until thoroughly combined and smooth.

3 Consume immediately.

KEY INGREDIENT: Banana

Bananas are one of the most popular fruits, but they aren't often noted for their health benefits. Even so, they are a nutrient-dense food that has anti-inflammatory properties. Bananas have the anti-inflammatory antioxidant quercetin. In addition, bananas also contain the powerful flavonoid kaempferol. A diet high in kaempferol is correlated with reduced serum interleukin-6 levels, an inflammatory cytokine.

Almonds, spinach, cacao powder, and flaxseeds all bring anti-inflammatory properties to this smoothie. You're also getting a good amount of vitamin E, omega-3 fatty acids, and antioxidants in this drink.

Even though there's spinach in this smoothie, you'll only be able to focus on the lovely combination of chocolate and almond butter. The frozen bananas bring a creaminess and naturally sweeten the smoothie. If you like chocolate and peanut butter together, you'll love chocolate and almond butter! This is an anti-inflammatory smoothie that tastes like a treat.

Per Serving
Calories: 323 | Fat: 17.3 g | Protein: 12.7 g | Sodium: 228 mg
Fiber: 11.5 g | Carbohydrates: 33.7 g | Sugar: 8.6 g

PEACHY STRAWBERRY DESIRE SMOOTHIE

Serves 1

INGREDIENTS

1 cup frozen peaches
1 cup frozen strawberries
1 cup roughly chopped bok choy
1 cup unsweetened vanilla almond
  milk
¼ teaspoon pure vanilla extract
3 tablespoons hulled hemp seeds
¼ cup whole almonds
Handful of ice (optional)

1 Place all ingredients in a large
   blender.
2 Blend the ingredients on high
   until thoroughly combined and
   smooth.
3 Consume immediately.

KEY INGREDIENT: Bok Choy

Bok choy is one of those powerhouse vegetables that provides excellent anti-inflammatory benefits, but it isn't an ingredient you'd normally find in a smoothie. There's no reason why you shouldn't rotate the greens you use in smoothies, and bok choy is a particularly nutritious choice. Bok choy is loaded with vitamin A, vitamin C, manganese, and zinc. It also contains omega-3 fatty acids and alpha-linolenic acid (ALA), which works to keep chronic inflammation at bay. Bok choy also has a higher concentration of beta carotene and vitamin A than any other variety of cabbage.

Pair bok choy with frozen peaches and strawberries with vanilla extract, and you'll forget you're drinking such a healthy smoothie! Hemp seeds add some protein to this smoothie, and the whole almonds add to the anti-inflammatory power.

Per Serving
Calories: 530 | Fat: 34.5 g | Protein: 22.7 g | Sodium: 227 mg
Fiber: 12.6 g | Carbohydrates: 41.7 g | Sugar: 22.6 g

STRAWBERRY BANANA OATMEAL SMOOTHIE

Serves 1

INGREDIENTS

1 medium banana, peeled and frozen
1½ cups frozen strawberries
2 cups chopped romaine lettuce
¾ cup rolled oats
1 cup unsweetened vanilla almond
  milk

1 Place all ingredients in a large
   blender.
2 Blend the ingredients on high
   until thoroughly combined and
   smooth.
3 Consume immediately.

KEY INGREDIENT: Rolled Oats

Many people have heard that oats can help lower cholesterol numbers, but did you also know that oats can help reduce inflammation? It's true! Oats have special compounds called *avenanthramides*, which researchers believe play the biggest role in reducing inflammation. Avenanthramides are unique to oats and have been shown to reduce the inflammatory signals put out by the cells that line the blood vessels.

Even more, oats also have saponins, special phytochemicals that promote an anti-inflammatory environment systematically. This tasty smoothie also gets extra anti-inflammatory properties from the strawberries and romaine lettuce. Freeze your banana ahead of time for an extra-creamy smoothie. And using vanilla almond milk adds great flavor.

Per Serving
Calories: 513 | Fat: 8.8 g | Protein: 14.9 g | Sodium: 192 mg
Fiber: 18.2 g | Carbohydrates: 100.5 g | Sugar: 27.6 g

RASPBERRY LEMON TART SMOOTHIE

Serves 1

INGREDIENTS

1½ cups frozen raspberries
2 tablespoons fresh lemon juice
¾ cup water
½ teaspoon pure stevia powder

1 Place all ingredients in a large
  blender.

2 Blend the ingredients on high
  until thoroughly combined and
  smooth.

3 Consume immediately or store
  in an airtight container in the
  refrigerator up to 24 hours.

KEY INGREDIENT: Raspberries

The raspberry is truly a powerful berry. Raspberries have been shown to inhibit the production of the same enzymes that anti-inflammatory products like ibuprofen and aspirin do! Like blueberries, raspberries are also high in anthocyanins, which are shown to reduce chronic inflammation in the body. Raspberries have one of the highest antioxidant levels of any fruit, so they are one of the healthiest fruits you can consume. Oxidative stress in your body can lead to health problems like heart disease and diabetes, and the antioxidants in raspberries fight that cellular damage from free radicals.

This smoothie is reminiscent of sweet-tart candies, but in healthy smoothie form! If you like tart raspberry lemonade, you'll love this smoothie. The tart flavor is balanced by the natural sweetness of pure stevia powder.

Per Serving
Calories: 115 | Fat: 0.0 g | Protein: 2.6 g | Sodium: 2 mg
Fiber: 13.7 g | Carbohydrates: 27.2 g | Sugar: 10.1 g

PEAR GINGER SMOOTHIE

Serves 1

INGREDIENTS

- 1 large ripe pear, cored and quartered
- 2 cups baby spinach
- 1 tablespoon peeled, chopped fresh ginger
- 1 tablespoon fresh lemon juice
- ¼ cup whole almonds
- ¾ cup cold water
- 1 cup ice

---

1 Place all ingredients in a large blender.
2 Blend the ingredients on high until thoroughly combined and smooth.
3 Consume immediately.

KEY INGREDIENT: Fresh Ginger

Pears and ginger go together naturally, and what a great way to incorporate the fantastic inflammation-fighting ginger into your smoothie. Ginger has a long history of medicinal use, dating back to ancient times, including use as a strong inflammation fighter. One group of compounds in ginger that are shown to have anti-inflammatory effects are gingerols. Gingerols inhibit the synthesis of pro-inflammatory cytokines.

Ginger also contains a protein-digesting enzyme called *zingibain*, which has also been shown to reduce inflammation in the body. This anti-inflammatory action makes ginger excellent for reducing pain after intense physical exercise. As a result, this juice, and all of the recipes with fresh ginger, are excellent as recovery drinks. Research has shown that the anti-inflammatory actions are equal to anti-inflammatory drugs, with patients reporting the same amount of pain relief when using ginger instead of over-the-counter drugs!

There are even more inflammation fighters in this smoothie, including the baby spinach and almonds. A pear has a lot of natural sugars, which gives this smoothie a subtle sweetness to offset the spicy ginger. Ginger brings a nice bite to smoothies. If you find it too strong, you can always use less and work your way up to the full recipe amount.

Per Serving
Calories: 334 | Fat: 17.2 g | Protein: 10.6 g | Sodium: 48 mg
Fiber: 11.4 g | Carbohydrates: 37.9 g | Sugar: 19.4 g

VA-VA-VA-VOOM ENERGY SMOOTHIE

Serves 1

INGREDIENTS

¼ medium avocado, peeled and
  pitted
1 medium Granny Smith apple, cored
  and quartered
½ medium cucumber
1 cup spinach
1 cup chopped romaine lettuce
1 cup chopped kale, veins removed
1 medium banana, peeled and
  frozen
2 tablespoons chia seeds
1 cup cold water
1 cup ice

1 Place all ingredients in a large
   blender.
2 Blend the ingredients on high
   until thoroughly combined and
   smooth.
3 Consume immediately.

KEY INGREDIENT: Spinach

Leafy green vegetables like spinach have potent antioxidants that have been shown to reduce inflammation. Spinach contains two carotenoids, lutein and zeaxanthin. Research has shown that the higher the levels of these two carotenoids are in the blood, the lower the inflammation markers will be. Spinach also contains flavonoids, powerful antioxidants that protect against free radical damage within your body. Spinach is also a good source of vitamins A and C, manganese, zinc, and selenium.

If you want your smoothie to fight inflammation *and* give you loads of energy, this is the smoothie for you. Packing three cups of greens into this smoothie will energize you and keep you going! It's a great idea to include a lot of greens in your diet every day, and smoothies like this make it an easy task.

Per Serving
Calories: 388 | Fat: 11.1 g | Protein: 8.8 g | Sodium: 41 mg
Fiber: 20.0 g | Carbohydrates: 67.4 g | Sugar: 33.0 g

MIXED BERRY SMOOTHIE

Serves 2

INGREDIENTS

½ cup strawberry chunks
½ cup raspberries
½ cup blueberries
1 cup unsweetened vanilla almond milk
½ teaspoon pure vanilla extract

---

1 Place all ingredients in a large blender.

2 Blend the ingredients on high until thoroughly combined and smooth.

3 Consume immediately or store in an airtight container in the refrigerator up to 24 hours.

KEY INGREDIENT: Berries

Berries of all kinds have an anti-inflammatory effect, so why not triple up and put three of them in one powerful smoothie? Strawberries, raspberries, and blueberries, with their strong antioxidant profiles, bring their unique properties to this smoothie. All three berries are rich in flavonoids, which have been touted for their ability to block the production of molecules that promote inflammation, specifically the cyclooxygenase (COX) and lipoxygenase (LOX) enzymes.

Studies have shown that the plant compounds in berries can reduce the risk of serious diseases like cardiovascular disease and cancer. In addition to their anti-inflammatory properties, the three berries in this smoothie contain good amounts of vitamin C, vitamin K, manganese, folate, copper, and fiber!

Berries deliver great nutrition and taste delicious. This smoothie takes advantage of that flavor, which is complemented by a touch of vanilla.

Per Serving
Calories: 67 | Fat: 1.8 g | Protein: 1.4 g | Sodium: 90 mg
Fiber: 4.2 g | Carbohydrates: 13.4 g | Sugar: 7.4 g

TROPICAL GREEN SMOOTHIE

Serves 1
INGREDIENTS

1 cup frozen pineapple chunks
½ cup frozen mango chunks
1 medium ripe banana (frozen or not)
1 cup chopped kale, veins removed
3 tablespoons hemp seeds
1 cup cold unsweetened coconut
   water

1 Place all ingredients in a large
   blender.

2 Blend the ingredients on high
   until thoroughly combined and
   smooth.

3 Consume immediately.

KEY INGREDIENT: Pineapple

Pineapple is one of the sweetest fruits and therefore a great natural sweetener for both juices and smoothies. It can help offset the earthy or bitter flavor of many greens and make them more palatable. Pineapples are good for more than just their sweetening ability, though. They are also considered a powerful anti-inflammatory food because they contain bromelain. Bromelain is a protein-digesting enzyme that works similarly to anti-inflammatory drugs in the body. It is easily absorbed in the body without degrading or losing its biological activity. Research has shown that bromelain reduces pain and swelling, so it is especially helpful for athletic recovery, arthritis symptoms, or any type of physical trauma.

In addition to its anti-inflammatory action, bromelain has been shown to be helpful in a number of other conditions. Because it helps the body break down proteins, it's an excellent digestive aid. Research has shown that it even has a protective effect against cancer, cardiovascular disease, and diabetes. This powerful enzyme is what makes pineapple a smart dietary choice.

All of the sweet, tropical-tasting fruit in this smoothie totally masks the taste of the kale, so even the pickiest palates won't realize it's there. Hemp seeds add protein to this smoothie, which will help keep you full longer. Coconut water is hydrating and adds another tropical component. Plain water is a fine substitute if you don't have coconut water.

Per Serving
Calories: 458 | Fat: 15.2 g | Protein: 16.2 g | Sodium: 260 mg
Fiber: 10.9 g | Carbohydrates: 73.4 g | Sugar: 48.3 g

WAKE-ME-UP GREEN SMOOTHIE

Serves 1

INGREDIENTS

½ cup coconut water
Juice from 1 medium lime
1" piece fresh ginger, peeled and
  sliced
½ cup packed parsley
2 cups chopped kale, veins removed
1 medium Red Delicious apple, cut
  into chunks
½ medium banana
1 cup ice

1 Place all ingredients in a large
  blender.
2 Blend the ingredients on high
  until thoroughly combined and
  smooth.
3 Consume immediately.

KEY INGREDIENT: Lime

Citrus fruits such as lime are high in vitamin C, which provides protection against inflammation. Studies have found that moderate amounts of vitamin C can positively affect inflammation markers, reducing them significantly. Consuming lime juice is a great way to naturally increase your vitamin C intake.

This is the perfect smoothie to drink in the morning. Only lightly sweet, this is a smoothie that has a bite from the ginger, tartness from the lime, and a little bitterness from the greens. It tastes healthy and will make you feel healthy! It will quickly become one of your favorite ways to start the day.

Per Serving
Calories: 228 | Fat: 0.7 g | Protein: 4.4 g | Sodium: 156 mg
Fiber: 10.0 g | Carbohydrates: 54.2 g | Sugar: 33.7 g

MANGO ZINGER SMOOTHIE

Serves 1

INGREDIENTS

1 cup frozen mango chunks
½" piece fresh ginger, peeled and cut
into chunks
1 medium banana, peeled and
frozen
2 cups spinach
1 cup unsweetened vanilla almond
milk
3 tablespoons chia seeds
1 tablespoon fresh lime juice

---

1 Place all ingredients in a large
blender.

2 Blend the ingredients on high
until thoroughly combined and
smooth.

3 Consume immediately.

KEY INGREDIENT: Chia Seeds

Chia seeds are a good source of alpha-linolenic acid (ALA), an omega-3 fatty acid known for helping protect against inflammation. A number of studies have shown that increasing daily amounts of ALA helps reduce pain and joint pain in arthritis patients.

Chia seeds also contain quercetin, an anti-inflammatory antioxidant. Quercetin inhibits production of inflammation-producing enzymes in the body. In addition to being anti-inflammatory, quercetin has also been shown to have anticarcinogenic and antiviral properties.

Mangoes, spinach, ginger, limes, and almonds also have anti-inflammatory powers. Put all of these ingredients together, and you end up with a strong anti-inflammatory drink. You are going to love the texture frozen mango gives this smoothie.

Per Serving
Calories: 402 | Fat: 13.0 g | Protein: 10.6 g | Sodium: 233 mg
Fiber: 18.9 g | Carbohydrates: 70.6 g | Sugar: 37.9 g

Chapter 3

JUICES

Freshly juiced fruits and vegetables can add a tremendous amount of nutrients to your diet. While smoothies are made by blending the *whole* food, juices are made by extracting just the juice from the fruits and vegetables. Both are beneficial and have a place in a balanced, healthy diet.

You are able to consume more juice in one sitting than a smoothie because smoothies are more filling and caloric. Some people believe that juicing allows for quicker absorption of nutrients because the fiber is removed.

In order to make the juices in this chapter you'll need a juicer. Juicers are widely available in stores and online in every price range. The two types of juicers you'll find are centrifugal and masticating. The most economical of these two types are centrifugal juicers. Centrifugal juicers are higher-speed juicers, but they are not as efficient as the masticating style. A masticating juicer works at a slower speed and retains more of the vegetables' and fruits' nutrients. The juice from masticating juicers also lasts significantly longer than centrifugal juicers.

No matter which kind you choose, you'll find that making fresh juice at home is easy and delicious. Adding juicing to your daily routine is a surefire way to improve your health.

CARROT GINGER

Serves 1
INGREDIENTS

5 medium carrots
1 tablespoon peeled, coarsely
   chopped ginger

1 Prepare the carrots by chopping off the tops and tips and then cutting them into appropriate-sized pieces for your juicer.

2 Process the carrots and ginger through the juicer.

3 Strain through a fine-mesh sieve if desired.

4 Consume immediately over ice or allow to chill in the refrigerator before serving.

5 Can be stored in a glass airtight container in the refrigerator up to 12 hours if using a centrifugal juicer and up to 3 days if using a masticating juicer.

KEY INGREDIENT: Ginger

Ginger is so powerful because it contains a number of compounds that help fight inflammation. The gingerols in ginger have been shown to suppress the pro-inflammatory compounds cytokines and chemokines and fight off free radicals that can lead to inflammation. In addition to its anti-inflammatory benefits, ginger eases nausea, helps lower blood sugars, and protects against cardiovascular disease. The same compounds that fight inflammation have been shown to decrease glucose, total cholesterol, and triglycerides. Ginger also has antifungal properties, so it can help with related conditions, such as yeast infections and jock itch.

The sweet carrots in this juice recipe offset the spicy ginger. This is a great energizing juice that can help you get moving in the morning or get through an afternoon slump!

Per Serving
Calories: 109 | Fat: 0.5 g | Protein: 2.0 g | Sodium: 210 mg
Fiber: 0.0 g | Carbohydrates: 21.6 g | Sugar: 14.6 g

GREEN PINEAPPLE

Serves 2

INGREDIENTS

½ medium pineapple, peeled and
cut into chunks
2 cups packed baby spinach

---

1 Process the pineapple and
spinach through the juicer.

2 Strain through a fine-mesh
sieve if desired.

3 Consume immediately over ice
or allow to chill in the refrigerator before serving.

4 Can be stored in a glass airtight
container in the refrigerator up
to 12 hours if using a centrifugal
juicer and up to 3 days if using
a masticating juicer.

KEY INGREDIENT: Pineapple

In addition to containing the digestive enzyme bromelain, which has an anti-inflammatory effect, pineapples are
packed with health-promoting nutrients. They are an excellent source of vitamin C and manganese and are also a great
source of copper, vitamins B_6 and B_1, fiber, and folate. The
vitamin C in pineapple helps your body fight free radical
damage and helps keep inflammation at bay also.

Another bonus of consuming pineapple is that it may help
your mental health. Pineapple is a good source of the amino
acid tryptophan, which is used by the body to produce serotonin. Serotonin is the hormone associated with feelings of
happiness and well-being. This green juice is sweet and
loved by kids and adults alike.

Per Serving
Calories: 111 | Fat: 0.2 g | Protein: 2.1 g | Sodium: 25 mg
Fiber: 0.0 g | Carbohydrates: 26.9 g | Sugar: 22.4 g

POPEYE JUICE

Serves 2

INGREDIENTS

2 medium carrots
2 cups packed baby spinach
1 medium orange, peeled and
  segmented

1 Prepare the carrots by cutting
   off the tops and tips and cutting them into appropriate-
   sized pieces for your juicer.

2 Process the carrots, spinach,
   and orange through the juicer.

3 Strain through a fine-mesh
   sieve if desired.

4 Consume immediately over ice
   or allow to chill in the refrigerator before serving.

5 Can be stored in a glass airtight container in the refrigerator up to 12 hours if using a
   centrifugal juicer and up to
   3 days if using a masticating
   juicer.

KEY INGREDIENT: Spinach

Spinach has a long list of health benefits; Popeye favored it for good reason! It's one of the most nutrient-dense foods you can consume. It packs in a wide range of vitamins and minerals, including vitamins A, C, K, E, B_2, and B_6; niacin; folate; calcium; copper; iron; and manganese. That's just a partial list of the important nutrients found in this leafy green vegetable!

All of those nutrients contribute to spinach having a host of health benefits. Spinach gets its anti-inflammatory powers, in part, thanks to its high vitamin K content, which has been shown to suppress the production of pro-inflammatory cytokines. High vitamin K intake is also associated with low concentrations of several pro-inflammatory biomarkers.

In addition to the vitamin K, spinach also contains two unique carotenoids, neoxanthin and violaxanthin, that help fight inflammation. These two carotenoids are thought to reduce inflammation in the digestive tract after the consumption of spinach.

Per Serving
Calories: 58 | Fat: 0.2 g | Protein: 2.0 g | Sodium: 65 mg
Fiber: 0.0 g | Carbohydrates: 11.5 g | Sugar: 9.9 g

CELERY SUNSHINE

Serves 1

INGREDIENTS

2 medium stalks celery
3 medium apples
1 medium lemon, peeled and
  segmented

---

1 Prepare the celery stalks
by cutting them into the
appropriate-sized pieces for
your juicer.

2 Prepare the apples by coring
them and cutting them into
appropriate-sized pieces for
your juicer.

3 Process the celery, apples, and
lemon through the juicer.

4 Consume immediately over ice
or allow to chill in the refrigerator before serving.

5 Can be stored in a glass airtight container in the refrigerator up to 12 hours if using a
centrifugal juicer and up to
3 days if using a masticating
juicer.

KEY INGREDIENT: Celery

Celery is well known as a low-calorie food with a high water content. Oh, but there's so much more to this crunchy vegetable. While it's a good source of vitamin C, more than a dozen other antioxidants have also been identified in celery.

Its wide range of protective antioxidants is what makes celery a standout nutritionally. Celery contains a class of antioxidants known as *phenolic acids*. Phenolic acids have protective qualities and fight inflammation. It's been found that these antioxidants inhibit protein denaturation, which is associated with increased inflammation. Consumption of celery juice has been studied and found to have an anti-inflammatory effect by decreasing levels of pro-inflammatory cytokines.

While celery juice alone isn't the most palatable juice, when combined with apples and lemon, it's quite refreshing. This juice is the color of sunshine and is sure to brighten any morning.

Per Serving
Calories: 275 | Fat: 0.6 g | Protein: 1.6 g | Sodium: 70 mg
Fiber: 0.0 g | Carbohydrates: 67.0 g | Sugar: 59.3 g

SWEET PARSLEY

Serves 2

INGREDIENTS

1 cup packed parsley leaves
3 cups seedless purple grapes

---

1 Process parsley and grapes through the juicer.

2 Strain through a fine-mesh sieve if desired.

3 Consume immediately over ice or allow to chill in the refrigerator before serving.

4 Can be stored in a glass airtight container in the refrigerator up to 12 hours if using a centrifugal juicer and up to 3 days if using a masticating juicer.

KEY INGREDIENT: Parsley

Parsley is a wholly underrated herb. It may be an afterthought in recipes or used only as garnish by some, but it deserves much more attention. Parsley comes with a whole range of health benefits that are not insignificant. Parsley contains myricetin, which is a potent anticancer compound and also fights diabetes. Parsley can also help you combat bad breath, which is important even if it's not as serious! It's also worth noting that parsley is high in vitamin C and vitamin A.

Parsley is also an outstanding herb for its anti-inflammatory properties. Parsley contains the flavonoid apigenin, which has been studied for its anti-inflammation effects. It was found that apigenin inhibited the collagenase activity present in rheumatoid arthritis. Like spinach, parsley is also high in vitamin K, which been shown to suppress the production of pro-inflammatory cytokines.

Take a second look at parsley; it's more than just a pretty garnish!

Per Serving
Calories: 156 | Fat: 0.4 g | Protein: 1.5 g | Sodium: 21 mg
Fiber: 0.0 g | Carbohydrates: 39.9 g | Sugar: 35.3 g

KALE-ING IT

Serves 2
INGREDIENTS

2 medium carrots
1 medium apple
3 large kale leaves, veins removed
½ medium pineapple, peeled and
    cut into chunks

---

1 Prepare the carrots by cutting
  off the tops and tips and cutting them into appropriate-
  sized pieces for your juicer.

2 Prepare the apple by coring
  and cutting into appropriate-
  sized pieces for your juicer.

3 Process the kale leaves, carrots, apple, and pineapple
  through the juicer.

4 Strain through a fine-mesh
  sieve if desired.

5 Consume immediately over ice
  or allow to chill in the refrigerator before serving.

6 Can be stored in a glass airtight container in the refrigerator up to 12 hours if using a
  centrifugal juicer and up to
  3 days if using a masticating
  juicer.

KEY INGREDIENT: Kale

Kale has recently enjoyed a rise to popularity, and for good reason. This leafy green vegetable has a lot of goodness hiding in those leaves. Kale is high in vitamin K, vitamin A, vitamin C, vitamin B_6, manganese, copper, and iron. In fact, calorie for calorie, kale is higher in iron than beef is! Over forty-five different flavonoids have been discovered in kale, which help to make it a potent anticancer food.

Two nutrients in particular help kale with its inflammation-fighting power: vitamin K and the omega-3 fatty acid alpha-linolenic acid (ALA). Vitamin K can suppress the production of pro-inflammatory cytokines. ALA acts as an antioxidant and suppresses the production of inflammation-causing myeloperoxidase in the body.

While by itself kale may not be the best-tasting vegetable, in this juice it is amply sweetened by carrots, apple, and pineapple. This juice is an excellent way to enjoy the health benefits from kale.

Per Serving
Calories: 173 | Fat: 0.4 g | Protein: 1.7 g | Sodium: 50 mg
Fiber: 0.0 g | Carbohydrates: 41.9 g | Sugar: 35.0 g

BLACKBERRY SENSATION

Serves 1

INGREDIENTS

1 large apple
2 cups ripe blackberries

---

1 Prepare the apple by coring it and cutting it into appropriate-sized pieces for your juicer.

2 Process the apple and blackberries through juicer.

3 Strain with a fine-mesh sieve if desired.

4 Consume immediately over ice or allow to chill in the refrigerator before serving.

5 Can be stored in a glass airtight container in the refrigerator up to 12 hours if using a centrifugal juicer and up to 3 days if using a masticating juicer.

KEY INGREDIENT: Blackberry

It's a beautiful thing when delicious food also happens to have incredible nutritional qualities. That's the case with the splendid blackberry. Blackberries are a tasty fruit that rank highly on nutritional charts.

Like all berries, blackberries are blessed with an abundance of antioxidants. Blackberries contain high levels of anthocyanins and other phenolic compounds, mainly flavonols and ellagitannins. Ellagitannins have been established to have strong anti-inflammatory effects in the body, even though the mechanisms aren't totally clear. It is known that foods with high levels of antioxidants contribute to reduced oxidative stress from free radicals in the body, which can result in anti-inflammatory activity.

This juice is vibrantly hued, perfectly sweet, and pairs perfectly with your breakfast meal.

Per Serving
Calories: 166 | Fat: 1.1 g | Protein: 1.5 g | Sodium: 3 mg
Fiber: 0.0 g | Carbohydrates: 33.2 g | Sugar: 33.0 g

MINT REFRESHER

Serves 1
INGREDIENTS

1 large cucumber
¾ cup mint leaves

---

1 Prepare the cucumber by cutting off and discarding the ends and cutting the cucumber into appropriate-sized pieces for your juicer.

2 Process the cucumber and mint leaves through the juicer.

3 Strain with a fine-mesh sieve if desired.

4 Consume immediately over ice or allow to chill in the refrigerator before serving.

5 Can be stored in a glass airtight container in the refrigerator up to 12 hours if using a centrifugal juicer and up to 3 days if using a masticating juicer.

KEY INGREDIENT: Mint

Ah, mint. It's a refreshing herb that brings fresh flavor to any dish or drink. It's also loaded with health benefits. Mint is used to treat a variety of ailments, including digestive upset, headaches, dandruff, nausea, and skin conditions. It inhibits the growth of many different bacteria. Mint is also a stimulant, providing a natural energy boost.

Mint has traditionally been consumed as an anti-inflammatory for the lungs. Studies have been conducted that show promise that mint may be used to treat asthma in the future. One of mint's powerful nutrients, rosmarinic acid, was found to block inflammatory action in the body.

This juice is light and refreshing. For a stronger mint flavor, you can use a full cup of mint leaves. In addition to this refreshing juice, try adding mint leaves to your favorite salad or infuse your water with fresh mint leaves.

Per Serving
Calories: 48 | Fat: 0.3 g | Protein: 1.7 g | Sodium: 11 mg
Fiber: 0.0 g | Carbohydrates: 10.8 g | Sugar: 5.0 g

SWEET BROCCOLI

Serves 2

INGREDIENTS

2 cups pineapple chunks (about ½ medium pineapple)
1 large orange, peeled and segmented
1 cup broccoli florets

---

1 Process the pineapple, orange, and broccoli through juicer.

2 Strain through a fine-mesh sieve if desired.

3 Consume immediately over ice or allow to chill in the refrigerator before serving.

4 Can be stored in a glass airtight container in the refrigerator up to 12 hours if using a centrifugal juicer and up to 3 days if using a masticating juicer.

KEY INGREDIENT: Broccoli

Broccoli has a number of different anti-inflammatory compounds. The sulfur-containing substance in broccoli, glucosinolate, is shown to lower levels of C-reactive protein, which is a blood protein used to measure the level of inflammation in the body.

Broccoli has three different kinds of antioxidants, making it one of the top vegetables you can consume for its nutritional benefit. It fights inflammation, has anticancer properties, helps your body with natural detoxification, and has also been shown to help lower blood cholesterol levels.

Juicing broccoli is an excellent way to reap its nutritional benefits, and doing so with sweet fruits like pineapple and orange makes it taste great.

Per Serving
Calories: 117 | Fat: 0.2 g | Protein: 1.7 g | Sodium: 16 mg
Fiber: 0.0 g | Carbohydrates: 28.1 g | Sugar: 13.9 g

CITRUS CRUSH

Serves 1

INGREDIENTS

1 medium pink or red grapefruit, peeled and segmented

2 medium oranges, peeled and segmented

---

1 Process the grapefruit and oranges through the juicer.

2 Strain through a fine-mesh sieve if desired.

3 Consume immediately over ice or allow to chill in the refrigerator before serving.

4 Can be stored in a glass airtight container in the refrigerator up to 12 hours if using a centrifugal juicer and up to 3 days if using a masticating juicer.

KEY INGREDIENT: Grapefruit

Grapefruit is low in calories yet has impressive nutritional stats. It's an especially good source of vitamin C, which plays an important role in fighting inflammation. It's also a strong antioxidant that protects the body from free radicals, which have a pro-inflammatory effect. Vitamin C supplementation has been found to protect against certain diseases like coronary heart disease and gout, both of which have inflammatory components. The orange in this juice recipe adds even more vitamin C. This grapefruit and orange combo is also a great immune-system booster.

Grapefruit has a number of other health benefits as well. It's been shown to be great for your skin, help reduce your risk of developing kidney stones, and boost your metabolism.

This is an eye-opening juice recipe that's terrific in the morning.

Per Serving

Calories: 298 | Fat: 0.6 g | Protein: 1.9 g | Sodium: 1 mg
Fiber: 0.0 g | Carbohydrates: 72.2 g | Sugar: 61.5 g

DRINK YOUR SALAD

Serves 2

INGREDIENTS

1 medium head romaine lettuce
2 large carrots
1 medium cucumber
2 large lemons, peeled and
  segmented

---

1 Prepare the romaine by removing the core and chopping it roughly.

2 Prepare the carrots by removing the tops and tips and cutting them into appropriate-sized pieces for your juicer.

3 Prepare the cucumber by cutting off and discarding the ends and cutting the cucumber into appropriate-sized pieces for your juicer.

4 Process the romaine, carrots, cucumber, and lemons through the juicer.

5 Strain through a fine-mesh sieve if desired.

6 Consume immediately over ice or allow to chill in the refrigerator before serving.

7 Can be stored in a glass airtight container in the refrigerator up to 12 hours if using a centrifugal juicer and up to 3 days if using a masticating juicer.

KEY INGREDIENT: Romaine Lettuce

Romaine is a nutrient-dense leafy green vegetable. It's an excellent source of vitamins K and A and folate. Vitamin A has been shown to reduce inflammation and oxidative stress, and 2 cups of romaine lettuce, at just 16 calories, provides almost half of your daily requirement.

You'll also find a good amount of fiber, manganese, copper, vitamin B_1, vitamin B_2, iron, potassium, and vitamin C in romaine leaves. All of the vitamins and antioxidants in romaine lettuce can help boost your immune system, prevent signs of aging, promote healthy eyesight, and prevent cancer.

This juice is like eating a big salad, but in this juice version, nutrients are more quickly absorbed.

Per Serving
Calories: 80 | Fat: 0.9 g | Protein: 2.0 g | Sodium: 71 mg
Fiber: 0.0 g | Carbohydrates: 16.3 g | Sugar: 10.6 g

DEEP ORANGE

Serves 2

INGREDIENTS

2 large carrots
2 medium oranges, peeled and
  segmented

1 Prepare the carrots by removing the tops and tips. Cut into appropriate-sized pieces for your juicer.

2 Process the carrots and oranges through the juicer.

3 Strain through a fine-mesh sieve if desired.

4 Consume immediately over ice or allow to chill in the refrigerator before serving.

5 Can be stored in a glass airtight container in the refrigerator up to 12 hours if using a centrifugal juicer and up to 3 days if using a masticating juicer.

KEY INGREDIENT: Orange

Orange juice is one of the most popular juices on the planet. It turns out, if you love orange juice, that's a good thing, as it's helping you fight inflammation. Research suggests that some flavonoids found in oranges, such as hesperidin and naringenin, help suppress inflammatory responses in the body. Oranges also contain carotenoids, which have been shown to inhibit certain inflammatory responses. Furthering their inflammation-fighting powers even more, oranges also contain beta-cryptoxanthin, a phytochemical that has been shown to decrease the development of inflammatory joint conditions.

You can always juice plain oranges, but why not add carrots to the mix and increase the nutritional value? Carrots add even more vitamins and antioxidants to your glass of juice, and they are a naturally sweet vegetable!

Per Serving
Calories: 87 | Fat: 0.2 g | Protein: 1.7 g | Sodium: 49 mg
Fiber: 0.0 g | Carbohydrates: 18.7 g | Sugar: 17.2 g

OVER THE RAINBOW

Serves 3

INGREDIENTS

7 large rainbow chard leaves
2 medium apples
2 cups seedless purple grapes
1 cup pineapple chunks (about ¼
    medium pineapple)

1 Prepare rainbow chard by
  chopping the leaves and stem
  to appropriate-sized pieces for
  your juicer.

2 Prepare apples by coring and
  cutting them into appropriate-
  sized pieces for your juicer.

3 Process the rainbow chard,
  apples, grapes, and pineapple
  through the juicer.

4 Strain through a fine-mesh
  sieve if desired.

5 Consume immediately over ice
  or allow to chill in the refrigerator before serving.

6 Can be stored in a glass airtight container in the refrigerator up to 12 hours if using a
  centrifugal juicer and up to
  3 days if using a masticating
  juicer.

KEY INGREDIENT: Rainbow Chard

Rainbow chard is a variety of Swiss chard with vibrantly colored stalks. That color is thanks, in part, to the concentration of betalains present. These phytonutrients have been shown to suppress pro-inflammatory enzymes cyclooxygenase (COX) and lipoxygenase (LOX). Swiss chard also contains flavonoids like quercetin and kaempferol, which act as antihistamines and reduce allergic reactions and inflammatory responses in the body. All of these compounds acting together make rainbow chard an excellent anti-inflammatory food to include in your diet.

In addition, Swiss chard is one of the most vitamin- and mineral-rich green vegetables. It has been shown to be an excellent food for blood sugar regulation and cardiovascular health.

The apples, grapes, and pineapple work together to mellow out the stronger flavor associated with the rainbow chard, making this a tasty and nutritious juice recipe.

Per Serving
Calories: 159 | Fat: 0.4 g | Protein: 1.4 g | Sodium: 241 mg
Fiber: 0.0 g | Carbohydrates: 40.0 g | Sugar: 34.8 g

QUADRUPLE THREAT

Serves 1

INGREDIENTS

3 large collard greens leaves
1 cup seedless purple grapes
1 cup pineapple chunks (about ¼ medium pineapple)
1 tablespoon peeled, chopped fresh ginger

---

1 Prepare the collard greens by removing and discarding the tough stem and roughly chopping the leaves.

2 Process all ingredients through the juicer.

3 Strain with a fine-mesh sieve if desired.

4 Consume immediately over ice or allow to chill in the refrigerator before serving.

5 Can be stored in a glass airtight container in the refrigerator up to 12 hours if using a centrifugal juicer and up to 3 days if using a masticating juicer.

KEY INGREDIENT: Collard Greens

Collard greens are an excellent source of two key nutrients that are known to fight inflammation: vitamin K and alpha-linolenic acid (ALA). In addition to these two key components, collard greens also contain glucobrassicin. Glucobrassicin can be easily converted into indole-3-carbinol. This is significant because indole-3-carbinol can prevent inflammatory responses at a very early stage.

Another important thing to know about collard greens is that they contain a peptide called glutathione. This helps the liver cleanse, protects against cancer, and boosts immune function. In fact, it is believed that the levels of glutathione in our blood can be a predictor of how long a person will live!

This juice recipe is called Quadruple Threat because four potent foods are working together to fight inflammation. Collard greens get help from the grapes, pineapple, and ginger here.

Per Serving
Calories: 176 | Fat: 0.6 g | Protein: 1.4 g | Sodium: 22 mg
Fiber: 0.0 g | Carbohydrates: 47.8 g | Sugar: 40.2 g

PURPLE POWER

Serves 2

INGREDIENTS

¼ small head purple cabbage
3 cups seedless purple grapes

---

1 Prepare the cabbage by removing the core and cutting the ¼ of the head into appropriate-sized pieces for your juicer.

2 Process the cabbage and grapes through the juicer.

3 Strain with a fine-mesh sieve if desired.

4 Consume immediately over ice or allow to chill in the refrigerator before serving.

5 Can be stored in a glass airtight container in the refrigerator up to 12 hours if using a centrifugal juicer and up to 3 days if using a masticating juicer.

KEY INGREDIENT: Purple Cabbage

Cabbage is a cruciferous vegetable that contains sulforaphane. This compound makes red cabbage a potent inflammation killer. Sulforaphane regulates inflammation by altering the messaging molecules within the inflammatory system in the body. This also has a potent anticancer effect.

There are other nutrients in red cabbage that help control inflammation. Red cabbage contains thirty-six of the flavonoids known as anthocyanins, well-documented inflammation fighters known to reduce inflammation markers in the bloodstream. Cabbage is also an excellent source of vitamin K, which suppresses production of pro-inflammatory cytokines.

Cabbage has a mild bitter flavor, but when paired with sweet purple grapes, it is milder and easier to drink. The purple color of both these deeply hued ingredients makes a vibrant juice.

Per Serving
Calories: 166 | Fat: 0.3 g | Protein: 1.6 g | Sodium: 23 mg
Fiber: 0.0 g | Carbohydrates: 42.7 g | Sugar: 37.8 g

BASIL SMASH

Serves 1

INGREDIENTS

1 large cucumber
7 large strawberries, hulled
1 cup loosely packed basil leaves

---

1 Prepare the cucumber by cutting off and discarding the ends and cutting the cucumber into appropriate-sized pieces for your juicer.

2 Process all ingredients through the juicer.

3 Strain with a fine-mesh sieve if desired.

4 Consume immediately over ice or allow to chill in the refrigerator before serving.

5 Can be stored in a glass airtight container in the refrigerator up to 12 hours if using a centrifugal juicer and up to 3 days if using a masticating juicer.

KEY INGREDIENT: Basil

Basil is a beloved herb that provides lovely flavor in a variety of cooking applications. It just so happens to have anti-inflammatory properties, making it a wise choice to add to your anti-inflammatory drinks! Basil contains essential oils, such as eugenol, citronellol, and linalool. These essential oils are known to be enzyme-inhibiting oils, which help keep inflammation under control. Eugenol actually mimics the action of over-the-counter anti-inflammatory medications!

Studies have also shown that basil may have the ability to act as an adaptogen, helping your body react to stress and protect against the body's response to stressful environments.

The basil in this juice recipe pairs nicely with strawberry and cucumber, making this a lovely, refreshing spring or summer beverage.

Per Serving
Calories: 73 | Fat: 0.6 g | Protein: 1.6 g | Sodium: 7 mg
Fiber: 0.0 g | Carbohydrates: 16.8 g | Sugar: 11.3 g

GREEN MONSTER

Serves 2

INGREDIENTS

1 medium cucumber
2 stalks celery
1 bunch parsley, chopped roughly
2 medium limes, peeled and
  segmented
2 medium kiwifruits, peeled and
  chopped

---

1 Prepare the cucumber and celery stalks by cutting off and discarding the ends and then cutting the remaining portions into appropriate-sized pieces for your juicer.

2 Process the cucumber, celery, parsley, limes, and kiwifruits through the juicer.

3 Strain through a fine-mesh sieve if desired.

4 Consume immediately over ice or allow to chill in the refrigerator before serving.

5 Can be stored in a glass airtight container in the refrigerator up to 12 hours if using a centrifugal juicer and up to 3 days if using a masticating juicer.

KEY INGREDIENT: Parsley

Parsley is a rich source of flavonoids; folic acid; and vitamins A, C, and K. Looking closely at its anti-inflammatory properties, you can see it has more than one of its components at work. Parsley contains volatile oils, including myristicin, eugenol, limonene, and alpha-thujene. All of these oils may have anti-inflammatory properties. Myristicin has been studied and shown that it inhibits the expression of cyclooxygenase-2 (COX-2).

Eating parsley regularly is also thought to speed up the excretion of uric acid. Uric acid can increase join stiffness and pain for those who suffer from arthritis, so this action means parsley can help reduce pain.

This "monster" of a juice recipe garners a lot of nutrients from all of the green foods on its ingredient list and is worth adding to your routine.

Per Serving
Calories: 74 | Fat: 0.5 g | Protein: 1.7 g | Sodium: 45 mg
Fiber: 0.0 g | Carbohydrates: 17.3 g | Sugar: 10.1 g

BEET CITY

Serves 1

INGREDIENTS

2 small beets
3 medium carrots
1 stalk celery
1 medium lemon, peeled and
   segmented

1 Prepare the beets by peeling and cutting them into
   appropriate-sized pieces
   for your juicer.

2 Prepare the carrots by removing the tops and tips and
   cutting them into appropriate-
   sized pieces for your juicer.

3 Prepare the celery stalk by
   removing the ends and cutting
   it into appropriate-sized pieces
   for your juicer.

4 Process the beets, carrots,
   celery, and lemon through the
   juicer.

5 Strain through a fine-mesh
   sieve if desired.

6 Consume immediately over ice
   or allow to chill in the refrigerator before serving.

7 Can be stored in a glass airtight container in the refrigerator up to 12 hours if using a
   centrifugal juicer and up to
   3 days if using a masticating
   juicer.

KEY INGREDIENT: Beets

Beets are a unique source of betaine, known for its anti-inflammatory properties. Its anti-inflammatory action seems to come, in part, from its ability to interfere with pro-inflammatory signaling cascades. Betaine has also been shown to suppress pro-inflammatory cyclooxygenase-2 (COX-2). Interesting to note is that betaines target cell-signaling pathways at the molecular level, which means they have a similar mode of action to selective COX-2 inhibitor drugs such as aspirin and ibuprofen. Food is truly medicine in this case!

Raw beets are shown to retain betaine levels better than cooked beets, so juicing is an excellent option for getting the most nutrition from your beets. Beets are also a good source of folate, manganese, copper, and potassium.

Per Serving
Calories: 127 | Fat: 0.6 g | Protein: 1.3 g | Sodium: 286 mg
Fiber: 0.0 g | Carbohydrates: 27.8 g | Sugar: 21.8 g

GREEN PAPAYA

Serves 2

INGREDIENTS

1 medium-large papaya
1 medium romaine heart

1 Prepare the papaya by peeling, removing seeds, and cutting it into appropriate-sized pieces for your juicer.

2 Prepare the romaine heart by removing the core and cutting it into appropriate-sized pieces for your juicer.

3 Process the papaya and romaine through the juicer.

4 Strain through a fine-mesh sieve if desired.

5 Consume immediately over ice or allow to chill in the refrigerator before serving.

6 Can be stored in a glass airtight container in the refrigerator up to 12 hours if using a centrifugal juicer and up to 3 days if using a masticating juicer.

KEY INGREDIENT: Papaya

Papaya contains a protein-digesting enzyme, papain. Papain (and other proteolytic enzymes, like the bromelain found in pineapple) modulates the inflammatory process in the body. It has been shown to reduce the swelling of mucous membranes and reduce capillary permeability. Papain increases the production of immune cells that speed healing. Papain also stimulates the digestion of proteins and fats and helps improve nutrient absorption.

In addition to anti-inflammatory papain, papaya is an excellent source of vitamins A and C. It's a good source of fiber, folate, magnesium, potassium, vitamin K, and copper as well. The potent antioxidants in papaya also contribute to its inflammation-fighting abilities.

This tropical fruit makes a lovely juice that pairs well with greens.

Per Serving
Calories: 156 | Fat: 0.9 g | Protein: 1.4 g | Sodium: 34 mg
Fiber: 0.0 g | Carbohydrates: 36.2 g | Sugar: 31.1 g

SWEET BABY RADICCHIO

Serves 1

INGREDIENTS

3 baby radicchio leaves
2 medium carrots
2 cups pineapple chunks (about ½ medium pineapple)

1 Prepare the radicchio leaves by chopping them into appropriate-sized pieces for your juicer.

2 Prepare the carrots by removing the tops and tips and cutting them into appropriate-sized pieces for your juicer.

3 Process the radicchio leaves, carrots, and pineapple chunks through your juicer.

4 Strain through a fine-mesh sieve if desired.

5 Consume immediately over ice or allow to chill in the refrigerator before serving.

6 Can be stored in a glass airtight container in the refrigerator up to 12 hours if using a centrifugal juicer and up to 3 days if using a masticating juicer.

KEY INGREDIENT: Radicchio

Radicchio, like most leafy vegetables, is rich in a number of key nutrients that help fight inflammation. Its bright red leaves indicate the presence of certain phytonutrients, one of which is ellagic acid. Ellagic acid is shown to block pro-inflammatory signaling pathways, in turn decreasing chronic inflammation. Radicchio also contains quercetin. Quercetin is a powerful flavonoid that inhibits production of inflammation-producing enzymes.

Radicchio also contains inulin, which helps support the body in many ways. Inulin promotes the discharge of pancreatic juices, indicating it can help aid digestion. Inulin is also a substance that can help regulate blood sugar levels.

Carrots and pineapple add to the nutrient level of this juice and also contribute to its sweetness since radicchio is not a naturally sweet vegetable.

Per Serving
Calories: 196 | Fat: 0.4 g | Protein: 1.3 g | Sodium: 92 mg
Fiber: 0.0 g | Carbohydrates: 47.8 g | Sugar: 38.4 g

Chapter 4

COLD DRINKS

What are you drinking on a daily basis? There's no reason why you can't make all of your everyday drinks inflammation-fighting drinks! The cold drinks in this chapter consist of the refreshments you probably already consume on a regular basis: milk, iced tea, lemonade, and even alternatives to sodas and sports drinks. In this chapter you'll find a number of nondairy milk recipes. Dairy is thought to cause inflammation, and it's easy to use alternatives that taste great and are often lower calorie than cow's milk. All of the drinks in this chapter are lower in sugar than most mainstream drinks you may be accustomed to and are all naturally sweetened or unsweetened. The last thing you want to do is counteract the anti-inflammatory ingredients you're utilizing with refined sugar! These recipes will help you replace your everyday drinks with inflammation-fighting drinks.

BASIC UNSWEETENED ALMOND MILK

Serves 4
INGREDIENTS

½ cup raw, whole, unsalted almonds
6 cups filtered water, divided

---

1 Cover the almonds with 2 cups filtered water in a small bowl and allow to soak at least 8 hours.

2 Use a fine-mesh strainer to drain and rinse the almonds.

3 Place the almonds in a large blender and add 4 cups filtered water to the blender.

4 Blend on high until smooth.

5 Strain the milk through a nut milk bag or cheesecloth.

6 Transfer to an airtight container and store in the refrigerator up to 5 days.

KEY INGREDIENT: Almonds

This recipe for unsweetened almond milk does double duty: it helps you eliminate inflammatory cow's milk from your diet while also using an ingredient that helps you fight inflammation. Smart!

Almonds are full of healthy polyunsaturated and monounsaturated fats, and they are also a great source of vitamin E. Not only are almonds thought to be anti-inflammatory, but they are a nutrient-dense food that has also been shown to help lower cholesterol. The almond milk you buy in the store if often filled with unnecessary ingredients, so making your own at home is a fantastic way to control what's going into your body. This recipe is economical, as it uses the least amount of almonds needed to create a milk. It's best for using in cooking or baking but not necessarily for drinking alone since it's not as creamy or flavorful as other milks.

Per Serving
Calories: 70 | Fat: 7.0 g | Protein: 3.0 g | Sodium: 0 mg
Fiber: 0.0 g | Carbohydrates: 1.5 g | Sugar: 0.5 g

ICED MOCHA LATTE

Serves 1

INGREDIENTS

1 cup cold coffee

1 tablespoon coconut oil

1 tablespoon full-fat canned coconut milk

2 teaspoons erythritol

1 tablespoon raw cacao powder

Ice, as needed

1   Place all ingredients, except ice, in a small blender.

2   Blend on high until thoroughly combined and frothy.

3   Fill a glass with ice and pour the latte over ice to consume immediately or store in an airtight container in the refrigerator up to 2 days.

KEY INGREDIENT: Raw Cacao Powder

In addition to raw cacao powder being an antioxidant powerhouse that fights inflammation, it is packed with a number of nutrients that provide health benefits.

The most common nutritional deficiency worldwide is iron deficiency. One of the great benefits of consuming raw cacao powder is that it's the most abundant source of plant-based iron. This is especially beneficial for vegans and vegetarians who don't consume animal products. Raw cacao powder is also one of the richest plant-based sources of magnesium, which happens to be another one of the most common nutritional deficiencies in the world. Magnesium is an important nutrient for both brain and heart health.

As you can see raw cacao powder is a great choice for fighting inflammation and delivering key nutrients to your body!

Per Serving
Calories: 168 | Fat: 16.3 g | Protein: 1.6 g | Sodium: 5 mg
Fiber: 1.0 g | Carbohydrates: 11.4 g | Sugar: 0.0 g

CREAMY VANILLA WALNUT MILK

Serves 4

INGREDIENTS

1 cup walnut pieces
6 cups filtered water, divided
1 teaspoon pure vanilla extract
1 tablespoon pure maple syrup

---

1 Cover the walnuts with 2 cups filtered water and soak at least 8 hours.

2 Use a fine-mesh strainer to drain and rinse the walnuts.

3 Place the walnuts in a large blender, along with 4 cups filtered water, vanilla extract, and maple syrup.

4 Blend on high until smooth.

5 Strain the milk through a nut milk bag or cheesecloth.

6 Transfer to an airtight container and store in the refrigerator up to 5 days.

KEY INGREDIENT: Walnuts

Walnuts are a smart choice for a dairy milk alternative. They have an excellent nutritional profile, and using them as milk is a great way to include them in your diet. In fact, of all the nuts, walnuts are the richest source of omega-3 fatty acids. Walnuts are also a good source of vitamin E, which is important for immune system function. These powerful nuts have been well studied for their protective benefits to the heart and circulatory system.

Walnuts have a number of elements that are known to fight inflammation, including alpha-linolenic fatty acid, the amino acid L-arginine, and phenolic antioxidants. Researchers have found that walnuts inhibit the production of the neurotransmitter substance P and bradykinin, which increase pain and inflammation in the body. The anti-inflammatory nutrients found in walnuts are also thought to have anticancer benefits.

Per Serving
Calories: 204 | Fat: 18.7 g | Protein: 4.6 g | Sodium: 1 mg
Fiber: 0.0 g | Carbohydrates: 5.6 g | Sugar: 3.9 g

CREAMY VANILLA ALMOND MILK

Serves 4

INGREDIENTS

1 cup whole almonds
5 cups filtered water, divided
1 teaspoon pure vanilla extract
1 tablespoon pure maple syrup

1 Cover the almonds in a small bowl with 2 cups filtered water and allow to soak at least 8 hours.

2 Use a fine-mesh strainer to drain and rinse the almonds.

3 Place the almonds in a large blender, along with 3 cups filtered water, vanilla extract, and maple syrup.

4 Blend on high until smooth.

5 Strain the milk through a nut milk bag or cheesecloth.

6 Transfer to an airtight container and store in the refrigerator up to 5 days.

KEY INGREDIENT: Almonds

The regular consumption of almonds has been shown to lower C-reactive protein levels, a key marker of inflammation and an independent risk factor for heart disease. Almonds may also be cardioprotective because they reduce the inflammation of blood vessels and for their ability to help lower LDL cholesterol levels. In addition, almonds contain the compound salicin. Salicin is a natural anti-inflammatory agent that converts to salicylic acid inside the body. This is the same active ingredient in aspirin!

Almonds are also high in vitamin E, which is shown to nourish and have an antiaging effect on your skin. The type of vitamin E found in almonds is known to be a powerful antioxidant that fights free radical damage and oxidative stress.

This Creamy Vanilla Almond Milk is a creamier, thicker almond milk than the basic version found earlier in this chapter. It's great for drinking or when you want more almond flavor.

Per Serving
Calories: 202 | Fat: 17.0 g | Protein: 7.6 g | Sodium: 0 mg
Fiber: 0.0 g | Carbohydrates: 6.7 g | Sugar: 4.7 g

CHERRY LIMEADE

Serves 6

INGREDIENTS

4¾ cups water, divided
¾ cup fresh lime juice (from about 4
  large limes)
2 cups pitted sweet cherries
½ cup erythritol

1 Combine 4½ cups water with the lime juice in a medium pitcher.

2 In a small saucepan, bring the cherries, erythritol, and ¼ cup water to a simmer over low heat.

3 Allow the cherry mixture to simmer, stirring occasionally, for 5 minutes.

4 Remove the cherry mixture from the heat and allow to cool.

5 Place the cherry mixture in a small blender and blend on high until you have a smooth purée.

6 Transfer the cherry purée to the pitcher and stir until it is combined with the limeade.

7 Allow to chill in the refrigerator before serving.

8 Serve over ice. May be stored in the refrigerator up to 4 days.

KEY INGREDIENT: Cherries

Cherries have a lower glycemic index than most fruits and are packed with nutrients. Their deep crimson hue indicates that they have an abundant amount of antioxidants and that they are rich in one type of antioxidant in particular: anthocyanins. Consumption of foods with high concentrations of anthocyanins is linked to decreased risk of several chronic inflammatory diseases, including cardiovascular disease, diabetes, and cancer.

Fresh or frozen cherries can be used for this drink. Frozen may be preferred for convenience since they are already pitted. If frozen are used, no changes to the recipe are necessary. The cherries give this limeade its bright pink color naturally and provide terrific flavor. Lemons can easily be substituted for the limes to make this cherry lemonade.

Per Serving
Calories: 39 | Fat: 0.1 g | Protein: 0.7 g | Sodium: 0 mg
Fiber: 1.2 g | Carbohydrates: 26.8 g | Sugar: 7.1 g
Sugar Alcohol: 16.0 g

UNSWEETENED RASPBERRY ICED TEA

Serves 4
INGREDIENTS

4 cups plus 2 tablespoons water, divided
4 green tea bags
6 ounces fresh raspberries
Ice, as needed

---

1 Place 4 cups water and 4 tea bags in a glass airtight container and place in the refrigerator.

2 Let the tea cold brew for 5 hours in the refrigerator.

3 Meanwhile, heat the fresh raspberries with 2 tablespoons of water in a small saucepan over medium heat.

4 Allow the raspberries to simmer until they are completely broken down, about 5 minutes.

5 Remove from heat and use a fine-mesh strainer to remove the seeds.

6 After 5 hours, remove the tea bags from the water. Combine the tea and raspberry purée.

7 Serve over ice. May be stored in the refrigerator up to 4 days.

KEY INGREDIENT: Raspberries

Those who are interested in anti-inflammatory foods for their antiaging effects will want to consume raspberries frequently. Raspberries contain ellagic acid, a polyphenol compound present in a lot of berries, but at the highest levels in raspberries. Ellagic acid is just one of the anti-inflammatory phytonutrients found in raspberries, and studies have found that it prevents collagen degradation by blocking matrix metalloproteinase production. In addition, it diminishes the production of pro-inflammatory cytokines. That means it helps prevent wrinkles and skin issues caused by inflammation!

Ellagic acid does more, however, than just combat aging. It's been shown to help prevent overactivity and overproduction of a number of pro-inflammatory enzymes, which can have a positive effect on inflammation in the body. For example, ellagic acid seems to help with excessive inflammation associated with Crohn's disease.

In addition to ellagic acid, raspberries are an excellent source of vitamin C, manganese, and fiber. They also have a good amount of B vitamins, folic acid, copper, and iron. The raspberries make this unsweetened tea an inviting, bright pink color and add just a touch of flavor.

Per Serving
Calories: 24 | Fat: 0.2 g | Protein: 0.5 g | Sodium: 0 mg
Fiber: 2.8 g | Carbohydrates: 5.8 g | Sugar: 1.9 g

BETTER SWEET TEA

Serves 8

INGREDIENTS

8 cups water
8 green tea bags
¼ cup erythritol
Ice, as needed

1 Place 8 cups water and 8 tea bags in a glass airtight container and place in the refrigerator.

2 Let the tea cold brew in the refrigerator for 5 hours.

3 After 5 hours, remove the tea bags from the tea.

4 Add erythritol and stir until dissolved.

5 Serve over ice. May be stored in the refrigerator up to 4 days.

KEY INGREDIENT: Green Tea

Green tea has a long history in China and very early on was ingrained as a fundamental part of Chinese society. Today it's used by traditional Chinese medicine practitioners to reduce heat, relieve headaches, aid digestion, and offer other health benefits. Green tea is loaded with antioxidants, like many of the inflammation-reducing foods highlighted in this book. It has two especially impressive compounds that help it fight inflammation: epigallocatechin gallate (EGCG) and quercetin. In studies, EGCG has been shown to reduce inflammation markers. Quercetin fights inflammation by suppressing inflammation pathways and functions. This is why green tea is a great choice when making iced tea.

Instead of sweetening this Better Sweet Tea with refined white sugar, which can cause inflammation, erythritol is used. Erythritol is a natural sugar alcohol that is found in plants. It does not induce an insulin response or change glucose metabolism in the body. This makes it a smart choice for sweetening your tea. It can be found in the natural section of most well-stocked grocery stores.

Per Serving
Calories: 2 | Fat: 0.0 g | Protein: 0.0 g | Sodium: 0 mg
Fiber: 0.0 g | Carbohydrates: 6.7 g | Sugar: 0.0 g
Sugar Alcohol: 6.0 g

BLUEBERRY LEMONADE

Serves 6

INGREDIENTS

4¾ cups water, divided
1 cup fresh-squeezed lemon juice
(from 4–5 large lemons)
2 cups blueberries
½ cup erythritol
Ice, as needed

1 In a large pitcher, mix together 4½ cups water with lemon juice.

2 Heat the blueberries, ¼ cup water, and erythritol in a small saucepan over medium heat.

3 Bring the blueberry mixture to a simmer and allow to simmer 5 minutes.

4 Remove the blueberry mixture from the heat and allow to cool.

5 In a large blender, blend the blueberry mixture on high until you have a smooth purée.

6 Add the blueberry purée to the lemonade and stir until well combined. Strain if desired.

7 Serve over ice. May be stored in the refrigerator up to 4 days.

KEY INGREDIENT: Lemon

Lemons are often used for flavoring in cooking, but many people overlook their tremendous health-promoting properties. Lemons feature phytonutrients with antioxidant and antibiotic effects and are an excellent source of vitamin C.

Lemons contain beta-cryptoxanthin, which belongs to a class of carotenoids. Beta-cryptoxanthin is a strong antioxidant that prevents free radical damage. It is thought that this helps it protect against the oxidative damage that can result in inflammation. One population-based, prospective study computed the dietary carotenoid intakes of subjects using diet diaries. It was found that a modest increase in beta-cryptoxanthin, such as is found in one glass of orange juice, significantly lowered one's risk of developing inflammatory disorders such as rheumatoid arthritis by 40 percent. This presents a strong case for drinking healthy lemonade!

Store-bought lemonade is made with loads of refined sugar and often doesn't even use real lemon juice. Skip the grocery store stuff and make it at home without refined sugar! It's so much easier than most people assume, and you'll reap the health benefits.

Per Serving
Calories: 36 | Fat: 0.1 g | Protein: 0.5 g | Sodium: 0 mg
Fiber: 1.3 g | Carbohydrates: 26.0 g | Sugar: 5.9 g
Sugar Alcohol: 16.0 g

BLUEBERRY SWEET TEA

Serves 8

INGREDIENTS

8 cups plus 2 tablespoons water, divided
8 green tea bags
1 cup blueberries
¼ cup erythritol
Ice, as needed

---

1 Place 8 cups water and 8 tea bags in a glass airtight container and place in the refrigerator.

2 Let the tea cold brew in the refrigerator for 5 hours.

3 Meanwhile, in a small saucepan, heat the blueberries, 2 tablespoons water, and erythritol over medium heat.

4 Bring the blueberry mixture to a simmer and allow to simmer 5 minutes. Remove from heat and allow to cool.

5 In a large blender, blend the blueberry mixture on high until you have a smooth purée.

6 After 5 hours, remove the tea bags from the tea.

7 Add the blueberry purée to the tea and stir until well combined. Strain if desired.

8 Serve over ice. May be stored in the refrigerator up to 4 days.

KEY INGREDIENT: Blueberries

Blueberries give this sweet tea a powerful upgrade! They are deeply pigmented and have a unique combination of phytonutrients. Blueberries have a wide range of flavonoids that give them a host of health benefits. While they are best known for their anthocyanin flavonoids, they also have two other unique anti-inflammatory phytonutrients, resveratrol and pterostilbene. Both of these belong to the group of compounds known as *stilbenoids*. These two powerful phytonutrients have been studied for their effects on pathways in inflammatory conditions and were found to down-regulate Akt phosphorylation (a well-known marker for inflammatory conditions). Pterostilbene was also found to suppress inflammatory edema and down-regulate inflammatory mediators.

Nature is a beautiful thing because these wonderful properties also contribute to the incredible flavor in blueberries. In addition to their health benefits, blueberries improve the taste of your beverages, like this Blueberry Sweet Tea!

Per Serving
Calories: 12 | Fat: 0.1 g | Protein: 0.1 g | Sodium: 0 mg
Fiber: 0.4 g | Carbohydrates: 9.4 g | Sugar: 1.8 g
Sugar Alcohol: 6.0 g

MACA CHOCOLATE MILK

Serves 4

INGREDIENTS

4 cups unsweetened vanilla almond milk

8 pitted dates

½ cup raw cacao powder

1 tablespoon maca root powder

¼ teaspoon pure stevia powder

1 Place all ingredients in a large blender.

2 Blend on high until the dates are thoroughly combined and the mixture is completely smooth, 1–2 minutes.

3 Chill before serving. May be stored in an airtight container in the refrigerator up to 5 days.

KEY INGREDIENT: Maca Root

Maca is a starchy root vegetable that is grown in South America. You won't find it served at restaurants or even in your grocery store, though. Thankfully, this superfood is found in powder form in most health food stores and is readily available online. Maca root was first used by the Incas over 2,000 years ago. They relied on it for its ability to give them sustained energy and endurance. It's easy to see why it was so important to the Incas when you discover that the maca root has more than fifty-five different beneficial phytochemicals.

Maca root has many medicinal purposes. It's been shown to enhance your memory and your mood and give your immune system a boost. It's used for its antiaging properties as well as treating adrenal fatigue. One way it's thought to help with inflammation is by regulating inflammatory hormones like cortisol. Maca has also been found to reduce inflammation at the cellular level.

This Maca Chocolate Milk is rich and creamy and tastes much more indulgent than it is!

Per Serving

Calories: 125 | Fat: 4.0 g | Protein: 4.1 g | Sodium: 180 mg
Fiber: 4.9 g | Carbohydrates: 21.7 g | Sugar: 10.2 g

WATERMELON MINT MOCKTAIL

Serves 2

INGREDIENTS

2 cups cubed watermelon
1 tablespoon raw honey
6 whole mint leaves
Ice, as needed
½ cup sparkling water

---

1 Place the watermelon cubes and honey in a large blender.

2 Blend the watermelon and honey on high until you have a smooth liquid.

3 Place the mint leaves in the bottom of a cocktail shaker. Use a muddler to muddle the mint leaves until they are just broken down slightly.

4 Fill the cocktail shaker with ice.

5 Add the watermelon mixture to the cocktail shaker and add a lid. Shake the cocktail shaker vigorously for 20 seconds.

6 Fill two glasses with ice. Strain the contents of the cocktail shaker evenly into the two glasses.

7 Top each glass with ¼ cup sparkling water.

8 Consume immediately.

KEY INGREDIENT: Watermelon

Nothing says summer like watermelon. Even though watermelon is 92 percent water, it still contains plenty of nutrients. Watermelon provides good amounts of vitamins C, A, and B_6. The anti-inflammatory benefits from watermelon come from a number of phytonutrients, with the standout being lycopene. Watermelons have one of the highest levels of lycopene among all fruits and vegetables. In fact, watermelons have a higher concentration of lycopene than red tomatoes, which are famous for their lycopene content. The lycopene in watermelons is also highly bioavailable. Lycopene is significant because it suppresses various pro-inflammatory cytokines. Be sure to give the watermelon a chance to ripen. Using ripe watermelon is important; the redder the fruit, the more lycopene it contains.

This is a refreshing drink that takes full advantage of watermelon's natural sweetness. Instead of a cocktail, why not fight inflammation with this mocktail?

Per Serving
Calories: 77 | Fat: 0.4 g | Protein: 1.0 g | Sodium: 1 mg
Fiber: 0.7 g | Carbohydrates: 20.3 g | Sugar: 18.1 g

MANGO LIME FIZZ

Serves 2
INGREDIENTS

1 medium mango
1 cup water
2 tablespoons lime juice
Ice, as needed
½ cup club soda

1 Peel the mango, remove the core, and cut the mango into chunks.

2 Place the mango chunks, water, and lime juice into a large blender.

3 Blend on high until the ingredients are thoroughly combined and smooth.

4 Fill two medium glasses with ice.

5 Pour the mango mixture over the ice. Add ¼ cup club soda to each glass and stir.

6 Consume immediately.

KEY INGREDIENT: Mango

Mango is a sweet, luscious fruit grown mostly in the tropics that is high in many nutrients. Luckily, it's available year-round in grocery stores. Mangoes are a great source of vitamin C, B vitamins, fiber, and copper. Mangoes have been shown to help lower blood glucose levels and help manage high blood pressure. Mango is high in vitamin B_6, which makes it a great food for a healthy brain, as vitamin B_6 and other B vitamins are crucial for maintaining healthy neurotransmitters. As for its anti-inflammatory effects, one study showed that consuming mango led to decreased intestinal inflammation and levels of pro-inflammatory cytokines.

This Mango Lime Fizz makes a refreshing, delicious, and healthy soda alternative for those who crave carbonation in their drinks.

Per Serving
Calories: 104 | Fat: 0.5 g | Protein: 1.4 g | Sodium: 13 mg
Fiber: 2.8 g | Carbohydrates: 26.4 g | Sugar: 23.2 g

COCONUT LIME SPORTS DRINK

Serves 4
INGREDIENTS

3 cups unsweetened coconut water
1 cup water
½ cup fresh lime juice
¼ teaspoon sea salt
½ teaspoon pure stevia powder

1   In a medium container, combine the coconut water, water, and lime juice.
2   Add the sea salt and stevia powder and stir until dissolved.
3   Consume immediately or store in an airtight container up to 1 week.

KEY INGREDIENT: Coconut Water

Coconut water is a naturally hydrating drink that can help replace electrolytes lost during rigorous exercise. Electrolytes are important minerals that play crucial roles in your body, including maintaining proper fluid balance.

Research has shown that both young and mature coconut water has anti-inflammatory properties. In one study, coconut water was found to have the same ability as ibuprofen to suppress inflammatory responses in the body. Researchers haven't concluded what the exact mode of action is, but the results of lowered inflammation in the body were clear.

With no added sugars or artificial flavors or colors, this sports drink is a much smarter option for hydrating.

Per Serving
Calories: 41 | Fat: 0.4 g | Protein: 1.4 g | Sodium: 287 mg
Fiber: 2.1 g | Carbohydrates: 9.3 g | Sugar: 5.0 g

UNSWEETENED ICED CINNAMON COFFEE

Serves 1
INGREDIENTS

1 cup brewed coffee
¼ teaspoon ground cinnamon
¼ teaspoon pure vanilla extract
1 tablespoon full-fat coconut milk
Ice, as needed

1   Place all ingredients, except ice, in a small blender.
2   Blend on high until the ingredients are thoroughly combined.
3   Fill a glass with ice. Pour the coffee mixture over ice.
4   Consume immediately.

KEY INGREDIENT: Cinnamon

Cinnamon is one of the most delicious spices and is used frequently in baking to add a warm depth to coffee cakes, crisps, and more. Not only does cinnamon have a lovely flavor, but it also comes with a host of health benefits. Cinnamon has been used for its medicinal properties for centuries. It is considered antimicrobial, antifungal, and antidiabetic and is known to help control blood sugar levels. Cinnamon gets its anti-inflammatory fighting powers from two powerful compounds, E-cinnamaldehyde and O-methoxycinnamaldehyde. Both of these compounds have been shown to decrease chronic inflammation through the down-regulation of nitric oxide and TNF-α production.

Cinnamon is especially high in antioxidants, which help fight inflammation caused by oxidative stress. In fact, it ranks seventh for antioxidants of all foods, spices, and herbs on the Oxygen Radical Absorbance Capacity (ORAC) scale.

Per Serving
Calories: 35 | Fat: 3.0 g | Protein: 0.6 g | Sodium: 5 mg
Fiber: 0.4 g | Carbohydrates: 1.1 g | Sugar: 0.2 g

STRAWBERRY SAGE LEMONADE

Serves 6

INGREDIENTS

1 cup lemon juice (from 4–5 large
lemons)
4¼ cups water, divided
1 pound strawberries, hulled and cut
in half
1 cup sage leaves
½ cup erythritol
Ice, as needed

1   In a large pitcher, combine the lemon juice with 4 cups water.

2   In a medium saucepan, heat the strawberries, sage leaves, erythritol, and ¼ cup water over medium heat and bring to a boil.

3   Once the mixture is boiling, use the back of a wooden spoon or a potato masher to mash the strawberries.

4   Reduce the heat and let the mixture simmer 3–4 minutes. Remove from heat and allow to cool.

5   Transfer the strawberry mixture to a large blender. Blend the strawberry mixture on high until the strawberries and sage are thoroughly combined and you have a smooth purée.

6   Pour the purée into the lemonade and stir well.

7   Serve over ice. May be stored in the refrigerator up to 4 days.

KEY INGREDIENT: Sage

Many herbs have been used for holistic remedies for centuries. Sage has some powerful compounds in its leaves that contribute to the anti-inflammatory effect it has. Carnosic acid and carnosol are the main anti-inflammatory compounds present in sage and its sister herb, rosemary. These compounds have both antioxidant and antimicrobial properties. Studies have shown that these compounds target multiple pathways associated with inflammation and cancer.

Sage also contains several antioxidant enzymes, including superoxide dismutase (SOD) and peroxide, and rosmarinic acid, which is a potent anti-inflammatory agent. Rosmarinic acid is readily absorbed by the body and is often recommended for patients with inflammatory conditions like RA and atherosclerosis.

Sage adds a unique and sophisticated flavor to this lemonade recipe. It pairs very well with strawberries, which of course also add to the anti-inflammatory abilities of this drink.

Per Serving
Calories: 33 | Fat: 0.2 g | Protein: 0.8 g | Sodium: 2 mg
Fiber: 1.8 g | Carbohydrates: 24.6 g | Sugar: 4.3 g
Sugar Alcohol: 16.0 g

ROSEMARY COCONUT COOLER

Serves 1

INGREDIENTS

1 cup unsweetened coconut water
1 tablespoon rosemary leaves
¼ teaspoon pure stevia powder
Ice, as needed
1 cup club soda

1 Combine the coconut water, rosemary leaves, and stevia powder in a small blender.

2 Blend on high until the ingredients are thoroughly combined.

3 Pour the coconut water mixture over a tall glass of ice. Add the club soda and stir.

4 Consume immediately.

KEY INGREDIENT: Rosemary

Rosemary has similar inflammation-fighting compounds to sage. Two of the compounds found in rosemary that fight inflammation are apigenin and diosmin. These two compounds have an anti-inflammatory effect through their ability to prevent your body from producing prostaglandins, which are responsible for causing an inflammation reaction throughout your body. The compound rosmarinic acid present in rosemary also fights inflammation in this way.

Rosemary is common in cooking but less common in drinks. Paired with coconut water, club soda, and a little stevia, this drink with inflammation-fighting rosemary makes a healthy alternative for anyone who enjoys soda. Its unique flavor is perfect for adult palates.

Per Serving
Calories: 47 | Fat: 0.6 g | Protein: 1.8 g | Sodium: 301 mg
Fiber: 2.8 g | Carbohydrates: 9.4 g | Sugar: 6.0 g

GINGER ALE

Serves 6

INGREDIENTS

For the Ginger Syrup
2 cups water
1½ cups peeled, chopped fresh
  ginger
½ cup pure maple syrup

For the Ginger Ale
4½ cups club soda
1½ cups Ginger Syrup

1 First, make the Ginger Syrup. Heat the water and ginger in a small saucepan over medium-low heat to a very low simmer.

2 Let the water simmer, with the pan partially covered, for 45 minutes. Keep the simmer very low.

3 Remove from heat and cover. Let steep 20 minutes.

4 Strain the ginger through a fine-mesh sieve, pushing down on the ginger with the back of a wooden spoon to release all liquid.

5 Add maple syrup to the ginger mixture and stir to combine. Ginger Syrup may be kept in an airtight container in the refrigerator up to 1 week.

6 For each serving of Ginger Ale: pour ¾ cup club soda into a glass. Top with ¼ cup Ginger Syrup and stir to combine.

KEY INGREDIENT: Ginger

Ginger originated in Southeast Asia over 5,000 years ago and was considered a luxury. It was widely cultivated and traded in other countries. Ginger has been traded throughout the centuries and prized for its medicinal merits. It became a highly sought-after commodity in Europe. In the Middle Ages, just one pound of the coveted spice was worth as much as one sheep.

While for thousands of years ginger was purported to be used for the treatment of a variety of ailments, like many herbal remedies, much of the information was passed down by word of mouth and there wasn't always scientific evidence to back the claims. Today, however, ginger has been studied extensively for its medicinal properties and health benefits. It is widely accepted that there is ample scientific evidence and research to support ginger's role as an antioxidant, anti-inflammatory agent, anti-nausea compound, and anticancer agent, as well as the protective effect of ginger against a host of other diseases.

Per Serving
Calories: 70 | Fat: 0.0 g | Protein: 0.1 g | Sodium: 40 mg
Fiber: 0.1 g | Carbohydrates: 18.0 g | Sugar: 15.9 g

SPARKLING WATERMELON LIME DRINK

Serves 8

INGREDIENTS

5 cups watermelon cubes
½ cup fresh lime juice
5 cups unsweetened lime-flavored
  sparkling water

---

1 In a large blender, in batches
if necessary, blend the watermelon cubes until they are
completely smooth.

2 Transfer the watermelon juice
to a large pitcher. Stir in the
lime juice and sparkling water.

3 Allow to chill before serving.
Serve over ice. May be stored
in the refrigerator up to 4 days.

KEY INGREDIENT: Watermelon

Watermelon is such a hydrating fruit, so it makes a smart choice to include in drink recipes. It is high in potassium, making it a natural electrolyte that can help regulate the action of nerves and muscles in your body. Watermelon also has an alkaline-forming effect on the body, which can help counteract the effects of consuming too many high acid–producing foods, such as meat and dairy.

While the lycopene in watermelon is one compound responsible for the fruit's anti-inflammatory action, there are more at work. Another compound found in watermelons, Cucurbitacin E, also contributes to its ability to fight inflammation. Cucurbitacin E is an anti-inflammatory agent because it blocks pro-inflammatory cyclooxygenase enzymes.

Per Serving
Calories: 32 | Fat: 0.1 g | Protein: 0.6 g | Sodium: 1 mg
Fiber: 0.4 g | Carbohydrates: 8.5 g | Sugar: 6.2 g

ORANGE STRAWBERRY FIZZ

Serves 1

INGREDIENTS

4 large strawberries, hulled
1 tablespoon water
Ice, as needed
¾ cup fresh orange juice
¼ cup soda water

1 In a small blender, blend the strawberries and water on high until they form a smooth purée. Set aside.

2 Put the ice in a glass. Pour the orange juice in the glass and top it with the soda water.

3 Stir in the strawberry purée.

4 Consume immediately.

KEY INGREDIENT: Strawberries

Strawberries are among the most popular fruits consumed throughout the world. Not only are these berries scrumptious, but they are also highly nutritious and health-promoting. Strawberries score approximately a 40 on the glycemic index. This is a low number compared to many fresh fruits. Researchers have found that consumption of strawberries following a meal has a positive impact on the regulation of insulin and blood sugar levels. Strawberries contain a number of anti-inflammatory polyphenols, including ellagitannins. The ellagitannins in strawberries have been found to block inflammatory actions in the body.

This Orange Strawberry Fizz is another great soda alternative and is a beautifully colored drink.

Per Serving
Calories: 106 | Fat: 0.3 g | Protein: 1.8 g | Sodium: 13 mg
Fiber: 1.8 g | Carbohydrates: 24.9 g | Sugar: 19.1 g

CHERRY SODA

Serves 4
INGREDIENTS

For the Cherry Syrup
1½ cups fresh pitted sweet cherries
1½ cups water
½ teaspoon pure stevia powder

For the Cherry Soda
3 cups club soda
1 cup Cherry Syrup

---

1 First, make the Cherry Syrup. Heat the cherries and water in a small saucepan over medium heat to a simmer. Allow to simmer 10 minutes.

2 While the cherries and water are simmering, mash the cherries to release more flavor.

3 Remove from heat and strain the cherries through a fine-mesh sieve. Use the back of a wooden spoon to remove as much liquid from the cherries as possible.

4 Stir in stevia. Cherry Syrup may be stored in an airtight container in the refrigerator up to 1 week.

5 For each serving of Cherry Soda: pour ¾ cup club soda into a glass. Top with ¼ cup Cherry Syrup and stir to combine.

KEY INGREDIENT: Sweet Cherries

There are different varieties of cherries, including sweet and tart cherries. Both sweet and tart cherries are known for their health-promoting properties. A number of human studies have been done researching the health benefits of cherries. The cumulative results of these studies show that cherries have been found to reduce oxidative stress in the body, decrease markers for inflammation, decrease muscle soreness after exercise, decrease blood pressure and arthritis symptoms, improve sleep, and decrease triglycerides and HDL ratios in obese patients. Polyphenols, melatonin, carotenoids, and vitamins E and C all contribute to the antioxidant and anti-inflammatory properties of cherries. All together, these nutrients form a powerful anti-inflammatory punch that can have a positive effect on many aspects of your health.

If you like to drink soda every day, this is an excellent replacement. Make a double or triple batch of the naturally sweetened Cherry Syrup to have on hand whenever a craving for soda hits.

Per Serving
Calories: 11 | Fat: 0.0 g | Protein: 0.2 g | Sodium: 37 mg
Fiber: 0.0 g | Carbohydrates: 2.7 g | Sugar: 2.5 g

Chapter 5

TONICS AND SHOTS

While all the recipes in this book are designed to have anti-inflammatory effects through their ingredients, this chapter has recipes that were designed for specific ailments and needs. Tonics are drinks that can help you heal or feel better. Whether you are suffering from insomnia, digestive troubles, or a cold, there is likely a recipe in this chapter that is designed to help.

Fair warning: These recipes were not developed based on taste. Instead, they were designed specifically for their medicinal qualities. Some happen to taste great naturally, but all of the drinks, regardless of taste, have powerful healing ingredients that can help you if you're seeking natural solutions to whatever is ailing you.

The shot recipes can give you a quick anti-inflammatory boost. Like the tonics, many of them were designed for specific health concerns or to be used preventively. They are easy to consume quickly, and some of them may become part of your daily routine.

PASSION TONIC

Serves 1
INGREDIENTS

1 cup unsweetened pomegranate
  juice
1 teaspoon maca root powder

---

1 Pour the pomegranate juice
  into a glass.
2 Stir the maca root powder into
  the pomegranate juice until it
  is completely dissolved.
3 Consume immediately.

KEY INGREDIENT: Pomegranate

Pomegranates have become famous for their antioxidant abilities. That is thanks mostly to the powerful antioxidants found in their juice and peel called *punicalagins*. These punicalagins are such strong antioxidants that pomegranate juice has been found to have three times the antioxidant activity than that of red wine and green tea.

The effect of such a powerful antioxidant is decreased inflammation. One study found that diabetics who consumed 125 milliliters of pomegranate juice each day had lower levels of the inflammatory markers C-reactive protein and Interleukin-6 than previously.

Pomegranates are one of the most well-known fruits for increasing libido. Paired with maca root powder, which is known to balance hormones, this Passion Tonic is also an excellent choice for improving your sexual health.

Per Serving
Calories: 154 | Fat: 0.4 g | Protein: 1.4 g | Sodium: 22 mg
Fiber: 1.3 g | Carbohydrates: 36.7 g | Sugar: 32.5 g

GOOD MORNING TONIC

Serves 1
INGREDIENTS

Juice from ½ medium lemon
1 cup warm or room temperature
  water

---

1 Pour the lemon juice into the
  water and stir to combine.
2 Consume immediately, preferably upon waking in the
  morning.

KEY INGREDIENT: Lemon

You most often hear of the rich amount of vitamin C in lemons, but did you know they are also full of folate, vitamin B_6, magnesium, calcium, phosphorus, and vitamins A and E? Lemon juice is also a natural solvent that attacks the uric acid that causes joint pain and inflammation.

In addition to its anti-inflammatory benefits, there are a number of reasons why drinking lemon water in the morning is a good idea. Drinking lemon water first thing in the morning can help get your body ready for digesting food throughout the day. Lemon water is hydrating and can flush the digestive system, a good idea first thing in the morning. There is evidence that lemon juice can help stimulate proper stomach acid and bile production. This flushing of the digestive system is good for clear skin, and the vitamin C content of lemon juice helps with collagen production.

Per Serving
Calories: 3 | Fat: 0.0 g | Protein: 0.1 g | Sodium: 0 mg
Fiber: 0.1 g | Carbohydrates: 1.1 g | Sugar: 0.4 g

SLEEPING BEAUTY TONIC

Serves 1

INGREDIENTS

1 cup tart cherry juice
1 tablespoon apple cider vinegar
1 tablespoon raw honey

1 Combine cherry juice and apple cider vinegar in a glass.

2 Add the raw honey and stir until dissolved.

3 Consume immediately.

KEY INGREDIENT: Tart Cherries

Tart cherries are working double duty in this tonic. First, they fight inflammation thanks to the anthocyanins they contain. Tart cherries actually have a unique blend of anthocyanins that aren't present in other anthocyanin-rich fruits, even blueberries! Tart cherry juice was specifically studied for its pain-reducing qualities. Runners who drank tart cherry juice reported less pain after races than those who did not drink it, and they also had significantly lower inflammation biomarkers.

In addition to their inflammation-fighting powers, tart cherries are also known to be an incredible sleep aid. Tart cherries are a natural source of melatonin, a hormone responsible for regulating the sleep-wake cycle. This tonic would be an excellent one to include in your daily routine, as regular consumption of tart cherry juice is shown to help people fall asleep faster and sleep longer. In fact, researchers have discovered that drinking tart cherry juice two times daily can increase sleep time by up to ninety minutes!

Per Serving
Calories: 206 | Fat: 0.0 g | Protein: 1.1 g | Sodium: 15 mg
Fiber: 0.0 g | Carbohydrates: 51.4 g | Sugar: 42.3 g

HEALTHY HYDRATION TONIC

Serves 1
INGREDIENTS

½ medium cucumber, cut into chunks
1 large strawberry, hulled and cut in
   half
½ cup coconut water
Ice, as needed

1 In a small blender, combine
   the cucumber, strawberry, and
   coconut water.

2 Blend the ingredients on high
   until thoroughly combined and
   smooth.

3 Strain through a fine-mesh
   sieve. Serve over ice.

4 Consume immediately or store
   in an airtight container in the
   refrigerator for 24 hours.

KEY INGREDIENT: Cucumber

Cucumbers are a natural fit for drink recipes. Cucumbers contain up to 95 percent water, so they can help keep you hydrated. Even with all that water, cucumbers contain a good number of nutrients, including vitamin K, B vitamins, copper, potassium, vitamin C, and manganese.

Cucumbers help you fight inflammation in a number of ways. Cucumbers contain an anti-inflammatory flavonoid called *fisetin*. It's been found that fisetin inhibits the pro-inflammatory enzyme cyclooxegynase-2 and inhibits the activation of mitogen-activated protein kinase. In addition, cucumbers contain quercetin. Studies show that quercetin can reduce inflammation by down-regulating nitric oxide synthesis expression.

This tonic recipe contains hydrating, nutritious ingredients and is great to include in your day when you're especially dehydrated or going to be in a situation that warrants extra hydration.

Per Serving
Calories: 45 | Fat: 0.4 g | Protein: 2.0 g | Sodium: 129 mg
Fiber: 0.4 g | Carbohydrates: 9.4 g | Sugar: 6.4 g

BERRY BEAUTY TONIC

Serves 1

INGREDIENTS

1 cup unsweetened coconut water
½ cup blueberries
1 teaspoon acai berry powder
2 tablespoons lemon juice
¼ teaspoon pure stevia powder
Ice, as needed

---

1 Place all ingredients except ice in a large blender.
2 Blend the ingredients on high until thoroughly combined and smooth.
3 Fill a large glass with ice and pour the drink over the ice.
4 Consume immediately.

KEY INGREDIENT: Acai Berry Powder

Acai berries have long been a staple in the diet of Indian tribes, but in recent years they have grown in popularity as a superfood health-conscious individuals want to include in their diets also. One reason is that acai is filled with antioxidants such as anthocyanins; polyphenols; and vitamins A, C, and E. It's also a good source of B vitamins, magnesium, potassium, phosphorus, manganese, iron, copper, calcium, and zinc.

The anti-inflammatory properties acai berries boast are due to the combination of antioxidants. Many of the antioxidant compounds found in acai berries have been shown to block inflammatory pathways in the body.

Those same antioxidants make this a potent tonic for beautiful hair and skin. The acai berry's high number of antioxidants makes it helpful for skin regeneration and preventing early signs of aging.

Per Serving
Calories: 111 | Fat: 2.2 g | Protein: 2.4 g | Sodium: 254 mg
Fiber: 6.0 g | Carbohydrates: 23.3 g | Sugar: 14.1 g

ANTIAGING TONIC

Serves 1

INGREDIENTS

1 cup unsweetened pomegranate juice

1 teaspoon dried amla powder

---

1 Add the pomegranate juice to a small glass.

2 Stir in the amla powder until it is dissolved.

3 Consume immediately.

KEY INGREDIENT: Amla Powder

The list of health benefits associated with amla, also known as *Indian gooseberry*, is long. It's high in vitamin C, phosphorus, calcium, iron, and vitamin B complex. Amla has been associated with aiding hair growth, improving eyesight, lowering the risk of macular degeneration, boosting immunity, treating menstrual cramps, and helping control diabetes. It's also great for controlling chronic and acute inflammation. Studies have shown that consuming amla powder results in similar anti-inflammatory effects as taking anti-inflammatory drugs.

Amla is full of antioxidants that are effective in reducing cellular damage that results from aging. Paired with another potent antioxidant fruit, pomegranate, this makes a powerful antiaging tonic. Look for dried amla powder in your local health food store. It is also readily available online.

Per Serving

Calories: 137 | Fat: 0.4 g | Protein: 0.4 g | Sodium: 22 mg
Fiber: 0.3 g | Carbohydrates: 33.7 g | Sugar: 31.5 g

FIRECRACKER DETOX TONIC

Serves 1

INGREDIENTS

1½ cups water
1 tablespoon apple cider vinegar
1 tablespoon lemon juice
¼ teaspoon ground cinnamon
¼ teaspoon ground ginger
⅛ teaspoon cayenne pepper
1 teaspoon raw honey

1 In a small saucepan, combine the water, apple cider vinegar, lemon juice, cinnamon, ginger, and cayenne pepper over medium heat.

2 Heat the ingredients until they are warm, stirring constantly.

3 Pour into a mug and stir in the raw honey. Serve warm.

4 Consume immediately.

KEY INGREDIENT: Cayenne Pepper

Cayenne pepper is often used to add spiciness to cooking but less often is considered for its health benefits. That should change, though, because cayenne pepper brings a lot of health-promoting properties to the table. It can help digestion and upset stomach; relieve gas, diarrhea, and cramps; improve poor circulation; and even help lower cholesterol. The healing powers of cayenne pepper can be attributed to a compound it contains called *capsaicin*. Capsaicin has anti-inflammatory effects because it inhibits the enzyme activity of COX-2 in the body.

The cayenne pepper gives the heat to this Firecracker Detox Tonic. All of the ingredients work together to aid your body in the natural detox process. This is an exceptional tonic with which to start or end each day.

Per Serving
Calories: 29 | Fat: 0.1 g | Protein: 0.2 g | Sodium: 0 mg
Fiber: 0.5 g | Carbohydrates: 8.0 g | Sugar: 6.3 g

MUSCLE CRAMP RELIEF TONIC

Serves 1

INGREDIENTS

1 cup unsweetened coconut water
¼ cup lite canned coconut milk
1 medium orange, peeled
2 tablespoons baobab fruit powder
Ice, as needed

1 Place all ingredients except ice in a large blender.

2 Blend the ingredients on high until thoroughly combined and smooth.

3 Fill a large glass with ice and pour the drink over the ice.

4 Consume immediately or store in an airtight container in the refrigerator up to 24 hours.

KEY INGREDIENT: Baobab

Baobab is a traditional African medicinal plant. In its native environment it is called "the tree of life." Baobab fruit grows in pods and has a tart, sweet taste. The pulp is taken out and turned into a powder that is worth seeking out. Dried baobab fruit powder is rich in antioxidants, magnesium, potassium, calcium, and protein. The fiber in baobab fruit powder acts as a prebiotic, which helps maintain healthy bacteria in the gut and helps keep inflammation in control.

Mineral depletion can lead to muscle cramping, so eating foods rich in minerals can help prevent muscle cramps. Baobab fruit is high in key minerals thought to play a critical role in relieving muscle cramps: potassium, calcium, and magnesium. Paired with the electrolytes found in coconut water, this tonic is perfect for athletes and highly active individuals.

Per Serving
Calories: 181 | Fat: 4.0 g | Protein: 2.8 g | Sodium: 255 mg
Fiber: 12.2 g | Carbohydrates: 36.2 g | Sugar: 22.8 g

HERBAL DIGESTIVE TONIC

Serves 1

INGREDIENTS

5 mint leaves
2 sage leaves
1 sprig rosemary
1 teaspoon peeled, chopped fresh
  ginger
1 cup plain, unsweetened kombucha

---

1 In a medium bowl, muddle together the mint leaves, sage leaves, rosemary, and ginger.

2 Add the kombucha to the muddled ingredients.

3 Strain through a fine-mesh sieve.

4 Consume immediately.

KEY INGREDIENT: Kombucha

When you think of bacteria, you may think of it as a cause of getting sick. It's important to realize, however, that there is good bacteria and bad bacteria. In fact, each of us has a complex ecosystem of bacteria within our bodies known as our *microbiome*. Most of the bacteria lives in our digestive system. Some scientists believe that up to 90 percent of disease can be traced back to the gut and the health of the microbiome. Our food choices play an important role in maintaining the health of our microbiome. Having the right amount of good bacteria and a healthy microbiome has a big part in fighting chronic inflammation. Kombucha is a probiotic-rich beverage that helps promote good bacteria in the gut, thus helping fight inflammation.

Kombucha is also known to help digestion through its unique combination of organic acids, enzymes, and probiotics. The herbs in this drink are also specifically chosen for their digestive properties.

Per Serving
Calories: 31 | Fat: 0.1 g | Protein: 0.1 g | Sodium: 10 mg
Fiber: 0.2 g | Carbohydrates: 7.5 g | Sugar: 2.0 g

COLD-BUSTING SHOT

Serves 1

INGREDIENTS

1 clove garlic
2 tablespoons water
1 tablespoon raw honey

1 Finely chop the garlic and allow it to sit 10 minutes.

2 Meanwhile, in a small glass, combine the water and honey.

3 Add the chopped garlic to the water and honey mixture.

4 Consume immediately.

KEY INGREDIENT: Garlic

Garlic has been used medicinally for centuries. It has been used to offer protection against cancer, heart disease, and infections. The health benefits of garlic can be attributed to the organosulfur compounds it possesses. Sulfur compounds play a critical role in your health, helping the cellular detoxification system and the health of your joints and connective tissue, as well as with oxygen-related metabolism. One particular organosulfur compound thought to be associated with garlic's anti-inflammatory action is thiacremonone. Thiacremonone is believed to play in important role in controlling inflammation by suppressing inflammatory activity in the body.

Consuming raw garlic is thought to have a powerful effect on fighting the common cold. Take this Cold-Busting Shot one to two times a day when you're feeling under the weather.

Per Serving
Calories: 67 | Fat: 0.0 g | Protein: 0.3 g | Sodium: 0 mg
Fiber: 0.1 g | Carbohydrates: 18.3 g | Sugar: 17.3 g

ENDURANCE-BUILDER SHOT

Serves 1

INGREDIENTS

2 tablespoons coconut water
1 teaspoon spirulina

1 Place the coconut water and spirulina in a small blender.

2 Blend on high until the ingredients are thoroughly combined.

3 Consume immediately.

KEY INGREDIENT: Spirulina

Spirulina is a freshwater blue-green algae that is noted for its exceptional nutritional profile. It's often touted as the world's most nutrient-dense food. One unique characteristic of spirulina is that it's high in protein, especially for a plant food. Even more unique is that 65 percent of spirulina is a *complete* protein, containing all of the amino acids the body needs. It's also one of the best plant sources of iron; it has, ounce for ounce, twenty-six times the amount of calcium as milk, and it is a great source of B vitamins. Spirulina is also a rich source of omega-3 fatty acids and the fatty acid known as gamma linolenic acid, both of which are known for their anti-inflammatory properties.

Studies have shown that spirulina is effective for increasing endurance and reducing muscle damage from exercise. This is a great shot for athletes and fitness buffs to consume daily.

Per Serving
Calories: 11 | Fat: 0.2 g | Protein: 1.6 g | Sodium: 55 mg
Fiber: 0.4 g | Carbohydrates: 1.7 g | Sugar: 0.8 g

APPLE CIDER VINEGAR SHOT

Serves 1

INGREDIENTS

1 tablespoon apple cider vinegar
2 tablespoons water

1 In a small glass, combine the apple cider vinegar and water.

2 Consume immediately.

KEY INGREDIENT: Apple Cider Vinegar

Apple cider vinegar is made from fermenting apples. This process develops prebiotics, which feed the good bacteria in your gut. This helps maintain a healthy microbiome, which can reduce overall inflammation in the body.

Taking a shot of apple cider vinegar, diluted with water, every day is a healthy habit to maintain. Apple cider vinegar has been shown to have a myriad of health benefits. In addition to its ability to help your body fight inflammation, it can help regulate blood sugar levels, improve skin health, lower cholesterol levels, reduce blood pressure, and relieve symptoms of acid reflux.

Per Serving
Calories: 3 | Fat: 0.0 g | Protein: 0.0 g | Sodium: 0 mg
Fiber: 0.0 g | Carbohydrates: 0.1 g | Sugar: 0.1 g

WHEATGRASS SHOT

Serves 2

INGREDIENTS

1 medium Granny Smith apple
1 cup packed wheatgrass (approximately 25 grams)

1 Prepare the apple by coring it and cutting it into appropriate-sized pieces for your juicer.

2 Process the apple and wheatgrass through the juicer.

3 Consume immediately or store in a glass airtight container in the refrigerator up to 12 hours if using a centrifugal juicer and up to 3 days if using a masticating juicer.

KEY INGREDIENT: Wheatgrass

Wheatgrass is a type of young grass in the wheat family. Despite the name, wheatgrass is a gluten-free edible grass. It's often consumed for its health benefits because it's a concentrated source of a number of important nutrients. You will find iron; calcium; magnesium; amino acids; and vitamins A, C, and E in wheatgrass. Wheatgrass is also one of the world's richest forms of chlorophyll. Chlorophyll has been shown to be effective against cancer, to help protect against the hazards of radiation, to be antimicrobial, and to be effective for wound healing. Studies have shown that wheatgrass has significant anti-inflammatory activity in cases of chronic inflammation. This Wheatgrass Shot is a good daily, overall health-promoting shot.

Per Serving
Calories: 43 | Fat: 0.0 g | Protein: 0.4 g | Sodium: 1 mg
Fiber: 0.0 g | Carbohydrates: 9.2 g | Sugar: 8.0 g

HANGOVER CURE SHOT

Serves 1

INGREDIENTS

1 medium beet
1 teaspoon peeled, coarsely
 chopped fresh ginger

---

1 Prepare the beet by peeling it
 and cutting it into appropriate-
 sized pieces for your juicer.

2 Process the beet and ginger
 through the juicer. Do not
 strain.

3 Consume immediately. Can
 be stored in an airtight container in the refrigerator up to
 12 hours if using a centrifugal
 juicer and up to 3 days if using
 a masticating juicer.

KEY INGREDIENT: Beets

While beets are an anti-inflammatory food, there are other health benefits that come along with eating (or juicing) beets. The same unique phytonutrient that helps beets be a potent anti-inflammatory agent, betaine, makes this vegetable a great choice if you've drunk too much alcohol. The betaine pigments are what give beets their bright crimson color, and they also help facilitate the body's natural detoxification process. They trigger the detoxification process and aid in the elimination of toxins.

While the beet helps eliminate toxins in this recipe, the ginger will help with upset stomach. If you're feeling the effects of alcohol, this is a good shot to turn to.

Per Serving
Calories: 31 | Fat: 0.0 g | Protein: 1.4 g | Sodium: 63 mg
Fiber: 0.0 g | Carbohydrates: 5.9 g | Sugar: 5.6 g

IMMUNITY-BOOSTER SHOT

Serves 1

INGREDIENTS

1 small orange, peeled
½ teaspoon peeled, chopped fresh
   ginger
½ teaspoon raw honey
⅛ teaspoon cayenne powder

---

1 Using a citrus press or your hands, squeeze the juice from the orange into the container of a small blender. It should yield approximately ¼ cup juice.

2 Add ginger, raw honey, and cayenne powder to the blender and blend on high until all ingredients are thoroughly combined and smooth.

3 Consume immediately.

KEY INGREDIENT: Raw Honey

The medicinal value of honey has been known since ancient times. It was often used as an ointment and wound healing agent because of its antimicrobial properties. Aristotle noted that honey was "good as a salve for sore eyes and wounds." In modern times, honey's ability to assist with wound healing has been demonstrated.

Even though honey consists of mainly sugar and water, it also contains vitamins, minerals, and antioxidants. The antioxidants help prevent oxidative damages that can lead to inflammation. Recent studies have also shown that honey inhibits the activity of pro-inflammatory COX-2.

Honey that's been heated can lose a lot of its health benefits, so it's important to use raw, unprocessed honey.

The immunity-boosting ingredients in this shot make it useful at the very first signs of sickness.

Per Serving
Calories: 37 | Fat: 0.1 g | Protein: 0.5 g | Sodium: 0 mg
Fiber: 0.2 g | Carbohydrates: 9.7 g | Sugar: 8.2 g

ELDERBERRY SYRUP SHOT

Serves 32
INGREDIENTS

¾ cup dried elderberries
3 cups water
1 cinnamon stick
4 whole cloves
1 tablespoon peeled, chopped fresh
ginger
1 cup raw honey

1 In a large pot, bring the elderberries, water, cinnamon stick, cloves, and ginger to a boil.

2 Reduce the heat to medium-low, cover, and simmer until the liquid has reduced by half, about 30–40 minutes.

3 Allow the liquid to cool, then strain through a fine-mesh sieve.

4 Press all the liquid out of the berries using the back of a wooden spoon.

5 Add the raw honey and stir until combined.

6 Store in an airtight container in the refrigerator up to 2 months. Recommended 1 tablespoon shot daily as a preventative measure and up to 2–3 shots daily when ill.

KEY INGREDIENT: Elderberries

Elderberries are grown in the United States and were traditionally used by Native Americans, who benefited from every part of the plant. Elderberries are found in a number of Native American folk remedies and are used for relieving cold and flu symptoms, reducing congestion, alleviating arthritis pain, treating upset stomach and gas, and promoting healthy detoxification. Research has shown that, indeed, consuming the extract of elderberries helps reduce the duration of the flu by three days! Elderberries are a good source of vitamins A, C, and B_6; potassium; and iron. In addition, elderberries are antioxidant rich, which could contribute to their anti-inflammatory properties.

Elderberry syrup is used both as a preventative measure to prevent illness and also to shorten its duration. It's best taken every day during the cold and flu season.

Per Serving
Calories: 34 | Fat: 0.0 g | Protein: 0.1 g | Sodium: 0 mg
Fiber: 0.0 g | Carbohydrates: 9.3 g | Sugar: 8.7 g

PREGAME SHOT

Serves 2

INGREDIENTS

3 baby radicchio leaves
1 medium pink or red grapefruit

1   Prepare the radicchio leaves by chopping them into appropriate-sized pieces for your juicer.

2   Prepare the grapefruit by removing the peel and cutting the fruit into appropriate-sized pieces for your juicer.

3   Process the radicchio leaves and grapefruit through the juicer.

4   Strain through a fine-mesh sieve if desired.

5   Consume immediately or store in a glass airtight container in the refrigerator up to 12 hours if using a centrifugal juicer and up to 3 days if using a masticating juicer.

KEY INGREDIENT: Radicchio

Radicchio is bitter and, like many bitter foods, it is good for your gut health. In addition to its anti-inflammatory properties, radicchio is an excellent digestive aid. The inulin in radicchio promotes healthy digestion and also helps balance blood sugar levels. Compounds in radicchio stimulate the liver to produce bile, a fluid that helps the body digest fatty foods. This is called Pregame Shot because it's especially helpful to take before consuming a heavy meal.

Per Serving
Calories: 50 | Fat: 0.1 g | Protein: 1.1 g | Sodium: 2 mg
Fiber: 0.0 g | Carbohydrates: 11.6 g | Sugar: 8.6 g

CONGESTION-FIGHTING SHOT

Serves 2
INGREDIENTS

1 small handful young mustard greens
1 teaspoon peeled, coarsely
  chopped ginger

---

1 Prepare the mustard greens by cutting off the ends and chopping them into appropriate-sized pieces for your juicer. You should have approximately 2 cups chopped mustard greens.

2 Process the mustard greens and ginger through the juicer.

3 Strain through a fine-mesh sieve if desired.

4 Consume immediately or store in a glass airtight container in the refrigerator up to 12 hours if using a centrifugal juicer and up to 3 days if using a masticating juicer.

KEY INGREDIENT: Mustard Greens

Mustard greens are a nutritionally dense vegetable that is especially high in antioxidants, namely vitamin A and vitamin C. Antioxidants help prevent cell damage caused by oxidative stress. When free radicals damage cells, chronic inflammation can result. Therefore, eating foods high in antioxidants is a good way to prevent inflammation in the body. Mustard greens are also extremely high in vitamin K, another critical nutrient for reducing inflammation.

Mustard greens have a spicy mustard flavor and are helpful, along with raw ginger, in helping to relieve congestion. If you often wake up congested, this shot will help clear your airways.

Per Serving
Calories: 6 | Fat: 0.0 g | Protein: 0.8 g | Sodium: 5 mg
Fiber: 0.0 g | Carbohydrates: 0.6 g | Sugar: 0.4 g

IMMUNITY-BOOSTING TONIC

Serves 1

INGREDIENTS

2 medium oranges
1 teaspoon camu camu powder
Ice, as needed

1 Use a citrus juicer or your hands to squeeze the juice from the oranges into a glass.

2 Stir in the camu camu powder until it is completely dissolved.

3 Add ice and consume immediately.

KEY INGREDIENT: Camu Camu Powder

Camu camu is a shrub found in the swamp or flooded areas of the Amazon rainforest. Its berries look similar to cherries and are one of the highest vitamin C foods on the planet. The camu camu berry has ten to sixty times the vitamin C content of an orange! In addition to its extraordinarily high vitamin C content, camu camu also contains manganese, iron, copper, magnesium, calcium, potassium, and zinc. It also contains the carotenoid lutein, known for its anti-inflammatory action. Lutein is shown to inhibit pro-inflammatory proteins in the body.

Camu camu's high vitamin C content makes it a good choice for boosting your immune system function. It has a naturally sour flavor, so it works well with sweeter orange juice. You can find camu camu powder in a health food store or online.

Per Serving
Calories: 94 | Fat: 0.2 g | Protein: 1.2 g | Sodium: 1 mg
Fiber: 0.3 g | Carbohydrates: 21.2 g | Sugar: 13.9 g

GLOWING SKIN SHOT

Serves 1

INGREDIENTS

¼ cup packed cilantro leaves
¼ cup unsweetened coconut water
1 tablespoon lemon juice

1   Place all ingredients in a small blender.
2   Blend the ingredients on high until the cilantro is thoroughly broken down and combined with the liquid.
3   Consume immediately.

KEY INGREDIENT: Cilantro

Cilantro has an impressive list of nutrients and health benefits. It's a great source of vitamins A, C, and K and B vitamins. In addition, cilantro provides minerals like potassium, calcium, manganese, iron, and magnesium. It's also high in antioxidants, including superstars like quercetin, kaempferol, rhamnetin, and apigenin. A lot of powerful nutrition is packed into those green leaves!

Research shows that cilantro can help lower cholesterol, lower blood pressure, and support healthy cardiovascular function. It has also been shown to help accelerate the removal of toxins from the body and to prevent neurological inflammation.

Cilantro has natural antihistamines, so this shot is perfect for relief from skin irritations.

Per Serving
Calories: 14 | Fat: 0.2 g | Protein: 0.6 g | Sodium: 64 mg
Fiber: 0.8 g | Carbohydrates: 3.5 g | Sugar: 1.9 g

Chapter 6

HOT DRINKS

From teas to lattes to hot cocoa, hot drinks can warm your body and soul. Sipping on a hot beverage in the afternoon is a ritual I've come to love. It's so common to purchase hot drinks from coffee shops that may taste delicious but don't do you any favors when it comes to your health. Instead of choosing a warm drink that is full of sugar and causes inflammation, why not use foods that fight inflammation and make your own warm, comforting drinks at home? That's exactly what you'll find here.

This chapter covers all of your favorite hot drinks that are made especially with ingredients that will help reduce inflammation. Most of them take just minutes to make and are full of nutritional benefits. It's time to ditch the coffee-shop drinks and make your own anti-inflammatory hot drinks!

MEXICAN HOT CHOCOLATE

Serves 2

INGREDIENTS

1 cup lite canned coconut milk

1½ cups unsweetened almond milk

1 teaspoon ground cinnamon

¼ teaspoon chili powder

1 teaspoon pure vanilla extract

¼ cup pure maple syrup

¼ cup raw cacao powder

1 In a small saucepan over medium-high heat, whisk to combine the coconut milk, almond milk, cinnamon, chili powder, vanilla extract, and maple syrup.

2 Bring the mixture to a boil, reduce the heat, and simmer 5 minutes until it thickens slightly.

3 Whisk in the cacao powder and remove from heat.

4 Serve warm. Store any leftovers in an airtight container in the refrigerator up to 48 hours. May be reheated.

KEY INGREDIENT: Raw Cacao Powder

Cacao beans are high in polyphenols, which work with your body to reduce inflammation. They are shown to have a range of cardiovascular-protective properties and boast *forty times* the antioxidants of blueberries. Another benefit? Cacao is the highest plant-based source of iron. Yes, you're doing your body a big favor by drinking this Mexican Hot Chocolate!

This hot chocolate drink is sweetened with an unrefined, natural sweetener: maple syrup. Maple syrup contains antioxidants and is a rich source of minerals like manganese and zinc. One study showed that maple syrup has twenty-four different antioxidants. These antioxidants can help reduce free radical damage, which causes inflammation.

Per Serving

Calories: 249 | Fat: 10.1 g | Protein: 2.9 g | Sodium: 156 mg
Fiber: 3.6 g | Carbohydrates: 36.9 g | Sugar: 24.4 g

GREEN TEA WITH GINGER AND LEMON

Serves 1

INGREDIENTS

1 cup water
1 tablespoon peeled, chopped fresh
  ginger
1 tablespoon lemon juice
1 teaspoon raw honey
1 tea bag green tea leaves

1 In a small saucepan, combine the water, ginger, and lemon juice and bring to a boil over high heat.

2 Remove from heat and strain the ginger from the water and transfer the water to a teacup.

3 Stir honey into the water until it is dissolved.

4 Steep the tea bag in the water 3 minutes.

5 Consume immediately.

KEY INGREDIENT: Green Tea

Green tea contains quercetin, a chemical compound that has strong anti-inflammatory properties. Green tea is one of the most health-promoting things you can drink. Studies have shown that regularly drinking green tea can help prevent diseases like heart disease and stroke, and consuming it daily is correlated with longer life spans.

Here green tea is paired with fresh ginger for extra protection against inflammation. Lemon juice also provides health benefits along with antioxidant-rich raw honey. Be sure to wait until you remove the water from the heat to add the raw honey so you protect the important enzymes present in the honey.

Per Serving
Calories: 30 | Fat: 0.1 g | Protein: 0.2 g | Sodium: 0 mg
Fiber: 0.2 g | Carbohydrates: 8.7 g | Sugar: 6.3 g

MORNING DETOX TEA

Serves 1

INGREDIENTS

1½ cups water
2 tablespoons lemon juice
1 tablespoon apple cider vinegar
1" piece fresh ginger, peeled and
  sliced
1 teaspoon raw honey

1 In a small saucepan over medium heat, combine the water, lemon juice, apple cider vinegar, and sliced ginger and bring to a simmer. Simmer 2 minutes.

2 Strain the ginger from the mixture and pour tea into a teacup.

3 Stir in the raw honey.

4 Serve warm immediately or store in an airtight container in the refrigerator up to 48 hours. May be reheated.

KEY INGREDIENT: Fresh Ginger

Ginger is used in a number of recipes in this book, and that's because it's one of the top inflammation-fighting foods. It's evident that it will help your body fight inflammation and is advantageous to include in your diet as often as possible. Ginger has such strong anti-inflammatory properties that it's often used to reduce pain in arthritis patients.

Although our bodies do a great job of naturally detoxing, this morning tea can help that natural process. It contains ingredients that can aid detox, such as lemon juice and apple cider vinegar. This is a lovely and health-promoting way to start each morning!

Per Serving
Calories: 31 | Fat: 0.0 g | Protein: 0.2 g | Sodium: 0 mg
Fiber: 0.2 g | Carbohydrates: 8.5 g | Sugar: 6.7 g

GOLDEN MILK

Serves 2
INGREDIENTS

For the Turmeric Paste
¼ cup turmeric powder
½ cup water
¾ teaspoon black pepper

For the Golden Milk
2 cups unsweetened almond milk
½ teaspoon Turmeric Paste
¼ teaspoon ground cinnamon
¼ teaspoon ground ginger
½ teaspoon pure vanilla extract
½ teaspoon coconut oil
2 teaspoons raw honey

1 First, prepare the Turmeric Paste: Mix the turmeric powder and water in a small saucepan over low heat, stirring until a paste is formed.

2 Once you have a paste, stir in the black pepper.

3 This recipe provides more Turmeric Paste than you'll need for this Golden Milk recipe, so cool and store the extra in a glass jar in the refrigerator up to 2 weeks.

4 Next, combine the almond milk, Turmeric Paste, cinnamon, ginger, vanilla extract, coconut oil, and honey in a small saucepan and gently heat over low heat.

5 Whisk well to ensure you combine the paste, oil, and spices.

6 Serve warm. Store any leftovers in an airtight container in the refrigerator up to 48 hours. May be reheated.

KEY INGREDIENT: Turmeric

Turmeric has been used holistically for centuries. A spice common in India, its bright yellow color gives this hot drink its name. In Southeast Asia, it is so highly regarded that it's used not only as a principle spice but also as a component in religious ceremonies.

Curcumin is the active ingredient that gives turmeric its anti-inflammatory effect. Curcumin isn't easily absorbed by your body; it does better when paired with black pepper, and that's why you find black pepper on the ingredient list for this Turmeric Paste. Some studies also suggest that it's more easily absorbed when consumed with fat, so coconut oil provides that.

Turmeric has gained the attention of many in the modern medicine field, indicated by the fact that it's been the subject of over 3,000 scientific publications in the last twenty-five years. The results of numerous studies prove that turmeric is a powerful anti-inflammatory agent that can be used to help combat a number of inflammatory-related diseases and conditions.

Per Serving
Calories: 65 | Fat: 4.1 g | Protein: 1.1 g | Sodium: 180 mg
Fiber: 1.3 g | Carbohydrates: 8.7 g | Sugar: 6.4 g

PUMPKIN SPICE LATTE

Serves 2

INGREDIENTS

2 cups vanilla walnut milk
½ cup brewed coffee
¼ cup pumpkin purée
2 tablespoons erythritol
1 tablespoon pure vanilla extract
½ teaspoon pumpkin spice

1 Combine all ingredients in a small saucepan.

2 Whisk until all the ingredients are thoroughly combined.

3 Gently heat over medium-low heat, whisking occasionally, until the drink is hot, about 5 minutes.

4 Serve hot. Store in an airtight container in the refrigerator up to 2 days. May be reheated.

KEY INGREDIENT: Pumpkin

Pumpkin-spiced drinks have risen to extreme popularity so much in recent years that if you see the acronym PSL in October, you know exactly what it means. The problem is that most of these Pumpkin Spice Lattes are made without any real pumpkin at all and are filled with inflammatory ingredients like dairy and refined sugar. You can make a much healthier, anti-inflammatory Pumpkin Spice Latte at home with this simple recipe.

By adding pumpkin purée (canned works just fine) to your latte, you're adding a good amount of fiber, vitamin A, vitamin C, vitamin B_6, copper, and manganese. Pumpkin boasts a high level of the antioxidant beta-carotene. Beta-carotene is known to help protect eye health, improve respiratory health, and protect the body from free radical damage. That protection also helps keep inflammation at bay.

Per Serving
Calories: 92 | Fat: 3.7 g | Protein: 1.4 g | Sodium: 142 mg
Fiber: 1.8 g | Carbohydrates: 20.6 g | Sugar: 6.1 g
Sugar Alcohol: 12.0 g

COFFEE, ELEVATED

Serves 1

INGREDIENTS

1 cup brewed coffee
1 tablespoon coconut oil

---

1 Pour hot, brewed coffee into a mug.

2 Add the coconut oil and stir until it is melted into the coffee.

3 Consume immediately.

KEY INGREDIENT: Coconut Oil

Coconut oil can be confusing, as there is a lot of contradictory information you can find as to whether it's beneficial for your health or not. While coconut oil is composed of saturated fats, it has a special kind of fats called *medium chain fatty acids*. These unique fats include caprylic acid, lauric acid, and capric acid. One indication that these medium chain fatty acids are beneficial is that lauric acid is one of the primary lipids found in breast milk. Medium chain fatty acids have been shown to be beneficial for brain, skin, immune system, and thyroid health.

Coconut oil is at work here to fight inflammation. The lauric acid in coconut oil has anti-inflammatory properties. Some studies have shown it to reduce inflammation better than leading medications.

Per Serving
Calories: 119 | Fat: 12.8 g | Protein: 0.3 g | Sodium: 4 mg
Fiber: 0.0 g | Carbohydrates: 0.0 g | Sugar: 0.0 g

MATCHA VANILLA LATTE

Serves 1

INGREDIENTS

¼ cup hot water
1 teaspoon matcha powder
1 cup lite canned coconut milk
¼ teaspoon pure stevia powder
⅛ teaspoon ground cinnamon
¼ teaspoon pure vanilla extract
2 teaspoons raw honey

1 Mix together the hot water and matcha powder in a coffee mug until the matcha is dissolved.

2 In a small saucepan over medium-low heat, whisk together the coconut milk, stevia powder, cinnamon, and vanilla extract. Heat until the mixture is hot, 2–3 minutes.

3 Pour the coconut milk mixture into the coffee mug with the matcha. Stir in the raw honey until dissolved.

4 Consume immediately.

KEY INGREDIENT: Matcha

Matcha, consumed in Japan for almost 1,000 years, was traditionally reserved for royalty and spiritual leaders. Today it is widely available at most supermarkets and is the only tea where you consume the whole tea leaf. This unique fact is what makes it special and abundant in health benefits.

Matcha is an antioxidant powerhouse, surpassing even the most antioxidant-rich foods like blueberries and dark chocolate. Although the mechanisms are not yet fully understood, the antioxidants in matcha, called *catechins*, are shown to have strong anti-inflammatory effects. Matcha is also known as an anti-inflammatory agent partly because of the chlorophyll it contains. Matcha is five times higher than regular green tea in chlorophyll, which interferes with the growth of bacterial-induced inflammation.

Matcha is also fantastic for sustained energy throughout the day thanks to L-theanine, an amino acid found in all green teas. It has also been found to have a calming effect for people who suffer from anxiety, as it binds to the same brain cell receptors as glutamate, producing an inhibitory effect.

Although matcha has an earthy flavor, it is masked with vanilla, coconut milk, cinnamon, honey, and stevia in this tasty latte.

Per Serving
Calories: 200 | Fat: 13.5 g | Protein: 0.6 g | Sodium: 15 mg
Fiber: 0.7 g | Carbohydrates: 16.0 g | Sugar: 11.7 g

CLOVE TEA

Serves 1
INGREDIENTS

1 tablespoon whole dried cloves
1 cup water
1 teaspoon pure maple syrup

1 Using a mortar and pestle, coarsely grind the whole cloves.

2 Combine the coarsely ground cloves and water in a small saucepan over medium-high heat and bring to a boil. Turn off heat immediately after the mixture boils.

3 Cover the pan. Allow to steep 3 minutes.

4 Strain through a fine-mesh strainer into a mug.

5 Stir in maple syrup.

6 Consume immediately.

KEY INGREDIENT: Cloves

Cloves are the dried flower buds of the Syzygium aromaticum tree. In the culinary world, they are a wonderful spice that brings a unique, warming flavor to whatever they are added to. Not only do they have fantastic sweet and spicy flavor, but they also have tremendous health benefits. Cloves have been shown to have antifungal, antiviral, antioxidant, anticancer, and anti-inflammatory properties. Eugenol is the compound at work fighting inflammation. It works, similar to many anti-inflammatory compounds, by blocking pro-inflammatory COX-2.

This Clove Tea, which pairs perfectly with maple syrup, is a lovely way to enjoy all the health benefits of cloves.

Per Serving
Calories: 32 | Fat: 0.6 g | Protein: 0.4 g | Sodium: 18 mg
Fiber: 1.2 g | Carbohydrates: 7.7 g | Sugar: 4.1 g

GINGERBREAD LATTE

Serves 1

INGREDIENTS

¼ cup full-fat coconut milk
1 teaspoon blackstrap molasses
¼ teaspoon pure stevia powder
Pinch ground cinnamon
Pinch ground ginger
Pinch allspice
Pinch ground nutmeg
1 cup brewed hot coffee

1 In a small saucepan, whisk together the coconut milk, blackstrap molasses, stevia, cinnamon, ginger, allspice, and nutmeg.

2 Heat the milk mixture over medium-low heat until it is warm, about 5 minutes, whisking frequently.

3 Pour the coffee into a mug and stir in the milk mixture.

4 Consume immediately.

KEY INGREDIENT: Coffee

Those of you who love your morning cup of coffee will be pleased to hear that it's more than just a way to help you wake up. Coffee brings a number of health benefits. Studies have shown that drinking coffee is associated with a lower risk for Alzheimer's disease and Parkinson's disease, and it even lowers the risk of some types of cancer. In two large studies over an eighteen- to twenty-four–year period, coffee was also associated with living longer, showing a 20 percent lower risk of death among men who drank coffee and a 26 percent lower risk of death among women who drank coffee.

Coffee is a rich source of polyphenols, powerful antioxidants. It is the polyphenols that are believed to bring coffee its anti-inflammatory benefits.

Per Serving
Calories: 133 | Fat: 11.4 g | Protein: 1.5 g | Sodium: 13 mg
Fiber: 0.2 g | Carbohydrates: 7.2 g | Sugar: 5.3 g

SPICED CRANBERRY DRINK

Serves 4

INGREDIENTS

3 cups whole cranberries
1 cup fresh orange juice
4 cups water
1 cinnamon stick
2 whole cloves
⅓ cup pure maple syrup
⅓ cup erythritol

---

1 Combine all ingredients in a large pot and bring to a boil.

2 Reduce the heat and allow the ingredients to simmer, stirring occasionally, for 20 minutes.

3 Strain the ingredients through a fine-mesh strainer, using the back of a wooden spoon to push the juice from the remaining cranberries.

4 Serve warm. Store in an airtight container in the refrigerator up to 4 days. May be reheated.

KEY INGREDIENT: Cranberries

Cranberries are rich in antioxidants known to fight inflammation. In addition to powerful anthocyanins, cranberries are also a good source of vitamin C and vitamin E. Studies have shown that consuming cranberries increases the total antioxidant capacity in the bloodstream.

Inflammation and oxidative stress in the body both have detrimental effects on your cardiovascular health. The ability of cranberries to fight inflammation and oxidation through the presence of antioxidants makes them excellent at protecting cardiovascular health.

This Spiced Cranberry Drink is an excellent fall and winter drink that would be a wonderful addition to holiday gatherings. It is sweetened naturally with erythritol, and fresh orange juice and pure maple syrup also add a natural sweetness. The orange juice provides extra vitamin C as well, making this an exceptionally nutritious drink recipe.

Per Serving
Calories: 123 | Fat: 0.1 g | Protein: 0.7 g | Sodium: 5 mg
Fiber: 0.6 g | Carbohydrates: 45.6 g | Sugar: 24.1 g
Sugar Alcohol: 16.0 g

COLLAGEN COFFEE

Serves 1

INGREDIENTS

1 cup hot brewed coffee
2 tablespoons plain collagen protein
  powder

1 Pour the coffee into a mug.
2 Stir in the collagen protein until
   it is dissolved.
3 Consume immediately.

KEY INGREDIENT: Collagen Protein

Collagen is the most abundant protein in your body. As you age, your body's natural collagen production slows down. Today, animal collagen is available in powdered form, allowing you to replace lost collagen in your body and reap the health benefits. Consuming collagen (not using it topically in beauty products but actually ingesting it) is associated with improving the health of the skin, hair, nails, and teeth; reducing joint pain and degeneration; and protecting your cardiovascular health. Studies have demonstrated the anti-inflammatory properties of collagen. One study reported that collagen was 25 percent more effective than standard anti-inflammatory drugs at reducing joint pain.

Plain collagen powder is odorless and tasteless, so adding collagen to your morning coffee is an easy way to add it to your daily routine.

Per Serving
Calories: 38 | Fat: 0.0 g | Protein: 9.3 g | Sodium: 58 mg
Fiber: 0.0 g | Carbohydrates: 0.0 g | Sugar: 0.0 g

REISHI MUSHROOM COFFEE

Serves 4

INGREDIENTS

For the Reishi Mushroom Tea
8 cups water
1 cup dried reishi mushroom pieces

For the Reishi Mushroom Coffee
4 cups hot brewed coffee

---

1 Start by making Reishi Mushroom Tea: Bring water to a boil in a medium saucepan.

2 Add the reishi mushroom pieces to the water and boil 30 minutes.

3 Turn off the heat, cover the pan, and allow to steep 15 minutes.

4 Remove the dried mushroom pieces and transfer the Reishi Mushroom Tea to an airtight container. The tea can be kept in the refrigerator up to 1 week.

5 To make each serving of the Reishi Mushroom Coffee, add ½ cup warm Reishi Mushroom Tea to 1 cup of hot brewed coffee.

6 Consume immediately.

KEY INGREDIENT: Reishi Mushrooms

Native to Asia, the reishi mushroom is an edible, medicinal fungus that's been used for thousands of years for its healing properties. Reishi mushroom is considered an adaptogen herb, which means it can help your body deal with the negative effects of stress. One such effect of stress is inflammation; therefore, reishi mushrooms are a powerful way to fight inflammation.

In addition to fighting inflammation, the reishi mushroom has been noted for its ability to fight fatigue, skin disorders, viruses, tumors, autoimmune disorders, heart disease, and sleeping disorders. Talk about a potent ingredient to include in your diet!

Alone, reishi mushroom tea is quite bitter and doesn't have a pleasant taste. Mixing it with coffee solves the problem and makes it easier to drink. Feel free to drink it alone, however, if you like the flavor!

Per Serving
Calories: 4 | Fat: 0.0 g | Protein: 0.4 g | Sodium: 4 mg
Fiber: 0.0 g | Carbohydrates: 0.5 g | Sugar: 0.0 g

TART CHERRY TURMERIC BEDTIME TEA

Serves 1

INGREDIENTS

1 cup tart cherry juice
1 cup water
1 tablespoon grated fresh turmeric
Pinch black pepper
Pinch ground cinnamon
1 chamomile tea bag
1 teaspoon raw honey

1 In a small saucepan, combine the tart cherry juice, water, turmeric, black pepper, and cinnamon.

2 Bring to a simmer over medium heat. Allow to simmer 5–7 minutes, until the liquid reduces by almost half.

3 Strain the mixture through a fine-mesh strainer and pour into a mug with the chamomile tea bag.

4 Allow the tea to brew 3 minutes.

5 Remove the tea bag and stir in the raw honey.

6 Consume immediately.

KEY INGREDIENT: Tart Cherry

Cherries have one of the highest levels of anti-inflammatory fighting power among foods. Specifically, the anthocyanins in cherries (the antioxidant compound in cherries that also gives them their bright red color) have been linked to reduce inflammation at levels compared to some pain medications. Cherries have also shown promise in treating arthritis and osteoarthritis—both conditions caused by inflammation—and in reducing the amount of circulating concentrations of inflammatory biomarkers in the blood.

Since the early twenty-first century the tart cherry has been promoted for its health benefits. Because of its positive effects on sleep quality and duration, this tea is perfect to drink before bedtime. In addition to helping you sleep, this Tart Cherry Turmeric Bedtime Tea is filled with inflammation-fighting ingredients.

Per Serving
Calories: 190 | Fat: 0.3 g | Protein: 2.0 g | Sodium: 19 mg
Fiber: 1.3 g | Carbohydrates: 45.8 g | Sugar: 31.1 g

MACA HOT COCOA

Serves 2

INGREDIENTS

2 cups unsweetened vanilla almond
  milk
¼ cup raw cacao powder
¼ cup pure maple syrup
2 teaspoons maca root powder

---

1 In a small saucepan over low
   heat, gently heat the almond
   milk until hot.

2 Whisk in the cacao powder,
   maple syrup, and maca root
   powder until well combined
   and no lumps remain.

3 Serve immediately. Can be
   stored in an airtight container up to 1 week. May be
   reheated.

KEY INGREDIENT: Maca Root

Inflammation in the body can be caused by a number of different lifestyle factors. One of those is stress, especially chronic stress. Maca root is an adaptogen, which means it is a plant that naturally helps the body adapt to stressors. Adaptogens have a special ability to adapt their functions to your body's specific needs. Because of this, including maca root in your diet can help your body deal with the elements of life that cause stress, such as busy schedules, demanding work tasks, or relationship issues, thus lowering overall inflammation in the body.

This Maca Hot Cocoa is a perfect drink when stress in your life is high and you need some time to relax and rejuvenate.

Per Serving
Calories: 192 | Fat: 4.0 g | Protein: 4.0 g | Sodium: 184 mg
Fiber: 4.0 g | Carbohydrates: 38.4 g | Sugar: 25.2 g

SPICED ELDERBERRY TEA

Serves 2

INGREDIENTS

2 cups water
2 tablespoons dried elderberries
¼ teaspoon ground cinnamon
¼ teaspoon ground ginger
1 teaspoon raw honey

1 Add the water, dried elderberries, cinnamon, and ginger to a small saucepan.

2 Bring the mixture to a boil, then reduce the heat to a simmer. Allow the mixture to simmer 15 minutes.

3 Strain the elderberries using a fine-mesh strainer.

4 Stir in the honey. Serve immediately. Can be stored in an airtight container in the refrigerator up to 2 weeks. May be reheated.

KEY INGREDIENT: Elderberry

Elderberry is a plant that is commonly used medicinally throughout the world. It is well known for its ability to fight cold and flu symptoms. It is also often used as a preventative measure against falling ill, as it has been shown to stimulate the immune system.

Elderberry contains a number of different polyphenol antioxidants. One in particular, kaempferol, has potent anti-inflammatory effects. It has been shown to modulate a number of different key elements in cellular pathway links to inflammation. Kaempferol is also known to have strong anti-cancer properties, with the ability to inhibit growth of cancer cells and preserve normal cell viability.

Elderberries are also high in anthocyanins, which contribute to their anti-inflammatory properties. Anthocyanins have been shown to inhibit activation of pro-inflammatory signaling pathways in the body.

You can find dried elderberry in your local health food store, and it is widely available for purchase online.

Per Serving
Calories: 15 | Fat: 0.1 g | Protein: 0.1 g | Sodium: 0 mg
Fiber: 0.0 g | Carbohydrates: 4.1 g | Sugar: 2.9 g

TURMERIC LEMON GREEN TEA

Serves 1

INGREDIENTS

1" piece fresh turmeric
2 tablespoons lemon juice
Pinch black pepper
1½ cups water
1 green tea bag

---

1 Peel and roughly chop the turmeric.

2 In a small saucepan, bring the turmeric, lemon juice, black pepper, and water to a simmer over low heat. Allow to simmer 3 minutes.

3 Turn off the heat, add the green tea bag, and cover the pan. Allow the tea to steep 3 minutes.

4 Remove the tea bag and strain the tea through a fine-mesh sieve.

5 Consume immediately.

KEY INGREDIENT: Lemon

Lemons are full of vitamin C, which is one of the most important antioxidants in nature. Anytime the body is exposed to free radicals, vitamin C helps neutralize them. That's one reason why vitamin C is such an important nutrient we need to make sure we're getting enough of. Vitamin C is also vital for immune system function. It's interesting to note that consuming fruits and vegetables high in vitamin C is associated with reduced risk of death from all causes. Lemons are an excellent way to help meet your vitamin C needs.

This tea recipe packs an anti-inflammatory punch with all of its ingredients and has a lovely flavor.

Per Serving
Calories: 9 | Fat: 0.1 g | Protein: 0.1 g | Sodium: 0 mg
Fiber: 0.2 g | Carbohydrates: 3.4 g | Sugar: 0.8 g

WARM WALNUT HONEY MILK

Serves 1

INGREDIENTS

⅓ cup walnut pieces
1 cup water
¼ teaspoon ground cinnamon
⅛ teaspoon pure vanilla extract
1½ teaspoons raw honey

1 Add the walnuts, water, and cinnamon to a small blender. Blend on high until the mixture is smooth.

2 Using a nut milk bag or a piece of cheesecloth, strain the milk into a small saucepan.

3 Heat the milk over medium-low heat until warm. Pour into a mug.

4 Stir in the vanilla extract and honey.

5 Serve immediately. Can be stored in an airtight container up to 1 week. May be reheated.

KEY INGREDIENT: Walnuts

Walnuts have a long, rich history, dating back to 7000 B.C. In fact, walnuts are the oldest tree food known to man. The walnut tree has always been highly revered, and its uses have included food, medicine, shelter, and dye and lamp oil.

Walnuts are a standout food because of their excellent nutritional composition. It has been found that walnuts have the highest levels of polyphenols of any nuts. Research has shown that walnuts can play a role in reducing the risk of cardiovascular disease and diabetes, both of which are related to inflammation in the body.

If you like to enjoy a warm drink before bed, this Warm Walnut Honey Milk is the perfect choice.

Per Serving
Calories: 161 | Fat: 12.9 g | Protein: 1.2 g | Sodium: 0 mg
Fiber: 0.0 g | Carbohydrates: 11.8 g | Sugar: 9.8 g

SLOW COOKER CHICKEN BONE BROTH

Serves 6

INGREDIENTS

Bones from 4 pounds chicken
8 cups cold filtered water
2 tablespoons apple cider vinegar
1 large onion, peeled and cut into chunks
2 large carrots, cut into chunks
3 stalks celery, cut into chunks
1 teaspoon sea salt
½ cup fresh parsley
3–4 sprigs fresh thyme

1 Put bones in a large slow cooker and cover them with water.

2 Add the rest of the ingredients to the slow cooker and allow it to sit 30–60 minutes before turning on the slow cooker.

3 Cook on low 8–24 hours. The longer time you can allow, the better.

4 Once you have finished cooking the broth, allow it to cool. Then remove the bones and vegetables from the liquid.

5 Strain broth through a fine-mesh sieve and use the back of a wooden spoon to extract all liquid from the ingredients. Repeat this procedure.

6 Store the broth in an airtight container in the refrigerator and consume within 3–5 days. May also be frozen up to 6 months.

KEY INGREDIENT: Chicken Bone Broth

Making homemade chicken bone broth is worth the time and energy it takes because the health benefits are impressive. Homemade chicken bone broth is full of minerals like calcium, phosphorus, magnesium, and potassium. Allowing the bones to sit in the liquid with apple cider vinegar before cooking is what helps draw these minerals from the bones. Bone broth also contains chondroitin sulfate and glucosamine. These are compounds that are sold as supplements to reduce inflammation, arthritis, and joint pain! Bone broth is known to heal the gut and boost the immune system, and it is great for hair, skin, and nails.

This broth is excellent for sipping on a daily basis to help reap the benefits. It can also be used for a base for your favorite soups and stews.

Per Serving
Calories: 32 | Fat: 0.3 g | Protein: 6.2 g | Sodium: 281 mg
Fiber: 0.3 g | Carbohydrates: 0.8 g | Sugar: 0.3 g

HOT SPICED APPLE ORANGE DRINK

Serves 1

INGREDIENTS

2 medium apples
1 medium orange
¼ teaspoon ground cinnamon
⅛ teaspoon ground ginger
⅛ teaspoon ground cloves

1 Prepare the apples by coring and cutting them into appropriate-sized pieces for your juicer.

2 Prepare the orange by peeling and cutting it into appropriate-sized pieces for your juicer.

3 Process the apple and orange through the juicer.

4 Strain the apple-orange juice through a fine-mesh sieve into a small saucepan.

5 Whisk the cinnamon, ginger, and cloves into the juice. Heat over medium heat until warm, about 3–4 minutes.

6 Consume immediately.

KEY INGREDIENT: Apples

"An apple a day keeps the doctor away"? Old wives' tale or truth? When you look at the nutritional information for the humble apple, it seems like a sound theory. Apples are a rich source of a number of powerful phytonutrients that can indeed keep your body healthy. All of the antioxidants in apples have been found to play an important role in cardio-vascular health. The numerous antioxidants found in apples have been shown to provide protection within blood vessels. One study indicated that one apple a day for four weeks significantly reduced blood levels of oxidized LDL cholesterol. A number of the antioxidants in apples, including quercetin and catechin, have been shown to have anti-inflammatory effects.

Per Serving
Calories: 229 | Fat: 0.5 g | Protein: 1.1 g | Sodium: 3 mg
Fiber: 0.0 g | Carbohydrates: 55.7 g | Sugar: 51.7 g

COCONUT CHAI ROOIBOS TEA LATTE

Serves 1
INGREDIENTS

1 cup water
1 red rooibos tea bag
½ cup lite canned coconut milk
1 teaspoon peeled, coarsely
  chopped fresh ginger
¼ teaspoon ground cinnamon
⅛ teaspoon ground cloves
⅛ teaspoon ground allspice
⅛ teaspoon ground cardamom
Pinch black pepper
1 teaspoon raw honey

1 In a small pan, bring the cup of
   water to a boil.

2 Place the tea bag in a mug
   and pour the boiling water
   over the tea bag. Allow the
   tea to steep 5–7 minutes.

3 While the tea is steeping,
   place the coconut milk, ginger,
   cinnamon, cloves, allspice,
   cardamom, and black pepper
   in a small blender.

4 Blend the ingredients on high
   until they are thoroughly combined and smooth.

5 Warm the coconut milk mixture in a small saucepan over
   medium heat until it is hot,
   about 1–2 minutes.

6 Remove the tea bag from the
   mug and add the coconut
   milk mixture.

7 Stir in the raw honey.

8 Consume immediately.

KEY INGREDIENT: Rooibos Tea

Native to South Africa, rooibos tea is an herbal remedy that's been used for centuries. The tea is extracted from the leaves of the Aspalathus linearis plant. Rooibos tea is highly regarded for its health benefits. A serving of rooibos tea provides nutrients like iron, potassium, zinc, manganese, copper, calcium, and magnesium. It's been shown to help keep hormone levels balanced, manage and prevent diabetes, help digestion issues, manage blood pressure, and prevent premature aging. Its anti-inflammatory properties result from a number of powerful compounds it contains, including quercetin.

Many of the spices in this tea recipe will also provide anti-inflammatory benefits, and it's a delicious, comforting drink.

Per Serving
Calories: 100 | Fat: 6.8 g | Protein: 0.2 g | Sodium: 9 mg
Fiber: 0.7 g | Carbohydrates: 9.3 g | Sugar: 5.9 g

US/Metric Conversion Chart

VOLUME CONVERSIONS

US Volume Measure	Metric Equivalent
⅛ teaspoon	0.5 milliliter
¼ teaspoon	1 milliliter
½ teaspoon	2 milliliters
1 teaspoon	5 milliliters
½ tablespoon	7 milliliters
1 tablespoon (3 teaspoons)	15 milliliters
2 tablespoons (1 fluid ounce)	30 milliliters
¼ cup (4 tablespoons)	60 milliliters
⅓ cup	90 milliliters
½ cup (4 fluid ounces)	125 milliliters
⅔ cup	160 milliliters
¾ cup (6 fluid ounces)	180 milliliters
1 cup (16 tablespoons)	250 milliliters
1 pint (2 cups)	500 milliliters
1 quart (4 cups)	1 liter (about)

WEIGHT CONVERSIONS

US Weight Measure	Metric Equivalent
½ ounce	15 grams
1 ounce	30 grams
2 ounces	60 grams
3 ounces	85 grams
¼ pound (4 ounces)	115 grams
½ pound (8 ounces)	225 grams
¾ pound (12 ounces)	340 grams
1 pound (16 ounces)	454 grams

OVEN TEMPERATURE CONVERSIONS

Degrees Fahrenheit	Degrees Celsius
200 degrees F	95 degrees C
250 degrees F	120 degrees C
275 degrees F	135 degrees C
300 degrees F	150 degrees C
325 degrees F	160 degrees C
350 degrees F	180 degrees C
375 degrees F	190 degrees C
400 degrees F	205 degrees C
425 degrees F	220 degrees C
450 degrees F	230 degrees C

BAKING PAN SIZES

American	Metric
8 x 1½ inch round baking pan	20 x 4 cm cake tin
9 x 1½ inch round baking pan	23 x 3.5 cm cake tin
11 x 7 x 1½ inch baking pan	28 x 18 x 4 cm baking tin
13 x 9 x 2 inch baking pan	30 x 20 x 5 cm baking tin
2 quart rectangular baking dish	30 x 20 x 3 cm baking tin
15 x 10 x 2 inch baking pan	30 x 25 x 2 cm baking tin (Swiss roll tin)
9 inch pie plate	22 x 4 or 23 x 4 cm pie plate
7 or 8 inch springform pan	18 or 20 cm springform or loose bottom cake tin
9 x 5 x 3 inch loaf pan	23 x 13 x 7 cm or 2 lb narrow loaf or pate tin
1½ quart casserole	1.5 liter casserole
2 quart casserole	2 liter casserole

Index

To Your Health!

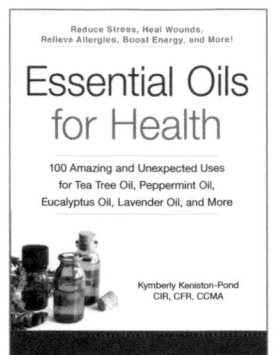

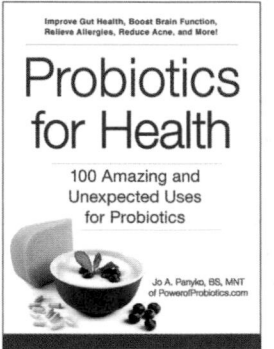

PICK UP OR DOWNLOAD YOUR COPIES TODAY!

adamsmedia
An Imprint of Simon & Schuster
A CBS COMPANY